LEWIS AND CLARK

Partners in Discovery

John Bakeless

Monty,
You'll always be
Lewis & Clark to me —
Thanks for sharing your
childhood discoveries with
me.
Yours,
[signature]
'79

DOVER PUBLICATIONS, INC.
Mineola, New York

Bibliographical Note

This Dover edition, first published in 1996, is a republication of the work
originally published by William Morrow & Company, New York, in 1947. The
large folding map that faced page 450 in the original edition is now on pages iv
and v of the present edition, printed at 60% of original size.

Library of Congress Cataloging-in-Publication Data

Bakeless, John Edwin, 1894– .
    Lewis and Clark : partners in discovery / John Bakeless.
        p.   cm.
    Originally published: New York, W. Morrow, 1947.
    Includes bibliographical references and index.
    ISBN 0-486-29233-9 (pbk.)
        1. Lewis, Meriwether, 1774–1809.   2. Clark, William, 1770–1838.
    3. Explorers—West (U.S.)—Biography.   4. Lewis and Clark Expedition
    (1804–1806)   5. West (U.S.)—Description and travel.   I. Title.
    F592.7.L675   1996
    917.804'2—dc20   96-19433
                                                                          CIP

Manufactured in the United States of America
Dover Publications, Inc., 31 East 2nd Street, Mineola, N.Y. 11501

to Bellamy Partridge

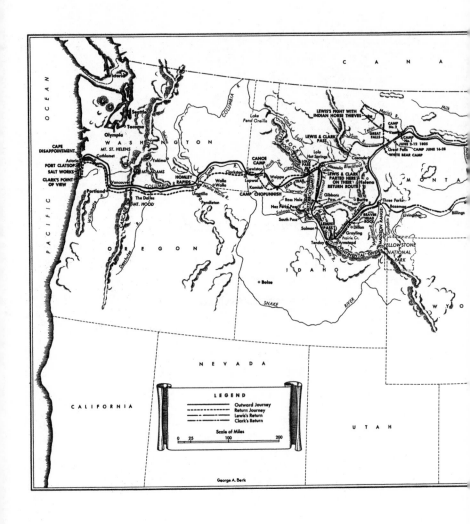

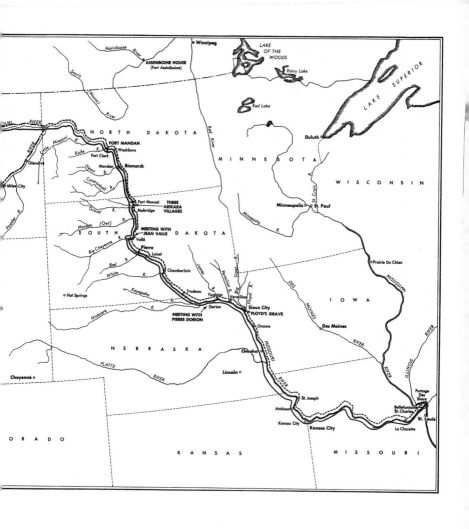

Preface

HISTORY offers few opportunities for a joint biography of this sort, in which two men's lives are so closely linked that they can be told as one. Beaumont and Fletcher and the Brothers Goncourt are perhaps the only other examples. The fame which resulted from the Lewis and Clark expedition was so great that it has overshadowed their other achievements and has overshadowed also the length and intimacy of their friendship. It is, therefore, necessary to emphasize the fact that this book is a biography of the two explorers, not merely the story of their explorations, however large the story of the expedition may bulk in any account of their careers.

Completion of this study has been much delayed by nearly six years of active duty in the second World War. Preliminary research, begun in 1939, was carried forward steadily until Pearl Harbor, after which the pressure of general staff duties became so great that it had to be laid aside entirely. On my return to reserve status early in 1946, I was enabled to devote my entire time to the book through the grant of a post-service Guggenheim Fellowship, which by a curious coincidence exactly equalled the Congressional grant for equipping the Lewis and Clark Expedition. Fortunately, a field trip as far as Nebraska in 1940 had already enabled me to see most of the important original documents. In February, 1946, I visited Virginia and Tennessee to consult local archives and in the winter of 1946-1947 I completed my study of the Lewis and Clark trail and of material contained in private collections and local archives from Pennsylvania to Oregon.

Though the book contains an immense amount of hitherto unknown material—for example, Lewis's correspondence with the War Department, just prior to his death, and Clark's comment on hearing of the tragedy—I have not attempted to mark it as such in the notes. Specialists will have no difficulty in recognizing it; others will not be interested. As this is a biography rather than a study in local history and local geography, I have not entered into the innumerable disputes as to the exact location of innumerable Lewis and Clark camp sites, though there is no doubt that some of them can be accurately determined.

To avoid encumbering the pages with foot-notes, all documentation has been placed in the back of the book. For the few passages of dialogue, authority will be found there. I have not "fictionized," nor have I invented conversation.

In such a study, I have naturally incurred innumerable obligations for friendly aid and criticism. These are acknowledged elsewhere. I can here express only my special obligations to Mr. George Libaire, who first suggested the subject; to the John Simon Guggenheim Memorial Foundation for the grant which made the final field study possible; to the publishers' editorial staff, whose searching criticism vastly improved the book; and to my wife, who labored with me in the archives, typed endless notes and much of the manuscript, and motored me 18,500 miles during the course of the research.

John Bakeless

Great Hill,
Seymour, Conn.
4 August 1947

Contents

Illustrations

Maps by George A. Berk.
Detail maps are found on pages *116, 126, 151, 245, 267* and *331*.
A map of the entire route is found on pages *iv/v*.

chapter I: Mr. Jefferson needs a Secretary

S O CLOSE had the election been that it looked for a time as if there would be no President at all in March of 1801. The decision had to be made by Congress, and even Congress was barely able to choose in time for the inauguration. It was past the middle of February, 1801, before Mr. Thomas Jefferson knew that he, and not Colonel Aaron Burr, would be the third President of the United States. Colonel Burr, accepting the office of Vice-President in graceful disgust, filled one term with injured dignity and then fell upon evil courses.

No one was very happy about the election. It was unpleasant for Mr. Jefferson to reflect that he owed the office to his political arch-enemy, Alexander Hamilton, who, changing his mind at the last minute, had allowed enough of his supporters to vote for Jefferson to give him victory. It was bitter

for Burr to be defeated; to be defeated by Hamilton's maneuvers was bitterest of all. To Hamilton, Mr. Jefferson was
only a little less dangerous than Burr. His election meant a
triumph of "republicanism," dangerous French political
principles, the rule of the masses, and the defeat of the aristocratic Federalist party which Hamilton thought the only
salvation of the new nation.

Surrounded as he was by the bitterest political dissension
as well as by disloyalty, the new President needed someone,
at least a private secretary, whom he could trust implicitly.
Mr. Jefferson was from Albemarle County in Virginia. His
thoughts kept turning to a fair-haired, blue-eyed Albemarle
County youngster, just past his middle twenties, from a plantation on Ivy Creek, a few miles from Mr. Jefferson's estate
at Monticello, on the opposite side of Charlottesville. Knowing the lad and his family, Mr. Jefferson much preferred him
to the numerous other young men who had for some time
been applying for the secretaryship.

The young man's name was Meriwether Lewis. Except
for his height and his bow legs, he looked a little like Napoleon, or so a school friend thought. He was a moody, serious
fellow, with a passionate love for endless rambles, the woods
and fields, or wild country of any kind. His manners, though
good, were stiff, his bearing awkward. His letters were far
from having a secretarial finish. His literary style, though
clear enough, was hardly polished. He wrote a fair hand,
but, despite his enthusiasm for education, his grammar was
dubious, and nothing on earth would ever teach him to spell.
Most people would have said that a worse private secretary
for the President of the United States could hardly be imagined.

But Mr. Jefferson knew all this, and none of it disturbed
him. He really had very little need of ordinary secretarial
services. Using his right and left hands with equal ease, he
wrote most of his letters himself and, ever a lover of mechani-

cal devices, did his own copying quickly and easily with a letter-press—in a day when most officials were still having duplicates for filing laboriously copied out by hand.

No, no. None of these things really mattered. This particular secretary was going to have duties—some very special duties—in the next year or two, though Mr. Jefferson was not yet ready to admit all that he was planning. Perhaps it was not all quite clear yet, even to himself.

For the last twenty years or more, Mr. Jefferson—who had himself never traveled more than 50 miles west of his own estate at Monticello—had dreamed of exploring the vast, empty, unknown lands beyond the Mississippi River, then the westernmost boundary of the United States. A dabbler in most of the sciences, he rather thought that prehistoric mammoths might still be living there, even though the nineteenth century was now beginning. After all, their bones, teeth, and tusks—fresh, not fossilized—were still lying about on the ground in Kentucky. Indians told him that they had seen the great shaggy beasts alive. Mammoths fascinated Mr. Jefferson. A box of their bones was a sure way to his heart. He also heard that somewhere in the vague western wilderness there was a huge mountain of pure salt. Doubtless there were many other wonders.

He had dreams of taking the entire fur trade away from the British, securing it to America by diverting it down the Missouri to St. Louis. To be sure, the Missouri River was not American—not yet; and neither was St. Louis or any of the other territory that he wanted to explore. But Mr. Jefferson had ideas of his own how that might be adjusted.

During all the long years in which he had been thinking about those huge blank spaces on the map, Mr. Jefferson had made one effort after another to get them filled in. His last effort had been nine years earlier, in 1792. When young Meriwether Lewis, now his prospective secretary, had begged to join that expedition, Mr. Jefferson had refused—the boy was barely eighteen. In the end, the 1792 expedition turned out to be just one more of Mr. Jefferson's futile series of western exploration schemes, one after another of which had had to be abandoned.

Nine years earlier, Mr. Jefferson had been merely Secretary of State. He was President now, with power enough to send out exploring expeditions as he pleased, if he could get an appropriation from Congress. Young Lewis was just the right age by this time, but what on earth had become of him? All Mr. Jefferson knew was that he had joined the army, been commissioned, seen service on the frontier. A year or two earlier, he had been on recruiting duty around Charlottesville. Where was he now? General James Wilkinson, commander-in-chief of the army, could certainly find out.

Mr. Jefferson decided to write not one letter but two. The first, a covering letter which enclosed his momentous note to Meriwether Lewis, was addressed to General Wilkinson. It would never do to antagonize the pompous little general by snatching away one of his officers without consulting him, as deferentially as possible.

Mr. Jefferson had so completely lost track of Meriwether Lewis that he did not even know he had been promoted captain. Would the general find "Lieut" Meriwether Lewis, asked the President, "not knowing where he may be"? If General Wilkinson approved of its contents, he was to hand Lewis an enclosed letter, with its offer of the post of private secretary to the President of the United States: "a general acquaintance with him arising from his being of my neighborhood has induced me to select him if his presence can be dispensed with without injury to the service."

No tactful brigadier has ever made difficulty for a President about a subaltern more or less. General Wilkinson complied at once.

At the very moment when Mr. Jefferson was writing his two letters, Captain Meriwether Lewis, Paymaster of the First

United States Infantry, was on his way back through the wilderness to Pittsburgh, having completed one of his periodic journeys down the Ohio River, up the Mississippi, and then cross-country to Detroit, paying the scattered troops of his regiment. On March 5, 1801, Captain Lewis reached the deputy quartermaster-general's depot in Pittsburgh. News of the "republican" Mr. Jefferson's election to the Presidency had just been received—dismal news for a predominately Federalist army, but joyful news to the intensely republican Captain Lewis, who defended Jeffersonian principles in vehement political discussions with his brother officers and who even carried Frenchified "republicanism" so far as to address his own mother as "Citizeness."

Already delighted by news of the election, the young officer was astonished by the President's offer. As Albemarle gentry, the Jefferson and Lewis families had always been well-enough acquainted, but Captain Lewis had never dreamed of anything like this.

In view of his recent "appointment to the Presidency of the U. S.," Mr. Jefferson wrote, he would require a private secretary. The Albemarle philosopher was happy to offer the post to his young friend from Ivy Creek; and he was careful to word his offer so that, although Lewis—remembering the expedition of 1792, for which he had volunteered—would understand plainly enough what was really in the President's mind, no one else could even guess. Mr. Jefferson explained that he especially wanted Captain Lewis as private secretary, because he would be able "to contribute to the mass of information which it is interesting for the administration to acquire."

Now, just what information could the President of the United States so urgently require from a regimental paymaster, aged twenty-six? Mr. Jefferson, who had not been a diplomat for nothing, very neatly dropped a few more hints in words that would be vague to General Wilkinson, but

clear enough to Lewis: "Your knoledge of the Western country, of the army and of all it's interests & relations has rendered it desirable for public as well as private purposes that
you should be engaged in that office." If he accepted, Captain
Lewis was to advise Mr. Jefferson at once, "wait on Gen
Wilkinson & obtain his approbation, & his aid," then "repair
to this place."

"Knoledge of the Western country"? The captain's years
in what was then the westernmost part of the United States
had certainly qualified him for travel into even wilder country farther westward. The army's "interests & relations"? The
army's only relations at the moment were with Indians—the
Missouri country was also full of Indians. "Public as well as
private purposes"? Captain Lewis knew well enough what
one of Mr. Jefferson's constant purposes had been as far back
as he could remember.

This was the western exploration scheme again! Disguised,
of course. And just as well, too, since General Wilkinson had
for years and years been a spy in the pay of the Spaniards
who held that western country along the Mississippi and Missouri, which they called Louisiana.

Captain Lewis rushed off an eager letter of acceptance—
setting the President right on that little matter of rank, incidentally. By March 22, the captain had three horses—a brown,
a bay, a sorrel mare—ready to carry him and his baggage,
together with some official papers, to Washington. Disposing
of a paymaster's responsibilities is no great matter, if the
accounts balance, and Captain Meriwether Lewis was one of
the most meticulous mortals that ever lived. There was no
trouble with the accounts.

Over the mountains, through Pennsylvania and Maryland,
to the new capital of the United States was a long journey
in those days, with clumsy pack horses stumbling under their
burdens over bad roads and winding trails, delaying even an
eager traveler. It was April before the new secretary reached

Washington, to find that President Jefferson had gone off to Monticello before his first month in office had elapsed. A note left behind him—correctly addressed this time, as his new secretary was gratified to see, to "Captain" Lewis—directed him either to follow the President to Albemarle or settle down in the new "President's House," where the steward would look out for him.

Lewis was to live there as "one of my family," the President wrote. Knowing that money was none too plentiful at the Lewis plantation on Ivy Creek, Mr. Jefferson tactfully pointed out that this arrangement would save the expense of food and lodging. The salary would be only "600 D." a year—not much, but better than a captain's pay.

There was also—though so far nothing explicit had been said—the stirring prospect of great events to come, of which this very private secretary would know the inner secrets. Mr. Jefferson was not a man to lose time. A message would soon be on its way to the American Minister at the court of the great Napoleon, who had already compelled Spain to return Louisiana to France. The Mississippi Valley was vital to the future of America. Would the Emperor of the French sell part of Louisiana?

If the prospects at which the President had so far only hinted should ever become realities, Meriwether Lewis would need a trusty friend. Captain Lewis's thoughts—perhaps at once, certainly within the next few months—began to turn toward a plantation near Louisville, Kentucky, where dwelt a red-headed lieutenant under whom Lewis had served while still a lowly ensign, as the army then called its second lieutenants.

chapter 2: The Clarks and the Lewises

THE red-headed lieutenant's name was William Clark. He was a civilian now, having resigned from the Regular Army five years earlier, after adventurous service in the Indian wars. During his last few months in the Regulars, he had commanded a "Chosen Rifle Company" (ordinary infantry carried muskets), in which Ensign Meriwether Lewis, four years younger than himself, had been a very junior officer.

Flaming red hair had been a Clark characteristic ever since an ancestor had fallen in love with a red-head and married her, a generation or two earlier. Family tradition held that every red-headed Clark was bound to distinguish himself, and it is certainly true that the most celebrated of the six Clark brothers are George Rogers Clark, conqueror of the Revolutionary Northwest, and William Clark, eighteen years his junior, explorer of the Pacific Northwest—both of whose nimble brains were covered by thatches of the most brilliant red, though the hot temper usually associated with it rarely appeared.

No one knows when or how Meriwether Lewis and William Clark first became acquainted. It is true that old John Clark and Ann Rogers Clark, his wife, had for a time lived in Albemarle County, not many miles from the Lewis plantation, but they had moved away to Caroline County long before red-headed Billy, their youngest son, was born.

The Clarks, like the Lewises, were old Virginia stock. The family was Scottish, perhaps from Argyllshire. The first pair, known to their descendants only as "Clark & wife," reached Virginia at Jamestown some time toward the end of the seventeenth century. One child, known only as "Son Clark," wandered with his wife to Georgia, there to vanish forever from the genealogy. Another son, William John Clark, said to have been born aboard ship in 1680, was the father of Jonathan Clark.

His son, John Clark (1724/25–1799), father of the explorer, William Clark, married his second cousin, Ann Rogers (1734–1798), when she was fifteen years old, and produced a family of six sons and four daughters. Of the sons, all were soldiers—five in the Revolutionary War, for which only Billy was too young. Four of the sons became general officers. Whether the second son, General George Rogers Clark, or the sixth, General William Clark, was the most distinguished of the soldier sons it would be profitless to dispute.

There is no doubt that Frances was the most fatally charming of the daughters. There was something about black-haired Fanny that stirred young men to the wildest admiration. Her brother William adored her. One of her suitors fainted dead away at the news that she had married another. Eventually the enchanting Fanny married and survived them both, to make yet a third husband happy.

Not long after their marriage, John Clark took his bride to a small plantation of a scant 400 acres near Charlottesville. Here, in a log cabin tucked away in a small ravine, were born the first three children—Jonathan, George Rogers, Ann, and possibly also the fourth child, John. The cabin has long since vanished, though its spring still supplies water for a modern plantation house, but a huge roadside boulder now bears a bronze plate marking the general vicinity.

Mr. Jefferson knew the Clarks nearly as well as he knew the Lewises, for his father's land ran near John Clark's cabin, occasionally he had done legal work for them, and he had been Governor of Virginia while George Rogers Clark was fighting Virginia's wars in the Northwest. The round hilltop that Thomas Jefferson was to make famous as Monticello was not far away. Part of the land had been deeded to the elder Jefferson in exchange for a bowl of punch—only that and nothing more—one of those princely gestures possible when land was cheap and family friendships dear. The deed, still extant, states that the land is sold "for and in Consideration of Henry Weatherburns biggest Bowl of Arrack Punch to him delivered at and before the Ensealing and delivery of these presents the Receipt where of the said William Randolph doth hereby Acknowledge." Henry Weatherburn was the keeper of the Raleigh Tavern in Williamsburgh—whither Virginia gentry habitually resorted—which had a reputation for mixed drinks. According to legend, it cost a guinea to fill the Raleigh's biggest punch bowl, but even in those days five dollars was a small price for 200 acres. Albemarle still knows that land as "the Punchbowl Tract."

Within thirty years after John and Ann Clark settled there, Albemarle County had become one of the most charming parts of Virginia, with their friend Thomas Jefferson as its leading citizen. But in the mid-eighteenth century it was still half-settled country and for some years it remained a wild, not wholly pleasant place to live. Neither was it very profitable, being beyond tidewater, on which the larger plantations depended for the export of tobacco.

Some time between 1756 and 1758, John Clark inherited a much better plantation close to the Spottsylvania line in Caroline County, about 25 miles from tidewater on the Rappahannock, where sailing vessels could lie along docks in the river to load tobacco. Here, in a six-room house heated by five fireplaces grouped around a central chimney, the Clarks lived for something over two decades and a half, through all the turmoil of the Revolution and for a short time after its close; and here, on August 1, 1770, William Clark was born.

Meantime, the Lewis family had remained at their plantation, "Locust Hill," on Ivy Creek, about seven miles west of Charlottesville, which then consisted only of a Court House, a tavern, and about a dozen houses. "Locust Hill" stood on one of those slight elevations with which Albemarle is studded and on which the early planters loved to build. From it, one has a splendid long view across rolling field and woodland till the mountains close it off at last, in some places at the distance of a single mile, elsewhere at 30. The longest view of all is westward.

The Lewises' blood was Welsh. They were descendants of a certain Robert Lewis, born at Brecon in Wales, in 1574, whose son, also Robert Lewis, had emigrated to America in 1635. Thereafter, through various generations, Lewis had succeeded Lewis until the birth of the explorer's father, William Lewis, at a date which cannot be exactly fixed, but which was about 1748. He married Lucy Meriwether (1752–1837), daughter of Thomas Meriwether of Cloverfields, and brought her home to Locust Hill.

Meriwether Lewis, born August 18, 1774, was the second child of the marriage. There was an elder sister, Jane, and a younger brother, Reuben. William Lewis was the first cousin of his bride's father, but in eighteenth-century Virginia and Kentucky the marriage even of first cousins was not unknown. In England, well on into the next century, the great Charles Darwin married a first cousin and, like John Clark and William Lewis, begat a brilliant progeny. Even Kentucky thought it odd, however, when Reuben Field, one of the heroes of the Lewis and Clark Expedition came back from his adventures and married his own niece!

Not much is known about Lieutenant William Lewis, who fades from his famous son's story when Meriwether Lewis is only five years old. He was a reasonably prosperous planter, having inherited from his father 1,896 acres on Ivy Creek—600 of which he later sold—with slaves to work it. He had grown up in greater prosperity, since Robert Lewis, his father, was wealthy enough to leave similar bequests to all nine of his children. The family seems to have been harmonious—at least, his sister Mary entrusted William completely with her share of the estate.

Lieutenant Lewis went off to war in the company commanded by Captain John Fleming, at least as early as February, 1776. He probably saw service of some kind near Yorktown, which later gave rise to the story that he had been in the siege that led to Cornwallis's surrender. Actually, he died in 1779, two years earlier, though one of his friends was sufficiently mixed up about it to make oath that he died "shortly after the siege of York." In the year of his death, he was the third signer of Albemarle County's special declaration of independence from the British king.

He is said to have served in the Revolution without pay and to have borne his own expenses—a degree of patriotic devotion just one degree beyond that of George Washington, who did indeed decline an officer's pay, but let his country meet his expenses, doubtless somewhat heavier than a line lieutenant's.

In November, 1779, Lieutenant Lewis returned to spend a short leave with his three children and his wife, at Cloverfields, her girlhood home. Crossing the Secretary Ford of the

Rivanna while the river was in flood, his horse was swept away and drowned. He himself swam ashore, reached Cloverfields with a bad chill, and died there of pneumonia, November 14, 1779. He asked to be buried in the little family "burying ground," just behind the plantation house, where his body still lies, marked with a simple modern stone (and the wrong date!), while his wife lies at Locust Hill.

Lieutenant Lewis left his plantation, £520 in cash, and various chattels, most of which, under the Virginia law of primogeniture, went to his eldest son, Meriwether, though his widow retained dower rights. The inventory of his estate includes 24 slaves and 147 gallons of whisky. The estate continued to prosper and when the widow, who had long since become Mrs. Lucy Marks, died in 1837 she left 49 slaves. The slaves were valued at between $600 and $100 each, except three—a little Negro girl valued at five dollars and two Negros valued at "oo.oo," perhaps pickaninnies, perhaps very old slaves. It was fifty years before his family finally secured the bounties due Lieutenant Lewis for his service in the Revolution.

Virginia widows in those days remarried as speedily as possible—sometimes in such haste that the second husband became executor for his predecessor's estate. No one was in the least surprised, therefore, when within less than six months after her first husband's death, on May 13, 1780, Mrs. Lewis became the wife of Captain John Marks. Family tradition says she was following the advice of her first husband, as he lay dying.

John Marks was a respectable Virginian, connected by marriage with Mr. Jefferson, who had risen to the rank of captain in the Continental Line, resigning in 1781 because of ill health. Not long after his marriage to the young and pretty Widow Lewis, he became interested in prospects of wealth to be won from new lands in Georgia. It was a day of speculative land crazes. General John Matthews, well

known in Albemarle, had, like many another Revolutionary
soldier, kept a sharp eye out for real estate while engaged in
his campaigns. Returning to Virginia when the Revolution
was over, he persuaded a number of families to emigrate with
him to new lands along the Broad River, in Georgia. With
this group of emigrants went the Marks family, including the
boy, Meriwether Lewis.

Like most journeys in the backwoods, this one was not
without tribulation. Delayed en route for several days, Captain Marks decided to send his family ahead, putting the
wagons in charge of an overseer, who, once out of his em-
ployer's sight, inevitably got drunk. Mounting a draft horse,
the fragile-looking Mrs. Marks took charge of the little car-
avan herself, leading it safely to its promised land in Georgia,
where her husband eventually joined her.

From the brief period the youthful Meriwether Lewis
spent with his mother in the Broad River settlements, one
legend lingers, showing the quick wit and readiness in emergencies that he was to demonstrate later on the Lewis and
Clark Expedition. When an Indian scare spread along the
Broad River, the white settlers first gathered for defense in
one of the cabins, then decided they were too few to defend
it, and finally fled for concealment to the forest. With typical
pioneer rashness, some hungry refugee lighted a fire and began cooking—a sure way of attracting any prowling Indians
that might be looking for scalps thereabouts. A distant shot
created another alarm. Men rushed for their rifles. There
was general confusion, amid which only the little Lewis boy
kept his head sufficiently to douse a bucket of water over the
fire. He can hardly have been more than ten, but already he
was a woodsman, accustomed to hunting alone at night from
the time he was eight years old. "He acquired in youth hardy
habits and a firm constitution," said a family friend. "He
possessed in the highest degree self-possession in danger"—as

the Indian scare showed and as the exploration of a continent was to show later.

The boy Meriwether did not stay long in the Broad River settlements, for about 1788, as letters to his mother show, he was back in Albemarle. Three years later, his mother was widowed again. Hunter though he was from childhood and frontiersman though he became, Meriwether Lewis was thus very much his mother's boy. Lieutenant William Lewis had gone off to war when his son was only two, had died when he was four, leaving at most vague memories in the child's mind. Though there is no reason to suspect that John Marks was anything but an indulgent stepfather, Meriwether knew little of his care. The boy soon left the wild Georgia back-woods and returned to Albemarle, where he could live with his mother's kin, labor at the studies which the preternatu-rally grave youngster took with immense seriousness, and—young as he was—keep an alert eye on the family property. By 1791, John Marks was dead and his widow soon returned to Albemarle for good, relying on her eldest son from his 'teens onward for financial guidance, protection of her dower rights, and sage counsel on the education of the other chil-dren. There were two more children now, John Hastings Marks and Mary Marks, the favorite of her half-brother Meriwether.

Like everybody else in Albemarle, the Lewis brothers, Meriwether and Reuben, adored their mother—a Virginia lady of the patrician breed, a benevolent family autocrat, with a character so sharp and definite that her twentieth-cen-tury descendants still refer to "Grandma Marks" with relish, as if they had known her in person. She was a woman who would have delighted that twentieth-century descendant of the Meriwethers who writes for the press on love, marriage, and female excellence, and who is known to an immense public as Dorothy Dix.

"She was sincere, truthful, industrious, and kind without

limit," wrote a Georgia neighbor. Meriwether Lewis "inherited the energy, courage, activity, and good understanding of his admirable mother." With the good understanding went intellectual interests. Lucy Marks treasured her small library, a rarity on the average plantation. She could not buy books enough to fill three rooms, like her friend Mr. Jefferson, who owned a series of large libraries, but her appraisers thought her little collection worth 30 dollars, the modern equivalent of several hundred dollars, and she valued it so much that she was careful to leave directions in her will for its equal division among her children.

To all these merits, she added both culinary and medical talents. One reason why Mr. Jefferson knew the Lewis family so well was that "Merriwether Lewis' mother made very nice hams"—better ones than even Monticello could produce. That is an achievement Virginians know how to value rightly. Mr. Jefferson's plantation overseer records that "every year I used to get a few for his special use."

There were always herbs in the garden at Locust Hill. Lucy Marks needed them, not only for cooking, but also in her medical practice, for she was a famous "yarb doctor," treating half the sick in the Albemarle countryside from her store of simples. No wonder her famous son knew just the right decoction of choke-cherry twigs when fever assailed him on the wild Missouri, or that he was able to care for his sick soldiers so successfully that amid all the hardship and disease of the expedition only one man died. No wonder, either, that her other two sons, Reuben and John, both became physicians.

But this Virginia lady was no mere bluestocking. "Her person was perfect," said an appreciative male acquaintance, "and her activity beyond her sex"—as indeed it was. When a sedate and spectacled old lady between seventy and eighty, "Grandma Marks" was still dashing about Albemarle on horseback to attend the sick, riding miles at a time and thinking very little of it. Even in old age, she retained "refined features, a fragile figure, and a masterful eye." Thoroughly feminine, with a housewifely pride in her elaborate store of family silver, much praised for her personal charm and delicate beauty, the explorer's mother was, in emergencies, nevertheless remarkably handy with a rifle. The early life of Albemarle was not without its own refinement, but it was a refinement mingled with the sturdy self-reliance of the frontier.

A party of boisterous and drunken British officers, paroled prisoners from Burgoyne's captured army who had been sent down to Albemarle to while away captivity as best they might, burst into Locust Hill one evening and blew out the lights. The child Meriwether must have been looking on. He saw his mother call her slaves, jerk her rifle down from its peg, and drive the too playful officers out of doors. Perhaps this incident, or Tarleton's cavalry raid on Charlottesville, or Tarleton's looting at the Meriwether estate of Cloverfields helped to develop in Lewis that intensely anti-British feeling of which a Canadian trader among the Mandan Indians complained, years afterward. Lewis's memory, curiously enough, was the defense of Locust Hill long after he and his mother were both dead. Not British officers but Phil Sheridan's troopers, riding that way just before Appomattox, threatened the plantation. One glimpse of Meriwether Lewis's Masonic apron was enough. House and lands were left unmolested.

The story of Mrs. Marks and the deer became a treasured family tradition. A hunting party from Locust Hill and neighboring plantations pursued their quarry all day long without success. Meantime their hounds brought the buck to bay on the lawn at Locust Hill, where the exquisite mistress of the house rushed out and shot it. When the crestfallen hunters returned at last, empty-handed, the buck, already transformed into a smoking saddle of venison, awaited them in the dining room, amid the profusion of table silver for which Locust Hill always had a reputation.

The plantation house was burned about 1838, but descriptions of it still remain. The first builder erected a tiny house of logs—one room, a little hall, a stairway leading to an upper hall, and a small half-story chamber. The later house, as Meriwether Lewis knew it, was the original log cabin, now boarded over, with two additions built on. The lower floor by that time included a dining room, a special "preacher's room," kept ready for itinerant Methodist divines, three other bedrooms, and a long passage where in later years the chests of the explorer son were stored.

Five huge locust trees, which gave the house its name, are gone, but their descendants flourish. The little family graveyard, characteristic of the South, remains—silent, lonely, overgrown with briars, but with the graves of Lucy Marks and her son Reuben Lewis still easily identifiable among the others.

The Meriwether family looked after their young kinsman well when he returned from Georgia to Albemarle. Uncle Nicholas Meriwether exercised unofficial oversight, while William D. Meriwether was officially appointed guardian and submitted accounts regularly to Albemarle Court. These accounts and his own letters tell the story of Meriwether Lewis's education.

A few very wealthy young Virginians used to attend the English universities. Others, like Mr. Jefferson, went to William and Mary, which included an Indian school and had six professors, all enjoined to celibacy under Virginia law. Planters who could afford it employed private tutors. But the sons of most Virginia gentry went to small schools kept by local parsons, where they learned Greek, Latin, mathematics, history, and modern languages, meantime developing in their own woods and fields the keen interest in natural history characteristic of Virginians of the day. Mr. Jefferson,

MRS. JOHN MARKS. *Mrs. Lucy Marks was the mother of Meriwether Lewis; . . . "refined features, a fragile figure, and a masterful eye."*

JULIA HANCOCK. *"Judy," as Clark called her, after whom he named Judith's River, Montana, married him on January 5, 1808.*

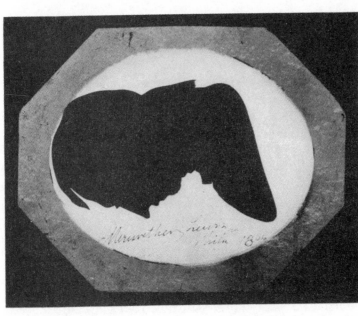

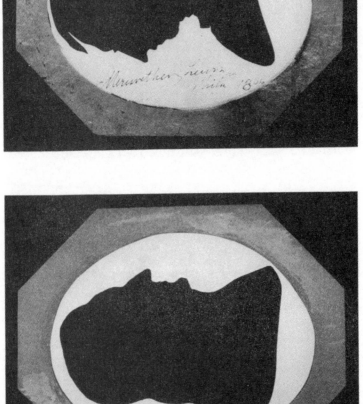

FATHER AND SON. *On the left is the silhouette of Captain William Lewis. The silhouette on the right shows Meriwether Lewis at the age of twenty. Both are published here for the first time.*

PERRY T. RATHBONE

Madison, Monroe, Washington himself studied in these little schools, whose masters were often men of fine scholarship and great ability. They were vastly superior to the wandering schoolmaster with no textbook except his own manuscript on "ciphering," under whom Meriwether Lewis had commenced his studies in Georgia.

Letters to his mother tell of Meriwether's difficulty in finding a schoolmaster in Albemarle. During the winter of 1787–1788, he writes that he has applied to Parson Matthew Maury. But Parson Maury at the moment was not keeping school and was not very eager to accept the new boy from Georgia, "as what we would wish to learn would interfere with his Latin business." By spring, however, he had "set in" with the parson, a main attraction at whose school seems to have been Miss Milly Maury, the parson's daughter, for whom Lewis developed a vague sort of sentimental attachment. Though "there had been some tenderness between them," as a relative wrote later, it was only puppy love. Young Meriwether's head was too full of plans and hopes, an eager interest in study, a still more eager interest in the woods, to take any girl very seriously. But Milly Maury never forgot him. As an old woman she still spoke affectionately of "Mirwether," and she is said, as she lay dying, to have asked to see once more the picture of the schoolboy who had become the dashing young officer, the President's secretary, the great explorer, and who had loved her once.

Lewis remained in Maury's little school two years. It was not particularly expensive. The accounts show, in June, 1788, an entry: "To paid the Rev Mathew Murray for Schooling" —seven pounds. In January, 1789, Mr. Maury received thirteen pounds and in July two pounds for tuition and board.

The next year, Lewis was sent to Dr. Charles Everitt, a prominent Albemarle physician who doubled as a schoolmaster. It was an unhappy choice, for Dr. Everitt was in bad health and was personally "of an atrabilious & melancholy

temperament: peevish, capricious & every way disagreeable."
The doctor had extraordinary ideas of discipline. He delighted to perch a boy on a three-legged stool, leaning against
the wall with two legs propped up on stones. Watching slyly
for a drowsy moment, he would slip up, kick out the stones,
and send his inattentive pupil crashing to the floor.

"We disliked the teacher," wrote one of Lewis's fellow
students, "his method of teaching was as bad as anything
could be. he was impatient of interruption We seldom applied for assistance, said our lessons badly, made no profi-
ciency, and acquired negligent and bad habits."

The same writer left a description of Lewis as a schoolboy:
"Meriwether Lewis, afterwards distinguished for his expedition up the Missouri was one of our schoolmates. He was
always remarkable for perseverance which in the early period
of his life seemed nothing more than obstinacy in pursuing
the trifles that employ that age: a martial temper: a great
steadiness of purpose self-possession, and undaunted courage.
His person was stiff and without grace, bow legged, awkward,
formal and almost without flexibility: his face was comely &
by many considered handsome. It bore to my vision a very
Strong resemblance to Buonaparte."

A very little of Dr. Everitt was enough. The boy was transferred to the school run by the Rev. James Waddel, who,
although a Presbyterian minister, held an Episcopal parish.
Tall, fair, erect, with light blue eyes which, when Lewis
studied under him, had not yet begun to fail, he was a "very
polite scholar" and a Doctor of Divinity of Dickinson College. The schoolboys saw him with a white linen cap as part
of his "domestic costume," but he walked abroad in the dignity of a "large, full-bottomed wig, perfectly white." Its
grandeur offset a palsied and deformed hand with fingers that
had never grown to normal size—relic of the doctor's boyish
effort to extract a rabbit from a hollow tree with a misapplied
hatchet.

Young Meriwether, who always took study seriously, had hoped to study further with Parson Maury. But his elders, as he wrote his brother Reuben, decided that he had now "got well acquanted with the English Grammer, and mite learn Geogrphy at Home. Upon this, I concluded to stay at Uncle Peacy Gilmers, and go to School to a Master in the Neighbourhood, (as there was none in the Neighbourhood at Cousin Williams) in Order to get acquanted with Figurs, where I am now Stationed. . . . I should like very much to have some of your Sport, fishing, and hunting, provided I could be doing Something, that will no Doubt be more to my advantag herafter."

This boyish attitude became characteristic of the man. While he was wintering among the Mandan Indians on his way across the continent in 1804 and 1805, his thoughts still turned to the education of his half-brother at Locust Hill. From the wildest part of the wild West, he wrote his mother gravely: "You may rest assured that as you reguard his future p[r]osperity you had better make any sacrefice of his property than suffer his education to be neglected or remain incomple[te]." Before that, he had been equally concerned about Reuben's education.

He paid one visit to his mother in the summer of 1790, for the guardian's accounts contain the entry: "To Cash for traveling expences to Georgia." It was the last time he would see John Marks, who died the next year. In April, 1792, he writes his mother that he has quit school entirely and will set out, as soon as his carriage is ready, to bring her back to Locust Hill. The carriage is said to have been built for him by skilled slave artisans of his friend, Mr. Jefferson.

There is a legend that Meriwether Lewis already knew William Clark and even that they had been schoolboys together, but nothing is really known of Clark's education. According to tradition, he had developed an intense interest in Indians by the age of four, something so normal in small boys that it would hardly be worth mentioning except that William Clark grew up to spend his life, first fighting Indians, then exploring among them, and finally serving as the government's leading expert in dealing with them. By tradition, too, he was especially devoted to his much older brother, George Rogers Clark, was greatly interested in George's Revolutionary campaigns, and joined in his later, post-Revolutionary campaigns against the Indians. However slight his formal schooling, it would be difficult to imagine a better preparation for the life William Clark was to lead than this early, intensely practical instruction under a veteran in woodcraft, Indian lore, and rough, frontier soldiering. At some time during these early years he also learned the drawing and map-making that he was later to put to good use in the army and to still better use on the Lewis and Clark Expedition.

Both of the growing boys owed much to the sheer richness and variety of Virginian life. Despite post-Revolutionary hardships, Virginia in those days was a safe and comfortable little world, urbane and civilized, with leaders like General George Rogers Clark, Mr. Jefferson, Mr. Madison, Mr. Monroe, who combined wide-ranging intellectual tastes with the habits of men of action. Mr. Jefferson, friend of both the Lewis and the Clark families, constructed a new version of the Testament to suit himself, corresponded with the great French zoölogist, Cuvier, on scientific matters, played the violin, read Homer, indulged in invention and architectural design, meditated political philosophy, established religious freedom, collected books, founded a university, interested himself in seeds, plants, and mammoths. That he was a practicing attorney, Governor of Virginia, Minister to France, Secretary of State, Vice-President, and twice President of the United States were minor matters.

After desperate forays on the Revolutionary frontier, George Rogers Clark whiled away the leisure of his later years reading, hunting, fishing, corresponding with a few chosen friends in different parts of the Continent—pursuits which he enlivened, it must be admitted, by a good deal of heavy drinking. Like Mr. Jefferson, like Meriwether Lewis, and like many other Virginia gentlemen of the day, both George Rogers Clark and William Clark had a lively interest in nature and in rudimentary science.

"I dont suppose there is a person living that knows the Geography and Natural History of the back Cuntrey better if so well as I do myself," wrote George Rogers Clark. "It hath been my study for many years."

Everyone agreed with Mr. Jefferson: "Botany I rank with the most valuable sciences." The altheas Mr. Jefferson brought back from France still grow in Albemarle. So does the broom he brought from Scotland, not altogether to the joy of modern farmers. The new classification of plants and animals devised by Linnaeus keenly interested Virginia, where the great Swedish taxonomist had two botanical correspondents. The Oxford botanist, Dillenius, even delayed the publication of a scientific tome until material from Virginia colleagues arrived.

Yet about this early plantation life, there was nothing merely bookish, secluded, or impractical. Every gentleman was the head of a highly organized group of small industries. Besides their agricultural pursuits, plantations did their own manufacturing, including carpentry, spinning, weaving, tailoring, blacksmithing, cooperage, building, and milling. Everyone shot, fished, rode—although a German baroness, wife of the captive commander of Burgoyne's German troops, managed to shock all Albemarle when she rode astride.

Though no longer hostile, the Pamunkey and Mattapony Indians were still about, clustered in villages from which they came to sell game and fish to the plantations. Even in the twentieth century, they still bring the Governor of Virginia annual tribute of wild game on Thanksgiving Day.

In such surroundings, both boys grew up through happy childhoods, graduating early into men's responsibilities. Even more than Clark, young Meriwether Lewis loved the wilderness and solitude. Mr. Jefferson himself observed that, from childhood, the lad was habitually off in the woods around Locust Hill, alone, coon hunting through the night. Lewis himself commented, as a young man, on the inveterate propensity for "rambling" that had early taken hold upon him. Even on the expedition, thousands of miles from civilization, he sought still greater solitude. The boats were too crowded. He was always eager to be off along the wild shores of the desolate Missouri, perhaps with two or three of his men—best of all, alone.

His guardian was indulgent. The accounts describe the purchase of "1 pr Knee Buckls," "10 Vest buttons," "2 hanks Silk," "1 Pin Kniff." There are frequent entries for "poct Money"—sometimes, alas! only a few pence, but on other occasions as much as six shillings. Other entries are hard to explain in the upbringing of a growing boy—"1 quart Whiskey for Negroe Wench" (was that medicine for a sick slave?) or "1 Quart Rum & 1 lb Sugar." But, as the Albemarle County Court gravely approved it all, everything must have been all right.

Perhaps the best evidence of a vigorous, active boyhood is the rate at which young Meriwether Lewis wore out his stockings. The guardian is always buying him "worsted hoes," "plad Hoes," or just plain "thread Stockings."

chapter 3: *Lieutenant Clark fights Indians*

AFTER the Revolution, Congress had fallen into the usual folly, which recurs after every American war: it decided there would never be another. If that was true, there was no use having an army, and besides, standing armies were "inconsistent with the principles of republican government," likely to be "destructive engines for establishing despotism."

By the middle of 1784, the army had already dwindled to 700 men. An Act of June 2, 1784, further reduced it to 80 men who guarded stores—25 at Fort Pitt and 55 at West Point and other magazines. Captain Alexander Hamilton's old battery of artillery was chosen to survive, and remains in the United States army to this day as Battery D, Fifth Field Artillery—sole link between the modern G.I. and the soldiers of the Revolution. Henceforward, the Congress, in its wisdom, proposed to entrust the national defense to 700 militia from each state, to be called out for a single year at a time. Infallibly, it had selected the worst possible system of defense.

It was joyful news among the wigwams. Though the Indians wasted no time perusing reports of legislative proceedings, they were quick to find the soft spots on the white men's frontier and to take the measure of the untrained and ill-equipped militia. Though it was a few years before the fatal nature of this piece of Congressional foolishness was realized on the safe and smug eastern seaboard, its results were instantly and tragically apparent among the western settlements. It was a glorious opportunity for massacre, of which the redskins took full advantage.

What could the United States do about it? Precisely nothing. Militia could hardly be raised, trained, and sent marching to the western frontier before their year was up, and it was time to go home. There was an immense waste of time, money, and effort in going through the same process, year after year.

Nor did the sole threat come from the Indians. The Spanish were pressing north and east along the Mississippi. His Catholic Majesty, the King of Spain, looked askance at settlements of these brash Americans anywhere upon the great river that he hoped soon to make exclusively his own. The British remained blandly in the frontier forts of the American Northwest that they had promised, under the treaty of peace, to evacuate. It took more than diplomatic protests in London to throw redcoats out of a log fort in the woods, as young Clark was soon to see for himself.

Within a year, Congress was forced to extend enlistment to three years and authorize one extraordinary regiment of Regulars—eight companies of infantry and two of artillery, a queer anticipation of the "combat team" of World War II. In 1786, this was changed into a still queerer "legionary corps." The evil word "army" was thus avoided, because the people of the safe and settled East were still suspicious of a regular army. Some of the country members of Congress, wrote Rufus King, "laugh and say the Indian war is only a political one to obtain a standing Army."

Most of this was merely Congressional paper work. Defense of the helpless settlers was still entrusted to a force of less than a thousand men, scattered in little wilderness garrisons across Ohio and Indiana from Pittsburgh to Vincennes, whose presence worried the Indians not at all. The painted warriors held high carnival and gathered in the scalps. Between the close of the Revolution and 1790, more than a thousand settlers had been killed by Indians in Kentucky alone, and the raiders were even more active in Ohio. One of Clark's brothers was killed by Indians on the Wabash about this time.

British agents helped on the bushwhacking. Announcing the end of the Revolutionary War to the tribes, they explained that "the hatchet was only laid down, but not buried." From Philadelphia, the American capital, a British agent wrote the Governor of Upper Canada: "The Indian War must not be allowed to subside; a peace must if possible be prevented." Indians being what they were, that was not very hard.

The Indians were especially quick to take up British suggestions of hostility because they were disturbed by the sudden, post-Revolutionary flow of white settlers westward. Immigrants by the hundreds were floating down the Ohio with all their household goods, slaves, and livestock in flatboats capable of carrying from 20 to 70 tons, or in swift keelboats, or in crude dugout canoes made of a single huge tree trunk or even of two trunks joined together. William Clark here saw for the first time the kind of dugout with which he was to struggle up the Missouri and down the Columbia later, for many a weary mile. According to one estimate, 1,000 boats went down the Ohio in 1785—the entire Clark family in one of them.

Their patriotism in the Revolution had cost the Clarks heavily. When there was no other way to support his army, General George Rogers Clark had drawn upon his father. Virginia refused to reimburse the family for these expenses. The general's own land claims were in a state of wild disorder. Creditors pressed claims of their own vigorously against the Clarks. Thus was already laid the foundation for that series of lawsuits, claims, counter-claims, and general business confusion which plagued the last years of George Rogers Clark, and which his brother William struggled most of his life to straighten out.

John Clark's family decided to seek new fortunes in Kentucky. In 1784 they set out for Pittsburgh, where they remained icebound until the Ohio River was open in the spring of 1785. Floating down the river to Louisville, they took up new estates there. Here they settled, the aging parents, distinguished sons, daughters, slaves, and fifteen-year-old William, who, like Meriwether Lewis, began to assume a man's business responsibilities when he was hardly more than a boy. When he was only sixteen, as a surviving letter shows, he was already being consulted about the purchase of equipment for his brother's mill; but it was all good training—cornmills turned out to be surprisingly helpful among the Indians a few years later.

Disturbance among the Indians grew with each new boat. From underbrush by the river banks, black eyes gleamed angrily in copper faces. Potshots flashed from tangled thickets. Warriors dashed out in canoes from coves along the shore, killed whom they could, scalped the dead, stole what they found, and disappeared.

Still the white men came. Kentucky was plainly lost to the red man. Ohio would be lost too. Many of the older chiefs remembered well enough how they had been driven from their eastern lands. They were alarmed by a map which Congress foolishly allowed to be published, showing the proposed creation of two more states. Though the Indians did not see the map, news of it spread swiftly through the woods, to be sullenly discussed in wigwams and cabins and by council fires.

They refused to observe treaties of 1784 and 1785 granting land in Ohio to the white man. Fraud and compulsion had tricked them, the red warriors said. They wanted a new treaty making the Ohio River forever a boundary between white and red.

The federal government seemed quite unable to deal with the red menace. By the spring of 1786, 1,500 Wabash warriors were on the warpath—"Encouraged by the British Traders from Detroit, and their own Inclination," according to George Rogers Clark. There was danger that the western settlers would secede to form a more aggressive government of their own. "Under the present system," wrote one of them, "we cannot exert our strength, neither does Congress seem disposed to protect us."

In the autumn, Colonel Benjamin Logan received definite orders from General George Rogers Clark to clean out the Shawnee settlements, which he did more expeditiously than completely. His militia were "out" only twenty-seven days, killed ten chiefs—including Daniel Boone's Shawnee foster-father, Black Fish—burned over two hundred Indian cabins, and destroyed about 15,000 bushels of corn. Young William Clark may have been one of the 400 to 500 militia who rode on this foray. He is said to have been with his brother in the Indian fighting with which the year closed. George Rogers Clark moved overland with 1,000 men, fortified himself at Vincennes, Indiana, and brought the Wabash Indians temporarily to terms. If they continued to fight after this, the elder Clark brother warned them, the Americans would "send a great many Families to take possession of your Lands and make a Conquest of them Forever." This was the one thing the redskins dreaded most, as the old Indian fighter very well knew.

Minor raids on both sides continued, however, until in August, 1789, Colonel John Hardin led 200 mounted volunteers across the Falls of the Ohio, killed more Indians, and destroyed more Wabash towns. With this group went William Clark, now nineteen. He spent the winter of 1789–1790 helping guard against the Indian retaliation that followed.

By 1790, it was apparent that reliance on scouts, patrols, and militia raids was hopeless. President Washington had had quite enough of guerrilla war. The militia would be called into Federal service and systematic Indian campaigns would begin. That put the matter into the hands of Brigadier General Joseph Harmar, commander-in-chief, and General Arthur St. Clair, governor of the Northwest Territory—both of whom proceeded to immediate and inglorious defeat.

Harmar, after burning some corn and villages, got himself ambuscaded, and was so closely pursued that even Cincinnati was threatened. Indians came boldly into the town in the night, and even stole the horses of officers attending a ball. When the enemy interfered with officers' dancing, it was time to call a halt. The luckless brigadier faced a court of inquiry in 1791, was acquitted of negligence, and delighted everyone by resigning.

Next year, while Meriwether Lewis was still slaving at his books in Albemarle, young William Clark was "out" again on General Charles Scott's "blackberry campaign," a name due to supply failure which forced the men to subsist on blackberries. A letter to Jonathan Clark dated May 30, 1791, remarks: "Y^r. Brother, *William* is gone out, as a cadet, with Genl. Scott, on the Expedition. He is a youth of solid & promising parts, and as brave as Cæsar."

Just what a "cadet" was in a frontier army, no one is ever likely to know. As William Clark was now approaching twenty-one, he was probably training on active duty for a commission to be awarded when he came of age, much like an *aspirant* in the French army.

Clark was serving under a fine but very tough commander. Scott had fought under Braddock at fifteen and all through the Revolution. "Brave and means well," Washington wrote in an acidly confidential little list of officers that he kept, but "of inadequate abilities for extensive command." Worse still: "by report, is addicted to drinking."

Scott set out toward the end of May, 1791, burned several Indian towns, and destroyed cattle, hogs, and provisions. The Indians gave chase as the column withdrew, and for a time there was a running fight, with the combatants strung out over several miles. Provisions ran low and once it was necessary to halt and make canoes—the sort of thing with which the Lewis and Clark Expedition was to become dolefully familiar.

Nevertheless, Scott brought his troops safely back and turned over 41 Indian prisoners to Federal troops. He was particularly pleased because he had broken his Kentucky volunteers of their bad habit of scalping the dead. Still glowing with this humanitarian triumph, the men were mustered out at Louisville. Some genius in the War Department got around to countermanding the whole expedition—in orders issued July 9!

Clark is also believed to have been one of about 500 men whom Colonel James Wilkinson, led into the Indian country in August of the same year. After much floundering in bogs and country "pondy in every direction," they found and burned a number of Indian towns. The strange admiration of the pre-eminently loyal Clark for Wilkinson (who eventually became as great a traitor as Benedict Arnold) may date from this period. They had already been associated on Scott's expedition.

General St. Clair now led into the Indian country the largest force yet sent out, with which he made by far the largest fiasco. There is no proof that Clark was with this expedition, but it is hard to believe that he was willing to be left behind. St. Clair had 4,000 men, ten field guns, and 200 women. One child was born during the campaign. It may be doubted whether these ladies were on a much higher plane than the soldiers, whom their disgusted adjutant-general described as "the offscourings of large towns and cities; enervated by idleness, debaucheries and every species of vice." Chaste nineteenth-century historians very strongly imply that all these women were the soldiers' wives. The queer thing is that some of them apparently were, though why any husband should drag his spouse into that howling wilderness, no one will ever know. Pioneer women faced many hardships, but they did not ordinarily go along on campaigns.

The staff work was bad as bad could be. Pay failed. Axes bent. The pack saddles were too big for the horses—fit only for elephants, as one indignant officer spluttered. Two traveling forges arrived without anvils. For a time, the whole force had only one cross-cut saw and only one "froe"—a wedge for splitting logs. Discipline was bad. Three men had to be hanged. St. Clair would have been glad to delay, but President Washington was impatient. Orders to go ahead were "express and unequivocal."

On October 18 there was a major disaster—the liquor gave out. The militia began to "talk loudly of returning home." Sixty of them, starting off in a body, had to be pursued by Regulars.

A band of Shawnee scouts under the redoubtable Tecumseh had for some time been hanging on the American flank, observing all this. The Indians were sure of victory for they had just seen a miracle. A medicine man had consulted the spirits. Two long rows of warriors sat silent in the forest that night while a large brush fire blazed at one end. From this, as the flames kindled, a large blacksnake emerged. It was, a startled white beholder said, "apparently 20 feet in length, and ran through the whole line with its head as high as the Indians' heads." The warriors fell into line behind the creature, yelling with all their might, until the snake escaped into the darkness. This was plainly a sign from the Great Spirit—anyone could see that. They attacked next day.

It was the old story—green troops, hasty training, bad discipline, lack of reconnaissance, surprise, panic, massacre. The camp women drove skulking soldiers from under the wagons "by firebrands and the usual weapons of their sex." But where the officers had failed, not even the camp followers could control the rout.

One woman known as Red Nance led all the fugitives, possibly because she realized the special value of her flaming red scalp. She ran as long as she could with her screaming baby in her arms, then pitched the child into the snow, and ran on. The Indians picked up the infant, took it back to Sandusky, and reared it as their own.

But Red Nance had been right in not trusting herself to Indian mercy. The Indians killed such women as they caught by driving stakes through their bodies and into the ground. Dead soldiers were later found with their mouths filled with dirt—a bit of aboriginal satire on American greed for land. One belated straggler told a horrible tale of slipping away from the battlefield, where the dead lay scalped and ghastly. Each still warm and bloody head had a little mist rising above it in the chill November air. They looked, he said, like pumpkins scattered about a cornfield.

chapter 4: Lieutenant Clark and General Wayne

SOMETHING had to be done to wipe out this series of defeats or the Indians would soon be beyond control. President Washington looked over his list of possible leaders. He remembered most of them—not very favorably. They had served under him in the Revolution, and he had his doubts about them all. It is strange what a low opinion the Revolutionary commander-in-chief entertained of his officers. From the lot, with numerous misgivings, he selected Anthony Wayne, "a brave general and nothing else." However, the times seemed to require a brave general, and Washington gave him the command in April, 1792. Wayne was only fifty and in vigorous health except that—like most other eighteenth-century generals—he suffered from the gout.

The Senate, indulging in the usual inanities about peace,

proposed more Indian treaties. Wayne was sent out with his hands tied by instructions to negotiate before fighting. The redskins, however, relieved him of this worry by gleefully butchering both peace commissioners—Colonel John Hardin, Clark's former commander, and Major Alexander Trueman, of the Fourth Sub-Legion, in which William Clark was now a lieutenant.

In spite of the murders, Indian negotiations continued. A delegation of chiefs visited Philadelphia, where they were received with the diplomatic protocol due ambassadors and dined with Washington. But as they promptly got drunk and persistently and joyfully stayed so, the cause of peace was not much advanced. Another peace conference at the mouth of the Detroit River led to no better result, except that the diplomats managed to stay sober. The Indians continued to demand the Ohio River as a permanent boundary. So far as they were concerned, it was that or nothing. Why negotiate? It was more profitable to get drunk.

When he reached his headquarters in Pittsburgh, Wayne made the embarrassing discovery that he had practically no forces to command. Such troops as remained were in a state of contagious timidity. Half of headquarters were still in mourning for Major General Richard Butler, killed in St. Clair's defeat. The soldiers who had shared that disaster, still shivering in their shoes, filled the few recruits who trickled in with terrifying tales of Indian fury. Virginia settlers remarked lugubriously as the rookies passed: "What a pity such a likely parcel of young men were going to be slaughtered by the indians as Genl. St. Clair's army was."

It was all very bad for morale. New arrivals stayed with the colors just long enough to drink up the bounty money paid them for enlisting, then vanished. Many never reached Pittsburgh at all. One major lost 50 recruits west of Carlisle. A cavalry officer lost seven dragoons. When a false alarm spread one night that Indians might attack Pittsburgh, a third of the sentries slipped off in the darkness. All were dissatisfied with Wayne's discipline as too severe, the Spanish spies reported.

Terrified by the St. Clair disaster, Congress had in March of 1792 enlarged the forces to six regiments. General Henry Knox, Secretary of War, organized them into a single "Legion of the United States." Wayne divided this into four "Sub-Legions." Regiments were done away with and the rank of colonel disappeared. Each Sub-Legion had its own infantry, cavalry, artillery, and "riflemen"—the latter distinct from ordinary infantry. The act creating the Legion was passed March 5, 1792, and on March 7, young William Clark was commissioned lieutenant of infantry and assigned to the 4th Sub-Legion on September 4, the day it was created. He became adjutant and quartermaster a year later.

When the cold weather came, Wayne moved his command a little way down the Ohio, to a new camp, "Legionville." Here his soldiers built log shelters, and here Clark and the rest settled down to a winter of drill, maneuvers, target practice, and bayonet training—plenty of bayonet. Wayne remembered the victory with unloaded muskets and cold steel that had made his reputation at Stoney Point. He took his troops out into the woods to skirmish, for if they fought at all, it would certainly be in wilderness. The winter raged. The snow fell. The drills and skirmishing went on. Mad Anthony wanted an all-weather army.

It was good training for Lieutenant Clark. The Lewis and Clark Expedition would spend two winters in wilderness log forts. When the time came, Clark knew all about building and defending them.

Eventually the winter grew so cold that the men's cloth hats were inadequate. The army knocked off drill and maneuvers for a few days and went bear hunting. Thereafter Clark and the Legion wore bearskins—homemade and not, perhaps, so impressive as the Coldstream Guards', but very practical. Each Sub-Legion had plumes of its own color—white for the 1st, red for the 2nd, yellow for the 3rd, and green for the 4th.

Even the color of the men's hair was prescribed. This was more sensible than it sounds. Uniformity is essential to discipline, but in a day when men wore either long locks or colored wigs, uniformity was hard to get. Apparently, Wayne solved the problem by putting all the black-haired men in the 1st and 3rd Sub-Legions and letting the rest powder their hair if it was the wrong color! At any rate, the fair-haired Meriwether Lewis eventually went into the 2nd Sub-Legion and the blazing red head of William Clark into the 4th. Later, Lewis was transferred to Clark's company under Clark's command. Doubtless both polls were subdued to an appropriate sameness of hue by the government allowance of two pounds of flour and one-half pound of rendered tallow for the hair. Or perhaps Wayne made them all wear wigs. Honest redskins had been greatly surprised to find soldiers with two scalps at Braddock's defeat and for years afterwards.

It is remarkable how completely Wayne avoided the habitual errors of the American at war. Previous defeats had been due to the use of half-trained troops. Wayne drilled his men endlessly before he let them fight. The militia, with far too much faith in their own valor, scoffed at the precision of the Regulars. On the frontier, they insisted, you could win with odds at "one Indian to four Regulars, and two Indians to one Kentuckian." Harmar and St. Clair had tried to instill in the Kentucky woodsmen the Regular Army's ideas of discipline—with dismal unsuccess. Wayne knew better. "When Wayne was out," says an old manuscript, "he left the militia to their own officers—and all went on peaceably & well."

In the past, shortage of supplies had led to disaster. Wayne built a line of forts and patrolled the ground between them, so that rations and ammunition came up on time. Careless in reconnaissance, the Americans had been repeatedly surprised.

Wayne agreed with his opponent, Chief Little Turtle, that "a good general is never surprised." When the Spaniards looked dangerous, he sent young Lieutenant Clark off to find out exactly what they were doing. He kept up a constant reconnaissance in the Indian country ahead of him, using scouts who had lived with the Indians, spoke their languages, knew their ways.

Prominent among these was Captain William Wells, a white prisoner adopted by the Miamis, who had married into the family of Chief Little Turtle and had fought with the Indians against Harmar and St. Clair. Dim recollections of a white childhood revived as Wayne's army approached. He took Little Turtle to the Maumee River. There he pointed, Indian-fashion, toward the sky. Until the sun reached the spot to which he pointed, they would still be friends; but after that they would be enemies, for Black Snake, the Miami warrior, was going back to the white men. The philosophical Little Turtle, with amazing magnanimity, let him go.

Convincing Wayne of his loyalty, Wells joined up as chief scout, commanding a group of four, which included another adopted Indian, Henry Miller, and Robert M'Clelan, with whom Lewis and Clark were to have a memorable meeting on the Missouri. Constantly operating ahead of the army, the little band of woodsmen had some astonishing adventures. Sent out one day to bring in a prisoner for questioning, Wells, Miller, and M'Clelan saw a smoke, slipped through the underbrush, and came upon three Indians camped in open ground. Creeping under a fallen tree, they decided to kill two and run down the third. M'Clelan was selected for the chase. Portioning out the Indians to right and left as their prey, Wells and Miller fired. Both warriors fell dead, as M'Clelan bounced out, tomahawk in hand, and dashed after the third. The fugitive, jumping twenty feet off a steep bank, had the bad luck to land in mud so soft that he sank to his waist. As his pursuer leaped down upon him, there was a savage hand-to-hand with knife and tomahawk until Wells and Miller arrived, to find them both helplessly stuck in the mud. When they had dragged their prisoner out and washed him off, they discovered that he was white—Miller's brother Christopher, whom the Indians had also adopted.

In the spring of 1792, young Lieutenant Clark was near home. His diary shows that he reached Fort Washington (Cincinnati) on May 15. On the 22nd, he was delivering letters for General Wilkinson in Lexington. He amused himself there until June 2, buying shoes, buckles, knee buckles, and a toothbrush, and otherwise enacting the role of dashing subaltern. His accounts show expenditure of 1 s. 6 d. for a barber's services, which must have exhausted the tonsorial talents of Kentucky, and he gave 3 s. "To Boy For Playing."

When Wayne actually moved into Indian country at Fort Washington in 1793, Clark was kept busy "on commands." His diary shows him preoccupied with supply problems and the health of his men. In May, 1793, the entry "all day at the corn" appears repeatedly, until he has "finished the corn halling." Other entries report "one man very sick. I blead him and Gave him a swet a Fale ague. . . . I was ob[liged] to punish one man for Filth, . . . one man sick the usual Fale ague. . . . I inspect into my mens Clothing arms and accoutaments."

Like his friend Lewis, Clark was a great believer in constant inspections, knowing only too well the chronic carelessness of the average soldier. Later, on the expedition, they held one inspection after another, until they were absolutely sure that their men were ready for any emergency.

On May 27, he started his command for Fort Washington (Cincinnati), passing on the way "2 Companys of horrid looking invuleads." Indian sign having been reported two miles down the river, on June 2 he noted: "I inspected into my men's equipments to Day, obliged to punish one for neglect of Duty & one for sleeping on his post Last night."

Next day he ran into deserters coming down the river by canoe. When they landed and tried to escape, a sergeant and seven men gave chase and caught them. Clark started his prisoners back to headquarters and went on, with various minor adventures. He was ill. His oxen got away in the woods. One died, and it took some time to round up the others. Indians were heard a few miles above him, crossing the river in the fog, but there was no attack.

In June he was ordered down the Ohio, ostensibly to carry corn and other supplies to the Chickasaw Indians, who lived conveniently close to the Spanish posts. Taking the precaution of giving his men "2 Extra Gills" of whisky, he got his boats loaded and, with a third and final gill to celebrate, pushed off. After taking his cargo to the Tennessee and Cumberland River valleys, he visited his home near Louisville on the way back and was at Fort Washington again in early September. After delivering stores at Fort Jefferson, a northerly outpost, he joined the army as it passed there on October 11.

The Spanish intelligence service kept a sharp eye on the comings and goings of this troublesome young lieutenant—"an enterprising youth of extraordinary activity"—who kept turning up in places where the Spanish did not in the least want him. They knew well enough that his "supply" mission to the Chickasaws might be a cloak for Wayne's intelligence and that he was probably sent to ascertain what aid the Americans could expect from the Chickasaws if—as for a time seemed likely—it came to a fight with the Spanish. The Spanish Governor, Gayoso de Lemos, tried the good old military intelligence method of interrogating casual travelers. They had seen Clark's flatboat, concealed in a small stream, with smoke rising from a campfire near it. De Lemos knew well enough whose it was, but when his spies tried to get inside they complained bitterly, though privately, of Clark's precautions: "His flatboats came well covered and locked with key so that it was not possible to see anything of what they contained."

The Spaniards were worried over Wayne's expedition because they were not sure which way it was really heading. If it attacked the Indians or the British, well and good. But Wayne had nearly 100 flatboats and he might sweep suddenly down the Ohio and into the Mississippi, where Spanish and American interests were always in conflict. They were further disturbed by the illicit efforts of the too-enterprising French Minister in Washington, the notorious Citizen Genêt, who was trying to organize against the Spaniards a French military expedition, to be composed of Americans from the western country, with Lieutenant Clark's elder brother, George Rogers Clark, as a French major-general. The Spanish spies probably knew that George Rogers Clark had already received his French commission. They may even have found out that Mr. Jefferson's friend, André Michaux, who was Genêt's agent as well as a botanist, had made a very secret visit to the elder Clark. It did not make them any happier to have the younger Clark floating up and down the Ohio and Mississippi, so close to Spanish territory.

In the following May, Clark wrote his brother Jonathan that "the Spaniards are much alarmed" over the erection of the American Fort Massac, well down the Ohio close to the Mississippi. They had "re-inforced the garrison of New Madrid, (50 miles below Ohio) with 150 regular troops, 5 galleys, each 60 men; have all the militia under pay, with a vast number of Indians for the purpose of opposing Gen[l]. [George Rogers] Clark in an expedition against their country." The Spanish excitement was needless. President Washington had quashed the whole scheme; but young Lieutenant Clark had managed to get complete plans of all the Spanish river galleys and their armament.

Harmar and St. Clair had been willing to go on taking chances until each took one chance too many. Mad Anthony knew it wouldn't do. Camps had to be fortified, on ground marked off by staff officers who went ahead with the advance guard. However weary the men might be at the end of a day's struggle along wilderness trails, they had to fell trees, build log barricades, and surround them with an abbatis—felled trees with sharpened branches pointing outward, the equivalent of modern barbed wire. Half a mile forward, half a mile in the rear, companies of infantry stood guard all night. When the army moved in the morning, the camp of the night before was kept garrisoned until the next camp had been fortified. The soldiers grumbled mightily—but they slept with their scalps.

Wayne's precautions were needed, for there were plenty of Indians about. On October 17, 1793, a train of 28 wagons, bringing up supplies under command of Lieutenant John Lowrey, of the 2nd Sub-Legion—to which Meriwether Lewis was later assigned—was attacked at Ludlow Springs, about seven miles north of Fort St. Clair. Lowrey's 90 soldiers eventually drove off the Indians, but not until they had killed the lieutenant, his ensign, and thirteen of the men. This is supposed to have been the first engagement in which the great Tecumseh took part as a minor war chief, not merely as a leader of scouts. Lieutenant Clark noted in his diary that the Indians also got away with nine or ten prisoners and some 70 stolen horses.

By November, Wayne realized that he could not end the campaign that autumn. It was the wrong season for Indian fighting, anyhow. "I consider the Indian formadable only when he has a choice of time and ground," he wrote. "In the *fall* of the year he's strong, ferocious and full of spirits—corn is in plenty and venison and other game everywhere to be met with; in the *spring* he is half-starved, weak and dispirited." The moral was, attack in the spring. He began building Fort Greenville, about six miles beyond Fort Jefferson. Its stockade enclosed 50 acres, on which the men built cabins for the winter. He was doing on a large scale what Lewis and Clark would do on a small scale at Fort Mandan on the Missouri in 1804–1805, and at Fort Clatsop on the Pacific, in 1805–1806.

In spite of an influenza epidemic, Wayne also pushed a force still farther ahead to the scene of St. Clair's defeat, where he built Fort Recovery, "a work impervious to savage force." A burial party under Wilkinson had not found all the bodies, and the bones of massacred soldiers lay all about, some of the skulls still showing the marks of scalping knives. Here and there lay St. Clair's lost artillery. The field guns of that day were merely bronze tubes, closed at one end, without elaborate breach and sighting mechanisms to rust. These were still good. Wayne fired a salute to the fallen— three times three from their own guns.

While the soldiers sweated at their axes, Lieutenant Clark, in November, accompanied his friend, General Wilkinson, and a party of friendly Chickasaws back to Fort Washington for supplies. He was again sent down the Ohio, lost two men by desertion, was held up by floating ice, did some hunting, and—disaster dreaded by all officers—lost government property. His diary dolefully notes: "loes a Publick Rifle."

January, 1794, at Fort Vincennes, was much gayer than garrison life at Fort Greenville. Clark managed to attend eight balls in a little over a month and diverted himself with cards. Indians arriving for council in February were drunk and quarrelsome most of the time. Once Clark notes: "some Indians get angry with me and thretn. Play cards with Evins." After more card games with Evins, he was back at Fort Washington on April 7, 1794, ready for action which was not long in coming.

He wrote his brother Jonathan that he had been "nearly ¾ of my time on command's," mostly at Vincennes and on the Wabash. "It appears that all active & Laborious commands fall to me"—a lieutenant's usual fate. The worst of it was that "This last com[man]d was not only Labor but I like to have starved." While on the Wabash, he had had to go twenty days without provisions, depending only on his rifle. Ascending the Ohio, his flank guard chased off several small parties of Indians, though without killing any.

After a few weeks at Fort Washington, he was ordered in May, 1794, to escort a pack train of 700 horses carrying clothing and rations to Fort Greenville. To guard this long column, he had 60 or 70 infantry and twenty dragoons. Eighteen miles out the advance guard—six infantrymen and about nine dragoons—were attacked and all the infantry killed. Clark, although ill, got his rear guard of infantry forward, there was about fifteen minutes of firing, the dragoons charged. The Indians escaped with a few pack horses that had broken loose in the excitement.

The moment the fighting ceased, Clark improvised a breastwork of kegs and baggage as a precaution against a new attack, but it soon became apparent that the Indians had retreated. Though his party had lost eight men, they had the scalp of only one Indian; but blood on the ground showed that the Happy Hunting Grounds must have received several other inmates. Indians always carried off bodies, if they could, to spare the dead warriors the disgrace of being scalped.

Like every other lieutenant in military history, Clark had an aggrieved feeling that the commanding officer did not properly appreciate him, especially in this skirmish: "My merit for my disposition and officer like conduct in the mentioned fray has not been sufficiently rewarded," he wrote his brother Jonathan, explaining in a parenthesis "no cred^t. for my disposition only for my supporting the front. Kissing goes by favor." The resentment against Wayne which his diary begins to show a few weeks later may have been caused by this incident.

His health doubtless had something to do with his bad humor. He mentions illness three times in his diary for

April. On the 15th: "I took a puke verry sick." He mentions being ill again on the 18th, and then on the 20th notes once more: "I am verry sick." It was the beginning of the illness which forced his resignation from the army within two years.

In spite of his belief in spring campaigns against Indians, Wayne was not able to move forward until mid-summer of 1794. He started at last on July 28, 1794, with 2,000 Regulars of the Legion and 600 Kentucky riflemen, while 900 more Kentuckians were hurrying from Fort Washington, trying to catch up. Nervous Kentucky sentries gave too many needless alarms the first night and forced the troops to turn out repeatedly; but at least these annoying interruptions to a good night's sleep showed an alertness notably lacking in earlier Indian campaigns.

It was hard traveling. The weather was hot. "No water except in ponds, which nothing but excessive thirst would induce us to drink," wrote one of the officers. The mosquitoes were "larger than I ever saw." On July 30, according to Clark, they "proceeded with usial Velocity—Through Thickets almost impervious, thro Morassies, Defiles, & beads of Netles more than waist high & miles in length & on the left flank crossed the water Course on which F. Recovery Stands, more then one Dozen times."

Beaver Swamp, eleven miles beyond Fort Recovery, stopped the column for two or three days. A hundred men splashed ahead to open the road, with scouts out around them and a company of infantry to protect them, while the engineers built a 70-yard bridge across the swamp for the rest of the army.

When they finally came out into open country on August 1, Lieutenant Clark noted with satisfaction that the men for the first time caught a glimpse of the whole column on the march. The effect on morale was very satisfactory.

Soon they began to run into abandoned Indian towns, and

at the junction of the Maumee and Auglaize Rivers Lieutenant Clark noted that some of the Indian cabins were still
burning. The Indians had "left every appearance of haveing
gorne off with precipation and the greatest consternation,
which must afford a mortifying proof of the great advantage
we have let Slip."

The last sentence is a sneer at Anthony Wayne, which refers to a squabble between Wayne and Wilkinson over correct tactics. Throughout the winter of 1793–1794, Wilkinson
had been scheming to get Wayne dismissed, so that he himself could take over the command. Though he had failed in
this, his intrigues had delayed supplies long enough to frus-
trate Wayne's favorite plan for a spring attack.

Around him, Wilkinson had gathered a group of officers
who, without open insubordination, seized every opportunity
to ridicule their commander. Wayne was "Mars," the "Old
Horse," "Old Tony." There were jokes about "Tony Lump-
kin." When members of the group spoke of "the General,"
as Clark sometimes does in his diary, they meant Wilkinson.
As Clark throughout his career was the very soul of loyalty
to the United States, he can hardly have had any suspicion
of Wilkinson's treason. He had no way of knowing that, for
at least a year, Wilkinson had been keeping the Spaniards
fully informed of American military affairs. They themselves described him as "a confidant and pensioner of ours."
"Pensioner" was almost too modest a word—Carondelet paid
Wilkinson $12,000 in one lump sum.

Clark had been associated with Wilkinson on earlier wilderness campaigns, where friendships ripen fast if they ripen
at all. He had no previous acquaintance with Wayne. As
junior officers often do, he adopted uncritically the ideas of
a respected senior. The experienced and loyal Wayne was in
his eyes a complete numskull, the plausible and disloyal
Wilkinson an infallible tactician. After August 7, the lieutenant's diary is bitterly hostile to his commander-in-chief.

When it became apparent that the Indians were withdrawing from their villages, Clark was quite sure that Wayne had made a dreadful mistake in refusing to attack, as Wilkinson wanted him to: "The Scheeme was perposed & certain Suckcess insu[r]ed if attempted—Genl. Wilkinson Suggested the plan to the Comd^r in Chief, but it was not his plan, nor perhaps his wish to Embrace So probable a means for Ending the War by compelling them to peace—this was not the first occasion or oppertunity, which presented its self to our observant Genl—for Some grand stroke of Enterprise, but the Comd^r in Chief rejected all & every of his plans."

The event showed that Wayne's tactics led to complete and overwhelming victory. There was never any real chance of surprise. Now that the Canadian documents are open, it is easy to see that the Indians were well informed of American movements most of the time. Simcoe, a former American Tory leader who had become Governor of Upper Canada, was able to send Lord Dorchester an exact map of the American march as far as Fort Recovery.

On the very night of Clark's sarcastic entry in his diary, an Indian was detected skulking about the camp. Kentucky riflemen brought him down. The fact that Wayne had already gone to bed gave Lieutenant Clark occasion for further sardonic reflection: "had this Alarm been well founded & the Enemy on our Heels, the old Gentleman, would have been caught [a]Sleep for he had already gone to bead to give ease to his infurmities & was so fast in the arms of Morpheus as to give Some trouble to wake him understanding the cause of the Bustle." However that may have been, Wayne occupied the Indian village of Grand Glaize next day (August 8).

The problem now was to keep the Indians uncertain of his intentions and thus keep their forces divided. Harmar's expedition had gone northwest down St. Mary's River to the upper course of the Maumee. St. Clair had tried to follow the same route. Wayne shrewdly let rumors slip that he, too, would go the same old way, thus keeping the Indians in that area to defend their villages. He then let slip a second crop of rumors that he would move northeast to attack the British at Fort Miamis, near modern Toledo.

However thoroughly he deceived the Indians, Wayne never deceived the astute Simcoe, who had fought him in the Revolution, knew how his mind worked, guessed correctly what he would do, and got ready to fight him. The British Fort Miamis, built in 1764, had fallen to pieces. Simcoe decided in the spring of 1794 to rebuild it and put in a garrison. The British fort stood on American soil, but what of that? Simcoe was a virulent Tory with a bitter hatred of the new nation that had ousted him. "All the speeches sent by Simcoe are as red as blood," a communicative Pottawatomie prisoner told the Americans. "All the wampum and feathers are red; the war hatchets are bright red; even the tobacco is painted in that color."

Cautious as always, Wayne halted to fortify again. Sweating in the August heat, his soldiers built a new stronghold. Wayne called it Fort Defiance—"I defy the English, the Indians, and the devil to take it," he remarked stoutly. He revealed his true intentions for the first time when he started a road northeast, down the Maumee River, toward the British fort. Nine miles beyond Fort Defiance, he built Fort Deposit, to guard his baggage, while the Indians to the West, aware at last where he was going, skurried through the wilderness around him to gather near Fort Miamis. There were two minor brushes on August 17 and 18.

Though fully ready for battle, Wayne himself did not expect it. Only a day before his victory, he was betting Wilkinson ten guineas and a quarter-cask of wine that there would be further peace negotiations. On August 14, he sent the scout, Christopher Miller, with a flag of truce to tell the Indians he would not attack them if they would withdraw or make peace: "Brothers, be no longer deceived or led astray by the false promises & language of the bad white men, at the foot of the Rapids." Playing for time, the Indians asked for ten days to think it over. Refusing, Wayne prepared to move.

It was rainy on the morning of August 20, 1794, and Wayne, like a good general, looked out for the comfort of his men. Since there was no longer any particular reason for haste, he held them in Fort Deposit until seven or eight o'clock. Even when it did move out, the Legion found the going difficult. A terrific storm some time before had knocked down trees in all direction. Fallen timbers lay all about, the trunks criss-crossed in slow decay. The British were nowhere to be seen. They had prudently abandoned their advanced post and were shut up snugly in Fort Miamis.

Indians were somewhere ahead, though Little Turtle had concealed them so cleverly that the American scouts could find no sign of their presence. The Indians had been waiting for days. On the 18th, they heard Wayne would come, and they fasted in preparation for the battle. Little Turtle's scouts, who had bumped into the American advance on the 17th, had overestimated its speed. They now sent back word that Wayne would not arrive until the 19th, and again the warriors fasted. By the 20th, everyone was hungry and, as the weather was bad, the chiefs decided battle was unlikely. Large numbers went off down the river to get food at Fort Miamis, four miles away.

A small party of Kentuckians were riding well ahead of Wayne's main body. From clumps of tall grass, invisible Indians suddenly fired. The Kentuckians whirled their horses and rode for their lives into the advancing Legion. For a few minutes there was amazing confusion. Leading elements of the column broke and ran. They threw a light infantry company into such disorder that its commander had to withdraw 40 yards to establish contact with units on his right that were standing firm. Here a battalion of riflemen reinforced them.

Wayne spurred forward, gout or no gout, though he had had to be lifted into the saddle that morning. Wilkinson hesitated to advance, for fear of ambush. The artillery sprayed the Indians with grape and canister. Wayne sent the dragoons forward, their long blades gleaming, their horses leaping the fallen trees, into the tall grass from which the fire was coming. It was a cavalry charge in the grand manner. The Indians scuttled for the woods.

Now was the time when the endless years of drill and discipline Wayne had inflicted on his grumbling Legion counted at last. Reinforcements were tumbling into the Indian line, but straight against it, loading and firing on the run as they had been trained so long, went the steady Regulars of the Legion. Somewhere among them was Clark, and probably Lewis also. The Indian reinforcements were exhausted after running four miles to reach the battle. As the Legion closed with its bayonets agleam, the warriors decided, as some of them remarked later, that they did not like "the sharp end of the stick." The infantry punched through the Indian line, while the Kentuckians were still trying to penetrate the tangle on the flank. Sauwaseekau, brother of Tecumseh, was killed, but Tecumseh himself survived to lead his battered Shawnees home. With his rifle so badly damaged that it would not fire, he borrowed a shotgun, rallied his warriors, and held his ground until the main Indian force gave way.

Wayne's troops chased the Indians a mile or two down the river, after which they paused to be "refreshed with ½ gill of Whiskey which they much required." Rushing up to Fort Miamis for refuge, the defeated warriors were horrified to find the gates barred against them by their quondam British friends, even the gaps in the abbatis blocked, and the garrison standing to arms. "Their Panic," said a British officer, "was so great, that the appearance of fifty Americans would have totally routed them."

As Wayne moved down to the British fort, a new issue

MERIWETHER LEWIS by Charles Willson Peale (1741-1827).
*Along with the Peale portrait of Clark, it now hangs in Independence
Hall, Philadelphia, where Peale opened his famous Museum in* 1802.

WILLIAM CLARK by Charles Willson Peale, about 1807. *"Family tradition held that every red-headed Clark was bound to distinguish himself." Both William Clark and his elder brother, George Rogers Clark, had flaming red hair, although not hot tempers.*

arose. Fort Miamis was no ordinary blockhouse but the scientific handiwork of a really good military engineer. The powerful earthworks were screened by a ditch and a wide abbatis. Inside was Major William Campbell with about 200 British troops.

Although the British were occupying American territory and although Wayne outnumbered them at least fifteen to one, President Washington was not looking for another war. Not until June did Wayne receive authority to drive the British out of Fort Miamis—if he had to. "But no attempt ought to be made unless it shall promise complete success; an unsuccessful attempt would be attended with pernicious consequences."

The caution of these instructions suggests the anxiety everyone felt at the prospect of a new war with the Mother Country. Governor Simcoe was already planning to lead a British-Indian invasion of the United States. If Wayne attacked Fort Miamis, he would send a British force strong enough to rouse the Indians again and defeat him. Before the American government could learn that hostilities had begun, he planned a surprise attack that would drive swiftly through New York State and, along the Delaware and Susquehanna valleys, into Pennsylvania. He intended to burn "every Mill on the forks of the Susquehanna down to Northumberland or Sunbury, and on the Delaware to Minesink." Simcoe thought that Vermont and Kentucky would remain neutral —there was enough unrest in both states to make that entirely possible. The series of interchanges between Wayne and Major Campbell were not, therefore, nearly so comic as they sound today, for on them hinged the possibility of a new war that might have destroyed the United States.

On the morning after the battle with the Indians, a gate in the palisade of Fort Miamis opened, and a British officer with a flag of truce emerged. American outposts received the note he presented, but begged him to get back into the shelter of his own fort again, "as the woods were full of Rifflemen, and they were affraid of his safety from accidents." In other words, you could never quite tell what a Kentucky volunteer would do next. Campbell wanted to know "in what light I am to view your making such near approachs to this Garrison," adding, "I know of no War existing between Great Britain and America."

Wayne replied that Campbell's fort was "far within the acknowledged Jurisdiction of the United States of America," where British troops had no business whatever. "Were you intitled to an Answer, the most full and satisfactory one was announced to you, from the Muzzels of my small Arms yesterday morning in the Action against the hoard of Savages in the vicinity of your Post, which terminated Gloriously to the American Arms—but had it continued until the Indians &c were drove under the influence of the Post and Guns you mention—they would not have much impeded the progress of the Victorious Army under my command." Lieutenant Clark thought this "pompious"—as in fact it was—but it kept the British quiet. Campbell, though he retorted that such a reply "fully authorizes me to any Act of hostility," was wise enough not to try "that dreadful decision, which perhaps is not intended to be appealed to, by either of Our Countries."

Wayne personally reconnoitered the British fort, coming within pistol shot and, sad to say, using "the most gross and illiberal language to the British soldiers on duty in it." He was so close that a British lieutenant felt *"absolutely* certain that he could have killed the bravo with his pistol." Simcoe had pointed out in advance the exact spot from which he thought Wayne would reconnoiter. Later he wrote triumphantly: "I know Mr. Wayne so well that he actually did reconnoitre at the express point where I said he would come."

Campbell now complained that the close approach of armed American troops was an insult to the British flag, whereupon Wayne demanded that he evacuate American soil. All he got from Campbell was the tart reply: "I certainly will not abandon this Post."

Each party having with all this rhetoric invited the other to get out and both parties having declined, eighteenth-century honor was satisfied. When, after a few days, Wayne began to withdraw his forces, Campbell promptly notified the notorious Canadian Indian agent, Alexander McKee. McKee had every reason to stir up the Indians again if he could, for the Kentucky volunteers had with special gusto destroyed his house and crops, remembering the innumerable raids against Kentucky that McKee had directed.

It was no use. The Indians, disgusted by the British refusal to fire on the Americans, had had quite enough. The celebrated Delaware chief, Buckongehelas, as he paddled his canoe dolefully up the Maumee to make peace with Wayne, even paused long enough to send a contemptuous message ashore to Major Campbell—who really had behaved with courage and discretion. The Indians continued to reproach the British for their failure to fight for the next two decades.

About twenty Indian scouts followed the American column at a respectful distance, but they did not attack. Clark heard them on the night of the 25th: "The Savages was round my redoubt late at night, making most Dreadfull yells Howling like wolves, & crying like owls, which Kept me up all night & my Men under arms, expecting hourly a charge from the Enemey, as I was 300 yds. from Camp."

During the autumn, Clark nearly ruined his military career forever by a bit of carelessness while on guard. By good luck, the officer of the day was too stupid to notice it, and the lieutenant's blunder remained a secret between his conscience and twentieth-century readers of his manuscript diary:

"8th Oct. 94.—I being on guard for two months past & for the first time Caught, or lay my self liable to be Broke & ruined for ever, viz: the officer of the day Visited my guard last night,

> & I had neglected giving out to my sentinals the Countersign,
> & approached my Picquet without being challenged. had this
> officer known his duty, & had me arrested, I should have been
> Broke, unquestionably. I can but be astonished to View what
> a little fault will ruin an officer in the Army."

With the rest of the troops, he was back at Fort Wayne during the autumn, after riding off with Wilkinson to visit two of the earlier battlefields on the way. He had sufficiently forgiven Wayne by this time to feel obvious gratification at dining "with the Comd^r in Chief, by his perticular Invertation." After that the critical entries in his diary ceased, and his admiration of Wilkinson slowly waned. Some of his army friends seem to have felt that Lieutenant Clark took himself a little too seriously, anyway. One early satirist labeled a book of company records: "Company Book of Lt. Clark's & Wayne's Wars"—a jest now permanently preserved in the National Archives of the United States.

With the rigors of the campaign over, the lieutenant relaxed in the cheerful society of army wives at Fort Washington, who were "much Galanted by the officers." Not all of them, however. The aristocratic youngster was disgusted by a major's wife: "as she was of *low* burth & less breading she is not noticed at all." He also had time for a little mild flirtation with Louisville young ladies. In fact, he enjoyed himself so much that in the spring of 1795 he was late reporting for duty; but he wrote his sister Fanny that the general "at my arrival was more favourable then I had any reason to expect, from my inatention to his orders to riturng at a Stated time." He asked Fanny to tell him all about the girls he knew, especially "miss ——," since he suffered from "long and painfull absence from her Conversation." Later he is eager to know what girls are getting married and all about dances at Louisville, adding lugubriously: "Miss F —— is Cruel."

chapter 5: Tipple tax war: the Whisky Rebellion

SINCE Mr. Jefferson refused, as yet, to send him off to western adventure along the wild Missouri, Meriwether Lewis turned to adventures nearer home. Rebellion was brewing in western Pennsylvania, where angry farmers were threatening armed rebellion against the new-fangled excise tax that Alexander Hamilton had introduced.

The trouble was whisky. The Scotch-Irish settlers around Pittsburgh believed in whisky, of which they produced, sold —and drank—a great deal. Western Pennsylvania thought its raw and fiery fluid so far from sinful that the local clergy often swallowed a glassful neat, in preparation for godly and powerful oratorical flights in the pulpit. Even a bishop, in full canonicals, once paused in a barroom on his way to confirmation, though it must be said on the bishop's behalf that he was not at the moment drinking whisky. All his Right Reverence wanted was a tumbler of pure brandy.

None of this in the least disturbed the faithful, who in some cases paid their parsons' salaries in kegs of sound "Monongahela rye." Everybody drank whisky—drank it so copiously that, according to an early local historian, "in many parts of the country you could scarcely get out of sight of the smoke of a still-house."

Women drank whisky. Storekeepers kept whisky on the counter, as a quick means of supplying eager customers. Farmers stored barrels of whisky in their cellars. Whisky was served at christenings, weddings, wakes, and funerals—flavored with tansy, mint, or maple sugar, or just drunk plain.

All this was largely an economic matter. The frontier farmer raised far more grain than he could either eat or sell. His horse could carry only four bushels of rye over the long, rough road to the Philadelphia market. There was no profit in that. The same horse could carry the distilled product of 24 bushels of the same rye, slung in two eight-gallon kegs across its back. A farmer's whisky brought only 40 or 50 cents a gallon in the West, and might bring as little as 25 cents. But in the East, where Monongahela rye had a reputation of its own, a farmer could double his prices. Two eight-gallon whisky kegs meant about sixteen dollars, and that was real money. The American Revolution had helped the trade along by cutting off the old supply of Jamaica rum.

It was all a very virtuous and workable solution of the grain problem—a pleasant solution, too, for everyone.

In other words, what the western counties of Pennsylvania wanted was whisky; what they did not want was Alexander Hamilton's excise tax on whisky. "Why we should be made subject to a duty for drinking our grain more than eating it, seems a matter of astonishment to every reflecting mind," one group of petitioners plaintively concluded.

When, in 1790, the Federal excise law was passed in spite

of their indignant protests, the tough Scotch-Irish farmers remembered what they had done a few years earlier when George III had likewise presumed to impose an unpopular tax. They talked wildly of secession. They threatened to join Canada, go west, seize Indian lands—in short do almost anything except pay taxes on their tipple. Everyone was far too much excited to think of merely raising prices and passing the tax on to thirsty consumers.

Eventually, they took up arms in open rebellion against the United States, with what President Washington, in his stately way, called "symptoms of riot and violence." To be a little more specific than President Washington cared to be, the "symptoms" consisted of shooting at the unhappy official who was trying to collect the tax, arresting him, holding him prisoner, seizing his papers, burning down his house, and finally compelling him to run for his life.

By August 4, 1794, the embottled farmers were so completely out of hand that United States Judge James Wilson certified to the President, without the least exaggeration, that the "laws of the United States are opposed, and the execution thereof obstructed by combinations too powerful to be suppressed by the ordinary course of judicial proceedings, or by the powers vested in the Marshal of that district." His Honor was simply quoting the language of the Constitution. Washington called out the militia of the nearest states, Pennsylvania, New Jersey, Maryland, and Virginia. Here was adventure, ready-made. Meriwether Lewis joined the Virginia militia under the Revolutionary veteran, General Daniel Morgan.

The expedition moved in two columns. The Pennsylvania and New Jersey troops assembled at Carlisle, making fearful havoc of the farmers' chicken coops as they passed. The Virginia and Maryland troops, Meriwether Lewis among them, gathered at Cumberland. President Washington visited both camps with a view to encouraging the men and marched with them as far as Bedford, Pennsylvania. The commander of the whole expedition was General Henry Lee, Governor of Virginia. Strange irony: The father of Robert E. Lee was suppressing rebellion against the United States!

The campaign did not amount to much. When the first troops reached Pittsburgh in October, the ringleaders among the "Whiskey Boys" had fled. Far down the Ohio, Clark with Wayne's forces could see them pass. One of his fellow officers wrote on November 2, 1794: "The whiskey run boys or insurgents from Fayette Washington Westmoreland & Allegheny were arriving at this time." Wayne seems to have made no effort to stop them. Twenty-five went down the river in a single boat. David Bradford, leading spirit in the revolt, escaped to Spanish territory, alone in a canoe, taking up Spanish lands at Natchez. The militia arrested a number of "whiskey rebels" who had failed to get away and who were taken east for trial, with some minor brutality.

By the latter part of November, the rebellion was over and most of the militia on their way home, having had on the whole a healthy outing and very little more. Nobody had been killed; only a few had died of disease or accident. They had enjoyed a complete triumph and had spent some pleasant evenings in Pittsburgh, "agreeably in Company with a great number of Gentlemen of and belonging to different Volunteer Corps, in singing and drinking of Brandy, & c."

Meriwether Lewis's share in all these martial proceedings was equally pleasant, though not at all heroic. His unit had been late in reaching the scene. On October 4 he wrote his mother from Winchester that the Virginia militia "now cut a moste martial figure; we shall this day draw all our acoutrements and receive our first lesson. We have mountains of Beef and oceans of Whiskey and I feel myself able to share it [with the] hartiest fellow in camp." On the 13th he wrote again to say that his next station would be Fort Cumberland. He had heard that the insurgent leaders had fled, leaving their followers "on the mercy of an insulted Government."

The campaign was to go on, "our leading men being determined entirely to consume every attum of that turbulent refractory sperit that exists among them." In December he hoped to visit Kentucky to look after his mother's land claims there. Otherwise the state would declare the lands vacant.

Not quite all the militia went home when the Whisky Rebellion was over. A small force, most of them volunteers, remained near Pittsburgh under General Morgan, to make sure that the now chastened mood of the "Whiskey Boys" should continue.

Lewis was, for a time at least, among these. He had thoroughly enjoyed the campaign—a vigorous march in crisp fall weather, much excitement, very little risk, some rain and discomfort, a bloodless and immediate victory. Small wonder that he wrote his mother on November 24, just after the main force had started home: "I am quite delighted with a soldier's life."

Lucy Marks, like all mothers of all sons in all wars, wanted her son at home. But the exuberant young adventurer had other ideas: "so violently opposed is my governing passion for rambling to the wishes of all my friends that I am led intentionally to err." It was all due, he thought, to "this Quixottic disposition of mine." His mother was not to worry. His life was no more dangerous than at home on Ivy Creek.

This, to be sure, was not quite true, but it was in the same comforting vein that he used later in a farewell letter to his mother before the Lewis and Clark Expedition plunged into the unknown West. He retained a touch of the shrewd man of business. He saw fine opportunities to acquire lands and would still do what he could about his mother's claims. Army life was fairly comfortable.

"We are all agreeably fixed in our houses and enjoy not only most of the comforts of life but many of its luxuries on very moderate terms. . . . The Insergiants are the same at hea[r]t they ever were, and I can see no honour or profit to be gained by living at the expence of the publick without rendering her any service." He sent regards "to all the girls," announcing that he would bring "an Insergiant Girl to se them next fall bearing the title of Mrs. Lewis." If there really was such a girl, he soon forgot her.

Although eligible for discharge in May, his enthusiasm led him to join up for summer operations and eventually to transfer to the Regulars, retaining the rank of ensign, which he had already won. He entered the 2nd Sub-Legion May 1, 1795.

Four years junior to Clark in age, he was three years junior to him in the army. He writes his mother proudly that he has had "an epaulet" sent from Philadelphia. Ensigns, cornets, and lieutenants wore a single epaulet on the left shoulder, captains a single epaulet on the right. It gave junior officers an amazingly lopsided appearance. Officers usually postponed having their portraits painted until they had attained the better-balanced dignity of two epaulets, but there is one print of Lewis as captain, with his left shoulder looking singularly bare and unadorned.

Not long after this he was on his way down the Ohio to join Wayne's forces. The famous partnership began about this time, when Lewis was assigned to the "Chosen Rifle Company" which William Clark commanded. It is not clear just when this happened. Clark himself said in a letter written in 1811: "Capt. Lewis was appointed an Ensign and arranged[assigned] to the company which I commanded a fiew months before I resigned." As Clark resigned from the army July 1, 1796, he must have had Lewis as a junior company officer either late in 1795 or early in 1796.

The two friends cannot have been long together, for Clark was absent during most of the autumn of 1795. In September, Wayne ordered him down the Ohio with dispatches "to the Governor or Genl. Commanding the Spanish armament said to be fortifying at the Chickasaw Bluff"—modern Memphis,

Tennessee. He was also to carry out certain "other instructions," which were carefully left unspecified.

If the Spanish were fortifying on the American side of the Mississippi, Wayne knew that he might have to move his army there. He would then need extensive and accurate military intelligence. He set Clark to work collecting it, at once. The lieutenant was off down-river by the middle of the month, traveling in a barge with a crew of one sergeant, one corporal, and fifteen soldiers.

Compared with the full and detailed intelligence report that he later submitted to General Wayne, Clark's diary of this voyage is a masterpiece of bland and innocent deception by silent omission. Clark knew that he might be seized and searched by the Spaniards. He must also have suspected that his boat had been examined by Spanish espionage agents on at least one of his previous trips. He had long since learned the value of keeping everything under lock and key (the Spanish agents seem to have been technically too unskilled to pick even the simple locks of that day), and he now took the additional precaution of making his written notes as innocent as possible. Read by an outsider, they would have meant nothing—merely a record of the length of each day's run, direction of currents, islands, animals killed by hunters, military precautions against Indian attack, and a list of the boats he met.

In tone, this diary differs, just enough to make the difference perceptible, from his other diaries. All the notes are just a little too long, just a little too detailed, with just a little too much data, and its innocence is just a little too elaborate. One wonders as one reads why Clark is going to so much trouble over topographical minutiæ, to which in his other notebooks he pays very little attention.

One wakes up with a start when one picks up the next document, the final intelligence report, as Wayne saw it. Clark had been employing the ancient trick, well known to every intelligence agent who aspires to a long life, of writing down only such memoranda as would appear innocent if intercepted or captured. He was at the same time noting with the most incredible alertness every detail of possible future military importance, but he was keeping all this in his head. Not a scrap of paper, not a written note relating to this part of his report exists, but on his return he was able to write out in the most admirable detail everything Wayne might need to know.

To the enlisted personnel of Clark's little command, who probably had no idea that they were engaged in international espionage, the journey must have seemed just another river voyage. They paused for minor repairs at Fort Massac, met a French and a Spanish pirogue, killed a great many bear and some wild turkeys, saw Indians, "put the arms in order," posted a strong guard, had some target practice, and then put their arms in "prime order."

The commander went ashore with surprising frequency for personal reconnaissances, which seemed strangely detailed as to distances, fortification sites, and possible roads; but otherwise the trip was the usual monotonous routine of drifting, rowing, camping, and guard, day after day. Although Clark discouraged his men from having much to do with passing boats and even refused permission for them to go aboard one craft, he was himself making inquiries about the Spaniards all the way down the Ohio.

Near the mouth of the Cumberland River, passing travelers informed him that the Spanish had taken possession of Chickasaw Bluffs and were fortifying. They also reported that the Spanish Governor intended to build a fort on the Mississippi at the Iron Bluffs, just below the mouth of the Ohio near the place where, during the Revolution, George Rogers Clark had built Fort Jefferson—not, of course, identical with Wayne's fort of the same name in Ohio. Most of the Spanish militia from New Madrid, said the voyagers, had crossed the Mississippi to work on the new fortifications. This, if true, was important, for it meant Spanish control of both rivers.

Next day, Clark learned, from the American lieutenant in command at Fort Massac and from others, that the Spanish Governor had actually visited the Iron Banks. The Spaniards, some informants thought, were looking for cannon which the Americans were supposed to have hidden when they abandoned Fort Jefferson. There was no Spanish fort there yet, but it would be a good idea to examine the terrain.

On his homeward journey, Clark landed to make a careful study of the old site of Fort Jefferson. Information from others was all very well, but he wanted to see for himself. He found a place where a new road could be cut overland to the site of the old fort. He landed on an island opposite the site and examined it carefully from a safe distance. Only then, sure that the Spaniards had gone, did he make his own personal reconnaissance of the entire area. He also made careful notes on everything else of military importance—conditions that would affect the health of troops, water supply, elevations, river traffic, possible future economic value.

Clark turned his boat out of the Ohio into the current of the Mississippi at noon of October 1, 1795 and—knowing that he would soon be meeting Spaniards—landed to let his men make themselves as smart as possible. The United States army must make a good impression on officers of a foreign power, even in the back woods. At this interesting point, just before Clark's meeting with Governor Gayoso de Lemos, a page is lost from his diary—perhaps torn out by some earlier owner because of its special interest, perhaps destroyed by Clark himself as telling a little too much. The diary does not resume until October 8, when Clark has parted with the Spanish officials and is on his way back to headquarters. Fortunately, his report to Wayne covers the hiatus.

At four o'clock on the 2nd, when Clark's boat was within

600 yards of New Madrid, a Spanish guard hailed and ordered him ashore. The lieutenant put in close to shore and lay there, but did not actually land. A Spanish officer from the Governor's own galley came over in a boat to say that His Excellency Señor Don Manuel Gayoso de Lemos, Brigadier in the Royal Armies of Spain, and Governor, personally required the American Officer's presence aboard his galley.

It was a somewhat tense meeting, since the Spanish Governor had been collecting information on Clark for a year or more. There was a brisk but formally courteous conversation:

"Sir/ I am an american Officer, and am under orders from the Commander in Chief with a Message and Letter to the Commanding Officer of the Spanish Troops now at the Chicasaw Bluffs—or on the East side of the Mississippi—U.S." Clark put the last words in to see what De Lemos would say. Would the Spaniard admit that the Bluffs were United States territory?

"I am that person," replied De Lemos. "I command all this upper country—and the Chicasaw Cliffs is under my immediate Command."

(So the Spaniards *were* going to claim it!)

"I presume sir you are the Governor."

De Lemos admitted as much. Clark delivered Wayne's letter and passed on the latest news. The United States and Great Britain had concluded a treaty of amity and commerce, guaranteeing free navigation of the Mississippi. De Lemos expressed surprise—the Mississippi did not flow through British territory. Without comment on that, Clark asked for a reply as soon as possible, receiving it—with very un-Spanish promptness—at nine the next morning.

Wayne had pointed out that the Spanish troops, fortifications, and armed galley at Chickasaw Bluffs were illegally within American boundaries. The Spaniards were playing the same game of encroachment that the British had played at Fort Miamis and elsewhere. There was no war, said Wayne. The United States was peacefully disposed. But "the last aggression (if as above reported) on the part of the Spanish Gov't has an alarming aspect." By whose authority had the Spaniards "thus made usurpation into the territory of the U. S. and built a fort therein"?

"I must request therefore of you the favor of replying particularly to these questions by the bearer who is Lieut. Wm. Clark who comes under flag of truce."

De Lemos replied blandly that he had not occupied American territory. He had no wish to do so. The land on which his fort stood was legitimately Spanish, since it had been purchased from the Chickasaw Indians. As this was the time when Citizen Genêt was trying to precipitate a French attack on Spanish territory based on American soil, De Lemos pointed to "Threats of the French Republicans living in the U. S." as justifying his military preparations.

Clark tried in conversation to find out the nature of the Spanish claim to Chickasaw Bluffs but received only the same reply that De Lemos gave Wayne in writing—the Spaniards had bought the land from the Indians. The American lieutenant then asked the Spaniard bluntly whether that was his pretext for building the fort. De Lemos evaded the question with a shrug. It was "a Ministerial business" for which he could not account.

The Governor was, however, on the whole conciliatory, treated Clark with the utmost politeness, and regretted that he had not been able to go far enough up the Ohio to call formally upon Wayne.

Amid all this diplomatic palaver, Clark kept his eyes and ears wide open. He was eventually able to submit detailed drawings of the Spanish river fleet with full details of its numbers and armament; drawings of the fort at Chickasaw Bluffs; equally detailed figures on Spanish land and naval forces; some information as to the Indian opposition to

Spanish settlements; and an abundance of information on geography and river navigation. There is so much of this, most of it undated, that Clark must have been quietly collecting information on all of his river trips.

He was safely back at Fort Washington November 4, 1795, having proved himself the very model of a good intelligence officer.

chapter 6: Mr. Jefferson and his Secretary

IT WAS the last of Clark's adventures until he set off in 1804 upon the expedition. During the rest of 1795 and the first half of 1796, the two friends lived the monotonous lives of army officers commanding small units in Indian country. There were, doubtless, hunting trips and many of those wilderness rambles that Lewis had loved from childhood, but little else to break the dullness of garrison routine.

Lewis still enjoyed military life. "The general idea is that the army is the school of debauchery," he wrote his mother, "but believe me it has ever proven the school of experience and prudence to your affectionate son."

Clark, who had been in the army so much longer, was growing less enthusiastic. The illness from which he had suffered occasionally during Wayne's campaign was becoming

worse and worse. As his family had for months been suggesting that he return to civil life to aid in their business
affairs, he asked Wayne for leave to go home and look into
the matter. On July 1, 1796, he finally sent in his papers
and retired to Kentucky, there to begin that hopeless effort
to untangle the affairs of George Rogers Clark which occupied him at intervals nearly all his life. Between 1798 and
1811, he paid out over $10,000 on his brother's behalf. In
1797 he made a trip into Illinois, at least partly to handle
George Rogers Clark's interests, and he visited New Orleans
on business the following year.

Though their patriotism in the Revolution had brought
financial misfortunes down upon them, the Clarks were never
really poor. A return of William's property shows that he
owned 9,255 acres of land—though it is described as only second or third rate—five old Negroes, seven Negroes above sixteen years of age, three under that age, three Negro children,
and numerous horses. Part of this property came to him
under his father's will, in 1799. The most interesting legacy
was "one negro man named York also old York and his wife
Rose," together with other slaves. The younger York was the
famous Negro who was to make the transcontinental journey
with his master.

The legacy was not really so large as it seems, since the
property was burdened with debts, and the bequest of the
family estate at Mulberry Hill was more or less a trust to
William, as the family man of affairs. At one time he had to
sell off some of his own property to meet his brother's obligations, and only by becoming a surety himself was he able to
keep the old general out of debtor's prison.

Occasionally the government drew upon the knowledge
young Clark had gained in those interminable voyages up
and down the Ohio and the Mississippi. The War Department requested a description of old Fort Jefferson, which
George Rogers Clark had built and the ruins of which Lieu-

tenant Clark had examined for Wayne in 1795. Once Mr. Jefferson, a family friend with whom Clark had become well acquainted on various visits in the East, wrote asking the best location for a new fort near the mouth of the Ohio. One never knew when that location, so near the Spaniards, might assume renewed military importance. There were times when Mr. Jefferson thought a Spanish war nearly inevitable.

Lewis and Clark appear to have corresponded occasionally, though only one letter of these years has been preserved. This is dated from Washington, June 27, 1801, after Lewis had become secretary to Mr. Jefferson, asking "Mr. Clark" to secure plots and land certificates for land originally surveyed for John Marks on Brush Creek, in Ohio.

To this period belongs the commencement of the two romances of Clark's life. Riding along a Virginia road one day, young William came upon two little girls—neither of them much over twelve, if that—both trying to ride one balky horse, which like so many animals was quite aware that it could defy children with impunity. Switches produced no effect whatever.

Clark dismounted and led the horse a short distance. When he remounted and led the way, the girls' balky brute knew that it had met its master and meekly followed. The little girls were Julia, or Judy, Hancock and Harriet Kennerly, first cousins who had been brought up together as sisters. Clark made up his mind then and there to marry Julia, who within three years would be fifteen—as old as his own mother had been on her wedding day. In the end, he married both.

Lewis, meantime, was rising gradually in rank. After Clark left the army, his friend was transferred, November 1, 1796, to the First Infantry—which in the modern army has become the Third. He was promoted lieutenant March 3, 1799, the rank of ensign having been abolished on that date, and captain December 3, 1800.

In April, 1796, he conducted a terrain reconnaissance from

Lorimier's store in Ohio, near the St. Mary's and Auglaize Rivers. In October he set out from Detroit overland for Pittsburgh, losing his way once or twice and getting hungry enough to find some dubious bear's meat in an old Indian camp "very exceptable." In February and March, 1797, Lewis was in charge of a Wyandot warrior, otherwise unknown, called Captain Enos Coon, whose bill he paid at the Pittsburgh Inn run by William Morrow. It was his first experience in handling Indians.

In May, 1797, the lieutenant was back at Locust Hill on leave. Becoming attorney for his mother, he began arrangements to bring her slaves home from Georgia and decided to visit that state to look after her property before returning to duty. He sold part of his own Ivy Creek land to a certain Clifton Rodes and another part to his brother Reuben. He went west—on the Marks children's behalf, rather than his own—securing land claims in Ohio and 2,600 acres in Kentucky, the latter worth twenty cents an acre. He also bought back some of the Ohio lands that had been granted to John Marks and later sold. He remained, by modern standards, a large landowner all his life, his mother eventually inheriting more than 3,000 acres from him, though a good deal of this probably had very little value. For a short time in the latter part of 1797, he commanded the newly erected Fort Pickering, near Memphis. During most of 1798 and at least the first half of 1799, he was stationed in and about Charlottesville, on recruiting duty.

Some time in 1800, he went north again and was assigned to Captain Ferdinand L. Claiborne's Company of the First Infantry, when it was organized at Detroit in September. In Detroit he indulged in vigorous political argument, on one occasion overwhelming an unfortunate Federalist brother officer with his Jeffersonian "republican" arguments, somewhat to the amusement of the bystanders. Becoming regimental paymaster almost at once, he had little dull staff routine at

Detroit headquarters. Instead, his duties required frequent journeys through the wilderness and up and down the Ohio River between Detroit and Pittsburgh. On at least one trip down the Ohio, he traveled with a 21-foot bateau and a 48-foot pirogue. It was good training—he would be using just such craft on the expedition. Clark had already had experience with river vessels of the same sort. By a singular irony, one of the young officer's best friends in Pittsburgh was Tarleton Bates, brother of that Frederick Bates who later became Lewis's bitterest enemy.

Captain Lewis's departure from Pittsburgh was a permanent farewell to the army life he loved. As private secretary to the President of the United States, he lived for the next two or three years amid the ceremonious formality of official Washington, which even Mr. Jefferson, who hated ceremonial, could not quite eliminate. President Washington and President Adams had kept up almost royal state. The "republican" Mr. Jefferson ended all that at once. There were no more elaborate Presidential levees, even though the ladies of Washington tried—just once—to force the new President to continue holding them.

Foreign diplomats, disgusted at leaving the metropolitan elegance of Philadelphia for the raw new village of Washington, were furious when they found that the new President was also reducing diplomatic protocol to its barest essentials, entertaining as simply as a Virginia private gentleman in his own home. "No titles being admitted here," the new rule ran, "those of foreigners give no precedence." There was to be "perfect equality" between guests, "whether foreign or domestic, titled or untitled, in or out of office." It was especially galling to the Europeans because, as former Minister in Paris, Mr. Jefferson knew all about court etiquette. The rather stuffy British Minister was so offended by the informality of one Presidential dinner that Mr. Jefferson's friend, Mr. Monroe, then Minister in London, had to smooth things over with the Foreign Office. A Presidential secretary with a little more experience of diplomatic life than Captain Lewis possessed might, possibly, have provided just the social touch that would have prevented the incident. It was the kind of thing you couldn't learn on Ivy Creek or among the Indians. Still, nobody could have done anything about a slight mistake by the first Turkish Minister to the United States. Arriving at a startled White House in the turban and gorgeous brocaded robes of the Sultan's imperial court, His Turkish Excellency proved quite indifferent to everything except one of the slaves, a large, fat Negress. The mammy, His Excellency explained, reminded him of "his best and most expensive wife."

You couldn't blame the foreigners for not liking Washington. The streets were simply muddy lanes. The houses were hovels. The Capitol was unfinished. So was the White House —just a big square box of a place with a roof that leaked for the next three years, the eastern part still unplastered. Mrs. Adams had found the bare East Room a handy place to hang the family washing. There were not even stables. The President and his secretary had to keep their mounts at 14th and G Streets.

There was no church either. When President Jefferson and Captain Lewis made their first appearance at the converted tobacco barn with a hastily erected cross which was at first used for worship, they selected chairs at random. In spite of Mr. Jefferson's dislike of ceremonial, a tactful congregation thereafter left those chairs vacant until the President and his secretary made their regular appearance. Matters were not much better when the House of Representatives began to be used for Sunday worship. The Marine Band, already brave in their traditional red coats, did their best with church music. But, though the marines tried valiantly, they were not much use in accompanying psalms. Eventually the congregation sang without them.

In spite of disgruntled diplomats, life in the White House was extremely pleasant for Captain Lewis, as well as for the non-diplomatic guests he assisted Mr. Jefferson in entertaining. The art of living had always been well understood in Albemarle County. Mr. Jefferson improved matters by bringing his own French cook home with him from Paris. Though Yrujo, the Spanish Minister, complained that you had to send 50 or 60 miles to assemble the materials for a good dinner in Washington, Mr. Jefferson did well enough. His imported wines were the finest that would stand the ocean journey, and his intimate dinners were so lavish that even his French chef thought the President extravagant. "Republican simplicity was united to Epicurean delicacy."

As Mr. Jefferson had long been a widower and as his two married daughters could rarely leave their husbands, Dolly Madison, wife of the Secretary of State, served as his hostess. Mr. Jefferson entertained almost every day, though rarely with more than a dozen guests. Sometimes the guests were a little startling—his first Fourth of July reception included five Cherokee chiefs. When the President wished secrecy and complete freedom to converse without restraint, there were only four people at his table—presumably himself, Captain Lewis, and two guests on whose discretion one could rely.

Having learned all about espionage in Paris, Mr. Jefferson served his most intimate dinners without any servants at all. Becoming President did not mean that he had given up that passion for inventions and ingenious small devices which marked his whole life. Monticello was equipped with a weather vane that could be read from indoors, a clock which told the days of the week, a bed that pushed up to the ceiling, double doors which moved automatically as one. He could not introduce all this at the White House, but he did devise a set of movable circular shelves which passed clear through the wall of the White House dining room, returning loaded dishes that had been placed on them by servants who never entered the room at all and thus never heard what the President's guests were saying.

Servants and official secrecy did not mix. "Much of the domestic and even public discord," the President thought, "was produced by the mutilated and misconstrued repetition of free conversation at dinner tables, by these mute but not inattentive listeners."

A guest one day noticed a curious-looking piece of furniture. Mr. Jefferson obligingly opened it up. Inside stood a goblet of water, a decanter of wine, a plate of "light cakes," and a candle. With a smile on his ruddy, freckled, good-natured face, the President explained that he often sat up late. Here was everything he needed. He did not have to call a servant. Just another of his little inventions.

The President's work room, where the Lewis and Clark Expedition was thought out, was downstairs. Mr. Jefferson's long table concealed a set of carpenter's tools and some scientific instruments, while around the walls was a profusion of books, maps, globes, charts, and in the windows pots of roses and geraniums. His pet mocking bird—released from its cage when the President was alone—sat on his shoulder or flew about and, when Mr. Jefferson retired for his daily siesta, hopped along up the stairs after him, step by step.

The mocking bird and Meriwether Lewis were probably in closer and more intimate association with Thomas Jefferson, during the first two years of his administration, than any other living beings. The Presidency was not, in those days, the exacting office it has since become. A President had time to think, even time to tinker with carpenter's tools, as Mr. Jefferson loved to do—and also time to discuss with his specially chosen and trusted confidential secretary the great project that was closest to both their hearts. There was time also for long visits, twice a year, to the Albemarle they both loved, for Monticello was not yet finished to suit its exacting owner. During the President's visits to Monticello, his secretary is said to have lived in the story-and-a-half clapboard house on the estate known as Franklin, the home of William Bache, grandson of Benjamin Franklin. This was close enough to Mr. Jefferson's "little mountain" so that the young captain could ride back and forth as his duties might require, and close enough to Locust Hill to enable him to see his family easily.

Mr. Jefferson's meticulous personal account books contain a few entries relating to his secretary which show him traveling back and forth on various Presidential errands. Thus, on July 20, 1802, he "paid Capt Lewis on account 30.D"; on October 13, he gave an order "in fav^r. Thos. Monroe for Capt Lewis 14.68"; and on November 16, he "gave Capt. Lewis ord. on J. Barnes for 40.D for travell & expenses." Five days later, Mr. Jefferson "rec^d. back from Capt Lewis .50 of the money ante Nov. 16."

Life in Albemarle County was always much more to Mr. Jefferson's taste than life anywhere else in the world, and he managed to make at least two visits in 1801. For himself he reserved a suite of five rooms at Monticello, which no one else entered except by invitation—three rooms for his books, one for his office, one for his bedroom. Here he retired after an eight o'clock breakfast, taking his secretary along if he needed him. Guests—somebody was always visiting at Monticello—were invited to amuse themselves for the morning. Dinner was at four. Afterward, one walked on the terrace or strolled in the woods. The President played with his grandchildren until tea was brought in, and firmly withdrew at nine o'clock.

As Mr. Jefferson observed, his secretary's work was more in the nature of an aide de camp's than a mere secretary's, a life suited to Lewis's tastes and talents; "the care of our company," said the President, "the execution of some commissions in the town occasionally, messages to Congress, occasional conferences and explanations with particular members,

with the officers, and inhabitants of the place where it cannot
so well be done in writing, constitute the chief business. the
salary of 600 D. a year serves for clothes and pocket money."
Mr. Jefferson provided a slave and a horse. Lewis wrote a
cousin soon after reaching Washington:

"I feel my situation in the President's family an extreemly
pleasent one—I very little expected that I possessed the confidence of Mr. J——n so far as to have produced on his part,
a voluntary offer of the office of his private secretary—however
nothing is extraordinary in these days of revolution, and reform."

It was all very agreeable, and Captain Lewis was happy
enough, except for occasions when a curious, causeless melancholy descended on the moody fellow. Mr. Jefferson sometimes eyed his promising young secretary a little uneasily, as
he noted these fits of depression. There was no reason for
them. Captain Lewis had every reason to be content but Mr.
Jefferson had seen those moods before. A good many of the
young man's family had the same tendency. Mr. Jefferson
knew them well—a moody race, sometimes with positive melancholia. Still, they were always an able breed and Captain
Lewis, however unsuccessful with spelling and with girls, was
a youngster whose promise nobody could mistake. The more
his friend the President thought about it, the more he felt
sure that—melancholy or no melancholy—he had found the
right man for his long-cherished wilderness venture.

As secretary, Lewis handled confidential business deftly.
One of the first of his more delicate errands was to serve as
the President's confidential intermediary in an effort to relieve the anti-Federalist writer, James Thomson Callender,
who, while the Federalists were in power, had been sentenced
and heavily fined under the Alien and Sedition Laws, and
who was now in much distress. Abhorring the laws under
which Callender had been sentenced and feeling bound to
aid a journalist whose anti-Federalism he had encouraged,

the President sent Captain Lewis with a gift of $50 and a private message that the fine would be remitted as soon as matters could be arranged.

Sad to say, Callender took quite the wrong attitude. "His language to Captain Lewis was very high-toned. He intimated that he was in possession of things which he could and would make use of in a certain case: that he had received the 50 D. not as a charity but a due, in fact as hush money."

Callender was trying to blackmail Mr. Jefferson over an old scandal. Long ago, Mr. Jefferson "when young and single," had impetuously tried to make love to a "handsome lady." The lady in the case was married. She was also of quite irreproachable character. Disdainfully, she had put the indiscreet philosopher in his place, but a few papers had fallen into the wrong hands.

This old scandal did the threatening Callender very little good, for Mr. Jefferson, even though his red hair had faded to gray, was not the kind of man who submitted to extortion. On hearing Lewis's report of the conversation, he indignantly broke off all relations with the man, and wrote his friend Madison not to pay Callender an additional $50 that the President, out of his private pocket, had already forwarded to help meet the fine. Though Mr. Jefferson saw to it that the fine was eventually remitted anyhow, the ungrateful Callender was soon spreading the one scandal of Mr. Jefferson's life through the nation, together with a great many more, which—though there is no shadow of proof—still more or less cling to his name. It all ended abruptly a year or two later when Callender, drunk, managed to drown in three feet of water.

There is a similar scandalous story—widespread though absurd and completely without foundation—that, while living with Mr. Jefferson in Washington, Lewis was also involved in a love affair with a married woman—Theodosia, the brilliant and beautiful daughter of Aaron Burr, wife of the South

Carolina planter, Joseph Alston. Though there has never
been a scrap of evidence for this quite impossible tale, it has
nevertheless been soberly set forth in no less than four books,
all because a novelist looking for heart interest dreamed it
up about forty years ago. The fact is that Lewis and Vice-
President Burr's attractive daughter never even saw each
other, except perhaps for a few months in Washington or at
Burr's trial for treason in 1806, when Captain Lewis, as special representative of the prosecuting President, was hardly
likely to find favor with the defendant's adoring daughter.
While Theodosia was a young girl in New York, her supposed lover was far away on the Northwest frontier. She was
married February 2, 1801, was in Washington for the inauguration, and was on her way to South Carolina in March, while
Lewis and his pack horses were still hurrying across the wild
roads between Pittsburgh and the Capital. She visited her
father in New York in 1802 while Lewis was in Washington,
she was in South Carolina until long after Lewis and Clark
had set off for the Pacific coast.

It is likely enough that Theodosia may have visited Washington during the months she spent with her father in 1802;
and it would be natural for the President's dashing young
secretary to pay some attention to the Vice-President's fascinating daughter. There may even have been a little newspaper gossip—though no one seems able to find it now.

But the tale of a flaming and romantic love affair arose
solely because in 1916 Emerson Hough felt the need of a little love interest for his novel, *The Magnificent Adventure,*
which was based on the Lewis and Clark Expedition. Quite
rightly finding Theodosia the most agreeable girl of the period, he bestowed her affections upon Meriwether Lewis. The
unanimous howl of rage that arose from the indignant Burr,
Alston, and Lewis families appalled the too inventive scrib-
bler. "I have heard from many members of each family, quite
often to my unhappiness," he wrote after his book appeared,

admitting ruefully that he had made the whole thing up: "So far as I know the love affair between Meriwether Lewis and Theodosia Burr is wholly imaginary." One writer even avers that Lewis taught Theodosia to ride—at a time when he had probably never seen her; and wrote for her a manual of equitation—a subject which infantry officers usually leave to the cavalry.

chapter 7: Mr. Jefferson buys an Empire

MR. JEFFERSON soon decided that the time had come to grant at last the request that the adolescent Meriwether Lewis had made of him in 1792. There is no document to tell when the momentous decision was made, nor how long and eagerly the two discussed the great scheme, alone together in the new White House. At the very latest the decision had certainly been made some time in 1802, for Lewis was actively at work on preparations long before the year was over.

Mr. Jefferson took Congress into his confidence in a secret message, January 18, 1803, in order to get funds for the expedition. It was a very adroit bit of political writing. The President did not dare explain that he wanted to explore Louisiana because he intended to buy at least a part of it for, secret though his message was, almost any secret confided to

Congress was sure to leak out. Besides, he was by no means sure he would be able to buy even a part of Louisiana Territory. He did the best he could to persuade Congress, by pointing out the commercial advantages of promoting the Indian trade. Why not gain for America the wealth that was now going to England? The Missouri River Indians were already furnishing "great supplies of furs and peltry to the trade of another nation, carried on in a high latitude through an infinite number of portages and lakes shut up by ice through a long season." Although Louisiana was nominally French territory temporarily under Spanish administration, the British were coming overland to secure the most profitable Indian trade, all the way south to the Missouri, and then exporting to London down the Border Lakes, the Great Lakes, and the St. Lawrence. However illegal this might be, there was nothing whatever that the Spaniards could do about it. If the Americans, too, could trade along the whole length of the Missouri (Mr. Jefferson carefully refrained from raising the question how this was possible with the Spanish in control), they could probably develop an Indian trade along both the Columbia and the Missouri from the Pacific to the Atlantic, "possibly with a single portage from the Western Ocean." Not even Mr. Jefferson realized what a portage across the Rocky Mountains would be like, for no white man had yet seen the upper Missouri.

The expedition would be cheap, the persuasive enthusiast in the White House went on, requiring only "an intelligent officer, with ten or twelve chosen men—" George Rogers Clark had once suggested no more than three or four. The sole expense would be arms, instruments, and Indian presents. The usual land bounty paid after the Revolution would be sufficient reward for the soldiers—"their pay would be going on whether here or there," observed the President, with an encouragingly frugal air, as he asked Congress for an appropriation of only $2,500 "for the purpose of extending the external commerce of the United States." This, he hoped, would arouse no suspicion of the real plan when it appeared, as it inevitably must, in the newspapers, and the vague wording "while understood and considered by the Executive as giving the legislative sanction, would cover the undertaking from notice and prevent the obstructions which interested individuals might otherwise previously prepare in its way."

Mr. Jefferson's lifelong interest in the mysterious country between the Mississippi and the Pacific was partly personal and partly patriotic, partly scientific and partly political. He was intensely curious about new plants, new animals, unknown fossils, geography, Indians. For years he had been collecting vocabularies of the various Indian languages and dialects—there were certain to be fascinating new languages among the unknown western tribes.

He also hoped that after the purchase of New Orleans had opened the Mississippi to American commerce, western exploration would provide for the expansion of the nation. By 1802, control of the Mississippi, a problem long agitated, was becoming so vital that it had to be settled. The United States was in grave danger of one day discovering that a European power had shut it off from the western lands entirely and was in permanent control of one bank, perhaps both banks, of the great river. Spain as a neighbor had been bad enough. Now Louisiana was French again, which was worse; and it might become British, which would be worst of all. Another century might elapse before the wild lands were fully colonized, controlled, and garrisoned, whether by the French, the British, or the Americans. But in the end America would have to do something about Louisiana; and Mr. Jefferson characteristically wanted to know what the country was like before he tried to solve the problem it presented.

For years he had been slowly collecting information as to the Missouri-Columbia route across the continent wherever he could find it, and making what efforts he could to send

THE CLARK HOME. *"Mulberry Hill," Jefferson County, Kentucky, was the home of John Clark, father of William Clark. This photograph was taken some time before* 1896.

LOCUST HILL, *the Lewis home, burned down about* 1838. *This sketch (and at least two others) was made at the site many years later by Miss Nancy E. Scott, under the direction of her sister, Mrs. Sally T. Anderson, wife of a later owner who belonged to the Lewis family. The descriptive material and a plan of the house were given Mrs. Anderson by an old lady who had lived in the house as a child.*

INDIAN PEACE MEDAL, obverse and reverse. *This one was supposedly given to the Nez Percé chief, Twisted Hair, and was found near Clearwater River, Idaho, in 1899 during the construction of the Northern Pacific Railroad.*

AN "INDIAN COMMISSION" *issued in the name of President Jefferson to important chiefs. Note that Lewis signs as "Captain, First Infantry," and that Clark, actually a Lieutenant, uses "Captain on an Expedition for North Western Discovery."*

explorers out. His interest had first become active during the Revolution. The possibility of British exploration had been no threat to the American Colonies so long as they were a part of the British Empire, but it was dangerous to an independent United States of America. In 1782 he had conversed with "a Mr. Stanley," who had been captured by the Indians and taken to a river flowing westward—perhaps the Columbia itself, perhaps only one of the Missouri's tributaries, which flow to all points of the compass before they finally turn toward the Atlantic. Mr. Jefferson's interest thereafter was untiring.

Just as the Revolution ended, he became alarmed by news that the British were planning an exploration of Louisiana, beginning at the Mississippi and going on to that vague area known as California. On December 4, 1783, he wrote to George Rogers Clark: "they pretend it is only to promote knolege I am afraid they have thoughts of colonising into that quarter. some of us have been talking here in a feeble way of making the attempt to search that country. but I doubt whether we have enough of that kind of spirit to raise the money. how would you like to lead such a party? tho I am afraid our prospect is not worth asking the question." Old General Clark declined—he could not afford to undertake the venture; but he made suggestions then that the Lewis and Clark Expedition carried out more than twenty years later.

When he met the adventurous John Ledyard in 1786, Mr. Jefferson, recognizing a kindred spirit, tried three times to send him eastward across Siberia and thence across North America from Nootka Sound. Ledyard was a Connecticut Yankee with a roving foot, who had joined the British Marines to see the world with Captain Cook. That he had been in British service under Cook during the Revolution was not held against him in America, for the purely scientific purpose of Cook's voyage was fully recognized and American warships had been specially instructed not to molest his ship, should they fall in with it on the high seas.

Ledyard's first proposal was to attempt the whole journey across Siberia and North America, on foot, but Catherine the Great refused a passport. The disappointed Ledyard then took passage from London aboard a British vessel bound for Nootka Sound, in September, 1786. The ship had hardly left the Thames when it was overhauled and seized by British customs officers.

Nothing daunted, Ledyard made his way to St. Petersburg, where he had the good fortune to arrive while the obstructive Empress was visiting the Crimea. In her absence, and with the aid of the French Ambassador, he secured a passport and started for Siberia. There was no American diplomat to aid him, since the conservative Russian government feared the Red and dangerous radicalism of the United States—governed by that arch-rebel George Washington and a set of revolutionists who had taken arms against their lawful sovereign—and refused to have diplomatic relations of any kind with a new, upstart state known to be spreading the devilish poison of democracy.

With much hardship but without open official opposition, the passport carried Ledyard as far as Yakutsk, where suspicious Russian officials, not daring to halt the bearer of an imperial passport, tried to discourage and delay him by dilating on the dangers of his journey. Disregarding them, Ledyard pushed on as far as Irkutsk, where he met a British friend who had been with him on Captain's Cook's voyage, whom he incautiously accompanied back to Yakutsk. Officials there had by this time had opportunity to make inquiries at St. Petersburg. Imperial Catherine, returning to her capital to find that her wishes had been disregarded, issued orders promptly. Ledyard was arrested February 24, 1788, rushed eastward under guard, and dumped across the Polish frontier with a warning not to try to enter Rusia again or "he would certainly be hanged."

"The royal dame," Ledyard confided to his diary, "has taken me much out of my way."

Catherine herself told the French Ambassador, who had helped secure the passport, that "she would not render herself guilty of the death of this courageous American, by furthering a journey so fraught with danger." As imperial Catherine's past career had never been marked by any great scruple regarding human life, the French diplomat shrewdly suspected that all this fine talk "only disguised her unwillingness to have the new possessions of Russia, on the western coasts of America, seen by an enlightened citizen of the United States."

The indefatigable Ledyard visited Mr. Jefferson, then American Minister in Paris, assuring him that he would now try a journey westward from Kentucky to the Pacific coast. He paused in Cairo to dabble in African exploration and there died.

In 1790, the War Department proposed a secret reconnaissance of the Missouri River by Americans—disguised as Indians to escape notice by the Spaniards. General Henry Knox, Secretary of War, sent secret instructions to General Harmar to devise "some practicable plan for exploring the branch of the Mississippi called the Messouri, up to its source." He may have had some idea of sending the explorer on to the Pacific. In further secret orders, Harmar was told that the exploring party must be "habited like Indians in all respects, and on *no pretence whatever,* discover any Connection with the troops." Written orders were not to be carried.

Harmar selected Lieutenant John Armstrong, who got only as far as St. Louis and St. Genevieve. Though his son later asserted that Armstrong paddled a canoe some hundreds of miles up the Missouri, Armstrong's own report shows that all he did was collect geographical notes and copy a map, after which he turned back. The Armstrong journey was kept so secret that Mr. Jefferson and his secretary never heard of it.

In 1792, Mr. Jefferson was the leading spirit in the proposal of the American Philosophical Society to send the French botanist, André Michaux, across the continent. Even as early as this, Mr. Jefferson was especially interested in the Missouri route; aid to Michaux was conditional upon his going that way. The Society opened a subscription list, to which President Washington contributed $25 and Messrs. Jefferson and Hamilton $12.50 each, eventually raising $128.25. It was for this journey that Meriwether Lewis had proposed himself in vain.

Michaux set out from Philadelphia July 15, 1792, but the scheme was soon abandoned. The Frenchman was not quite the guileless man of science he professed to be, but a secret agent of revolutionary France, helping to organize Genêt's proposed raid by Americans on Spanish possessions in Louisiana. On his way westward, he visited George Rogers Clark, who had been commissioned major general in the French service, with proposals on Genêt's behalf. (It was not by any means the last time that ostensibly scientific exploration would be used to cloak military intelligence agents.) When President Washington got wind of what was afoot, the French raid and Michaux's exploration ended together.

Despite these failures of American exploration, the country over which Captain Lewis was to lead his expedition was not all *terra incognita*. As far as the Mandan and Minnetaree villages near Bismarck, North Dakota, about 1,500 miles above its mouth, the Missouri was fairly well known. Sixty-six years before Lewis and Clark started, the great French explorer, Verendrye, had visited the Mandans and when the French were expelled from Canada, British traders, coming overland from the Assiniboine, soon followed in his footsteps. As early as 1743, Verendrye's sons had even caught sight of

the Rocky Mountains, along whose eastern edges Peter Fidler
of the Hudson's Bay Company later explored.

Beyond the cluster of Indian villages near Bismarck, only
a few men had ventured and none of them had gone very
far. For two hundred and fifty years exploration had been
nibbling at the edges of the vast territory drained by the
Missouri. In 1720, a Jesuit father, sent out from France to
study routes to the Pacific had suggested two: one, overland,
after establishing trading posts among the Sioux; the other,
up the Missouri, the route that fascinated Mr. Jefferson, the
way that Lewis and Clark took in 1804.

Meantime, the Spaniards had done a little. Coronado had
marched north from Mexico, perhaps as far as Kansas, in 1540
and 1542. A certain Jacques d'Eglise, credited with being the
first Spanish subject to ascend the Missouri, had ventured
some distance up the stream as early as 1790, continuing his
exploration until 1792. Jean Baptiste Trudeau had reached
the river villages of the Arikaras in 1794–1795 and brought
back a detailed journal of his trip. The Scot, James Mackay,
setting out under Spanish auspices with orders to go to the
Pacific, gave up when he reached Nebraska, and returned,
bringing a map of the country with him. The exact route
of Lewis and Clark seems to have been anticipated by "an
old man," whose very name is now forgotten. This intrepid
soul lived among the Pawnees from about 1784 to 1794, traveled overland with other Indians, to the sources of the Missouri, and beyond them saw a large river flowing west. But
his adventure led to nothing further.

In 1798, when the days of Spanish dominion were already
numbered, Zenon Trudeau, the Spanish Lieutenant Governor, was looking for volunteers "to penetrate to the sources
of the Missouri, and beyond it if possible to the Southern
Ocean." Fortunately for America's future, he never found
the men he wanted. While Mr. Jefferson and Captain Lewis
were already planning the Lewis and Clark Expedition, in

May and September, 1802, François Marie Perrin du Lac ascended the Missouri as far as White River, in South Dakota, publishing his book *Voyage dans les deux Louisianes* in 1805, the year before Lewis and Clark returned. In the same year as Perrin du Lac, James Purcel (or Pursley) after a desperate little knife-and-rifle fight with the Kansas Indians on the Osage River, had pushed on to the headwaters of the Arkansas, where he was still hunting and trading in 1804, when Lewis and Clark were on their way up the Missouri. Another party had been caught by the Sioux, who—though the explorers never suspected it—were still dragging a survivor, Charles Le Raye, about with them when the American explorers reached Sioux country.

The Pacific coast was much better known; but the coastal explorers were sailors and traders, little concerned about the interior, though one British officer had gone 119 miles up the Columbia. Only Alexander MacKenzie, first white man to cross the continent north of Mexico, had come overland through Canada reaching the very spot where Vancouver's ship had touched only a few weeks after Vancouver had sailed away.

None of these men were really predecessors of Lewis and Clark. They were mostly rude rivermen, hunters, trappers, traders, or unwilling Indian captives, who went part way and then returned. No one else made the whole desperate journey, as Lewis and Clark did, through the upper Missouri River country, across the mountains to the Columbia's southern tributaries, and then down the great river to the sea; nor did any one else even attempt to bring back their detailed reports on geography, botany, zoölogy, minerals, Indian life and languages, or anything even remotely approaching the completeness of Clark's careful if sometimes inexact maps of the new lands.

The fact that his expedition would traverse territory not a single inch of which was American disturbed Mr. Jefferson no more when he was preparing to send out Lewis and Clark than it had when he was encouraging Ledyard and Michaux. Fearful of American expansion though they were, the Spaniards had encouraged American settlers to come to Louisiana to find homes. With a little diplomacy, Mr. Jefferson knew that he could secure the Spanish government's complaisance in admitting a party of explorers who would be traveling, not for political but merely for "literary" purposes—the odd word is Mr. Jefferson's own, for he was writing in a day when science had not yet ceased to be literate.

And further, a great idea was dawning. Amid much hushed and secret consultation, a mighty shuffling of maps and papers, Mr. Jefferson's negotiators were at work in Paris. Already there was some reason to hope that a part of Louisiana would be American before the Lewis and Clark Expedition started, though not even Mr. Jefferson then dreamed of the possibility of buying all Louisiana.

The Emperor Napoleon was at the moment in much more trouble than usual. His Caribbean possessions, especially San Domingo, had lately been in uproar. He had reconquered them, but the restoration of French rule had been costly. Toussaint l'Ouverture and his rebellious Negroes had been hard to handle. The Emperor needed money for he had promised to pay American claims for French spoliation during the undeclared but vicious Franco-American naval war, and where was the cash to come from? He would need a great deal more than the American claims required, for he was already thinking of starting another war with Great Britain, and wars with the British were always expensive.

If he did attack Britain, there was a practical certainty that the British navy would gobble up Louisiana. Mr. Jefferson, who understood the French government thoroughly from his service as Minister in Paris, played adroitly on Napoleon's fears. The Emperor was allowed to get the impression that the United States might join the British. Perhaps, Napoleon pondered, it had been a mistake to make the Spanish return Louisiana to France in 1800. Still the thing was done, and the secret had leaked out in the spring of 1802—Mr. Jefferson had known or guessed it even earlier. Even if the Spanish forces were still in actual possession, everyone had known for some months that Louisiana was legally French again and quite defenseless. A belligerent England could seize it with the greatest ease. If the British should strike northward from New Orleans or the American west across the Mississippi, there would be nothing Napoleon could do.

It was a situation which disturbed Mr. Jefferson very nearly as much as it disturbed the Emperor of the French. The decaying Spanish Empire had been relatively harmless, but after Louisiana had, on paper, been returned to France, the prospect of having as a neighbor the most powerful military nation in the world was, as Mr. Jefferson wrote to his friend, Mr. Monroe, "very ominous to us."

If the British conquered Louisiana, which in case of war they would have a perfect right to do, matters would be still worse. The new and weak United States would then have their late king as an uncomfortably close neighbor both to the West and to the North. Worst of all, the British, who would then control New Orleans, could strangle American trade down the Mississippi to the sea whenever they chose, as the Spaniards had done before. They would probably enjoy doing it. It is just possible that some such thoughts continued to linger in restless British heads until 1815, when Old Hickory's motley army smashed Wellington's veterans at New Orleans, once for all.

Alone in the White House with his secretary, young Captain Lewis, Mr. Jefferson pondered these matters at length. It is a tragedy that no record remains of these long midnight conversations.

Instructions went out to the American Legation in Paris. The American Minister, Robert R. Livingston, made certain

overtures to Talleyrand, Foreign Minister of France. Negotiations dragged. Mr. Jefferson dared not trust even diplomatic mailbags with all he wished to say—the secret was too
great. He rushed his friend and neighbor, James Monroe,
hastily to Paris as a special envoy. Livingston, eager for all
the credit, tried to hurry the negotiations to completion while
Monroe was still at sea. French diplomats were dilatory. Negotiations, for part of Louisiana only, continued to drag.

Then suddenly, one day, even before Monroe arrived, Mon-
sieur Talleyrand asked easily, as if it were the most casual
question in the world, what the Americans would give, not
for part, but for all of Louisiana. When Monroe landed, he
was as much astounded as Livingston. The Americans saw a
chance they had never dreamed of and, risking their careers,
cast to the winds their instructions to pay $2,000,000 for New
Orleans. To have communicated with President Jefferson
would have meant a delay so long that everything might have
been ruined. Napoleon was in a hurry. They struck the
bargain quickly. Louisiana—all of it—became American for
$15,000,000, though Monroe and Livingston knew very well
they had no authority whatever to pay so much; and Mr. Jefferson, believer in a strict construction of the new Constitution, felt quite sure he had no right to buy any territory at
all. He bought it all the same, though—wrestling with his
conscience later—he hoped he had not "made waste paper of
the Constitution." The Bonaparte family were filled with
impotent rage. Mr. William Pitt was aghast. Spain was dismayed. Mr. Madison feared that a rush to Louisiana would
"dilute the population." Many Americans thought the land
was worthless. But Louisiana was American for all that, and
Captain Lewis and his Corps of Discovery would soon be
ready to make good the paper claim by actually traversing
the country.

Three couriers with three separate copies of the treaty sped
westward across the Atlantic in three separate vessels, to make

sure that one at least would reach America quickly. The first arrived July 14, 1803, preceded by rumors. Mr. Jefferson's enemies were nearly as indignant as the Bonapartes, but the Senate, after sundry rumblings, ratified the treaty with commendable promptness on October 19, 1803. One day after he had himself received the treaty, Mr. Jefferson wrote the news to Captain Lewis, who had now for months been deep in preparation for the expedition which he proposed to lead up the Missouri, no matter whether it was French or American. Lewis passed the news on to his friend, Clark, in strictest secrecy, August 3.

Like so much governmental "hush-hush," most of this was little better than a form. Though Mr. Jefferson described the sale of Louisiana as "a bolt from the blue," it was only Talleyrand's sudden offer to sell the whole territory that was surprising. The President had known for some weeks, and probably much longer, that the negotiations were taking a favorable turn, even if he had no anticipation of the suddenness with which they were concluded or the vastness of the area he was securing for the United States. As early as June 19, Lewis had been able to write Clark that "very sanguine expectations are at this time formed by our Government that the whole of that immense country wartered by the Mississippi and it's tributary streams, Missourie inclusive, will be the property of the U. States in less than twelve Months from this date."

Even before the Senate had ratified the treaty, Mr. Jefferson was willing to take into his confidence a Spanish official with whom he was acquainted. This was Henry Peyroux de la Coudrenaire, commanding at St. Genevieve and St. Louis. To him, Lewis carried a letter. Mr. Jefferson could not "omit the satisfaction of writing to you by Capt Lewis, an officer in our army, & for some time past my Secretary. As our former acquaintance was a mixt one of science and business, so is the occasion of renewing it. you know that the geography of the

Missouri and the most convenient water communication from the head of that to the Pacific ocean is a desideratum not yet satisfied. since coming to the administration of the U. S. I have taken the earliest opportunity in my power to have that communication explored, and Capt Lewis with a party of twelve or fifteen men is authorized to do it. his journey being mere literary, to inform us of the geography & natural history of the country, I have procured a passport for him & his party, from the Minister of France here, it being agreed between him & the Spanish minister, that the country having been ceded to France, her minister may most properly give authority for the journey. this was the state of things when the passport was given, which was sometimes since, but before Capt Lewis's actual departure we learn through a channel of unquestionable information that France has ceded the whole country of Louisiana to the U. S. by a treaty concluded in the first days of May." He asked his friend to "give all the protection you can to Capt Lewis & his party in going and returning."

Mr. Jefferson's information was not quite correct. The treaty was dated April 30, 1803, though not actually signed until May 2. Louisiana belonged to the United States. Captain Lewis would be traveling through American territory, even if it was territory that no American had ever seen.

chapter 8: *Lieutenant Clark gets a letter*

IN CHOOSING his secretary to lead the expedition, Mr. Jefferson was picking the best man to be found in the United States, though even Meriwether Lewis was not quite the miracle of perfection he wanted. Strength and courage taken for granted, the leader of Mr. Jefferson's proposed expedition had to be a man of varied talents. He had to be a natural leader or he could never carry his little command through the dangers and hardships ahead of him. He had to be an expert woodsman with some knowledge of Indians or he would never get back alive. He had to have some scientific training or he could not make the maps, observations, and collections which were the main purpose of the expedition.

No one combined so many of the needed qualities as Captain Lewis, though not even his devoted friend in the White

House could take the infantry captain's qualifications as a man of science very seriously. As Mr. Jefferson wrote his friend, Caspar Wistar in a "perfectly confidential" letter of February 28, 1803:

> "we cannot in the U. S. find a person who to courage, prudence, habits & health adapted to the woods, & some familiarity with the Indian character, joins a perfect knoledge of botany natural history, mineralogy & astronomy, all of which would be desirable. to the first qualifications Capt Lewis my secretary adds a great mass of accurate observation made on the different subjects of the three kingdoms as existing in these states, not under their scientific forms, but so as that he will readily seize whatever is new in the country he passes thro, and give us accounts of new things only: and he has qualified himself for fixing the longitude & latitude of the different points in the line he will go over."

If he had already mastered navigation by February, 1803, Lewis had begun getting ready for the expedition fairly early in 1802. In the early months of 1803, he was still busier. One of his first concerns was to find an Indian interpreter of some kind, though it was hopeless to look for any man who knew all the dialects the expedition was certain to encounter. In early April, he was trying to buy "portable soup." He finally got it, but—except when they were very near starvation—the Lewis and Clark Expedition sometimes thought it would have been much better if he hadn't. It sustained life. Sometimes the expedition almost wished it wouldn't.

During late April, May, and probably June of 1803, Lewis was in Philadelphia and Lancaster, buying scientific instruments, cramming science, getting medicine from the famous Dr. Rush, of Philadelphia, and harrying the quartermaster depot for equipment. The arsenal at Harper's Ferry was also building him a wonderful iron boat, such a craft as only an army officer would ever have designed. Its iron framework was to be in two sections. When these were taken apart, the boat could easily be stowed away, since it would weigh less than 100 pounds. The expedition would travel by ordinary Missouri River craft until this became impossible. Then they would put their iron frame together, cover it with bark as Lewis had seen the eastern Indians do, and load it with 1,770 pounds. Not very experienced in naval architecture, Lewis wondered how to establish a proper curve for the body of this amazing craft. Presto! He had found it. "The curve of the body of the canoe was formed by a suspended cord." Gaily he named it the *Experiment*. Cheerfully his weary men carried the extra weight of that iron frame some thousands of miles. When all other craft failed, the *Experiment* would save them.

Mr. Jefferson had left the choice of a companion to the leader himself, the War Department obligingly providing a blank second lieutenant's commission to be filled in with any name Lewis might choose. Who should it be? A practical field soldier—there would probably be fighting. A leader—the difficulties would call for the highest qualities of leadership. A frontiersman and a bold one at that—the wilderness beyond the Mississippi was no place for a novice. Science? Well, Lewis was a fairly good amateur himself, but he would need a companion handy enough with pen and pencil to make maps and scientific drawings, for Lewis himself was no draughtsman.

Also, no matter how brave and skillful, his companion must be a congenial man. In the perpetual physical strain, the eternal discomfort, the ever-present danger of the wilderness, nerves can fray till tempers snap like a taut rope. That would never do. The men of the expedition, under a severe strain themselves, would be only too quick to sense any hint of friction between their commanders.

Lewis's thoughts turned at once to two of his army friends. He knew that he would find a congenial man as well as a

brave and able one in Billy Clark. Billy was a good soldier.
The admiring relative who thought him "as brave as Cæsar"
had been right. Having served in Lieutenant Clark's company, Lewis knew he was a leader. Billy could sketch, too.
He had illustrated his own intelligence reports to Wayne.
He was an experienced woodsman, with years of wilderness
campaigning. Besides, Mr. Jefferson was as well acquainted
with the Clarks as he was with the Lewises. It would be just
as well to make sure of Mr. Jefferson's approval.

Clark was, as the success of the expedition showed, a wise
choice. Amid hardship, strain, suffering, hunger, thirst, pain,
exhaustion, sickness, worry, imminent danger, across the continent and back (three years in all, if you count the period of
preparation), there was no dispute, no quarrel, no vital disagreement. On two trifling questions only were Captains
Lewis and Clark ever at odds. One was the palatability of
dog meat; the other was the necessity of salt.

But there was no certainty as yet that Clark would accept.
If not Clark, who else? Lewis's thoughts turned to Lieutenant Moses Hook, a brother officer in the First Infantry. He
decided to make the first offer to Clark and, if he refused, to
take Hook. The Secretary of War authorized Hook to place
himself under Lewis's command, "being informed by Capt.
M. Lewis that he and you have a mutual desire that you may
accompany him on his tour to the Westward."

Alas for Hook! Clark accepted at once. The Lewis and
Clark Expedition brought immortality to its leaders. The
Lewis and Hook Expedition vanished into the historical
limbo of things that might have been.

Lewis wrote Clark from Washington, June 19, 1803, after
plans for the expedition were well under way, clearly stating
his intention of exploring both the Missouri and Columbia
River valleys and going to the Pacific coast, and explaining
that he hoped to secure a return passage by sea, on one of the

vessels that put into the mouth of the Columbia to trade with the Indians. Then the great offer:

"If therefore there is any thing under those circumstances, in this enterprise, which would induce you to participate with me in it's fatigues, it's dangers and it's honors, believe me there is no man on earth with whom I should feel equal pleasure in sharing them as with yourself: I make this communication to you with the pevity [privity?] of the President, who expresses an anxious wish that you would consent to join me in this enterprise."

The expedition was going—treaty or no treaty—for Congress had given authority; but secrecy was still essential. Lewis told his friend the whole story of the negotiations with France; but, he wrote, "here let me again impress you with the necessity of keeping this matter a perfect secret."

Clark received the letter on July 16. Excitedly, he talked it over with his brother. Old General George Rogers Clark urged him to accept: "A fine field was open for the display of genius." Clark accepted next day: "This is an amence undertaking fraited with numerous dificulties, but my freind I can assure you that no man lives with whome I would prefer to undertake & share the Dificulties of such a trip than yourself." On the 24th, he wrote again: "My friend I Join you with hand & Heart."

Whether Clark joined the expedition or not, Lewis wanted him to find "some good hunters, stout, healthy, unmarried young men, accustomed to the woods, and capable of bearing bodily fatigue to a pretty considerable degree." The international situation was still too ticklish to let anyone know the exact destination of the Lewis and Clark Expedition. Recruits would have to join blindly, without knowing where they were to go; but plenty of adventurous young men were eager to join any expedition that was going anywhere. Lewis suggested that Clark could preserve secrecy "by holding out the idea that the direction of this expedition is up the Mississippi to its source, and thence to the lake of the Woods, stating the probable period of absence at about 18 months; if they would engage themselves in a service of this discription there would be but little doubt that they would engage in the real design when it became necessary to make it known to them, which I should take care to do before I finaly engaged them."

Alas for military secrecy! Clark agreed to spread the rumor suggested by Lewis, but he had to send the melancholy news that it had done very little good. The real aim of the expedition was already a matter of common gossip, "mentioned in Louisville several weeks agoe." Recruiting news was more cheerful. Clark had already tentatively engaged a few men "of a description calculated to work & go thru those labours & fatigues which will be necessary." He was discouraging young gentlemen of his own class, "as they are not accustomed to labour."

Lewis approved Clark's ideas in a letter of August 3. He didn't want young gentlemen either, but "if a good hunter or two could be conditionally engaged I would think them an acquisition, they must however understand that they will not be employed for the purposes of hunting exclusively but must bear a portion of the labour in common with the party." Hunters would be absolutely vital, as the expedition needed "an emensity of meat." It ate "4 deer, an Elk and a deer, or one buffaloe" daily.

As he had done when setting off for the Whisky Rebellion, as he did to the end of his days, Lewis tried to spare his mother anxiety by a few well-meant half-truths. In a farewell letter dated July 2, two days before he set out from Washington, he unblushingly assured her that crossing the wilds of the Missouri, the Rockies, and the Columbia, would be "by no means dangerous." Actually, the Lewis and Clark Expedition was anything but the peaceful scientific promenade that its leader sketched so airily.

Lewis can hardly have believed what he wrote, or expected Lucy Marks to believe it, either; but he wanted to reassure her as much as possible. Anyhow, she always loved to get long letters from her sons.

It is doubtful if Mrs. Marks was ever in the least deceived by this factitious optimism. She knew the danger. She also knew her son's habit of emerging scatheless, or nearly so, from very desperate doings, and that was all she could rely on to keep up her courage, though her neighbor, Mr. Jefferson, tried to help. He had his first word of Lewis in the autumn of 1804 "thro a channel meriting entire confidence"—probably one of the white wanderers the expedition met on the Missouri. This placed him at the mouth of the Platte on August 4. All accounts agreed that Lewis would "be through his whole course as safe as at home"—a very pious lie. Mr. Jefferson sent the false but comforting news to Reuben Lewis, "believing that this information would be acceptable to your self, his mother & friends."

During the whole length of the expedition, only one other letter came back out of the unknown West, in the summer of 1805. Then silence. Mr. Jefferson hoped, a little. Lucy Marks, in the plantation house on Ivy Creek hoped, or tried to hope, as much as she dared.

From Washington, by way of Harper's Ferry, Lewis went on to Pittsburgh. A month earlier he had arranged to have a wagon collect supplies he had left at Lancaster, Frederick, and Harper's Ferry and take them on to Pittsburgh. He was careful to order special handling for his precious box of mathematical instruments.

At Pittsburgh, he had endless difficulties with the boat builders, "a set of most incorrigible drunkards," who took twelve days to get his poles and oars ready; but, after many delays, he was off down the Ohio River on August 30.

Lewis had already secured military equipment at the old Schuylkill arsenal, now the Philadelphia Quartermaster Depot. What the arsenal could not supply, he purchased through Israel Whelen, Purveyor of Public Supplies, in Philadelphia. His equipment included astronomical instruments, the framework of his iron boat, an airgun, a swivel gun, blunderbusses, rifles, ammunition and accouterments, clothing, provisions, camp supplies, Indian presents, eighteen tomahawks, fifteen scalping knives, fifteen dozen pewter looking glasses, three pounds of beads, six papers of small bells, three dozen tinsel bands, two dozen earrings, 500 brooches, 72 rings, three gross of curtain rings to adorn copper-colored fingers or ears. The total cost was $2,160.41.

The main problem now was the selection of the best possible personnel from at least 100 applicants. The War Department had authorized him to call on the commanding officers at Massac and Kaskaskia for non-commissioned officers and privates and to recruit from civil life "such suitable Men as may be inclined to accompany you." Their total number was, originally, not to exceed twelve but these orders had to be changed.

When he left Pittsburgh, Lewis was still trying to keep the real purpose of the expedition secret. Even the Deputy Quartermaster General there thought he was going to "ascend Mississippi." He had with him seven soldiers, a river pilot, "three young men on trial they having proposed to go with me throughout the voyage," and his Newfoundland dog, Scannon.

Three miles downstream, he halted at Brunot's Island, estate of the Frenchman, Dr. Felix Brunot, who had originally come to America to aid his foster-brother, Lafayette. Some of the local settlers asked to see Lewis's airgun tested. Now, the airgun was one of the showpieces of the expedition, the like of which few Americans and no Indians had ever seen. It was a new arm, with which there had been much experiment in England during the latter part of the eighteenth century, though it was still a curiosity in America. British poachers found airguns convenient. Their pop was far less likely to bring irate gamekeepers down upon them than the blast of a fowling piece. Enough air could be pumped in for several shots so that—though not quite a repeater—the gun could be fired as fast as a man could drop in bullets, a great deal faster than anyone could load, wad, and prime a Kentucky rifle. Yet it was very nearly as powerful as a rifle. If ammunition ran out it would be the expedition's only means of killing game for food. It drew blood for the first time that day on Brunot's Island, when one of the curious civilians examining it inadvertently pulled the trigger and grazed the temple of a woman 40 yards away. She fell as if dead, but the wound turned out to be only a graze. At least, it showed what the gun could do.

The Ohio journey was tiresome and annoying. The boats leaked, shoals blocked the river so that Lewis had to borrow oxen from the local settlers to get them across. As he paid their charges, Lewis complained bitterly that they had "no filanthrophy." He picked up more cargo at Wheeling, pausing to rest his men, dine with the local gentry, and entertain them at a watermelon feast. At Wheeling one other man missed fame by a hair's breadth. Dr. William Ewing Patterson, son of the professor of mathematics at the University of Pennsylvania, asked to be taken along. Since an exploring expedition can always use a medical man and since this one had £100 worth of medicine with him, Lewis agreed to take him if he could be ready "by three the next evening." The dilatory doctor was too slow; Lewis went his punctual way at 3 P.M.

River travel grew easier as the lower Ohio grew deeper and Lewis began to enjoy himself. It was entertaining to watch his Newfoundland dog, Scannon, catch squirrels, large numbers of which were swimming the river. Scannon, "active strong and docile," killed them in the water and brought them to his master who thought squirrels "when fryed a pleasent food." No wonder Lewis refused a Shawnee's offer of three beaver skins for Scannon, who had cost twenty dollars—an enormous sum for a dog in those days.

Lewis "engaged George Drewyer in the public service as an Indian Interpretter," when he reached Fort Massac. Drouilliard, whose name no one on the expedition ever learned either to spell or pronounce, was a young French Canadian whose father had served with the British during the Revolution. A dead shot, an experienced woodsman, an old hand among the Indians, an expert in sign language, he was exactly the kind of man Captain Lewis was looking for. Farther down the river, at Louisville, they found Clark waiting for them. Lewis's diary does not note the meeting of the two leaders, but Clark's eldest brother, Jonathan, scribbled in his diary for October 26, 1803: "Capt Lewis and Capt Wm Clark set of on a Western tour—went in their boat to Mr. Temple's."

Turning out of the Ohio and up the Mississippi, they paused at Cap Girardeau to make the acquaintance of Louis Lorimier, an Indian trader who, during the Revolution, had helped the Shawnees to capture Daniel Boone. Ever a man with an eye for the ladies, Lewis was quick to note that the Shawnee Mme. Lorimier had been "very handsome when young" and that "the daughter is remarkably handsom & dresses in a plain yet fashonable stile or such as is now Common in the Atlantic States among the respectable people of the middle class. she is an agreeable affible girl, & much the most descent looking feemale I have seen since I left the settlement in Kentuckey."

Part of his enthusiasm may have been due to the supper, "really a comfortable and desent one," which the Lorimier ladies provided. The regrettable fact that an army commanded by Captain Clark's brother had burned $20,000 worth of Lorimier's Indian goods while attacking the Shawnees, some years before, did not come into the conversation. Without further adventure, they reached St. Louis.

Clark set up a base camp at Rivière du Bois, on the American bank of the Mississippi, since there had not yet been a formal transfer of Upper Louisiana and the Spaniards still controlled the west bank. This left Lewis free to move up and down the Mississippi, completing preparations. There were many minor difficulties. Clark, busily building boats at Rivière du Bois, could not get a whipsaw. The owner of a map they needed refused to let it be sent to them. William Henry Harrison, at Vincennes, hastily had it copied before returning it to the exigent owner. Lewis searched in vain for "hair pipes." He was delayed waiting for a friendly Kickapoo chief. Clark had to pacify a Kickapoo war party. There were such problems as tallow, lard, and finding French engagés who knew the river.

The local gentry, especially those in the Indian trade, were not always co-operative. Lewis indulged in one outburst to Clark: "Damn Manuel and triply Damn Mr. B. they give me more vexation and trouble than their lives are worth—I have dealt very plainly with these gentlemen, in short I have come to an open rupture with them; I think them both great scoundrels, and they have given me abundant proofs of their unfrendly dispositions towards our government and it's measures—these gentlemen (no I will scratch it out) these puppies are not unaquainted with my opinions." The "Manuel" who is thus feelingly condemned can only have been the famous fur trader, Manuel Lisa. Lewis was particularly annoyed by a threat to petition the American Governor at New Orleans against him.

In mid-winter he visited Kaskaskia and Cahokia, on the Mississippi, securing two of his best men from Captain Russell Bissell's company of the First Infantry. One of these, Sergeant John Ordway, a New Hampshire Yankee, Lewis must have known in 1800 and 1801, when they were both constantly in and out of the quartermaster's offices in Pittsburgh. Captain Bissell gave up Ordway without dispute, so far as the records show; but there was trouble when Lewis also asked for Patrick Gass, an old Regular who had fought Indians, had known Daniel Boone, and had become acquainted with the Clark family as early as 1793. He was a little man, standing only five feet seven, "poor but spunky," broad-chested and sturdy—a fine soldier and, best of all, an experienced carpenter, sure to be useful when the expedition had to build forts, cabins, and canoes. Bissell flatly refused to let two of his best men go. Determined to join the expedition, Gass contrived a very private interview with Lewis, who thereupon, armed with Presidential authority, overruled the disconsolate company commander.

Drouilliard rejoined Lewis's party at Cahokia, bringing eight men from Tennessee, in whom Lewis was somewhat disappointed, since there was "not a hunter among them." However, one was a blacksmith and another a "House-joiner," both of whom would be useful.

In spite of annoyances, Clark kept the organization of the expedition moving rapidly forward at Rivière du Bois. "I have not been from my Camp to any house since my arrival here," he wrote in mid-January. However, the veteran of Wayne's Indian campaign was not discouraged: "My Situation is as Comfortable as could be expected in the woods, & on the frontier."

Since Clark's day, the government has moved the mouth of Wood River up the Mississippi, and the vagrant Missouri has moved its own mouth downstream. But Clark from his camp could look directly up the muddy torrent of the Missouri, the way he was to go: "The Missouri which mouths imediately opposite me is the river we intend assending as soon as the weather will permit."

While Clark labored in camp, Lewis moved up and down the Mississippi, also engaged in preparations. He returned from Cahokia January 30; 1804, went to St. Louis in February, and was back in camp by March. Both officers, when in St. Louis, were hospitably entertained by Pierre Chouteau. Though he had not yet received his commission, Clark took command in Lewis's absence and the first known Detachment Order, February 20, 1804, refers to him as "Capt." In Detachment Orders of March 3, Lewis still refers to himself as "the Commanding officer"—Clark, technically, had not yet been recommissioned. Other orders read, "the Commanding officers." Theoretically, it is an impossible way to run a military organization, but it worked perfectly.

Sawyers were kept busy cutting planks for the boats, while blacksmiths hammered them together. The workmen were rewarded for their extra exertions by exemption from guard duty and an extra gill of whisky a day. Four men occupied in making maple sugar were also exempted from guard duty but got only half a gill. A "practicing party" was kept on the rifle range, firing one round a day "off hand," at 50 yards, the rifle of that day lacking the range of its modern descendant. Hunters were ordered to get back to camp in time for guard duty, which was quite as unpopular then as now. Though straggling was prohibited, some hunters carried iniquity so far as to visit "a neighbouring whiskey shop." One group of offenders had to be confined to camp for ten days.

"Robust helthy hardy young men" the enlisted explorers might be, but not all of them were soldiers yet and they needed discipline. It took some months, hundreds of miles of travel, a few courts-martial, several hundred lashes, and two dismissals from service before the "Corps of Discovery" was ready to face any hardship or danger that the plains, rivers, mountains, wild beasts, and Indians could produce, with unmatched discipline and courage.

Some of the best men were very troublesome at first. Detachment orders of March 3 emphasize that "the Commanding officer feels himself mortifyed and disappointed at the disorderly conduct of Reubin Fields, in refusing to mount guard when in the due roteen of duty he was regularly warned; nor is he less surprised at the want of discretion in those who urged his oposition to the faithfull discharge of his duty particularly Shields, whose sense of propryety he had every reason to believe would have induced him reather to have promoted good order, than to have excited disorder and faction."

This was read on parade, while the offenders squirmed. Both Lewis and Clark had been away, leaving camp, as usual, in charge of Sergeant John Ordway. Some of the robust, healthy, and hardy young men had not yet quite grasped the sacredness of sergeants. Lewis and Clark backed up their non-com: "The commanding officers highly approve of the conduct of Serg^t. Ordway." It was the right way to handle these two men, both of whom distinguished themselves on the expedition.

In April those men who were still technically civilians were formally enlisted and the detachment was organized into three squads with a sergeant in command of each, Ordway also acting as a kind of first sergeant. Other men were kept about the camp for a time. Later one of the newly enlisted men was dropped and Robert Frazer added in his place. Since there were only two commissioned officers, sergeants acted as officers-of-the-day and eventually served on courts-martial together with private soldiers, thereby anticipating a "reform" of courts-martial, recently much discussed.

Lewis was in St. Louis in March and was a witness of the formal transfer of Upper Louisiana to the American flag, adding his signature to the official record. New Orleans had been taken over months before, but affairs moved more slowly on the upper Mississippi. President Jefferson had long had troops ready to take possession. On March 8, 1804, a few American soldiers of the First Infantry (Lewis's regiment), commanded by Lieutenant Stephen Worrell, crossed to St. Louis and marched to Government House, ready for the ceremonies of transfer. Lewis was with them.

Next day, Lewis's friend, Captain Amos Stoddard, who was the authorized commissioner for both the French and the American governments, formally received transfer of Upper Louisiana from the Spanish Governor, De Lassus, on behalf of the French government only. On March 10, he solemnly received transfer of authority from himself, as French commissioner, to himself, as American commissioner, and began work as temporary civil and military governor.

Occasionally Stoddard appealed to Lewis for advice. After all, the ex-secretary knew what the President wanted. In March, being short of funds, he took Lewis's advice on getting a draft. Two days later he went with Lewis and Clark to inspect the old St. Louis forts and see what repairs they might need. When Indians began pouring into the village "to see their new father and to hear his words," Lewis, being by this time fully equipped for Indian trading, furnished tobacco and whisky for them.

A few days later, Congress passed the Louisiana Government Act, dividing the Purchase into a southern part, the Territory of New Orleans, and a northern part, the District of Louisiana, which was for a short time attached to Indiana Territory before it was made a separate Louisiana Territory, with the 33rd parallel dividing it from New Orleans Territory which eventually became the state of Louisiana.

When the explorers shoved off their boats in May of 1804, they knew almost everything that any white man knew about the country they were to traverse—though it would have astonished them to learn that in 1802 and 1803, while their own expedition was being so carefully planned, the Canadian trappers, Pardo and Le Raye, were already wintering on the Yellowstone and exploring in Montana.

It was, after all, easy to know everything about the Missouri country—there was very little to know. Mr. Jefferson, who had an agent collecting information in New Orleans, made haste to lay a description of his Louisiana Purchase before Congress. The information was somewhat startling. Somewhere in the new territories there was a mountain "of solid rock salt," said to be 180 miles long and 45 miles wide, "without any trees or even shrubs on it." Mr. Jefferson's enemies said derisively that there was probably an American eagle, also in solid rock salt, sitting on the top. Nothing was known of the Missouri Valley, beyond the Mandan villages, Mr. Jefferson said, "though the traders have been informed that many large navigable rivers discharge their waters into it." The presence of silver and copper was suspected. There was little mention of gold. Mammoths might not be the only strange creatures found there.

The two friends snatched up every bit of information they could secure—collecting, as Clark wrote, "what information we can of this river and its res[ourc]es so as we may make Just Calculations before we start." The only important data they seem to have missed were Armstrong's map and notes, which for another century were to slumber among General Harmar's papers, where no one ever heard of them.

The two leaders had been at pains to study the maps of Anville and Vancouver, besides the manuscript map that General Harrison had sent and John Evans's map, which Mr. Jefferson sent on January 13, 1804: "I now enclose you a map of the Missouri as far as the Mendans, 12 or 1,500 miles . . . it is said to be very accurate." A few days later Mr. Jefferson sent notes from Trudeau's journal and eventually he supplied a complete English translation of the whole thing.

Another of the Spaniards' early explorers supplied what facts he could in conversation. This was the Scot, James Mackay. Clark's papers still contain an empty wrapper labeled "Mr. Evins's sketches of the Missouri, present by Mr.

MacKay." Mackay allowed Clark to make excerpts from his journal.

Since Clark paid frequent visits to the village of St. Charles, he probably met and talked with the aged but vigorous Daniel Boone, who had long been collecting all the information he could regarding the country to the West. There was also information from a certain John Hay, who kept a winter station on the Assiniboine River. Perhaps from him Lewis learned of Peter Fidler's explorations along the edge of the Rockies for the Hudson's Bay Company.

The commanders also picked up a good deal of information from the rivermen who abounded in St. Louis and St. Charles, some of whom knew the first few hundred miles of the Missouri fairly well. On May 6, only a few days before they started, they secured information from Étienne Cadron, of St. Louis, who had visited the Saline on the forks of the Arkansas the winter before.

Two remarkable items of equipment were put together in St. Louis at the last moment, by Dr. Antoine Saugrain, a French refugee physician, who loved to dabble in science. Mr. Jefferson had asked for temperature records. According to well-attested legend, Dr. Saugrain scraped the mercury from the back of his wife's prized French mirror, melted down the glass, made tubes, ascertained where the mercury stood in them at freezing and at blood heat, and then graduated between those two extremes as best he could. He must have made several, for there is reference in the Journals to the breaking of "our last Th[er]mometer" as they crossed the Rockies. By curious irony, the wandering trader, Pierre Antoine Tabeau, already had a practical metal thermometer among the Arikaras, far up the Missouri.

Nearly twenty years before friction matches were generally known, Dr. Saugrain produced some for the expedition by putting sulphur on one end of a splinter of wood and then tipping it with phosphorus. Half a century later, the Nez

Percés still remembered the amazing speed with which Lewis and Clark made fire.

A final vexation arose at the last moment—the rank to be given Clark, who had resigned from the army as an infantry lieutenant. The popular idea is that Lewis and Clark were both captains, co-equal joint commanders. So they were—once they got into the field and away from officialdom; but that was their own little arrangement, which would have created a fine official frenzy if the War Department had ever found out about it. There is no doubt that President Jefferson and the War Department meant Lewis to be commander, but it was awkward for him to ask his old friend and company commander to serve as his subordinate. Mr. Jefferson had intimated that Clark was to have a captain's commission and Lewis himself had written: "your situation if joined with me in this mission will in all respects be precisily such as my own." For some reason it had been proposed to issue the commission in the Corps of Engineers and it was to be made permanent in the Regular Army, if Clark so desired on his return.

In the War Department, red tape began to unwind with dizzying speed. President Jefferson was promptly put in his place, a pompous letter from his Secretary of War overruling him on March 26: "The peculiar situation, circumstances and organisation of the Corps of Engineers is such as would render the appointment of Mr. Clark a Captain in that Corps improper—and consequently no appointment above that of a Lieutenant in the Corps of Artillerists could with propriety be given him, which appointment he has recd. & his Commission is herewith enclosed—his Military Grade will have no effect on his compensation for the services in which he is engaged." It would take the curious mind of a War Department clerk to explain why, if an infantry lieutenant could not be recommissioned in the engineers, he ought to go into the artillery!

Lewis delayed sending the bad news to Clark until May 6, 1804. Then, transmitting the second lieutenant's commission, he wrote: "it is not such as I wished, or had reason to expect; but so it is—a further explaneation when I join you.—I think it will be best to let none of our party or any other persons know any thing about the grade, you will observe that the grade has no effect upon your compensation, which by G—d, shall be equal to my own."

"My feelings on this Occasion," said Clark dryly, afterward, "was as might be expected."

Nobody, not even Mr. Jefferson, was ever allowed to know the secret, except Nicholas Biddle, who edited the Journals some years after the expedition had returned, and even he was pledged to secrecy. "I did not think myself very well treated," Clark wrote to his editor, in somewhat chaotic prose, "as I did not get the appointment which was promised me—as I was not disposed to make any noise about the business have never mentioned the particulars to anyone, and must request you not to mention my disapointment & the cause to anyone."

It was always "Captain" Lewis and "Captain" Clark to the men of the expedition; and, as both resigned from the army soon after their return and both were equally rewarded, the lieutenancy, however galling, made very little practical difference. It was a little embarrassing when they both had to sign the papers they gave the Indians. Lewis signed as Captain, First Infantry. Clark created himself "Captain of a Corps of Discovery," and the Indians were not critical. He was careful to tell Biddle later, emphatically underlining the words, that he and Lewis had been *"equal in every point of view."* He chose to regard the second lieutenant's commission that he actually held as "mearly calculated to autherize punishment to the Soldiers." Pocketing his pride, he stayed with Lewis because he "wished the expedition suckcess."

chapter 9: *The Corps of Discovery starts*

ON SUNDAY morning, May 13, 1804, everything was ready at last. Boats were loaded with provisions, ammunition, and Indian goods —"tho' not as much as I think ness^y. for the multitude of Ind^s. thro which we must pass on our road across the Continent," the cautious Clark noted. Although they carried 21 bales of presents for the Indians, they had taken too many red and white beads and not enough blue ones, a shortage the disastrous nature of which did not appear until much later. At least there were fourteen barrels of "parchmeal," holding two bushels each; twenty barrels of flour; seven barrels of salt, which ran out long before they reached the Coast; 50 kegs of pork; 50 bushels of meal; "Tools of every Description"; and abundant drugs and medical instruments.

Tucked away in Private Cruzat's personal baggage was one

other article of equipment which surely no exploring expedition had ever carried before. Cruzat had taken along his violin—which would have delighted that enthusiastic fiddler, Mr. Jefferson. It turned out to be one of the most useful things the expedition carried. The Indians were astonished at the music. Some of them even said politely that they enjoyed it. And all the weary way, Cruzat and his fiddle furnished music for the square dances which, even without feminine partners, were the chief recreation of the Lewis and Clark Expedition. Rare indeed were the occasions when the men were too tired to dance.

All of this was carried in three vessels: a 22-oar keelboat, or bateau, handled by the soldiers of the permanent exploring party; a large pirogue in which the hardy French rivermen commanded by their "patroon," La Jeunesse, strained at the oars, and another pirogue of six oars, rowed by soldiers not part of the Corps of Discovery, who were to be sent home in the spring.

The keelboat was the kind of craft which both of the officers and many of the soldiers had used on the Ohio—55 feet long, drawing three feet of water, and carrying one square sail. She was decked over for ten feet in the bow, with a cabin astern. Along the gunwales amidships, lockers were placed so that their lids could be raised to give additional protection in case of attack. It was a modification of the craft that George Rogers Clark had used in his early wilderness campaigns. William Clark would use vessels very much like it a few years later, when he was fighting the British in the War of 1812.

The only lack was Captain Lewis himself, who had gone over to St. Louis on business—officially, "to fix off the Osage chiefs," whom his host Pierre Chouteau had brought down the Missouri and was taking to Washington for a treaty; unofficially, to say good-by to a large number of girls. Girls, at the moment, did not greatly interest Clark. There was that little thing named Judy Hancock, growing up in Fincastle,

MISSOURI RIVER BOATMEN by Charles Bodmer. *This is one of a series of drawings by the artist who accompanied Prince Maximilian Alexander Philipp von Wied-Neuwied on his travels in the interior of North America. Although these pictures were made about thirty years after Lewis and Clark's expedition, the country and its inhabitants were virtually unchanged.*

BUFFALO AND ELK by Charles Bodmer. *Along the Missouri, "the party rarely lacked fresh meat of some sort—buffalo, antelope, beaver-tail and beaver-liver, the last two being especially appreciated by Lewis. Private Whitehouse observed that 'the Game is getting so pleanty and tame in this country that Some of the men has went up near enofe to club them out of their way.'"*

one of the two girls he had helped manage that balky horse—well, more of her hereafter.

Clark sent a messenger to tell Lewis all was ready but decided to start without him when he found Lewis could not get back to Rivière du Bois till next day. It would be easy enough to catch up with the expedition by riding overland to St. Charles. He wanted to start with the boats at once, for if the first few miles of river travel revealed errors in loading —they did, of course—he would need time to rearrange his cargo, while awaiting the arrival of the other commander.

The departure of the Corps of Discovery was extremely matter-of-fact. The local people gathered to say farewell, and the boats pushed off without ceremony of any kind. "I Set out at 4 oClock P.M.," says Clark's journal, "in the presence of many of the neighbouring inhabitents, and proceeded on under a jentle brease up the Missourie to the upper Point of the 1st Island 4 Miles and camped on the Island." The boats moved ahead to St. Charles next day.

As Clark had feared, his craft were badly loaded. Missouri rivermen placed the heaviest load in the bow, so that a boat hitting one of the hidden snags which studded the river would not ride up on it and tear out her bottom. Clark's soldiers, unused to the river, had loaded all the boats so that they were stern-heavy, and the experienced French engagés had failed to warn them of their error. Everything had to be done over at St. Charles.

Discipline was still as bad as bad could be. When they reached St. Charles, there was a ball, at which one of the men was found "behaveing in an unbecomeing manner." When he got back to camp he added disrespectful language to the first offense, and with two others, decided to celebrate their last contact with civilization by going AWOL. A court-martial, with a sergeant as president, sentenced two of them to 25 lashes on the bare back, but with a recommendation to mercy, which Clark approved. The worst sinner got 50 lashes,

which were duly administered at sunset the same day. Floggings of this sort were just the ordinary field punishment
usual in the army of the day. They were administered with
switches or ramrods, not with the heavy leather whips of the
British navy. If they had been, the sentences dealt out by the
expedition's courts-martial would have killed the offenders.

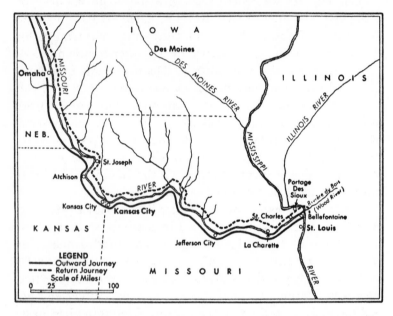

For the well-behaved, there was more festivity, including a
second ball, to which, Clark noted wistfully, "it is not in my
power to go." More cheerfully he noted, "Seven Ladies visit
me to day."

Lewis pushed on through a thunderstorm to join him on
the 20th, accompanied by his friend, Major Amos Stoddard,
other officers, and some gentlemen of St. Louis. He had bid-
den satisfactory farewell to his hostess, Mrs. Peter Chouteau
and—indefatigable romantic—to "some of my fair friends of
Sᵗ. Louis."

Clark had finished reloading while waiting for Lewis and everything was now ready. After consultation, the two commanders decided to make the final start at two o'clock on May 21, but a farewell dinner proved so very convivial that the Lewis and Clark Expedition started an hour and a half late, "under three Cheers from the gentlemen on the bank." Even so, they were delayed next morning "one hour for 4 frenchmen who got liberty to return to arrange Some business they had forgotten in Town." In spite of the forgetful engagés, they were moving again at six in the morning, stopping at Daniel Boone's Femme Osage settlement to pick up two men who had gone ahead to buy corn and butter.

Throughout the expedition, Lewis had most of the narrow escapes. His career as an explorer now very nearly ended, on its second day, when he fell from a 300-foot cliff. Luckily, he "caught at 20 foot" from the top.

At the little French trading settlement of La Charrette, they met Régis Loisel, just down from the Sioux villages along the Missouri, with the very latest information about the country ahead. Louis Labeaume, whom Lewis as Governor of Louisiana Territory later made an associate judge, had told them before leaving Rivière du Bois to look out for Loisel, who was somewhere up the Missouri, and for Loisel's assistant, Pierre Antoine Tabeau, who would have "much information in relation to that country." Loisel may have told them more about Tabeau, whom he had recently left among the Arikaras. At any rate, Lewis and Clark knew all about the man when they found him a few months later.

Loisel was not quite the guileless friend he seemed. Though he gave information to the Americans, he was listening carefully all the while to what they themselves had to say of their plans. A few days later, he was privately reporting to the Spaniards on the danger of American influence among the Indians; the danger of an American claim to all lands watered by the Missouri's tributaries; the peculiar menace of the

Lewis and Clark Expedition, which had "already set out to explore the way"; and, finally, the value to Spain of his own services, which he offered to combat the nefarious schemes of the United States. The former Spanish Governor rushed this to his superiors, warning that Nuevo Mexico was in danger and urging that Loisel be employed as a frontier agent to head off the Americans. At about the same time, the Spanish Governor of West Florida—much alarmed about the expedition, though not very well informed—was urging that Spanish troops be sent overland from Santa Fé or Chihuahua at once, either to capture Lewis and Clark or to force them back. His Excellency noted with dismay that already bets were being offered in Florida that the Americans would possess a Pacific port within five years.

Cursing an epidemic of boils, intestinal upheavals, mosquitoes, snags, a broken mast, snapping tow ropes, lost oars—and probably, in private, their commanders—the expedition crawled upstream against the stiff Missouri current. Hunters moved along the bank, shooting for the pot and meeting occasional friendly Indians. A shore party herded the expedition's horses, sometimes meeting loose horses on the prairie and gathering them in. Movement along the shore was not easy, for the Missouri is edged with steep bluffs of hard clay and the shore below was overgrown with thickets and trees, through which they had to fight their way. One of the officers was usually ashore. Lewis was soon off to the woods, collecting "many curious Plants & Srubs," noting a new birdsong, finding occasional Indian sign. Clark once got so far ahead of the boats that he had to camp by the shore and wait for them. Deer were plentiful, bear began to appear, there was some buffalo sign. The party jerked such meat as it did not eat on the spot.

On the 26th, the captains assigned special duties to their sergeants. One took the helm and saw that everything was shipshape, no small task for a soldier. A second commanded the guard amidships, managed the sail, watched the oarsmen, issued liquor, posted the guard, watched the shore en route, and posted the guard ashore. At each relief of the guard during the night, he reconnoitered for 150 paces around the camp with two soldiers. A third, in the bow, kept a sharp look-out for snags in the river, signals, and possible enemies. Never once relaxed, from start to finish, the expedition's constant alertness largely accounted for its success. To take the Corps of Discovery by surprise was quite impossible, and when armed and alert, they were amply able to defend themselves against any possible attack.

There was some traffic in the lower Missouri. A raft floating downstream brought word that the Osage band on the Arkansas River had contemptuously burned a letter announcing American annexation. Another raft bore three disconsolate hunters, returning from a year up-river, who had eaten all their provisions and, having exhausted their ammunition, had no way to get any more. Near Plumb Creek, on June 12, the expedition sighted two rafts and, pausing to buy buffalo grease from the raftsmen, met Pierre Dorion, veteran frontiersman who had spent twenty years among the Sioux and had been in correspondence with Clark's famous elder brother as early as 1780.

Fascinated by the adventurer's talk, the captains quizzed him till it was too late to go on, so that the rafters and the expedition camped together for the night, still talking. By morning, Dorion had been persuaded to turn back to the Sioux country, "with a view to get some of their Cheifs to visit the Presd^t. of the United S." Two days later they met another raft from Pawnee country, but none of these raftsmen were willing to turn back on a similar errand to the Pawnees.

A surprise inspection found some of the arms in bad order. Another inspection, a week later, found all the rifles clean —the men were learning. A careful record of course and distance began from the very start. Lunar or solar observations were made, even when it was necessary to fell trees to get a sight. Sergeant Floyd's diary notes on June 2: "we fell a nomber of trees at the pint for the porpas of oberservations." Both captains were keeping journals, and so were Ordway, Floyd, Gass, Whitehouse, and Frazer. Of these journals, Frazer's has been totally lost, and Gass's exists only in a printed version, much rewritten by a local schoolmaster and horribly "literary." The other manuscripts survive, though Ordway's disappeared for nearly a century.

There had been trouble with discipline from the first days at Rivière du Bois, and the relatively mild punishments which had been tried at first had failed to cure it. The captains, knowing that the thing had to stop before the expedition reached really dangerous country, prepared for severity. Four courts-martial were to meet before winter. On June 30, John Collins and Hugh Hall went before a court composed entirely of enlisted men, the first charged with being drunk on guard and letting Hall steal whisky, the second charged only with "takeing whiskey out of a Keg this morning." Collins received 100 lashes on the bare back and Hall 50 lashes, also on the bare back, at half past three that same afternoon.

On July 12, Alexander Willard was charged with "Lying down and Sleeping on his post" while on guard. As this might involve a death penalty, the two officers sat as the court, finding him guilty of a breach of the Articles of War "tending to the probable distruction of the party." He was sentenced to receive 25 lashes at sunset every night for four nights.

As the expedition passed the Platte River's junction with the Missouri, the commanders decided to halt for a few days and try to make friends with the Oto, Maha, and Missouri tribes. Almost at once there were two desertions. Moses B. Reed, one of the soldiers, and an engagé appropriately named La Liberté found the going too hard and disappeared. Suspecting that both men were at the neighboring Indian village, the captains sent Drouilliard and three soldiers back to arrest

Reed and "if he did not give up Peaceibly to put him to Death"—orders which Drouilliard was to remember to his own misfortune a few years later. Drouilliard's party caught both men easily enough but La Liberté escaped and apparently spent the next few years among the Otos. Reed also tried to escape but gave up when Bratton threatened to shoot him.

HOLDING A COUNCIL WITH THE INDIANS from Sergeant Gass's Diary. *"Lewis made the speech which became monotonously familiar as the expedition counciled with one tribe after another during the next few thousand miles: His Red children were now under the protection of a new father, the Great White Father at Washington. They must keep the peace. The Great White Father would send traders to supply them with all necessities."*

Besides his prisoner, Drouilliard also brought back a delegation of Oto chiefs, gay in colored buffalo robes and blankets. As soon as the red plenipotentiaries could be suitably welcomed, Reed faced a court-martial, which "only sentenced him to run the Gantlet four times through the Party & that each man with 9 Swichies should punish him." He was sent home in disgrace in the spring.

Strange to say, the Oto chiefs interceded for the deserter. Treated to a short dissertation on discipline, the savage humanitarians professed themselves satisfied and watched Reed run the gauntlet, then and there. As this eventful day was August 18, Lewis's birthday, it closed with an extra gill of whisky for everybody—except, presumably, Reed—and a strictly stag dance to the music of Cruzat's violin, which, the Journals say, he played "extreemly well."

In formal council with the Otos, Lewis expounded the new situation in Louisiana; and Indian speeches, in reply, courteously accepted the advice he brought from their great father in Washington. Presents and medals were distributed, as was customary, together with "certificates," or "Indian commissions," of which Lewis and Clark had brought a plentiful supply, in blank. One of these is shown in the illustration facing page 83.

It was disappointing to find that the grand chief of the Otos, together with many Oto and Missouri warriors, was absent, but the captains left a written "speech," hoping that some white trader would read and translate it for them. A copy, now in the National Archives, is the best surviving record of what the explorers told the Indians in speeches all the way to the Pacific: They had been sent "by the great Chief of the Seventeen great nations of America" to inform his red children of a "council" held with the French and Spanish—in other words, the Louisiana Purchase. As a result, "your old fathers the french and Spaniards have gone beyond the great lake towards the rising Sun, from whence they never intend returning to visit their former red children in this quarter." The red children must surrender French and Spanish flags and medals, receiving American flags and medals in return. The great American chief now controlled all the rivers and would "command his war chiefs to Suffer no vessel

to pass," except those of his own traders, who would soon
bring the Indians all the white man's goods they might desire. He would welcome the Oto chiefs if they came to visit
him. The document authorized any trader into whose hands
it might fall to bring chiefs to St. Louis. The council broke
up with a dram all round and the first of innumerable demonstrations of the airgun and "many Curiosities," which made
a great impression. It was plain that these white strangers
had big medicine.

Tragedy followed two days later. Capering too vigorously
while dancing with the Indians, Sergeant Floyd returned to
camp just in time to go on guard, badly overheated. He flung
himself down on a sandbar near the river, refusing the shelter
of a tent, and was soon seized with what Sergeant Gass described as "the cramp colic." It is just possible that he really
had appendicitis. On July 31, Floyd himself noted in his
personal diary: "I am verry Sick and Has ben for Somtime but
have Recoverd my helth again." He made no more entries
regarding his own condition, but Clark notes on August 19:
"Serjeant Floyd is taken verry bad all at once with a Biliose
Chorlick we attempt to relieve him without success as yet,
he gets worst and we are much allarmed at his Situation, all
attention to him." The next day the boats went on, though
Floyd was getting weaker—"no pulse & nothing will Stay a
moment on his Stomach or bowels."

He died just as they were approaching a bluff in what is
now Sioux City, Iowa. Knowing that the end had come,
Floyd turned to Clark with the quiet words: "I am going
away I want you to write me a letter." What he wrote or to
whom, no one thought to record, but there is an echo of his
family's grief and their faith in Clark in an undated letter of
his brother Nathaniel to a sister: "Dear Nancy: Our dear
Charles died on the voyage of colic. He was well cared for as
Clark was there." On the bluff overlooking the river, the

dead man's comrades dug his grave, fitted rough slabs of oak about his body, and rendered the honors of war.

"This Man at all times gave us proofs of his firmness and Determined resolution to doe Service to his Countrey and honor to himself," wrote Clark in the Journals; "after paying all the honor to our Decesed brother we camped in the Mouth of floyds River about 30 yards wide, a butifull evening." The solitary grave lay only a mile or two behind them. The men, allowed to elect his successor, chose Patrick Gass, who had already held a sergeant's warrant in the First Infantry.

The severity with which Willard, Hall, and Reed had been punished had not yet quite ended the bad discipline. On October 13, Private John Newman spoke mutinously to Lewis, was instantly arrested, and that very night went before a court-martial of enlisted men, over which Clark presided, though he took no part in reaching the verdict. The court sentenced Newman to receive 75 lashes and to be "discarded from the perminent party engaged for North Western discovery." That is, like Reed, he was no longer to be considered a member of the expedition, though since there was no immediate way of getting rid of them, both still had to be carried along. Newman was denied "the honor of mounting guard," and became simply a "labouring hand" aboard the red pirogue. Instead of guard duty, he was "exposed to such drudgeries" as might relieve the others.

His flogging, the day after the court-martial, horrified an Arikara chief who saw it as much as earlier floggings had horrified the Otos. The chief "cried aloud (or effected to cry)." Clark again explained the necessity of discipline. Quite so, replied the copper-colored humanitarian. He put his own warriors to death in such cases, but "his nation never whiped even their Children, from their burth."

Though the deserter Reed seems to have been indifferent to his disgrace, the wretched Newman did his utmost to atone all winter, until Newman penitent was almost more of a problem than Newman mutinous. In his eagerness, he exposed himself to such severe weather that his hands and feet were frozen. On his recovery he begged Lewis's forgiveness and asked to be taken on the rest of the journey.

"Although he stood acquitted in my mind," Lewis felt it "impolitic to relax from the sentence." Newman and Reed went down-river in the spring; but when the expedition was over, Lewis praised Newman for "the zeal he afterwards displayed for the benefit of the service" and recommended him for one-third of the gratuity given the others, since he had given one-third of their service. Reed, a deserter, was beyond forgiveness.

Newman's was the last court-martial of the expedition. His case and Reed's had produced the desired effect. Disgrace and dismissal were severer penalties than the lash. Having eliminated trouble-makers by the spring of 1805, the captains found their men entirely loyal, diligent, and devoted through all the perilous miles they traveled together.

Finding Indians was proving surprisingly difficult. So far, the only contact had been with the Otos. The Mahas, or Omahas, could not be found anywhere. The Sioux were equally elusive. Once the explorers found an Indian fire, still smoking, but the Indians themselves were gone. Again and again the white men set the prairies on fire, the accepted signal to come down to the river, but no Indians responded.

On August 27, as they passed the Rivière Jacque (the modern James, or Dakota), an Indian swam off to the pirogue, and when the boats turned in to the shore two more Indians greeted them with the news that a large Sioux camp was near. Dorion, who spoke Sioux, Sergeant Pryor, and a French engagé were sent to invite the principal chiefs to council at Calumet Bluff.

The Sioux, who at first appeared so friendly, were playing a double game. Toward the end of August, while the Corps of Discovery was still many miles downstream, there had been

more Indians about than they supposed. Keen black eyes
had long been watching their progress. The Sioux chiefs soon
received a report that "a party, an army, as they called it, of
soldiers were coming up the Missouri." A first council met
to decide between peace and war. Eventually it decided to
do nothing—just yet. The women and children were left un-

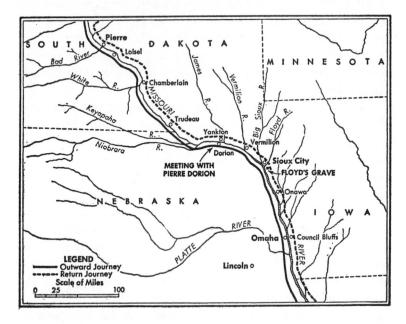

der guard in the villages, messengers were sent out with
orders to wandering Sioux bands, and all available warriors
swarmed down to the Missouri.

To the end of their days, neither Lewis nor Clark ever
learned that close at hand at this very moment was a white
prisoner, Charles Le Raye, whom the Sioux had been dragging about with them ever since they caught him in 1801.
He was kept carefully out of sight. Otherwise, he could have
told the exploring party a good deal more than the Sioux
wanted them to hear. But though the explorers knew noth-

ing of Le Raye, the captive knew all about them. Had he been able to reach them with full information, supplementing the hint that they received from a Maha prisoner, whom the Sioux were also holding, the captains would have been better prepared to deal with the fiercest of all the tribes.

Dorion and Pryor soon reappeared on the bank with five Sioux chiefs, 70 curious boys and warriors, and Dorion's son, whom he had found trading in the village. The white men rejoined the exploring party and the Indians—after being supplied with tobacco, corn, and kettles—were invited to visit the camp next morning.

The treacherous Sioux, for the moment, gave every appearance of being in a cordial mood. Pryor and Dorion, much to their embarrassment, were met by an escort with a buffalo robe ready to carry them into the Sioux camp—an honor reserved for chiefs of great importance. Hastily explaining that "they were not the owners of the Boats & did not wish to be carried," they accepted a fat dog, of which "they partook hartily and thought it good and well-flavored."

The chiefs and warriors came to council with the captains at noon, "Stout bold looking people, (the young men handsom) & well made," who were "Verry much deckerated with Paint Porcupine quils & feathers, large leagins and mockersons, all with buffalow roabs of Different Colours." Only a few had rifles, the rest being armed only with bows and arrows. There was nothing in their manner to suggest that a war council had been held only a few days before and that another was soon to gather for deliberation.

The captains and the Sioux chiefs met to smoke a more or less hypocritical pipe of peace under an oak tree, near which the American flag flew from a high staff. Lewis made the speech which became monotonously familiar as the expedition counciled with one tribe after another during the next few thousand miles: His Red children were now under the protection of a new father, the Great White Father at Washington. They must keep the peace. The Great White Father would send traders to supply them with all necessities.

All the chiefs received medals and clothing. The grand chief received an American flag and one of Mr. Jefferson's "Indian commissions." He was also given an artilleryman's coat, bedizened with gold lace, red in front and army blue elsewhere, together with a military cocked hat, complete with feathers.

Meantime, the young braves were building a bower of branches, to which the chiefs retired for deliberation. While the chiefs debated, the Indian boys shot their arrow at a mark, for prizes of beads bestowed by the explorers. Others were given Jew's harps, on which they twanged happily. Lewis demonstrated his airgun, firing at a tree. After a few shots, the Sioux ran eagerly to inspect the target and "Shouted aloud at the Site of the execution She would doe." When it grew dark, the young men put on their paint and danced, while the Americans threw presents to them, tobacco, bells, knives, tape, and binding.

After breakfast next morning, the chiefs, returning, sat down in a row with all their pipes pointing to the seats prepared for Lewis and Clark. After the two captains had been formally seated, the grand chief Weucha (The Shake Hand) promised peace and agreed to send Sioux chiefs to Washington with Dorion in the spring. When spring came and the Sioux war plans failed, some chiefs actually made the journey. Other chiefs and one warrior said the same thing, with the interminable circumlocutions of aboriginal oratory. Unanimously they asked for ammunition, traders, goods for their squaws, and "milk of great father"—in short, whisky. Clark secured a Sioux vocabulary, also some statistics, which revealed that the British were getting most of the Sioux trade.

Without knowing it, the Americans made one lifelong friend for the United States, probably among this first friendly band. A Yankton Sioux squaw had just had a baby. One of the white men wrapped the papoose in an American flag and proclaimed him an American. The child grew up to become the Yankton chief, Strike-the-Ree, who was enthusiastically pro-American all his life. Was he not an American himself? To the end of his days, Strike-the-Ree "remembered" the passage of Lewis and Clark, but unfortunately that was about all the information he could ever give.

Before departing, the expedition dropped Dorion off with a written commission, the right to display the American flag, and authority to employ a trader to take the Sioux chiefs to Washington. He was also left as a kind of one-man peace delegation, with instructions to end the war between the Sioux, Mahas, Pawnees, Poncas, Otos, and Missouris. It was a task that would have baffled a council of foreign ministers, for even the Sioux themselves were not quite sure with whom they were at war and with whom they were at peace. War parties were always going out, whenever the young men felt the need of scalps. Some bands were at war, others were at peace, a fact that may account for the hostile attitude of the next Sioux the expedition encountered. These chiefs rather thought that at the moment they were at war with twenty tribes and at peace with eight, but they were a little vague about it. Dorion finally went off with his Indians and a bottle of whisky, having so much on his mind that he forgot his camp kettle and had to send back for it.

On August 31, as the captains sat in council with the Sioux, the greatest disappointment of their journey was unconsciously being prepared for them in far-off Massachusetts. On that day, Captain Samuel Hill sailed out of Boston harbor in the brig *Lydia* on a voyage to China by way of the Columbia River and the Pacific coast, whither Lewis and Clark were also bound.

The expedition pushed on up the Missouri, pausing to map some "ancient fortifications," which skeptical modern scholarship suggests were nothing but natural sand formations. They were so much interested in a prairie dog village that the whole party except the sentry turned out with kettles and buckets in a vain effort to force a few of the stubborn little animals to the surface. It was not one of the outstanding successes of the Lewis and Clark Expedition, which poured five barrels of water down one hole without effect. The total capture was one wretched prairie dog.

Clark was partly consoled by the discovery of a huge fossil, "the back bone of a fish, 45 feet long tapering to the tale, Some teeth &c. those joints were Seperated and all Petrefied." It was certain to interest that passionate paleontologist, Mr. Jefferson, though Private Whitehouse described the great discovery succinctly if not very scientifically, as "a ruck of Bones on the Bank."

By the first week of September, everyone began to worry about Private Shannon, who had been sent out on August 26 to take the expedition's two horses along the bank. When he had not reappeared by September 4, a landing party went ashore without finding any trace of him. Colter, searching independently, rejoined the boats two days later to report that he could not find him either. As Shannon had little food with him and almost no ammunition, there was general alarm. It was clear that by this time he must be close to starvation, wherever he was. Men sent out with food supplies again failed to find him.

Finally, on September 11, the men in the boats saw a white man on horseback ride down to the bank. It was Shannon who, after mistaking an Indian trail for that of the expedition's shore party, had concluded the boats had passed him and had traveled far ahead at full speed to catch up—while the expedition, actually far behind, was doing its very best to overtake him. Having used up his food and all his ammunition, he had lived for twelve days on wild grapes and one rabbit, which he had killed by using a bit of hard wood when his bullets were all gone. Realizing that he would soon be too weak to travel, he had released one horse, keeping the other as an emergency ration, while he waited by the river, hoping that a trader's boat would come along and pick him up.

Clark philosophized: "thus a man had like to have Starved to death in a land of Plenty for want of Bullitts or Something to kill his meat." The men in the boats had been feasting on an abundance of buffalo, deer, antelope, elk, while the famished Shannon was looking for them. As the expedition went on, Shannon, being very young and wholly inexperienced in wild country, got lost so often that his comrades almost ceased worrying. When he was not losing himself, he was usually losing or forgetting his equipment.

Other men sent ashore to take charge of the horse did even worse than Shannon, for they let the Indians steal it. But this made very little difference, for Drouilliard and Shields soon came into camp proudly leading the other horse, which Shannon had had to turn loose a few days earlier.

Indians were now becoming more frequent. On the evening of September 23, four Sioux appeared on the bank, three of whom swam the river with the news that others were not far away. Five more Indians were seen on the shore, but no one could understand their language. Still uncertain what attitude these Sioux would take, the expedition anchored 100 yards out in the stream, putting no one ashore but the cooks and a guard. When a few Sioux boys came into camp, one of the engagés mustered enough of the language to learn that they were Teton Sioux; that their chiefs were coming to visit the Americans; and that "if their young men had taken the horse they would Git him again." The boys were sent back to their villages with a present of two "carrots," or twists, of tobacco, and an invitation to their chiefs to visit the white men next day.

Eighty lodges of Tetons were camped at the next creek upstream, and 60 lodges a little farther on. That meant nearly 1,500 Indians to deal with, who might be in either a friendly or a hostile mood. On the way up the river next morning, while getting out clothing and medals to use as presents at the council, the captains prudently made sure they had "prepared all things for Action in Case of necessity."

Everything went well at first. Gaily they named a strip of land in the river Good Humored Island. The boats came up one by one, while Lewis, first to arrive, was smoking with the chiefs—just across the river from modern Pierre, South Dakota. Though the Sioux seemed friendly enough, two-thirds of the men were kept alert in the boats, where they could not be overcome in a sudden rush and yet were ready for anything that might happen on shore.

Since Dorion had been left behind, there was no competent interpreter, a fact which may account for the unpleasant scene that followed; but there is no doubt that at least some of the Sioux were acting in bad faith. On the very day when one set of chiefs were meeting the Americans in council, another set of Sioux chiefs in another council were deciding to kill them. If the explorers had been able to explain their mission clearly, they might have won the Sioux over. As it was, Lewis could not even finish his speech for lack of adequate translation.

They presented a medal to Black Buffalo Bull, "Said to be a good Man," to The Partizan, soon to prove himself a very bad one, and to a few others. Matters might have gone better if the friendly and extremely influential chief Matowinkay had not happened to be absent.

Black Buffalo, according to the trader Tabeau, who knew him, was "of a good character, although angry and fierce in his fits of passion," like all Sioux. He was friendly to the white men, being "intelligent enough to know that it is to the interest of his nation to treat them kindly"; but although "frank and above-board" with his white friends, he found it necessary to disguise his feelings shrewdly in the presence of other Sioux, especially those not of his own band.

The same trader thought The Partizan a "monster of iniquity," greedy, envious, ambitious, vacillating between audacity and timidity. He had terrorized the Loisel party, to which Tabeau belonged, into giving him "presents" of unusual value. He "invariably found means to thwart the intentions of Black Bull and to make his pacific plans miscarry." Even among the Sioux themselves, Black Buffalo frequently had to restrain him. The two chiefs, walking together one day, met a squaw who had recently rejected The Partizan's amorous advances. Still angry over her rebuff, the chief tried to shoot her on the spot. After his rifle had missed fire two or three times, Black Buffalo ended the incident by remarking calmly: "This is enough; you see that the gun does not wish to kill."

With the tribe wavering between peace and war and a chief like The Partizan doing his best to stir up trouble, Lewis, Clark, and Black Buffalo found it difficult to prevent a fight. The Council having proved a failure, since it was impossible to understand each other, the explorers took the Indians over to their boats to see "such Curiossities as was Strange to them," including of course, the airgun. After this display the white men "gave them ¼ a glass of whiskey which they appeared to be verry fond of, Sucked the bottle after it was out & Soon began to be troublesom." The Partizan pretended to be drunk "as a Cloake for his rascally intentions" —it is hard to see how even an Indian could get genuinely drunk on a quarter of a glass. None of the Indians wanted to go ashore.

Eventually Clark landed himself, taking a boatload of presents; but, when he reached the shore, three young men seized the cable of his pirogue, while another warrior threw his arms around the mast. The Partizan, still pretending drunkenness, staggered against Clark, "verry insolent both in words & justures." Clark drew his sword while the three men with him prepared to defend themselves. Lewis ordered everyone in the boat under arms and manned his swivel.

Sioux warriors, with bows already strung, began to pull arrows out of their quivers.

There was some loud and angry talk, typical of Sioux who have no particular grievance but outnumber the other fellow and would rather like to find one. Clark, who after all had red hair, "felt My Self warm & Spoke in verry positive terms" —which luckily could not be completely understood. The Indians, insisting that one pirogue must be left behind, "as they were poor," refused to allow Clark to leave; "they S^d. they had Soldiers on Shore as well as he had on board. Capt. Clark told them that he had men and medican on board that would kill 20 Such nations in one day."

Though himself surrounded, Clark was able to get the pirogue back to the large boat, where Lewis promptly filled her with twelve soldiers and sent her back to shore. Their arrival caused a general exodus of all Indians except the chiefs and their personal attendants. Black Buffalo, taking hold of the rope himself, ordered his young men to clear out. Seeing the way open at last, Clark offered his hand to Black Buffalo and The Partizan, both of whom refused it. He boarded his pirogue and started back to join Lewis. Almost at once, Black Buffalo and three others—though not The Partizan, who remained surly—waded in after him and were taken aboard. The reason for this developed next day: they were good family men and wanted their squaws and children to see the boat!

The expedition pushed on about a mile that night and anchored off an island, which Clark named Bad Humored Island, "as we were in a bad humer." When they started off next day, the Sioux had broken up their secret council at the village inland, and the bank was covered with Indians for a distance of four miles. Clark did not think much of them, "Generally ill looking & not well made their legs Small generally," but he was in a jaundiced mood.

When they reached an excited crowd of men, women, and

children at the next village, Lewis took a small escort and fearlessly went ashore with Black Buffalo and his other Indian guests, who wished to let the squaws and children see the white men. After Lewis had been gone three hours, Clark became suspicious enough to send a sergeant to see how things were going. Lewis reported everyone was friendly, and eventually they both were ceremoniously carried in a decorated buffalo robe to a council with the chiefs, where they smoked the peace pipe. There was a feast, and a sacrifice of "some of the most Delicate parts of the Dog" to the American flag. Ten musicians beat skin drums and brandished rattles, while the squaws danced and the young men sang. But in spite of much cordiality this council, too, was a failure for lack of interpreters.

The Indians were equally agreeable next day, however, and there was another dance; but about noon a clumsy helmsman brought a pirogue broadside against the cable of the bateau, snapping it. As the current caught her, Clark had to order all hands to the oars, the Indians aboard got excited, and one foolish fellow yelled that the Mahas were attacking. This brought 200 warriors rushing to the bank, where 60 of them remained all night. Some Maha prisoners, held by the Sioux, had managed to whisper a warning to the white men, that the Sioux intended to stop the expedition.

A strong guard was kept on duty all night, and, if the boats could have anchored well out in the stream, there might have been no further trouble, though The Partizan had now arrived overland and was privately doing his best to stir up the warriors. Since her anchor was lost, however, the bateau had to tie up to shore, and when she tried to go in the morning, warriors seized the cable and refused to let go unless they were given tobacco. Lewis was on the point of slashing the cable with his sword and opening fire, but Clark finally handed some tobacco to Black Buffalo.

The pacific chief handed it to the other Indians, then

himself jerked the cable out of their hands, passed it to the
soldier at the bow, and himself got aboard. When they picked
up his son farther along the bank, Black Buffalo sent the
young man back to the turbulent tribe with a message from
Lewis and Clark: "if they were for peace Stay at home & do
as we had Directed them, if the[y] were for war or were De-
turmined to stop us we were ready to defend our Selves."

Though Indians were constantly showing up on the bank
for the next few days, there was no further hostility. The
Partizan himself appeared with three men and two squaws,
asking to be taken aboard and offering the squaws for the
entertainment of the soldiers. When this was refused, he
showed up again on a sand bar, asking to be put across the
river. Clark sent the pirogue to take him over.

When more Teton Sioux appeared on the river bank,
Lewis and Clark hove to, just long enough to send tobacco.
They told these Sioux, who were "verry selicitious for us to
land and eate with them," that they had been "treated badly
by some of the band below, after Staying 2 days for them,
we Could not delay any time, & referred them to Mr. Durion
for a full account of us and to here our Talk Sent by him to
the Tetons." Black Buffalo helped by throwing a small twist
of tobacco on the bank and telling them to "go back & open
ther ears." After all the expedition had been through, the
commanders decided that it was about time to "refresh the
men with a glass of whisky after Brackfast."

Black Buffalo, thoroughly frightened by a narrow escape
from upset in mid-Missouri, left during the afternoon. The
stern of the bateau caught on a submerged log and, as the
whole craft swung broadside to the swift current, she nearly
heeled over. Loose articles from the lockers went rattling
over the deck, while the chief ran and hid. Though heroic
exertions righted the bateau in time, Black Buffalo then and
there decided that life on the bounding Missouri billow was
not for him. Like all Sioux, he was happier on a horse than

anywhere else, especially on a boat. When the bateau put in
to shore, he got his rifle and told the captains that "he wished
to return, that all things were cleare for us to go on, we would
not see any more Tetons &c. we repeated to him what had
been Said before, and advised him to keep his men away,
gave him a blanket a Knife & some Tobacco, Smokᵈ. a pipe
& he Set out."

Though the expedition camped that night with everyone
on the alert, there was no attack. Black Buffalo may have
been a timid sailor, but his presence aboard while they traversed the Teton country had been useful. His parting comment that the explorers "would not see any more Tetons"
explains his accompanying the voyagers so far. All young
Indians are hot-headed. He knew The Partizan was stirring
them up. There might be an attempt at massacre, which his
presence would prevent. With their swivel, blunderbusses,
airgun, and rifles the explorers could have defended themselves but they would have had a hard time traveling and
fighting at the same time.

The rest of the voyage to the Mandan Village was uneventful, except for a meeting with a French trader named Jean
Vallé and some others, who had been trading with the Sioux
"300 Leagues up the Chien [Cheyenne?] River under the
Black mountains." Vallé described river courses, timber,
game, and the Cheyenne Indians to a group of highly atten-
tive listeners.

Occasional Indians on the banks received a cold reception,
since Lewis and Clark expected attack "every moment." One
Yankton Sioux simply wished to be ferried across the river;
but Sioux passengers being the very last thing the expedition
wanted at the moment, the commanders refused as gracefully
as possible, suggesting that he go back down the river and
discuss the inter-tribal peace problem with their friend Dorion. This was not very practical advice for a man who simply
wanted to get home to his teepee, squaws, and papooses with-

out swimming the muddy Missouri, but he finally disappeared when told that there were traders just below the last bend in the river. Other Indians, hailing from the banks, were haughtily ignored. One who swam into camp, begging for powder, had to be content with tobacco. Three others, begging for tobacco, got only good advice.

On October 8, the expedition made contact with the Arikaras, or Ricarees, at the lower of their three villages, a collection of conical lodges made of willow wattles covered with straw and five or six inches of mud, some of them 50 feet in diameter. The village, surrounded by fields of corn, beans, and the curious tobacco of the Arikaras, stood on an island just below the mouth of modern Rampart Creek (also called Oak Creek).

Seeing large numbers of Indians coming down to the shore, Lewis went over with two soldiers and interpreters, while Clark after making ready for defense in case of need, settled quietly down to "a pleasent evening all things arranged both for Peace or War." Lewis presently returned with two French-Canadians—Pierre Antoine Tabeau, of Loisel's expedition, about whom Labeaume had told them, and his assistant Joseph Gravelines, who had been with Tabeau only a few months.

Tabeau was a well-educated French-Canadian who, during the Revolution, had taken an oath of fidelity to the United States and who did everything in his power to assist the American explorers. As he was then living in the lodge of Kakawita, chief of the village, he was able to exercise a strong influence. Gravelines was of almost equal value since he had a remarkable speaking knowledge of Arikara, a peculiarly difficult language because the numerous dialects differed so greatly that even Arikaras of different bands could hardly understand each other. Lewis and Clark found him "an honest discrete man" and made much use of his services.

After spending years among them as a trader, Tabeau

described both the Sioux and Arikaras as: "stupid, superstitious, gluttonous, lewd, vindictive, patient by principle, fierce of temper, cowardly with men of like strength, fearless in assassinations, ungrateful, traitorous, barbarous, cruel, lying, thievish." Though he did not like them, he did know how to handle them. Partly because of Tabeau's influence and

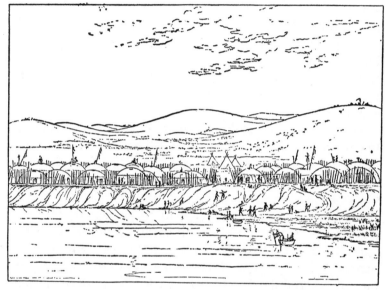

ARIKARA VILLAGE by George Catlin. *A typical Arikara village was "a collection of conical lodges made of willow wattles covered with straw and five or six inches of mud, some of them 50 feet in diameter."*

partly because of excellent interpretation by Gravelines, the Arikaras, in contrast to the Sioux, were very friendly. Indians from all three villages came pouring in to see the strangers. Three chiefs called, received presents of tobacco, and were told that the white men would council with them next day.

The real center of attraction was Clark's slave, York, whose journey up the Missouri soon became something very like a triumphal tour. White and red men the Arikaras knew well enough; but a black 'one, especially one with kinky hair, was something they had never dreamed of, in their wildest imaginings. Delighted to find himself of so much importance, York "did not lose the opportunity of [displaying] his powers Strength &c. &c." He was really a wild animal, he explained gravely. His master, Captain Clark, had captured him and tamed him. Being a sturdy fellow, York added a few convincing demonstrations of his physical strength, "Carried on the joke and made himself more turribal than we wished him to doe." The wondering redskins examined his sable body from top to toe, by no means sure that the blackness was anything more than paint.

York's experiences still to come would be even more flattering, though as yet the Indian ladies had not begun to take the highly personal interest in him that soon developed. Clark notes gravely that the Indians were "much pleased with my black Servant."

Tabeau and Gravelines came in for breakfast the next morning, providing much helpful gossip about the local situation among the Arikaras, to which the captains listened eagerly, before the council met. There was jealousy between the villages, and the Arikaras of the two upper villages feared that the explorers might create a "first chief" from the lower village. Such recognition from the Great White Father would add too much to the prestige of the Indians there. The copper color of his skin does not change the nature of a politician very much!

Chiefs of all three villages came to the council, however, probably because Tabeau had been busy with a little prairie diplomacy. The explorers, forewarned of existing jealousies, tactfully made a chief in each of the villages, then distributed presents, fired the airgun, set up a cornmill, and showed the Indians how it worked.

Taking two chiefs aboard, they went on upstream to visit the two upper villages, where they "Set talking on Various Subjects untill late," and went back to their own camp loaded with presents of cornbread, squashes, and beans. After the hostility of the Sioux, it was extremely pleasant. Before he settled down in his blankets for the night, Clark noted: "all Tranquility."

At next day's council matters were even better. Lewis's proposal that the Arikaras make peace with the Mandans under American protection made a great impression. It looked like a good chance for both tribes to escape Sioux oppression. The second chief, Lassel, offered to visit his Great Father in Washington and suggested that the explorers take Kakawita up-river with them to negotiate with the Mandans. There were further presents and for once it was the Indians who provided the white men with tobacco.

Though in after years they became extremely hostile, the Arikaras on this occasion made a good impression on the Corps of Discovery. Clark wrote: "they appear to be peacefull, their men tall and perpotiend, womin Small and industerous." Sergeant Patrick Gass observed "a great number of handsome and smart women" and thought the Arikaras "the most cleanly Indians I have ever seen on the voyage; as well as the most friendly and industrious." Clark, not quite so enthusiastic, qualified his praise by calling them: "Durtey, Kind, pore, & extravigent. pursessing national pride, not beggarly recive what is given with great pleasure."

The guileless Arikaras even gave implicit credence to the tall tales some of the white men told them. They had encountered, the soldiers said, an animal "without a mouth," which was "nourished only by breathing the smoke of the meat through the nose." Modifying Greek mythology, someone described a tribe of Amazons, who killed all male children, rearing little girls by hanging their cradles in the trees, Indian fashion, "where the air nourishes them." Chief Kakawita himself was extremely resentful when Tabeau expressed mild doubt of these very dull fantasies.

The only sour note was struck by Sergeant Gass, who tried Arikara tobacco and then obviously rather wished he hadn't. He noted disconsolately: "Their tobacco is different from any I had before seen: it answers for smoking, but not for chewing." It is no wonder he did not like it, for the stuff was mixed with buffalo tallow, and the plant from which it came was not the tobacco plant at all but an Arikara specialty. The best the French traders could say for it was that "when they lack other tobacco this satisfies them."

The explorers were astonished to discover that the Arikaras refused liquor unless paid to drink it. Drink made a man ridiculous: "they say we are no friends or we would not give them what makes them fools." Hence also the logical conclusion: "Since you wish to laugh at my expense, you ought at least to pay me." This attitude prevailed among several of the Missouri tribes for a few years, until more traders came, and the Arikaras, like other Indians, fell victims to the liquor craving. Clark was to spend much of his energy during his last thirty years trying to keep liquor away from the very tribes that now refused it of their own volition.

chapter IO: *A winter's tale: Fort Mandan*

REJECTING the proposals of one or two ardent Arikara damsels who wished to join the expedition on the spot, the explorers took aboard an Arikara chief, who was to carry peace proposals to the Mandans. Being a friendly individual, he proved a pleasant traveling companion, sometimes traveling in the bateau, sometimes rambling on shore with one of the captains, discoursing on the animals they saw about them.

Peace prospects began to look rather dim on October 22, when they passed the camp of a dozen or more Teton Sioux. Far from their own territory and presenting "the appearance of war," they were obviously on a horse-stealing and scalping expedition. The Indians told two contradictory stories to account for themselves, received no presents, and parted from the exploring party on terms of mutual suspicion. Lewis and

Clark were not surprised to hear complaints of horse-stealing and murder from the Mandans, a few days later, or to find themselves the victims of Sioux depredations, as the winter wore on. Equally alarming was the news that Indians had lately killed a Frenchman on his way to the British post on the Assiniboine.

Mandan Indians now began to appear, riding down to the edges of the high mud bluffs along the shore to watch the boats pass, with great curiosity. On the evening of October 25, some Mandans came into camp, including the son of a recently deceased chief, who had cut off both his little fingers in sign of mourning, or "marks of Savage effection," as Clark put it.

Next day's voyage had a still larger audience. There were crowds of Mandans along the shore in many places. The Arikara chief was set on shore to begin his peace negotiations, while the two officers visited the lower Mandan village, Matootonha. Taking two of its chiefs aboard, together with a supply of earthen pots and corn without which the Indians would not travel, the boats moved on up the river to the other Mandan village, Rooptaree.

The expedition was now 50 or 60 miles north of modern Bismarck, North Dakota. In the vicinity were five Indian villages. At Rooptaree the Mandan chief was Poscopsahe (Black Cat), while at Matootonha the principal chief was Shotaharrora, or "Coal"—an Arikara by blood, who had been adopted by the Mandans—with She-he-ke (Coyote, usually known as The Big White) and Kagohami (Little Raven) as subordinate chiefs. These were typical Mandan villages, much like those of the Arikaras, with large, warm, circular houses made of logs, upon which earth was thickly piled, with a single opening in the roof to let out the smoke. Council houses made in this way could accommodate 200 Indians, and family lodges, though smaller, were still commodious.

A little way up the Missouri, at the mouth of the Knife

River, was Mahaha, a village of the Wetersoon, or Soulier
Noir, Indians. Farther up the Knife River were two Minnetaree villages, Metaharta and Hidatsa, with the brutal chief
Kakoakis—usually known by his French name, Le Borgne,
because he had only one eye.

All these Indians were used to white men and on friendly
terms with each other. In the cluster of villages gathered the
few scattered traders who came up the Missouri and the Canadians who came overland from the Assiniboine, together
with wandering Indians from other tribes.

Lewis accompanied the two Mandan chiefs overland to
Rooptaree, leaving Clark to follow with the boats next day.
When Clark arrived, he brought with him a Canadian squaw
man, René Jussome, whom he had found living in one of
the riverside settlements with his Minnetaree wife and half-
breed children. Opinions of Jussome along the Missouri were
not too flattering. One Canadian described him as an "old
sneaking cheat," with a character "more despicable than the
worst among the natives." Another credited him with principles "much worse than those of a Mandane," plus "every
mean and dirty trick which they have also acquired from
their intercourse with a set of worthless scoundrels who are
generally accustomed to visit those parts."

However that may have been, Jussome knew Indians, with
whom he had been living for fifteen years, and he spoke
fairly good Mandan. Lewis and Clark found him useful,
though occasionally annoying, and full of valuable information about the local chiefs, which enabled the explorers to
go into council with some knowledge of the men with whom
they were dealing.

Indian chiefs, like the political leaders of other races, were
a very mixed lot. Poscopsahe was an admirable character.
"This man," said Clark, "possesses more integrety, firmness,
inteligence and perspicuety of mind than any other indian I
have met." She-he-ke was an amiable but rather weak char-

acter, not greatly respected by his tribe—a fat fellow, known as The Big White because of his light complexion, which was not much darker than that of a thoroughly tanned white men. Sergeant Gass thought him the "best looking Indian he ever saw," and a later visitor described him as "a fine looking Indian, and very intelligent."

Le Borgne was a brutal creature, gigantic in stature, with a huge aquiline nose and coarse features, glaring savagely out of his good left eye, while the white, opaque membrane that had destroyed the sight of the other made his appearance still more forbidding. One white acquaintance remarked that if his one eye had only been in the middle of his forehead, he would have made a good Cyclops.

Le Borgne was famous for his bold but brutal exploits. On one occasion, he entered a hostile village alone, by night, with no disguise except a blanket drawn over his head. Catching a young squaw alone in a lodge, he silently raped, killed, and scalped her, after which he withdrew safely, with a pleasant sense of duty done. Even to his own tribe he was a terror and he made an uncomfortable neighbor for the Lewis and Clark party, whom he privately despised, especially as he also despised their friend She-he-ke, whom he once described as a "bag of lies."

The council with the chiefs was delayed because violent winds kept some of the chiefs at Matootonha, on the south bank, from crossing the Missouri. The other chiefs, while waiting for the council, divided their time between the bateau, "which was verry curious to them viewing it as great medison," and York, who was an absolute novelty. Black Cat, grand chief of the Mandans, added to Jussome's characterizations of the chiefs with whom they would have to negotiate and walked up the Missouri for a mile and a half with the two captains to help them find a site for their winter fort as soon as possible. The site he suggested was good, but there

MINNETAREE VILLAGE IN WINTER by Charles Bodmer. *During the winter at Fort Mandan, there were two Minnetaree villages fairly close by, up the Knife River. "As for the Mandans and Minnetarees, it is doubtful how much real friendship they felt for the American party, especially in the beginning. One minor Minnetaree chief snubbed Lewis by the highly civilized device of announcing that he was 'not at home.'"*

INTERIOR OF A MANDAN LODGE by Charles Bodmer. *"In the vicinity . . . were typical Mandan villages, much like those of the Arikaras, with large, warm, circular houses made of logs, upon which earth was thickly piled, with a single opening in the roof to let out the smoke. Council houses . . . could accommodate 200 Indians, and family lodges, though smaller, were still commodious."*

was so little timber near it that they had to choose another place.

When the wind died and a fair day dawned, the council met. Le Borgne arrived by special invitation. There were now two Arikara chiefs, Ar-ke-tar-na-shar and Kakawita, who had come as ambassadors to make peace with the Mandans. Tabeau had been working quietly to influence the Arikaras toward peace. He had managed to keep a passing Mandan war party from attacking them, and pure good luck prevented the Arikaras from killing a few Mandans—either event would have ended any possibility of peace. All was harmony, except that the Minnetaree chief became restless as he listened to the very long speeches of the Great White Father's officers and finally remarked that he had to go home, as he feared his village would be attacked in his absence. One of the other chiefs rebuked him for such rudeness, and the worried Minnetaree subsided, while the torrents of elaborate prairie oratory flowed on.

At least one chief in each village received a medal, a flag, and a uniform coat with plumed hat, while the grand chief of each nation received the special medal with President Jefferson's portrait on it. The expedition's cornmill, which had made a great sensation, was presented to the Mandans. It had been brought along because Lewis and Clark originally intended to leave some of their men at the Mandan villages to "make corn" for food on the return journey. When they gave up this idea, the heavy iron mill was not worth carrying farther. The Canadian trader, Alexander Henry, saw it among the Mandans in 1806, still serving a useful purpose though not quite that for which it had been designed: "I saw the remains of an excellent large Corn mill, which the foolish fellows had demolished on purpose to barb their arrows, and other similar uses, the largest piece of it which they could not break nor work up into any weapon, they have now fixed to a wooden handle and make use of it to pound marrow bones to make grease."

The medals were not all received in quite the spirit that the captains intended. The Minnetarees, who privately thought them bad medicine, made haste to pass the dangerous trinkets on to other Indians with whom they were not on the best of terms, hoping to transfer the bad medicine with them. To be sure, the medals constituted official recognition of a chief's rank by the United States government; but the Minnetarees knew little of the United States and were not much impressed by what Lewis and Clark said about it. According to Alexander Henry, "they were all much disgusted at the high sounding language the American Captains bestowed upon themselves and their own nation wishing to impress the Indians with an Idea of their great power as Warriors, and a powerful people that if once exasperated could instantly crush into atoms all the nations of the earth &c. This manner of proceeding did not agree with those haughty Savages, they have too high an opinion of themselves." It took the Minnetarees and Mandans several years to grasp the idea that any nation really could be more powerful than themselves.

The flags, however, were another matter. Even the haughty Le Borgne draped himself in the flag for an adoption ceremony, and the Canadian, Henry, was much annoyed to be greeted by the Mandans in 1806 with a ceremonial display of the flag that the Americans had given them.

The Arikara chief, Ar-ke-tar-na-shar, received a silver dollar to wear as a medal, "with which he was much pleased." Kakawita received a genuine medal. Tabeau, the trader whom Loisel had left behind among the Indians and who had lived so long among them that he had no illusions left, thought him "perhaps of all the Ricaras the one who will make the best use of it," but he was, nevertheless, not a very edifying character. "Proud, alert, ferocious, cruel, and, con sequently, a great man," according to his guest, Tabeau, he was renowned among the Arikaras both for bravery and magic. Like the famous Maha Chief Blackbird, Kakawita had somehow secured a little poison, probably arsenic. When Blackbird, through his magic, announced that someone was going to die very soon, the prophecy invariably proved accurate. Kakawita seems to have used similar methods with similar success, achieving such a reputation that his envious fellow chiefs feared he was becoming too prominent. They had, according to Tabeau, at first hesitated to send him to make peace with the Mandans at all, "lest he receive too many great honors among the Mandanes and particularly some marks of distinction on the part of Captn Lewis."

There were various incidents before the council met a second time, as the chiefs had to be given time for deliberation. The prairie caught fire. Two Indians were burned to death, three were badly burned, and others had narrow escapes. When a half-breed boy was entirely unharmed by the fire, the Indians said the Great Spirit must have favored him because of his white blood. The skeptical explorers noted that the mother had assisted the Great Spirit by throwing a green buffalo skin over the child, so that neither he nor the grass around him burned, an incident which J. Fenimore Cooper later used in one of his novels. When the fire swept by the American camp, "it went with great rapitidity and looked Tremendious," but it did no harm.

She-he-ke, from the lower Mandan village came in late with another chief, asking to hear some of the white men's speeches. The two had not been able to attend the council because they had been hunting. She-he-ke duly received a belated medal, though he was less influential than the explorers thought, "not much distinguished as a warrior, and extremely talkative, a fault much despised amongst the Indians." Still, he was a chief and had to be treated accordingly.

The second council, held on October 31, was a great success. The Mandans agreed to make peace with the Arikaras, though they were tactless enough to add that it was only because they had already killed so many of them they were getting tired of it. The Minnetarees joined the peace movement, and delegations set off for the Arikara country. When it was all over, the grand chief of the Mandans called, resplendent in his new uniform and cocked hat, bringing his two sons with him. The call turned out to be unofficial. The little Indian boys just wanted to see the white men dance. As the Lewis and Clark Expedition habitually danced on the slightest excuse anyway, they "verry readily gratified him."

If the first necessity was making friends with the Indians, a close second was getting winter quarters built before the cold became unendurable. A long rest in dry, warm, weatherproof cabins with hearth fires was essential, for the constant dampness and growing cold, combined with the strenuous exertion and overheating incident to rowing, poling, and towing their heavy craft against the Missouri's current had begun to take their toll of the expedition's health. Clark had for a time been so crippled with rheumatism that he could not leave the party. One of the Field brothers was down with rheumatism in the neck. Cruzat had it in the legs. There had been an epidemic of boils and abscesses—sure sign of exhaustion. Lewis had been poisoned by minerals dissolved in the river water.

The site finally selected for Fort Mandan, the expedition's winter quarters, was on the left bank of the Missouri, downstream from the Mandan villages and just across from the site of the future army post, Fort Clark. There was plenty of timber here, and the fort would be near enough to the villages so that the white men could keep an eye on the Indians and also on the Canadian traders, for whom the villages were an important trading center. Six hunters went downstream to lay in a meat supply. Jussome and his family moved to the American camp so that his services as interpreter would

be constantly available. The men went to work in the wooded
bottom lands under the high clay bluffs along the river, fell-
ing trees, cutting the logs to length, and flattening a few for
the "puncheons" used as floor and ceiling of frontier log
cabins. Sergeant Gass, originally a house-builder, was in his
element.

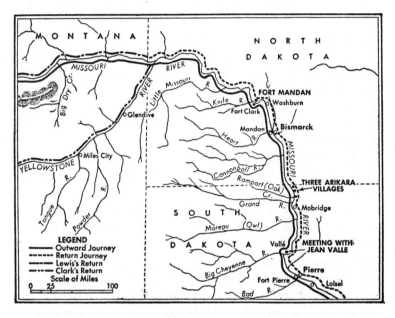

Clark, though still suffering from rheumatism, was busy
directing the building. Lewis was busy writing all day, apparently in the hope of sending a few preliminary reports,
which he and Clark had begun some time before, back with
a party of the engagés who at first wished to return immediately and were building their own canoe for the purpose.

Axes rang; a few men got hurt; Indians caught 100 wild
goats at a single haul by the ancient tribal trick of driving
them into a funnel-shaped corral. News spread that 50 lodges
of Assiniboines would winter with the neighboring Minne-

tarees. An aurora borealis so interested the sergeant of the
guard that he woke his commanders to see it. The wind began to blow hard and cold. Waterfowl passed overhead, going south. Cree and Ojibway Indians from the North began
to appear about the villages. Gravelines and some of the
engagés started down-river for Arikara country.

They had hardly gone when ice was running thick in the
river. Cargo was transferred from the boats to a new log
storehouse. By mid-November the huts were so far advanced
that the men could begin "dobing" them—that is, plugging
the cracks between the logs with mud. During the first two
weeks of November there is an eloquent gap in the journal
kept by Private Joseph Whitehouse, as if he were so exhausted
by swinging an ax all day long in the cold that he had no
energy left for his journal.

When Fort Mandan was finished, no Sioux war party had
any hope of success in attacking it. "The whole," said a Canadian observer, "is made so strong as to be almost cannon
ball proof." It was built in the form of a triangle, or, more
accurately, a slice of pie. The stout log cabins formed two
sides, opening inward. The base of the triangle was closed
by a semi-circular stockade of "amazing large Pickets." Clark
had seen the value of Wayne's elaborate fortification of wilderness camps and was doing the same thing.

Fort Mandan was not only strong, it was also warm. The
whole expedition moved in about the middle of November
to escape the cold, though the cabins were still unfinished.
The two commanders shared a separate cabin as living and
working quarters, while the men bunked together in small
groups. The white men needed shelter more than the Indians, who played lacrosse on the ice, stark naked, with the
thermometer at 26 degrees below zero.

The explorers were getting into their fort not a moment
too soon for their safety. On November 5, unknown to them
and to their Mandan friends, the Sioux had held another war

council, attended by many more warriors than had been on hand earlier. Attacking a strong blockhouse, defended by the airgun, the swivel, (specially adapted for mounting on stockades), blunderbusses, and plenty of well-aimed rifle fire, was not an inviting prospect. After much debate, the Sioux decided to invite the Arikaras to join them in a slaughter of the white men in the spring.

The Mandans themselves were not too peacefully inclined. Poscopsahe himself explained frankly that they meant to keep the peace with the Crees and Assiniboines only until they could make sure Lewis and Clark had been telling the truth about the Great White Father's beneficent intentions. If supplies did not come up the Missouri, they would pay no further attention to their promises of peace. The early explorer, Evans, had not kept his promise to come back with arms and ammunition. Lewis and Clark's promise of American trade might be equally false. It was not Evans's fault that he had failed to return. He had died in New Orleans five years earlier but the Americans apparently did not know of his death. All they could do was to reiterate their advice to keep the peace, assuring Poscopsahe that he certainly would receive supplies from American traders.

Such trade was of immense importance to the Indians along the Missouri River. Though traders had long been passing up and down the river from St. Louis, there had been so few that the Indians still were almost wholly dependent on British trade, overland from the base on the Assiniboine River. The Assiniboines and Crees held the country between the Mandans and the British, while the Sioux were between the Arikaras and the British. They were thus able to control the passage of white traders, picking out the best goods for themselves and cutting off the Mandans and Arikaras entirely, whenever they felt like it.

The traders moved only on sufferance of the tribes and always at great risk. They carried goods of immense value to the Indians, who could rob or slaughter them at pleasure, unless kept in good humor by extortionate "presents." There was no chance of a rescuing cavalry column or of white man's justice when a trader got into trouble in these early days. Though Wayne had subdued the eastern tribes, these western Indians, still inaccessible, had little idea of the white man's power and no fear of him whatever.

If the Americans could keep the Missouri trade route open, all this would change. Even the Sioux could not close the river as they could close the land routes, and the Assiniboines and Crees had no control over river traffic whatever. If Lewis and Clark spoke the truth, a new hope opened for all the Missouri River tribes.

All the Indians could, of course, have lived in entire independence of white traders, if they had wanted to. They had been doing so for centuries. One shrewd chief remarked, "In my young days there were no white men, and we knew no wants; we were successful in war; our arrows were pointed with flint, our lances with stone and their wounds were mortal." But, as every economist knows, there is no limit to human desires. Having once seen the white man's rifles, axes, knives, beads, and cloth, the Indians developed an insatiable appetite for them. Desires soon became necessities. Iron made better arrow points than flint. The white man's knives were sharper. The steel ax was infinitely superior to the stone one. Bad as they were, even traders' rifles were better weapons than the finest bows, and the tribe with the largest stock of them could easily conquer its neighbors.

All this, Lewis and Clark pointed out to the Mandans with that endless patience any dealing with Indians always requires: "we advised them to remain at peace & that they might depend upon Getting Supplies through the Channel of the Missourie, but it required time to put the trade in opperation."

Into the white men's camp on November 11, 1804, walked

a squaw—pregnant, though she was hardly more than a child. The Corps of Discovery's most remarkable member was about to join up, though no one at the moment realized it. This was Sacagawea, one of two little Shoshone girls who had been captured by the Minnetarees a few years before. Squaw prisoners were just livestock, of even less importance in the Indian scheme of things than squaws usually were, and the little Shoshone girls had a bad time, "forced to be wives for the men," according to Indian tradition. Traded from one warrior to another, Sacagawea was finally put up on a blanket by her current owner and gambled away to Toussaint Charbonneau, a squawman from Montreal, who had a special weakness for very young Indian girls. Eventually, Charbonneau acquired the other little slave as well.

This second "wife" of Charbonneau's also accompanied Sacagawea on her first visit to Fort Mandan; but, as the expedition left her behind when it started westward in the spring, no one now knows much about her. Her name may have been Otter Woman.

Toussaint Charbonneau, their husband, born in Montreal about 1759, had already been in the Indian country for at least ten years and had been living among the Minnetarees for about five. Characteristically, the first record of him—in the journal of the trader, John MacDonnell—shows him already deep in aboriginal love affairs, one of three men who set off "to court the Foutreau's daughter a great beauty." Two months later an old squaw, catching Charbonneau "in the act of committing a Rape upon her Daughter," wielded a canoe awl so handily that Charbonneau could hardly walk back to his canoe—"a fate he highly deserved for his brutality," says MacDonnell, with a virtuous air. When Lewis and Clark reached the Mandan country, he was living in the lower Minnetaree village, where he was well known to all the Indians, who had given him no less than five names, all slightly derisive: "Chief of the Little Village, "Man Who Possesses

Many Gourds," "Great Horse from Abroad," "Forest Bear," and another said to have been "not very refined."

Pitying the forlorn little prisoner-wife, who was so soon to become a mother, the explorers sent a gift of provisions, which led to a quarrel between Charbonneau and the jealous Jussome. When the baby, her first, was born on February 11, Sacagawea suffered severely in prolonged labor, which the two captains—whose rough and ready army medical experience did not include obstetrics—were unable to relieve. Finally, Jussome remarked that he had frequently hastened difficult deliveries by a dose of powdered rattlesnake's rattle. Lewis happened to have a rattle, two rings from which Jussome crushed in a little water and administered. Within ten minutes the baby was born though, as the Journals say, "what effect it may really have had it might be difficult to determine." The dose, being merely chitin, was in fact quite ineffective, but at least it did no harm.

As they came to know Charbonneau, the captains began to realize that, whatever his shortcomings, he and Sacagawea together would be a valuable team. Charbonneau could interpret so long as they were among the river Indians; Sacagawea's knowledge of Shoshone offered their only chance of conversing with the Rocky Mountain Indians. The squawman accepted their offer of employment, promising to take Sacagawea with him to the coast, leaving the other wife behind.

All might have gone smoothly but for the untimely arrival of three Canadian traders from the Northwest Company, who arrived toward the end of November, bringing four white voyageurs with them. The Americans had found other traders whom they had met on the Missouri friendly enough, but relations were less cordial with the newcomers. In general charge of the party was the veteran, Antoine Larocque, and with him were Charles McKenzie and Baptiste LaFrance. Stopping to inquire for Charbonneau at the Minnetaree village, "his usual place of residence," they learned to their surprise that he had already been employed as interpreter by an American exploring party. On their way to the Mandan villages next day, they met Lewis, accompanied by Jussome and Charbonneau, and paused for a fifteen-minute chat, after which Lewis invited them to visit Fort Mandan. When they met again, a day later, in Poscopsahe's lodge, Lewis agreed to let them share Charbonneau's services as interpreter.

This friendly beginning was soon followed by friction. The Northwest traders were none too pleased to find American troops arriving so promptly in the Louisiana Purchase and somewhat apprehensive as to the future of their own share of the Indian trade. LaFrance was soon found to be spreading rumors among the Indians and making "unfavourable & ill founded assursions." The captains were still more disturbed when they heard that Larocque was distributing British medals and flags to the local chiefs. Warning the Indian leaders "that those simbiles were not to be receved by any from them, without they wished [to] incur the displeasure of their Great American Father," they waited for a good opportunity to have it out with Larocque. This presented itself next day, when he visited Fort Mandan to find out why Charbonneau had failed to arrive, as promised.

Lewis and Clark "informed him what we had herd of his intentions of makeing Chiefs &c. and forbid him to give Meadels or flags to the Indians." According to Larocque, they explained "that the Government looked upon those things as the sacred emblems of the attachment of the Indians to their country." They again agreed to let him have Charbonneau as interpreter "on Conditions he did not say any thing more than what tended to trade alone." He was not to translate any remark directed against the United States, even if ordered to do so—"which," said the captains diplomatically to Larocque, "we are very far from thinking you would." Larocque, with some irritation, denied the whole thing, and was perhaps telling the truth, for he noted in his private journal: "As I had neither flags nor medals, I ran no risk of disobeying those orders, of which I assured them."

Seeing that Larocque was much interested in the future management of the Indian trade under American sovereignty, the explorers tried to persuade him that it would remain open to all, while the handicaps that the Spanish had imposed would be removed. "A very grand plan was schemed," wrote Larocque, "but its being realized is more than I can tell, although the Captains say they are well assured it will." The events of the next few years more or less justified his skepticism.

Each group resented the other's presence. To the Americans, the Canadians were alien intruders on territory which the United States controlled by right of purchase. Legally, Lewis and Clark were entirely correct, but international law meant singularly little along the wild Missouri. To the Canadians who had been trading there for years, the Americans were intrusive newcomers, no matter what parchments had been signed in Paris the year before.

Nevertheless, both parties were white men among a native population, and they contrived to maintain at least outward amiability—all, that is, except Lewis, who was never quite able to conceal his uncontrollable aversion to these "British." McKenzie remarks in his diary that he and Larocque "became intimate with the gentlemen of the American expedition, who on all occasions seemed happy to see us, and always treated us with civility and kindness. It is true, Captain Lewis could not make himself agreeable to us. He could speak fluently and learnedly on all subjects, but his inveterate disposition against the British stained, at least in our eyes, all his eloquence. Captain Clarke was equally well informed, but his conversation was always pleasant, for he seemed to dislike giving offense unnecessarily."

In spite of his anti-British feeling, Lewis spent a whole day tinkering with a damaged compass belonging to one of the Canadians and eventually returned it to him in good working order. The situation was slightly Pickwickian, though no one seems to have realized it. Lewis, the ardent British-hater, was himself of the purest British blood, like his companion Clark. The "British" whom he so industriously hated were all French except McKenzie, who was of Scottish birth.

Even the affable Clark joined Lewis, however, in refusing the bland proposal of Larocque that he should accompany the expedition when it started for the Rockies in the spring. Valuable though his experience would have been, his presence would have given the British too much information and might in later years have weakened American claims to Oregon territory. Both Lewis and Clark must have realized that the United States would eventually claim all the territory they traversed, even beyond the boundaries of the Louisiana Purchase.

The rebuff did not in the least deter Larocque. On their arrival in November, 1804, Lewis and Clark had made the mistake of sending a friendly message and a copy of their British passport to the Canadian trader, Charles Chaboillez, at Fort Assiniboine. Chaboillez promptly instructed the veteran, Daniel William Harmon, to take six or seven Canadians and two or three Indians up the Missouri as far as the Rockies, returning by November, long before Lewis and Clark could possibly reach the United States again.

When Harmon fell ill, Larocque went instead, setting off from the Assiniboine June 2, 1805, about two months after Lewis and Clark had resumed their westward voyage from Fort Mandan. With McKenzie and one other man, he explored Montana and Wyoming, though without reaching the Rockies. He was safely back on the Assiniboine by October 18, 1805, while Lewis and Clark were still on their way down the Columbia. Larocque was decent enough to tell some Rocky Mountain Indians whom he met "that probably they

would see in their lands some whites come from another
place, but that the latter were our brothers and we hoped
that they would not injure them."

As for the Mandans and Minnetarees, it is doubtful how
much real friendship they felt for the American party, especially in the beginning. One minor Minnetaree chief snubbed
Lewis by the highly civilized device of announcing that he
was "not at home." Some chiefs refused presents, and one
complained that "had these Whites come among us with
charitable views they would have loaded their 'Great Boat'
with necessaries. It is true they have ammunition, but they
prefer throwing it away idly than [sic] sparing a shot of it to
a poor Mandane." McKenzie wrote that "the Indians accepted of clothing, but, notwithstanding, they could not be
reconciled to like these 'strangers,' as they called them." Clark
had to protest to the Indians on one occasion because they
had compared the Americans unfavorably with the Canadians, but was met with the bland aboriginal excuse that this
was merely "in just & laftur."

Larocque, on the other hand, says that before the explorers
left Fort Mandan, the Indians had "grown very fond of them
though they disliked them at first." After Lewis and Clark
had gone, McKenzie, who understood more Mandan than the
Indians quite realized, was embarrassed to find Canadians
"despised" by the Indians, "and the American captains, whom
they hated till then, praised."

Le Borgne took a jaundiced view of the Corps of Discovery,
remarking on one occasion: "Had I these white warriors in
the upper plains, my young men on horseback would soon
do for them, as they would do for so many 'wolves,' for there
are only two sensible men among them, the worker of iron
and the mender of guns."

American prestige was much enhanced by Clark's prompt
armed support when a Sioux and Pawnee raiding party shot
up a small group of Mandan hunters with bows and arrows,

while nine horses and four Wetersoon Indians disappeared for good, probably into the hands of the same war party. The raid was a golden opportunity for a show of American power. An hour after the news came, Clark had an armed party of 23 men on the flank and rear of the Mandan village. He arrived so swiftly that the Mandans themselves were at first a little alarmed, until Clark "informed them that if they would assemble their warriors and those of the Different Towns, I would [go] to meet the Army of *Souex* &c. chastise them for takeing the blood of our dutifull Children." As there had been a snowstorm in the meantime, the Indians decided that the snow was too deep for pursuit.

"In the Spring after the Snow goes off we will raise the warriers of all the Towns & Nations around about us, and go with you," said the chiefs.

The Mandans were convinced that there had been Arikaras among the raiders. This was probably confusion, due to the Mandan habit of describing Arikaras as Pawnees, the tribes being closely related. The unexpected arrival of three genuine and friendly Pawnees at this inopportune moment nearly precipitated a minor massacre by the infuriated Mandans; but the chiefs forbade the proposed slaughter, assuring their warriors that the Americans would disapprove. As Mandan indignation threatened the laborious American efforts to make peace, Clark tried to salvage the results of his diplomacy; "you say the Panies or Ricares were with the *Seeaux*, some bad men may have been with the *Seeaux* you know there is bad men in all nations, do not get mad with the recarees untill we know if those bad men are Counternanc^d. by their nation."

The winter went swiftly, for there was plenty to do. Under frontier conditions, the mere effort to stay alive is a greater burden than snug and comfortable modern folk—steam-heated, well-fed, electric-lit—can readily imagine. Clark's journal notes, one busy winter day: "I am ingaged in Copying a Map, men building perogus, makeing Ropes, Burning Coal [i.e., charcoal], Hanging up meat & makeing battle axes for Corn"—the axes, for which there was an enormous demand, being hammered out by the expedition's blacksmiths to be traded for the Indians' corn. The Indians were so eager for iron that they would give six or seven gallons of grain for a piece four inches square. While this was going on, Captain Lewis was toiling at the lengthy report that had to go back to Mr. Jefferson in the spring. Small wonder that Clark notes a day or two later: "all hands employd."

Except when it was so bitterly cold that they dared not venture out, the explorers relied for their food on buffalo hunts, which were not always successful. Three hunters, failing to find game, lived for two days on the carcass of one wolf, the only thing they had been able to kill. When the half-starved men dragged themselves back to the fort, "they informed us that it eat very well," Private Whitehouse noted. It was by no means the last wolf that they would thankfully devour. Private Bratton used to remark in his old age that "the worst morsel of which he partook on the journey was an old she wolf that was suckling her young."

Both whites and Indians were frostbitten. Joseph Field "got one of his ears frosed," and York suffered still more severely. Clark blistered his feet so badly on "uneaven ice" that for a time he found it difficult to walk. Indians brought diseases and injuries of all kinds for the white magicians to cure. Together, the captains thawed out frozen feet, amputated frozen toes, and treated pleurisy.

A collection of small animals had to be kept alive to be sent to Mr. Jefferson in the spring, so that Fort Mandan became a fair imitation of a small zoölogical park. Four magpies hopped about a cage. A prairie hen was carefully nursed until the time came to ship her east. The expedition's only live prairie dog was carefully guarded to prevent escape—a serious problem for his keepers, since he could both dig and gnaw. Apparently this was the same animal that, on their way up the Missouri, they had captured by filling his burrow with water and forcing him to the surface.

The expedition also seized the opportunity to take Indian vocabularies, at the express wish of Mr. Jefferson, who for years had been making a comparative study of Indian languages. He had been careful to furnish Lewis and Clark with printed lists of certain common English words. Of each Indian tribe, as they passed, they were to inquire the equivalent, setting each Indian word down opposite the English. Fort Mandan was an ideal spot for the purpose, as there were villages of three different tribes near it and Indians of other tribes came in occasionally during the winter. It was a difficult task, however. The Indians could not imagine why anyone should want a vocabulary and "concluded that the Americans had a wicked design upon their country"—which was not far from the truth—while the vocabularies themselves were not always accurate. The amateur philologists had to use French interpreters, who could not always agree between themselves on the real meanings of Indian words.

There was some minor friction with the Indians. One warrior was affronted when Private Whitehouse whacked him over the knuckles with a spoon for misbehaving at table. A visiting chief, who "took a miff" because he was not flattered with sufficient attention, went fuming back to his village. A Mandan husband, not without reason, became jealous of Sergeant Ordway. The interpreters' wives formed a dangerous habit of letting Indians into the fort at night after the gates were closed. The Canadian, LaFrance, aided an Indian to make off with a white interpreter's horse.

Through it all, while Lewis worked over his reports in the little cabin that they shared, Clark was busy with maps and sketches, quizzing passing Indians for geographical information and combining their answers with his own topographical notes to make "a Connection of the Countrey."

When Christmas came, everyone was ready for a celebration. The Indians were told not to visit the fort, as this was one of the white men's great medicine days. The celebration opened with a volley from the rifles and a salute from the swivel. Captain Clark treated each man to a glass of brandy. They raised their flag and everyone had another glass of brandy. Some of the men went hunting, while the others cleared a room and began dancing "all without the comp^y. of the female Seck, except three Squaws the Intreptirs wives and they took no part with us only to look on."

At ten o'clock in the morning, everyone had another glass of brandy, and dinner was a Lucullan feast of flour, dried apples, pepper, and other priceless rarities, specially distributed so that, as Gass said, the enlisted messes could "celebrate Christmas in a proper and social manner." At half past two, the swivel was fired again to summon everyone to renewed dancing. "And So," says Private Whitehouse, "we kept it up in a jovel manner untill eight oC. at night."

New Year's Day was equally festive, opening with two shots from the swivel and a round of small arms, followed by a glass of "old ardent Spirits" all round. Shortly afterward, Captain Clark issued more of the same, and in the afternoon, drinks for the whole party were on Captain Lewis.

About ten o'clock, half the men went by invitation to the Mandan village "to dance"—or so they said. They took with them Cruzat's violin, a tambourine, and "a Sounden horn"—probably the expedition's bugle. They fired one round as a salute at the entrance to the village, marched in with their music playing, fired another round in the center of the village, and were rapturously welcomed, especially by the younger squaws.

Even without feminine partners, the enlisted men were enthusiastic dancers, whose antics never failed to amuse the Indians. This time there was an additional attraction: a Frenchman—probably one of the voyageurs—who danced "on his head." Clark and a few others followed the first group to the village later in the day. According to Ordway, they "danced in different lodges untill late in the afternoon." Clark and most of the men came back to Fort Mandan that evening, but six of the men stayed the night with the Indians. Next day Lewis and another party rushed off to the other Mandan village "a frolicking."

As the weather grew colder, the explorers found that they had made a bad mistake by leaving their boats in the river. They had, luckily, brought their most important supplies ashore, so that these vital reserves were safe enough by the time ice threatened to destroy the boats. The ice formed in a series of layers, with running water in between. When the men tried to cut it away, the water below rose so rapidly that they could not get at the ice farther down. They then decided to heat the water inside the boats by the old Indian device of dropping in hot stones, hoping this would melt the ice on the outside. It was no use. All the local fieldstone burst into small fragments when put in the fire. Sergeant Gass made a trip to a distant bluff to get stone of another kind, but the new quarry provided nothing better. As Sergeant Ordway remarked: "come to heat the Stone they flew in peaces as soon as they Got hot."

Finally, they made a rope of elkskin and built a windlass with which, after shattering the ice with iron spikes and axheads attached to long poles, they could haul their craft out of the river.

In mid-February, the expedition had its first real Indian trouble. Drouilliard, Frazer, Goodrich, and Newman, the latter with a broken rifle, met a party of 105 Indians, supposed to be Sioux, who took two of their horses and returned a third horse only after heated protests by the soldiers and also, strange to say, by one of the raiding Indians. The Sioux also stole two knives and a tomahawk, then returned the tomahawk. Though, in spite of all their plotting, this was their only triumph, the incident was very bad for American prestige. Lewis urged the Mandans to join him in pursuit; but, as most of the warriors were away hunting, he gave chase with 24 of his own command and a handful of Indians, only two of whom had rifles. The Sioux raiders, however, had such a long start that Lewis never caught up, though he found one of their bivouacs with the campfires still smoking, and he had the satisfaction of bringing back a ton and a half of buffalo meat. From Gravelines, who had been wintering with the Arikaras and had seen the Sioux war party that Lewis failed to catch, came warning that the Sisetoons, three bands of Teton Sioux, and the Yankton Sioux threatened war against the Indians "in this quarter" and intended to "kill everry white man they See." This, of course, was a result of the secret Sioux war councils, of which the white men still knew nothing definite, though by this time they must have begun to suspect a good deal.

Equally alarming was the news that Murdoch Cameron, a Canadian trader at St. Peter's, on the Minnesota River, was arming the Sioux. Cameron was only trying to help them drive off Ojibway raiders from the North, but there was no telling how the Sioux would use the extra rifles once they had secured them. If this fierce race of warriors were given firearms instead of bows and arrows, they would be still more dangerous. Fortunately, no other attacks developed.

The expedition just missed meeting one other American, a certain John Tanner, who had been captured and adopted by the Ojibways around Rainy Lake some years earlier. Tanner arrived at the Mouse River trading post, not far to the North, just after some of Lewis and Clark's men had visited there to make some small purchases. Supposing that the expedition would stay at the Mandan village for a long time, Tanner put off visiting them until it was too late. Years later he was to meet Clark as Governor of Missouri, tell his story, and receive Clark's help in bringing the half-breed Tanner children back to civilization.

In March, while preparations for departure were beginning, the ferocious Le Borgne arrived with something obviously on his mind. After the usual formalities of presents and pipe-smoking, the Minnetaree chief revealed his curiosity. "Some foolish young men" had told him that the Americans had with them a man who was completely black. Somewhat hesitantly, he inquired if such a being existed. The captains sent for York. Much surprised, the red-skinned chief examined the sable complexion. Surely this was just a white man, painted. Solemnly Le Borgne moistened a fingertip and tried to rub off the color. Even when the experiment failed, he was not quite convinced, until York took off his hat to display his kinky hair. Marveling, the great chief departed.

chapter II: *Aboriginal amours*

DANCING was not by any means the sole attraction that drew the men from their comfortable fort to the Mandan lodges. Lewis and Clark had long found certain aspects of aboriginal hospitality, however welcome to the men, somewhat embarrassing to their commanders. Among the Sioux, Arikaras, Mandans, and many other North American tribes, there existed the common primitive custom of providing a guest with literally *all* the necessities of life: food, lodging, presents, and—to the straightforward primitive mind, the greatest need of all—a temporary wife. The custom was both ancient and widespread. An English traveler in New York State in 1677 remarks that the Iroquois "invited us y^t when all ye maides were together, both wee and our Indyans might choose such as lyked us to ly with."

It was customary to offer an especially honored guest your wife, your sister, or your maidservant, either for the night or for the duration of his stay, all depending on the exact degree of honor you wished to show him. The guest, apparently, was not always allowed to follow the Iroquois custom and choose a lady for himself.

It was all regarded as an eminently respectable procedure, indeed so distinctly *comme il faut* that a guest's refusal of these hospitable offers was practically an insult to his host. Alexander Henry observed that Mandan husbands were "offended if their offers are not accepted of unless you can convince them of there being some good reason for your refusing to comply with their wishes, and that it is not out of contempt, they always expect payment for their complaisance, but a mere trifle will satisfy them, even one single coat button."

Once ordered to place herself at a guest's disposal, a squaw was not easy to get rid of. The English botanist Bradbury was horrified when a warrior, much pleased by a gift of silver ornaments, offered his sister. The traveler escaped only by giving the excuse that it was his turn to stand guard. Alexander Henry, about to leave a camp of friendly Indians, was at once assigned a fresh young squaw, his host's best wife, to go along as solace for the rigors of travel. With some difficulty, he managed to lose her in the bustle of departure. Another Canadian had to pacify the indignant squaw who had been offered to him and whom he had rejected, by paying to escape her favors.

Hospitality was combined with ordinary prostitution, which was also quite openly carried on. While Loisel's expedition was at his Missouri fort, just before the Lewis and Clark Expedition, a Sioux warrior offered his wife, "one of the prettiest of the village and, moreover, reputed discreet." In return for the woman's favors, a trader offered a knife, some vermilion, and a little tobacco.

"As the present appeared small because of her attractions," says Tabeau, "the husband pulls off the robe in which the Venus is wrapped through modesty and, in spite of some affected manners, increased, of course, the price of his goods by exposing it. The cavalier still hesitated, when the victim to whom the sacrifice was doubtless painful, but who feared, nevertheless, to lose the occasion of proving her submissiveness, remarked that knives with a green handle were not common; that the vermilion was a beautiful red; that the tobacco—in short, well, what else? At least, she speaks so well that they agree and the husband firmly holds the door."

To be respectable, these affairs had to be carried on with the approval of a husband or a brother. Any unchastity not thus officially approved was a black disgrace, though the aboriginal rules of conduct do not appear to have been any more rigidly observed than their civilized equivalent. Among the Arikaras, looseness was a privilege of married squaws only. Since young Arikara girls were supposed to remain chaste till marriage, careful parents took the precaution of fastening their daughters' skirts to the ground at night. Even this, according to the scandalized Tabeau, was "not proof against a lover who pleases; but, according to their law, that is a marriage."

With the consent of the husband, anything went. "All goes on often in the presence of and even by order of a jealous husband. This paradox will be no longer a paradox when it is understood that a Sioux, as a Ricara, is alive to this affront only when his wife, by a secret infidelity, departs from his house. Therefore, all that which meets with his approval, being in order, is not offensive and such a man, who would kill or at least turn out his wife upon the slightest suspicion, prostitutes her himself for a very small reward and it is seen that a wife has not yet been chastised for having failed in submission in like case.

"I have seen among the Bois Brulé a secret infidelity punished and a husband order his wife to be unfaithful."

Warriors who, with the usual Indian passion for gambling, had gambled away everything else they owned, had no compunction about staking their wives' favors; and girl prisoners like Sacagawea were casually put on a blanket and played for.

MANDAN SQUAWS by George Catlin. *At left is Sha-ko-ka ("Mint"), at right Mi-neek-e-sunk-te-ca ("Mink"). "One thing that made the Mandan girls especially attractive was the light color characteristic of many of the tribe, which had helped give rise to the legend of 'white Indians' descended from the mythical band of Welshmen supposed to have settled in North America some centuries before."*

"A Ricara lost at play the enjoyment of his wife for some days," Tabeau reports, "and he lay tranquilly at the foot of the bed, while the young man who had won received, in his sight, a thousand caresses." This happened in the lodge of the powerful chief, Kakawita, himself.

Illicit amours—that is, those to which the husband had not given his consent—were punished with characteristic Indian savagery when discovered, although Lewis and Clark's men had no great difficulty in affairs of this kind. The chief, Le Borgne, who was no model of marital fidelity himself, finding that his squaw had deserted him for a lover, sought her out in her father's lodge, whence the other man in the triangle had prudently disappeared. Le Borgne sat smoking quietly, while the old men of the village, guessing what was coming, hastily gathered in an effort to appease him. Finally laying aside his pipe, Le Borgne led his faithless spouse by the hair to the lodge door and there—while the distressed family did nothing whatever, since after all the squaw was his—neatly cut her down with his tomahawk. Yet, when in a milder mood, the same chief calmly handed another of his runaway wives over to her lover, with a wedding gift of three horses.

A Bois Brulé Sioux, who about this time caught his wife *in flagrante delicto*, commenced his family discipline "by removing her hair from the nape of the neck up to the brow and, stopping near the ears, he allows the hair and skin to hang down each side. He continues his work by mutilating her arms and hands and ends by a cut of the knife on the shoulder-blade." Another warrior simply cut his unfaithful wife into pieces, carrying her tongue back to camp with him for some inexplicable reason. Still another Indian husband settled his difficulties by slipping a heavy charge of gunpowder into the folds of his wife's blanket. When she approached a campfire that was throwing off sparks, the warrior's marital troubles were over.

Indian custom, to be sure, did not altogether approve of these severities, but no one ever did anything about them when they happened. A squaw, after all, is property, and surely a man may do as he wishes with his own. Husbands who were not inclined to be harsh, contented themselves with slashing off the tip of an unfaithful squaw's nose or tattooing her face in such a way as to disfigure her permanently.

The freedom with which the Indians offered their women at first startled, then delighted, the enlisted men of the expedition. Clark notes: "a curious custom with the Souix as well as the rickeres [Arikaras] is to give handsom squars to those whome they wish to Show some acknowledgments to." He says no more, and the men's own journals usually ignore such incidents with elaborate innocence. Yankton Sioux tradition, however, avers that there was a three-day carouse of the enlisted men and the squaws, in which only the captains declined to participate, when the Yanktons first met the expedition and before Teton Sioux hostility had developed. "The white men gave unlimited license to their baser propensities," according to Doane Robinson, who gathered up traditions afloat among the Sioux, some ninety years later.

The two officers seem—in the main at least, and perhaps entirely—to have remained aloof from all this license. There is a Sioux legend that Lewis was smitten by a young Sioux beauty named Willow Bark, who is said to have traveled with him in the boat when the expedition left her tribe's country. The Sioux warrior, Martin Charger, later claimed to be Lewis's grandson. There is, however, no mention of Willow Bark in the Journals, which do mention with much detail the Arikara squaw who really did travel in one of the boats for a while. As for Martin Charger, he was probably merely laying claim to the most distinguished ancestry he could think of. His story does not agree with Yankton tradition.

The Journals even say: "The Seauex we got clare of without taking their squars." The Sioux, however, are persistent individuals, and "they followed us with Squars two days." The Partizan even stood on the bank and yelled an offer of squaws across the muddy Missouri waters.

The expedition had no sooner reached the next village

than the Arikaras began to show the same exalted, if not very
refined, form of hospitality. Clark notes: "Their womin
verry fond of carressing our men &c," and mentions "2 young
squars verry anxious to accompany us." Sergeant Gass mentions "a great number of handsom and smart women" in the
Arikara villages.

The Arikara squaws were more brazen than the Sioux.

"It could be said that the latter do justice to themselves
and know the value of their favors," Tabeau wrote in his
diary—everyone on the Missouri seems to have kept a diary
in those days. But even Sioux virtue had its limits: "The
most inflexible is not proof against a prize of vermilion and
of twenty strands of blue beads." It is perhaps no accident
that the Lewis and Clark Expedition used up its supply of
blue beads far too soon.

The traveler Brackenridge, visiting the Arikaras a few years
after Lewis and Clark, found that "after dusk the plain behind our tents was crowded with these wretches, and shocking
to relate, fathers brought their daughters, husbands their
wives, brothers their sisters, to be offered for sale." His boatmen traded practically everything they possessed, even their
blankets and shirts, for the caresses of Arikara damsels. One
engagé returned to camp entirely naked, having given every
stitch he wore to the squaws. An Arikara chief inquired
whether there were no women where the white men lived,
for "one might suppose they had never seen any before."

Just as they had done among the Sioux, the commanders
tried not to know too much about what was going on among
the Arikaras. The original manuscript of their Journal says
primly that the entirely willing Arikara squaws were "put off
dureing the time we were at the Towns," but that is not
quite true. Nicholas Biddle, who wrote not only from the
Journals but also from indecorous information probably furnished by George Shannon, remarks that among both Sioux
and Arikara squaws "our men found no difficulty in pro-

curing companions for the night by means of the interpreters. These interviews were chiefly clandestine, and were of course to be kept secret from the husband or relations."

ARIKARA SQUAW by George Catlin. *Pshan-shaw ("Sweet Scented Grass") was an Arikara squaw. The tribe according to Clark, "appear to be peacefull, their men tall and perpotiend, womin Small and industerous."*

Being immensely admired by all the Indians who saw him, York had no need to keep his gallantries secret. Far from creating prejudice, his blackness added to his attractions and aided in his amours. The Indians, who had never seen or imagined so magnificent a being, were eager to take the most practical way "to preserve among them some memorial of this wonderful stranger." In this innocent effort either they or other tribes wholly succeeded—York's progeny were traceable for years afterward among many tribes along the Missouri and in the mountains of Idaho, where their kinky hair can still be detected. One friendly and admiring Arikara warrior took York home, presented his wife, and, delicately withdrawing, stood guard before his own door. When one of the white men came along looking for York, "the gallant husband would permit no interruption before a reasonable time had elapsed." Negro blood was traceable among the Mandans as late as 1889.

Getting finally clear of all these ardent damsels, the explorers took with them only an Arikara chief, but they had reckoned without Arikara perseverance. The tribe sent two young squaws, described as "handsom," to follow along the river bank. They caught up after a day's journey on foot, located the white men's camp on the opposite shore, and shrieked until a pirogue went across and found them, accompanied by a single brave. All three Indians were brought over to camp, where the squaws "pursisted in their civilities." The results of these civilities among the Galahads of the Corps of Discovery are not stated, except that again "the black man York participated largely in these favours."

One squaw remained with the expedition for the next three days. When other Arikaras appeared on the bank asking to see her, she at first hid herself but finally came out, went ashore to give one warrior—probably her husband—"a pair of ear-rings and drops for leave to come with us; and when the horn blew for all hands to come on board, she left them and came to the boat." That evening they found a camp of about 30 Indians, and the romantic Arikara lady finally decided to leave the white men and join the tribe once more.

The Mandan women had an especial reputation for loose

morals, which was well known to all white traders, for whom their village was a kind of center, partly because of its convenience for trade and partly because of the attractions of the squaws. The prim David Thompson, who visited the villages in 1797, was horrified to find that the voyageurs of his party were well acquainted with the reputation of the Mandan ladies, which "was almost their sole motive for this journey." After visiting the village he had to admit that a group of Mandan dancing girls, though they "were all courtesans," were "a sett of handsome tempting women." Clark, unbending in his old age, once discussed "the daughters of the Mandans and other tribes" with a casual acquaintance: "his eyes beamed with youthful fire and he assured me that they were the handsomest women in the world." One thing that made the Mandan girls especially attractive was the light color characteristic of many of the tribe, which had helped give rise to the legend of "white Indians" descended from the mythical band of Welshmen supposed to have settled in North America some centuries before. The light Mandan complexions seem to have been mainly due to the large admixture of white blood in the tribe, resulting from long contact with white traders coming overland from Canada, since, as David Thompson observes, their white visitors had never been "examples of chastity."

The expedition had arrived at the Mandan villages just before the buffalo medicine dances, primitive fertility rites intended to bring the buffalo, especially the cow buffalo, into the Mandan country where the hunters could kill them. This was a matter of life and death to the plains Indians, who depended on the immense buffalo herds for their principal meat supply and also for buffalo hides, which the plains tribes used for robes, bedding, tents, canoes, and clothing.

Young Mandans scouted about the plains, constantly on the alert for an approaching herd. When they found one, they made no attempt to do any hunting themselves, since this might have frightened the buffalo away before hunting parties from the villages could assemble for a larger kill. Instead, they returned at once to the villages to report. The old men of the village then formally announced that the buffalo cow was not far from the Mandans but she would come no nearer until the warriors made sacrifices in her honor. Then, says Tableau, who had often witnessed the ceremonies:

> "At once these good husbands bring in their prettiest wives (for they have several) to the temple of Paphos, wrapped in a single covering. A master of ceremonies arranges them on one side of the lodge and their husbands at the other. The nude old men bellow, roar, paw the earth, strike it with their heads and make the dust fly. At last, they imitate the bull in heat. During this fine performance, a small fire is lighted in the center of the lodge in which some odoriferous herbs are burnt and, in the smoke of which, the actresses come to be perfumed without much concern about decency. They then defile before a number of young men—equivalent to their own number —seated in a row. Each husband has put into the hands of the young man who has pleased him a little stick, which his wife recognizes in passing and which she seizes as if to take it away; but, the cavalier resisting, she drags him without much effort outside the lodge and, all the others doing the same, the company soon finds itself in couples on the prairie, where the old men, continually bellowing and keeping at a certain distance, seem to censure their weakness and to manifest their sorrow. On re-entering the lodge, the husbands thank them very humbly. The ceremony continues all night, the actors however, changing partners at each scene."

The Mandan abandon of these fertility rites was at first rather startling to the Americans, and Nicholas Biddle, who later edited the official edition of the Journals, taking refuge in the decent obscurity of a learned language, puts his descrip-

SHE-HE-KE by C.B.J.T. de St. Memin. *She-he-ke (Coyote, usually known as The Big White) was a subordinate chief of the Mandans. Lewis and Clark belatedly awarded him a medal, although he was "not much distinguished as a warrior, and extremely talkative, a fault much despised amongst the Indians.' " This portrait was done in crayon and is in the American Philosophical Society collection.*

ON THE UPPER MISSOURI by Charles Bodmer. *"The expedition crawled upstream against the stiff Missouri current. Hunters moved along the banks, shooting for the pot and meeting occasional friendly Indians. Movement along the shore was not easy, for the Missouri is edged with steep bluffs of hard clay and the shore below was overgrown with thickets and trees."*

tion into Latin. Clark, who does not seem to have known as much about this "curious custom" as Tabeau, describes only the part played by the old men of the tribe:

> "the old men arrange themselves in a circle & after Smoke a pipe which is handed them by a young man, Dress[ed] up for the purpose, the young men who have their wives back of the Circle go to one of the old men with a whining tone and request the old man to take his wife (who presents [herself] necked except a robe) and— (or Sleep with her) the Girl then takes the Old Man (who verry often can scarcely walk) and leades him to a convenient place for the business, after which they return to the lodge; if the old man (or a white man) returns to the lodge without gratifying the Man & his wife, he offers her again and again; it is often the Case that after a 2ᵈ. time without Kissing the Husband throws a new robe over the old man &c. and begs him not to dispise him & wife."

Tabeau remarks that though Lewis and Clark's men were witnesses of the ceremonies, the captains themselves held aloof from such goings on, as they had done among the Yanktons. David Thompson says that squaws who really loved their husbands and wished to remain faithful to them in spite of the necessities of the tribal ritual, deliberately selected impotent old men as partners.

These ceremonies sometimes went on for a fortnight, but in 1805 the buffalo cows put in a prompt appearance. "This early success," says Tabeau dryly, "the Mandanes attributed to the American soldiers, who were untiringly zealous in attracting the cow."

They must have been. "We Sent a man to this Medisan Dance last night," wrote Clark on January 3, 1805; "they gave him 4 Girls." It was just as well that the Americans were not at the Mandan villages during a summer festival of a similar nature, of which a Canadian observer remarks:

"Certainly there could be no performance more lascivious than the one I saw."

It was much the same all the way across the continent as it had been among the Sioux, Arikaras, and Mandans. The Flatheads, according to Sergeant Patrick Gass, writing while they were on the Pacific, were the only Indians who did not exhibit "loose feelings of carnal desire, nor appear addicted to the common customs of prostitution; and they are the only nation on the whole route where any thing like chastity is regarded."

The Sergeant preferred to hint at unutterable things rather than to discuss the amours of the expedition frankly. Some readers, he wrote at the Mandan village, might think "We ought to be prepared now, when we are about to renew our voyage, to give some account of the *fair sex* of the Missouri; and entertain them with narratives of feats of love as well as of arms. Though we could furnish a sufficient number of entertaining stories and pleasant anecdotes, we do not think it prudent to swell our Journal with them; as our views are directed to more useful information. Besides, as we are yet ignorant of the dangers, which may await us, and the difficulty of escape, should certain probable incidents occur, it may not be inconsistent with good policy to keep the Journal of as small and portable a size as circumstances will make practicable. It may be observed generally that chastity is not very highly esteemed by these people." Further, "the women are generally considered an article of traffic, and *indulgencies* are sold at a very moderate price. As proof of this I will just mention, that for an old tobacco box, one of our men was granted the honour of passing a night with the daughter of the head-chief of the Mandan nation. An old bawd with her punks, may also be found in some of the villages of the Missouri, as well as in the large cities of polished nations." The elaborate language suggests that the local schoolmaster who served as his literary assistant was engaged in toning down some of the sergeant's more lurid tales. It is a pity that no one has ever been able to find the lost manuscript original of Gass's diary.

In spite of all this laxity, Mandan husbands occasionally showed signs of jealousy. Sergeant John Ordway was a model soldier and a pillar of strength to the expedition, but he had his weaknesses, prominent among which were squaws, though none of this appears in his own diary, which might be read with edification by a bench of bishops. His most daring note, made while he was in the midst of his amorous exploits, reads only: "a nomber of Savages came Staying about our Garrison, espacally Several of the women." Clark's journal, however, tells a different story.

During his military service in the wild Ohio country, Ordway's thoughts had occasionally strayed to a girl named Betsey and a girl named Gracey, both of whom lived not far from his father's home, near Concord, New Hampshire. At Kaskaskia, the worthy sergeant had been much disturbed by a "flying report" of his "matrimonial engagement with Miss Nevens," who may have been identical with Gracey, or may have been still a third girl, for Ordway though a quiet, steady fellow, was also a romantic soul.

Denial of his engagement to Miss Nevens raised the question of Betsey, who had written him, just before the expedition started, "that She was offering herself a Sacrifice at the Shrine of Hymen." The news gave the sergeant some very mixed emotions—"not that I wish Betsey to loose an opportunity of enjoying connubial felicity by waiting for my return; but the probability is, that if She remains in a State of Celibacy till my return I may perhaps join hands with hir yet." These modified raptures being altogether too chill for Betsey, she had proceeded to get married to her more eager suitor.

Though he was later to marry his Gracey, when the expedition was all over, Ordway was at the moment fancy-free and in a receptive mood toward the Mandan ladies. Even before the buffalo medicine dances began—accepting the offer

of a generous and broad-minded Mandan husband—he had
taken over the warrior's squaw as a temporary wife-for-the-
night. It was all very amicable, but when Ordway had gone
cheerfully back to camp next day and the warrior had begun
to think things over, there was domestic altercation in the
Mandan's lodge. The squaw—who cannot possibly be described as erring, since she had only done as her husband
bade her—fled to the white men's fort, where she lived for
some days with the interpreters' wives.

That was the serious part. Her little affair with the dashing
white sergeant had been perfectly proper by Mandan morals
and Mandan etiquette. But running away from her husband's lodge, no matter how she had been treated there, was
a grave offense, for which the angry warrior might quite
legitimately have killed her.

He was, however, as above stated, a broad-minded Mandan.
He did not insist on exercising a deserted husband's full right
of punishment. All he did, when she finally returned to the
marital buffalo robe, was to beat his wife and stab her. Even
then, he exercised moderation, for he stabbed her only three
times, and no one knows how severe the beating really was.
Nevertheless, no matter how leniently she had been treated,
the Mandan lady didn't like it. She fled to the fort again,
whither her indignant spouse followed. This time their domestic altercation was both public and violent. The sentry
called Captain Clark just at the critical moment with the
news that an Indian was about to kill his wife at the interpreters' quarters. The bachelor Clark rushed down and read
the Mandan pair a little moral lecture on domestic hap-
piness:

"he the Husband observed that one of our Serjeants Slept
with his wife & if he wanted her he would give her to him,
We derected the Serjeant (O[r]dway) to give the man Some
articles, at which time I told the Indian that I believed not
one man of the party had touched his wife except the one he
had given the use of her for a nite, in his own bed, no man

of the party Should touch his squar, or the wife of any Indian, nor did I believe they touch a woman if they knew her to be the wife of another man, and advised him to take his squar home and live hapily together in future, at this time the Grand Chief of the nation arrived, & lectured him, and they both went off." Neither of the departing pair seemed very happy and it may be doubted whether the captain's advice to the lovelorn had any lasting good effect. Lewis would have been a more appropriate adviser. After all, Dorothy Dix belongs to his family.

It was a difficult position for the commanders, who do not seem to have persisted very long in any early efforts they may have made to keep the men away from the Indian women. Farther up the Missouri and along the Pacific coast, they gave up entirely and allowed the enlisted men to "fraternize" almost when and as they pleased, opportunities being frequent, especially for that notable curiosity, York.

The natural result of the white men's licentiousness appears in a note in Clark's Journal: "Several men with the Venereal cought from the Mandan women." Nearly three months later, he notes: "Generally helthy except Venerials Complaints which is verry Common amongst the natives and the men Catch it from them." It was a serious business in the confined quarters of the fort and in the still more confined boats in which they would resume the journey in the spring, though Canadian traders insisted that syphilis, though common among the Mandans, existed only in a mild form.

Nothing stopped the Indians, who kept right on offering their women. In mid-January, a leading war chief of the Minnetarees paid a visit to Fort Mandan, bringing his squaw, and "requested that she might be used for the night." Clark adds: "his wife handsome," but otherwise the Journal maintains a discreet silence. When the expedition finally set out for the Rockies, at least one Mandan squaw had to be firmly dissuaded from going along.

chapter 12: *The next leg*

SPRING came at last. The ice began to break. Soon the Missouri was in flood. "Gangs" of wild geese, ducks, and swans passed honking and quacking overhead. Buffalo, alive and dead, caught by the violent, muddy current, went whirling downstream among the cakes of ice. Clark admired the agility with which the Mandans leaped from ice cake to ice cake in their search for buffalo meat, hailing with especial delight the most thoroughly putrid carcasses, of which they were especially fond.

It would soon be time for both the Canadian traders and the American explorers to resume their journeys. While the Canadians looked to their horses, the Americans got their boats ready. The new canoes, made during the winter, were taken down to the riverside and calked. The old bateau and the pirogues were repaired.

Nine boxes were packed with specimens and curios for Mr. Jefferson—deer horns, a mountain ram's horns, elk's

horns, a Mandan bow and arrows, buffalo robes, Indian costumes, a bearskin, Indian pottery, botanical specimens, the
skeletons of various animals. The live animals from the
Fort Mandan zoo were carefully put aboard in improvised
cages. With this combined museum and menagerie went
Clark's new map, the "connection of the country" which
during the winter he had made by combining his notes, and
also a long letter to Mr. Jefferson, some journals, and a letter
to Lewis's mother. The consignment reached St. Louis safely
about July.

The party of returning soldiers and French engagés who
were to carry this precious cargo to St. Louis were in charge
of Corporal Richard Warfington, whose enlistment had ex-
pired. Joseph Gravelines, who had been wintering among
the Arikaras, was to serve as pilot and escort an Arikara chief
on a visit of state to the Great White Father. Though Kakawita had earlier brought word that several chiefs would go,
in the end only one was willing to take the risk. Warfington's party picked up the chief as they passed the Arikara
villages downstream—and an unfortunate venture it turned
out to be.

Warfington's party was small, for the captains had abandoned their original plan to send half their men home with
him, leave one fourth at the Mandan village to grow crops
for food on the way back, and cross the continent with the
fourth that remained—perhaps less than a dozen men. They
had by this time seen enough of the Indians to realize the
need of a larger force. Having tested their men on the long
journey up the Missouri and the severe winter among the
Mandans, the commanders rid themselves of the least valuable, and could rely completely on the 32 who finally set
forth with them on the long journey to the coast. The men
were in good spirits and—barring the unfortunate aftermath
of their Indian love-calls—in good health. Lewis was delighted
to note that they were all "zealously attached to the enter-

prise, and anxious to proceed; not a whisper of murmur or discontent to be heard among them, but all act in unison, and with the most perfect harmony."

About three weeks before they started, there was trouble with Charbonneau. The Canadian traders had been working on the shifty squawman, even inviting him to return to Canada with them, the result being that he suddenly demanded special privileges. He was not, he stipulated, to be subject to the captains' orders; he was not to do the usual camp duties; he was to be free to return when he pleased. Shrewdly guessing the real origin of the trouble, Lewis and Clark coldly dismissed him. It was the right treatment. Within a few days Charbonneau was beginning to make overtures, which were soon followed by a complete apology and an offer to perform all duties and observe ordinary discipline. Lewis and Clark gladly re-employed him, for though they could do without Charbonneau himself easily enough, Sacagawea's knowledge of the Shoshone language promised to be valuable.

Just after the Canadians had departed, the Americans set out. As the homeward-bound pirogue left the Mandan village for St. Louis, about five in the afternoon of April 7, 1805, and began to drop downstream, Clark with six small canoes and the two larger craft started up the Missouri, while Lewis rambled on foot ashore—alone and happy.

"Our vessels," he wrote exultantly, "consisted of six small canoes, and two large perogues. This little fleet altho' not quite so rispectable as those of Columbus or Capt. Cook, were still viewed by us with as much pleasure as those deservedly famed adventurers ever beheld theirs; and I dare say with quite as much anxiety for their safety and preservation. we were now about to penetrate a country at least two thousand miles in width, on which the foot of civilized man had never trodden; the good or evil it had in store for us was for experiment yet to determine, and these little vessels contained every

article by which we were to expect to subsist or defend ourselves. however, as the state of mind in which we are, generally gives the colouring to events, when the imagination
is suffered to wander into futurity, the picture which now
presented itself to me was a most pleasing one. enterta[in]ing
as I do, the most confident hope of succeeding in a voyage
which had formed a da[r]ling project of mine for the last
ten years, I could but esteem this moment of my departure
as among the most happy of my life."

He would have been less exultant if he had known the
shabby joke that fate was playing him at that moment. Two
days before, on April 5, the trading brig *Lydia,* of Boston,
Captain Samuel Hill commanding, had entered the Columbia River.

Lewis and Clark could not be quite sure that they had
outwitted the Sioux, though Tabeau and Gravelines, who
had been keeping their ears open all winter, had learned a
good deal about their hostile plans. In late February Gravelines had brought word from the Arikara villages that, though
the friendly Sioux chief, Black Buffalo, would keep his own
band quiet, the Sioux bands farther up the river intended to
attack the friendly Indian villages around Fort Mandan and
at the same time wipe out the white men, who were clearly
bad medicine. Sioux emissaries had visited the Arikaras to
suggest their joining in the attack; but these friendly Indians
disapproved of the scheme so strongly that they would not
even provide food for the visiting warmongers—by Indian
standards the sharpest rebuff possible.

The expedition's departure upstream instead ruined the
whole Sioux war plan. Sioux scouts suddenly reported that
"the soldiers" had gone beyond their reach, instead of coming
down the river where they could be easily attacked. On April
4, 1805, the whole Sioux camp, including women and children, moved to the Missouri's banks, but it was already too
late for successful pursuit. Corporal Warfington's party seems

to have had no difficulty in eluding them, though Lewis and Clark might have to reckon with them on the return journey.

Further information of Sioux plans is lacking, for their prisoner, Charles Le Raye, escaped on April 26 and made his way safely to the settlements. It seems never to have occurred to him to give anyone information about the expedition, though he had been hearing the Sioux discuss it all winter.

The going grew harder as the boats ascended the Missouri. "Hard riffles" and high waves became frequent. Tow-ropes were out every day and sometimes all day long, the men "towing & waiding in the water & holding the canoes from filling in the waves." Often they were up to their armpits in the cold stream and then had to climb out and scramble over the sharp rocks along the shores. Sometimes the banks were so slippery and the mud clung so tenaciously to their feet that they could not wear their moccasins. Earth and stones showered down upon them from the crumbling cliffs that edged the shore. Once or twice, in very bad weather, they could not travel at all.

"we to be Sure have a hard time of it oblidged to walk on Shore & haul the towing line and 9/10 of the time barefooted," wrote Private Whitehouse. They suffered so much from cuts and bruises on their bare feet that Lewis found some could hardly walk or even stand: "at least it is with great pain they do either. for some days past they were unable to wear their mockersons; they have fallen off considerably."

Even worse than the rocks were the prickly pears, whose thorns could pierce the toughest leather moccasins, a constant agony to the men on the tow-rope, who had to spend so much time watching for thorns that they could hardly handle the rope. Clark sat down by the campfire one evening and extracted seventeen thorns from his feet. Lewis, when he discovered that the prickly pears easily penetrated even a double thickness of dressed deerskin, "guarded or reather fortyfied" his feet with moccasin soles of hard, dried buffalo skin.

Charbonneau's stupidity almost ended the Lewis and Clark Expedition, once for all, on May 15. It had been a pleasant, easy day. Everything had gone so well that both captains went ashore at the same time, something they almost never dared to do. The pirogue, under full sail, was running easily up the Missouri with Charbonneau at the helm, though he was "the worst steersman of the party" and "perhaps the most timid waterman in the world." No one yet realized, however, quite how clumsy he was.

A sudden squall struck the sail. Charbonneau, at the helm, failed to respond. Looking 300 yards across the river, the two captains saw the craft heel completely over, then lie for an agonizing half minute on her side among the high waves. The man handling the brace of the sail, not knowing what else to do—he was, after all, a soldier not a sailor—clung to it till the wind jerked it out of his hands. By that time, it was too late. The boat was filling. Water was pouring over the gunwale.

On board there was a scene of wild confusion. Charbonneau dropped the tiller and called upon his Maker. Both captains tried to make their orders heard through the wind and across the roaring water. Finding that hopeless, they both fired their rifles, hoping to attract the men's attention. That failed too. Throwing down rifle and shotpouch, Lewis began unbuttoning his coat to swim out, before he realized how hopeless the effort would be.

Cruzat, in the bow, saved the day by bellowing a threat to shoot Charbonneau on the spot, if he did not take the helm again. Standing helplessly on the shore, the captains watched the pirogue fill and settle till her gunwales were barely above water. But she had not quite capsized. The awning over her deck had offered just enough resistance to the water. Struggling desperately, the men began to haul in the sail. Slowly she righted while, regardless of her craven husband's panic, Sacagawea, burdened with her baby though she was, began calmly fishing out of the river the articles which floated off the deck and past her place in the stern.

Still looking as if she would go under at any moment, the pirogue turned toward the shore. Cruzat set two men bailing with kettles that luckily happened to be on deck and, still more luckily, had not gone overboard. He himself took an oar and with two of the others coaxed the waterlogged craft ashore, with water lapping half an inch below her gunwale.

There was nothing to do but halt and see how much damage had been done. The pirogue carried the expedition's journals, instruments, books, and medicines. If it had gone clear over, the expedition would have been "deprived of nearly everything necessary for our purposes, at a distance of between two and three thousand miles from any place where we could supply the deficiency." Three of the men aboard, Charbonneau included, could not swim. Lewis himself thought that there was a hundred-to-one chance that, if he had tried to swim out himself, "I should have paid the forfit of my life for the madness of my project, but this had the perogue been lost, I should have valued but little." With the essentials of their equipment lost, they would have had to turn back.

Anxiously, the explorers unloaded the dripping, muddy cargo. Many of the medicines were ruined; others, though damaged, could still be used. The rest of the equipment could be dried out. Lewis could only hope that the ruined drugs would not be needed. Only a few articles had rolled off the deck and sunk. Sacagawea had saved almost everything that would float. Lewis, though he never shared Clark's liking for the Shoshone squaw, did full justice on this occasion to her "equal fortitude and resolution with any person on board."

There was some consolation for their mishap in the abundance and tameness of the game. Though the animals were emaciated after a hard winter, the party rarely lacked fresh meat of some sort—buffalo, deer, antelope, beaver-tail and beaver-liver, the last two being especially appreciated by Lewis. Private Whitehouse observed that "the Game is getting so pleanty and tame in this country that Some of the men has went up near enofe to club them out of their way." One fat and complacent wolf suffered himself to be slain with nothing more than an espontoon, a kind of halberd—spear and ax combined—that was still part of an army officer's equipment.

Not all the game was equally submissive. Scannon, Lewis's Newfoundland, made the mistake of trying to catch a beaver, probably the first he had ever seen. He was bitten so severely that he nearly bled to death. After his recovery, however, the big Newfoundland distinguished himself by his skill in catching wild geese and bringing them ashore for his master's benefit.

The Indians seemed to have abandoned the country, though Indian sign continued to appear. Once a lodge pole, one end splintered from dragging after a dog or pony on the march, floated downstream. Someone found a football, which looked very much as if it had belonged to Minnetarees. A series of old Indian encampments at intervals along the banks appeared to have belonged to a band of about a hundred lodges, who had been moving at leisure up the river some five weeks before. Sacagawea, called on to examine some old moccasins, said they were not Shoshone but must come from a tribe living east of the Rockies and north of the Missouri. Minnetarees again, the captains thought.

On June 2, 1805—while Drouilliard and Charbonneau, who had gone ashore, were having a desperate but eventually victorious battle with a grizzly, out of sight and hearing—the boats in a "Small Sprinkling of rain" were approaching the site of the modern village of Loma, Montana. Here the Missouri divides, the main stream coming in from the South while Maria's River comes in from the North. A third river, the Teton (Rose or Tansy), after just failing to unite with the main Missouri stream, turns until it flows into Maria's River, only a few miles from the point where the latter reaches the Missouri.

It had not been a bad day, in spite of the rain and the grizzly. The current for the last two days had not been so swift as usual and Private Whitehouse noted: "we git along verry well with the towing lines." After an eighteen-mile run for the day, they went into camp on the south side of the Missouri, near the fork.

Which stream was the Missouri—whose headwaters, the Minnetaree Indians had assured them, reached almost to the headwaters of the Columbia? No one as yet realized that still a third fork, where the Teton branches from Maria's River, was only a few miles ahead. It was hard enough to decide between the two nearly equal streams they could see, one of which was 362 yards wide, the other 200 yards. If they made the wrong choice, they would not be sure of it till they were well up in the Rockies. Returning to try the other fork would then mean at best a serious delay; and it might even leave them stranded in the Rockies in mid-winter. This, the commanders feared, might so discourage the men that the whole expedition would have to be given up.

The first thing to do was to reconnoiter both streams far enough to get some idea of their general direction, width, depth, and current. Accordingly, Sergeant Gass and two men took a canoe up the "South branch" (i.e., the real Missouri) while Sergeant Pryor also with two men, went up the north branch, now Maria's River. Other small parties went out on foot to look for high ground from which it might be possible to see the distant courses of the rivers. Lewis and Clark strolled off together to the highest land they could find at the forks, while the remaining men went to work dressing skins for leather clothing.

From their height of land, Lewis and Clark had "an exten-sive and most inchanting view; the country in every derection around us was one vast plain in which innumerable herds of Buffalow were seen attended by their shepperds the wolves; the solatary antelope which now had their young were dis-tributed over it's face; some herds of Elk were also seen; the verdure perfectly cloathed the ground, the weather was pleas-ent and fair; to the South we saw a range of lofty mountains which we supposed to be a continuation of the S. Mountains, streching themselves from S. E. to N. W. terminating ab-brubtly about S. West from us; these were partially covered with snow; behind these Mountains and at a great distance, a second and more lofty range of mountains appeared to strech across the country in the same direction with the others, reaching from West, to the N of N.W., where their snowey tops lost themselves beneath the horizon. this last range was perfectly covered with snow. the direction of the rivers could be seen but little way, soon loosing the break of their chan-nels, to our view."

The exploring parties came back without much to report. Both had gone ahead part way by canoe and then still farther on foot, leaving themselves barely time to get back to camp by evening, as ordered. Sergeant Gass reported that the south branch had a swift current and ran southwest. Pryor had found rather less current in the north branch, which seemed to run northwards as far as he had gone, ten miles.

The men of the expedition had by this time jumped to the false conclusion that their true course led up the north branch. The Missouri was a muddy river and so was the north branch, which was proof enough for them. The captains were not so sure. The north branch was muddy and sluggish with a bed of mud and gravel. That looked as if it flowed a long way through flat plains. The south branch was clear and swift with a bed of round, smooth stones. That looked as if it flowed directly from mountains not far distant.

The only way to be sure was to make a more complete reconnaissance. The captains decided to separate. Lewis would take Sergeant Pryor, Drouilliard, and four men up the north fork. Clark would take Sergeant Gass, York, and three other men up the south fork. The sergeants would be some use as guides as far as they had gone.

Both parties had a drink all round in preparation for an early start next morning. Lewis reflected as he prepared his pack that, in spite of all his years of soldiering, it was the first time he had carried his own pack, though he felt "fully convinced that it will not be the last." He was right about that.

Next morning, he headed for the highest land he could find along the north fork and took bearings on the distant mountains. Pushing on upstream, he soon found, as he had expected, that it ran through plains. Though game was plentiful most of the time, on one occasion the cautious Lewis had each man kill a prairie dog "to make shure of our suppers." As they killed five elk later, they did not need the prairie dogs; but Lewis, ever scientifically minded, had a few roasted anyhow, "by way of experiment," and found them very good.

By the third day, he was convinced that the north fork ran "too much to the North for our rout to the Pacific." Just to make sure, he sent two men forward to get on a hill and observe as far upstream as possible, while the rest of the group were getting two rafts ready to float downstream. When the rafts proved a failure, the party had to return on foot.

It was an adventurous journey. As they skirted the top of a 90-foot precipice, Lewis slipped and just saved himself from a fall by driving in his espontoon as a hand-hold. He had hardly recovered his balance when he heard a yell from Private Windsor, behind him: "Good God, Captain, what shall I do?" He looked back to see Windsor lying on his stomach with his right arm and leg clawing at vacancy while he hung on with his left hand and dug in with his left foot as well as he could. Concealing his alarm under an elaborate calm, though he expected to see the man crash down at any moment, Lewis mendaciously assured him that there was no danger. He must use his right hand to get his knife loose and with it dig a toehold for his right foot. When this was done, the imperturbable captain instructed Windsor to slip off his moccasins and crawl forward on hands and knees, with rifle in one hand, knife in the other. Calmed by his officer's self-possession, Windsor did as he was told and reached safety. Lewis sent the others by a less dangerous path.

They had to force their way down the river, sometimes in the stream up to their chests, at other times cutting footholds in the packed earth of the cliffs which edged the stream, while rain added to their misery. Nevertheless, they camped triumphantly that night with six deer for dinner, more than they could possibly eat, and an abandoned Indian lodge to give them shelter. Lewis concludes his journal for the day: "I now laid myself down on some willow boughs to a comfortable nights rest, and felt indeed as if I was fully repaid for the toil and pain of the day, so much will a good shelter, a dry bed, and a comfortable supper revive the sperits of the w[e]aryed, wet and hungry traveler."

When traveling proved somewhat better next day, giving him time for reflection, Lewis's thoughts turned to his cousin, Maria Wood, back in Albemarle—one of the innumerable girls with whom he had, at one time or another, more or less faintly fancied himself in love, and all of whom he invariably lost to others with no perceptible pangs. His men still thought this was the real Missouri, but Lewis had long since become certain it was an unknown river. In that case, it would require a name. Clark had already named two rivers for girls: "Martha's River" in honor of a certain "M. F.," otherwise unknown, unless she is the cruel "Miss F——" mentioned in a letter to his sister, and Judith's River, in honor of "Judy" Hancock.

Since he had explored the north fork and it was obviously his turn to name a river, Lewis called the stream Maria's River, "in honour of Miss Maria W——d. . . . it is true," his journal adds, "that the hue of the waters of this turbulent and troubled stream but illy comport with the pure celestial virtues and amiable qualifications of that lovely fair one; but on the other hand it is a noble river." It remains Maria's River to this day, though the "lovely fair one" never became Mrs. Lewis.

Clark's party had gone 40 miles up the south fork. Their first discovery, eight miles up the river, was "a beautiful spring where we refreshed ourselves with a good drink of grog," according to Sergeant Gass, who apparently agreed with Clark that a beautiful spring was no place to be drinking water.

Where Lewis had found only plains along the north fork, Clark soon found himself with snow-covered mountains to north and south—more evidence that the south fork led directly to the Continental Divide. By midday, Clark decided this was the proper route and started back by way of the Teton River, pausing to carve his name on a tree after the old custom of the Kentucky pioneers. He was back two days before the other party and was beginning to feel some alarm for their safety when Lewis returned, having covered 60 miles upstream as against Clark's 40.

Reunited at their base camp, Lewis and Clark found themselves, as usual, in complete agreement. Lewis came back from the north fork convinced it was the wrong way; Clark came back from the south fork, convinced it was the right one. Cruzat stoutly maintained that they ought to take the north fork. Though he was half blind, Cruzat had been taken along because he knew the lower river and "from his integrity knowledge and skill as a waterman had acquired the confidence of every individual of the party." He was, however, only a practical riverman, with no knowledge of topography. The rest of the enlisted men, knowing nothing whatever about the problem, agreed with Cruzat. When Lewis "indevoured to impress on the minds of the party" the captains' view of the matter, they remained unconvinced. But they were disciplined soldiers by this time, and "they said very cheerfully that they were ready to follow us anywher we thought proper to direct."

Lewis, after refreshing himself and his stalwarts with grog, gave himself the first evening in camp to "rest from my labours," while Clark busily plotted the course of the two forks. The two leaders decided to get rid of their big red pirogue and as much of the heavy baggage as possible, before leaving the forks. This would mean seven more hands for the other boats—badly needed hands, since work at the tow-rope, already difficult, was likely to grow worse. They would need the extra supplies cached at the forks on the way home.

The experienced Cruzat knew all about making "cashes" and the men went to work under his directions. Selecting a dry spot on higher ground, he cut the heavy prairie sod from a twenty-inch circle and laid it aside, digging down and enlarging the hole underneath but leaving the rest of the surface undisturbed. The earth was carried away and thrown into the river, so that there would be nothing to give wandering Indians any hint that buried treasure was near. When the excavation had been carried down six or seven feet, the bottom was hollowed out to receive any water that might seep in, and dry sticks were used to keep the contents of the cache from touching the moist earth. When the hole was nearly filled with the expedition's forge, tools, reserve rations, reserve ammunition, tin cups, traps, skins, and specimens, the contents were covered with leather, and earth was rammed in between this covering and the surface. A few days after the original twenty-inch circle of sod had been replaced, the grass had grown enough to conceal the hiding place completely. It was a common Indian method.

There was a good deal of other preparation. Men not engaged in digging were kept busy dressing skins to make clothing, which wore out rapidly from the combined effects of rocks, brambles, prickly pears, and Missouri River water. Since the blacksmith's tools now had to be stored, the party's arms were given a final overhauling and then inspected. The ingenious Shields renewed the mainspring of Lewis's airgun, which would have to be the mainstay of the party if ammunition ran out. Hereafter, only minor repairs would be possible.

There was always danger that Indians might find and rob the cache, in which case the expedition would be destitute. To guard against such a disaster, the captains buried four pounds of powder and some lead near their tent. Finding that they could still spare ammunition, Clark made some additional small caches of ammunition and a reserve ax. The pirogue was dragged out of the water and lashed to trees on a small island, so that floods could not sweep it away. The remaining canoes were calked and repaired, while all baggage was given a thorough drying—canoes always pick up more or less water from rain, splash, and leaks.

The party were in good spirits, though Sacagawea and Lewis were both ill. The others amused themselves in the evening, after a day of toil with "danceing and Singing Songes in the most social manner," with violin accompaniment by Cruzat, while Lewis dosed himself with medicine and bled Sacagawea. Both indomitable spirits were ready for travel when the time came.

At eight o'clock on the morning of June 11, Lewis, though still weak from his illness, swung his pack and started up the Missouri afoot with Drouilliard, Gibson, Joseph Field, and Goodrich. Drouilliard would interpret in case they met Indians, while Charbonneau remained with Clark for the same purpose. They had not gone far before Lewis realized that he had been over-sanguine as to his cure. By midday his illness was so much worse that he could not even eat. Violent intestinal pain increased, a high fever set in. By evening he realized that he could not go on at all.

Though he had brought no medicine and Clark's boats where the medical stores were packed would not even be starting until next day, he was not Lucy Marks's son for nothing. That vigorous old lady had been dosing half of Albemarle County with garden herbs and simples most of her life, and her son knew exactly what to do now. Choke cherry was abundant. He ordered the small twigs gathered, the leaves stripped off, and the twigs cut into two-inch lengths and boiled till they gave off a "strong black decoction of an astringent bitter tast." Taking a pint of this nauseous brew at sunset and another an hour later, Lewis found himself free of pain by ten o'clock. The fever abated, he broke into a gentle perspiration, had a good night's rest, and was off with his men at sunrise, feeling "quite revived," though by way of precaution he quaffed another pint of his choke cherry extract before starting. He was, in fact, so completely revived that he helped kill two grizzlies at ten o'clock, both bears falling at the first fire, which was a record for the expedition, thus far.

On the third day out (June 13), while the other three were off hunting, Lewis and Goodrich heard "the agreeable sound of a fall of water." Soon they could see spray, rising and disappearing like smoke. As they came closer they heard "a roaring too tremendious to be mistaken for any cause short of the great falls of the Missouri." Hurrying down the last hill, Lewis scrambled up a tangle of rocks about twenty feet high, opposite the center of the falls, and gazed at "the grandest sight I ever beheld." He had arrived at the season when the Missouri is in flood and the Great Falls were at their best, the water foaming over high masses of rocks, throwing up so much spray that the sun formed a rainbow above it. It was more than a magnificent sight—it was proof that they had chosen the correct route and really were on the main stream of the Missouri. These were the falls that the Indians had described to them.

So enthusiastic was Lewis that he hastily jotted down a description of the scene, then decided it was so inadequate he would cancel it, then decided he could do no better on a second attempt: "I wished for the pencil of Salvator Rosa or the pen of Thompson, that I might be enabled to give to the enlightened world some just idea of this truly magnificent and sublimely grand object, which has from the commencement of time been concealed from the view of civilized man."

Reflecting that his wish was "fruitless and vain" he set about the practical task of finding a camp site, arranging for a meat supply, and selecting a landing place for Clark's canoes. The even more practical Goodrich, who had never heard of Salvator Rosa or Thomson's *Seasons,* began fishing. The party feasted that night on buffalo hump, buffalo tongue, marrow bones (to which Lewis was partial), and trout. Flushed with his discovery, inwardly stayed by abundant food, Lewis rolled happily into his blankets.

chapter 13: Grizzly bears and rattlesnakes

THE tameness and abundance of game animals on the upper Missouri was not an entirely unmixed blessing. The grizzly bears which preyed upon the swarming game were equally numerous, quite as fearless as the deer and buffalo, and—unlike most wild animals—often ready to attack without provocation. They were huge brutes, often weighing well up to half a ton, astonishingly fast in spite of their bulk, ranging in color from yellowish to very light gray, so that the expedition's journals usually refer to them as "yellow" or "white bears." As yet unaccustomed to firearms, the grizzlies had no fear whatever of the crude one-shot rifles of the day and were extremely ferocious. They were so powerful that Spaniards, hunting with the lasso on the Pacific coast, found that even when roped a grizzly could walk off, towing two horses and their riders.

No white man at that time knew much about grizzlies. In fact, except for possible trappers, traders, and hunters who left no record, no white man had ever seen them. Even their tracks were curiosities. Edward Umfreville had heard stories about "the grizzle bear" by 1790 but he failed to find any. The explorer, Alexander McKenzie, saw tracks in 1795 and noted that "the Indians entertain great apprehension of this kind of bear, which is called the grisly bear," but the animals themselves he did not meet.

Neither Lewis nor Clark had ever seen a grizzly either, but during the long sojourn at Fort Mandan they had heard many an Indian tale about them, to which they had listened with a good deal of skepticism, though the Minnetarees had two warriors killed by bears that winter. Though Indians were occasionally able to kill grizzlies, the red hunters said, the grizzlies far more frequently killed Indians. It took six to ten warriors to kill a single bear, and even then the risks were so great that the same ceremonial preceded a grizzly hunt that preceded the setting forth of a war party. Lewis listened tolerantly. That might be true of Indians with bows and bad rifles; it would be very different with his expert riflemen.

Soon after the party left the Mandan village, grizzly tracks began to appear on the shore, especially around the carcasses of dead buffalo, and aroused much speculation. They were enormous. No one had ever seen anything like them. Sometimes a single footprint was eleven inches long and seven and one-half inches across. But no bears were to be seen; "the men as well as ourselves are anxious to meet with some of these bears," wrote Lewis, sublimely unaware how numerous and how close his own meetings with them were soon to be. He still doubted the Indian accounts of the beasts' ferocity. They seemed rather timid. Though more and more bear tracks continued to appear along shore, there were still no bears. They must, Lewis observed, be "extreemly wary and shy."

Consequently when, a few days later, Lewis and one of the men encountered two grizzlies together, they both fired at them simultaneously, without the least hesitation. They wounded both bears, but they also emptied both rifles at the same time, which in grizzly-hunting was a serious error. One bear fled but the other chased Lewis for 70 or 80 yards. He escaped because the bear was so badly wounded that the hunters were able to escape its rushes by dodging about over the prairie, until they could finally reload, fire again, and kill it. When all the excitement was over, this terror turned out to be nothing but a 300-pound cub.

Lewis still felt confident: "the Indians may well fear this anamal equiped as they generally are with their bows and arrows or indifferent fuzees, but in the hands of skillfull rifle-men they are by no means as formidable or dangerous as they have been represented." He was soon to change his mind about that!

Clark and Drouilliard together killed another grizzly, which did not die until it had reached a sandbar halfway across the river, after the hunters had fired ten bullets into it. This bear weighed 500 or 600 pounds and was eight feet seven and one half inches from nose to the hind feet. It had not proved really dangerous, though its amazing capacity to absorb bullets gave the expedition something to think about while they were boiling down its fat.

The expedition's muzzle-loaders did not have the shocking-power of a modern express rifle. With their low velocity bullets, it did very little good to shoot a grizzly unless your first shot hit him in the brain, the only shot that would "conquer the farocity of those tremendious anamals." Shot through the "lights" (lungs), entrails, or shoulder, the bear merely spouted blood in all directions, picked himself up, and showed his resentment by enthusiastically trying to kill you. Again and again, hunting parties pumped these bears full of bullets before they dropped them.

No one ever succeeded in putting a bullet into a grizzly's heart, and the brain was protected by large thick muscles covering the forehead and by a sharp projection of the heavy frontal bone. Only a perfect shot by a skillful rifleman could hit it. Few hunters cared for the extreme risks taken by one daredevil, whom the Pennsylvania trapper, Zenas Leonard, saw kill a grizzly with a single shot, some years after the Lewis and Clark Expedition. This man was cool enough to let the bear charge to within a few feet, when he thrust the muzzle of his rifle—endearingly named "Knock-him-stiff"— into the brute's mouth, and let drive with a one-ounce bullet. This, as the hero of the encounter remarked, gave the grizzly "a very bad cough," but it was not a method ever likely to become popular. A single slip or misfire meant certain death.

From this time on, the curiosity which the grizzly tracks had at first aroused was abundantly gratified. Bears now seemed to pop up all over the landscape, sometimes alone, sometimes in pairs, almost invariably willing to stand and fight it out, or even to attack. It took the party a very short time after they reached country swarming with grizzlies to discover that the Indian hunters had been entirely correct in their accounts.

Lewis himself began to revise his earlier opinion of grizzlies after a little experience: "I find that the curiossity of our party is pretty well satisfyed with rispect to this anamal, the formidable appearance of the male bear killed on the 5th added to the difficulty with which they die even when shot through the vital parts, has staggered the resolution [of] several of them, others however seem keen for action with the bear."

Private Bratton, being temporarily disabled by an abscessed hand, was one day given permission to vary the monotony of canoe travel by a solitary stroll ashore. Late in the afternoon, Lewis, glancing toward the bank, saw a white man running for his life. He could see him gesticulating and he could soon hear him yell. It was Bratton, who reached the safety of the boat so completely out of breath that for several minutes he could not even talk. He finally gasped out that he had had the folly to shoot at a grizzly while he was all alone, with no second rifle to support him. A single shot was all he got a chance to fire. Luckily, it was a hit. The aggrieved bear promptly gave chase but was so badly crippled that Bratton, after a half-mile run, got away.

Lewis, turning out seven hunters to follow the bloody trail, finally came up with the bear in a thicket of rosebushes and willow. Two shots in the head ended matters. Examination of the carcass showed that Bratton's bullet had smashed through the lungs, in spite of which the bear, after chasing him half a mile, had traveled over a mile farther before taking cover, had then dug itself a large hole, and was still "perfectly alive" when the hunters caught up, two hours later. It took two men to carry the hide, and the carcass yielded eight gallons of oil.

Lewis revised his opinion still further: "these bear being so hard to die reather intimedates us all; I must confess that I do not like the gentlemen and had reather fight two Indians than one bear."

In justice to the grizzlies, it must be said that most of them were probably not nearly so ferocious as the explorers thought. Like many wild animals, the grizzly is eternally curious. Many of the bears at which the expedition fired probably were approaching merely to see what these strange objects were, though curiosity turned to ferocity soon enough when they were wounded—as they usually were.

A few evenings later, the men in one of the rear canoes saw a grizzly lying in the open, about 300 yards from the river. Six hunters, landing out of the bear's sight, took advantage of a slight rise in the ground of the rolling prairie to creep up within 40 yards. Four of them let drive together, the other two holding their fire. All four bullets hit the bear, two going through his lungs. As the wounded animal charged, the other two also fired, one wounding him slightly and the other breaking his shoulder. These six wounds "only retarded his motion for a moment only." Unable to reload, all six men ran for the river with the bear, making fairly good time on three legs, behind them. Two men got the canoe afloat, where they were fairly safe, since no wild animal can swim fast enough to catch well-handled small craft. The other four hunters, hidden in the willows, hastily reloaded and again opened fire as chance offered, "but the guns served only to direct the bear to them." Two had to throw away their rifles and jump over a twenty-foot bank into the Missouri. The bear jumped after them, only a few feet behind the second man, but as it struck the river downstream from the fugitive hunter, it had the current of the Missouri against it. This gave time enough for one of the men still on shore to fire from the cliff's edge down into the river. Being in no danger himself, he could fire coolly and easily and so managed to put a ball into the brain. They dragged the carcass out of the water with eight bullets in it or through it.

The danger from these monsters, when wounded, cannot be exaggerated. In 1821 a man in Major Jacob Fowler's party was caught by a grizzly when his companion's rifle twice missed fire. Their mongrel bitch gallantly delayed the bear long enough for both men, one of them badly mauled, to scramble up a sloping tree. But, though grizzlies' huge claws are too blunt to climb vertically up a tree, this bear was able to crawl up the sloping trunk to renew the attack. The hunter, after coolly sharpening his flint, managed to fire at last, but not until the bear had gotten its jaws on the other man's head. When it was all over and the bear was safely dead, the injured man said: "I am killed that I Heard my

Skull brake—but We Ware Willing to beleve He Was mistaken—as He Spoke Chearfully on the Subgect till In the after noon of the second day When he began to be Restless and Some What delereous—and on examening a Hole in the upper part of His Wright temple Which We beleved only Skin deep We found the Brains Workeing out—We then Soposed that He did Heare His Scull brake." The man died next day.

There was a series of adventures with bears near the forks and the falls of the Missouri. Even experienced men like Drouilliard and Charbonneau had narrow escapes. While the rest of the party were approaching the forks, these two, hunting together, had encountered a "yellow bear" in a "bottom" near the river. It almost caught Drouilliard and, as he escaped, rushed after Charbonneau. As usual, the interpreter completely lost his head and in his excitement fired his rifle uselessly into the air while he ran, thus leaving himself completely defenseless. He managed to get away into the bushes, where he hid until Drouilliard put a bullet into the brain.

When the captains took separate parties up the two forks of the Missouri, each party met grizzlies. Lewis's men killed two without much effort, but Joseph Field, with Clark, had the narrowest escape of the expedition. Clark's party had gone into camp in an old Indian lodge at the top of a cliff, overlooking the river. Field went down to the river and stumbled suddenly on two bears. One, "an old hea bear," attacked just as Field discovered that the powder in his rifle was too wet to fire. He dodged the bear's first rush, though it came close enough to strike his foot, and fled, with the bear hot behind him. The rest of the party, hearing this uproar, ran to the edge of the cliff where they could see everything but could not get down the sheer wall of the bluff to get in a few shots at close range. However, they poured in as many shots as they could without hitting Field, and the noise of their combined shots and yells was enough to frighten the grizzly into the river. General opinion was that the bear "would have killed him if the rest of the party had not been in hearin to have fired at him which made him turn his course." Next day they ran into three more bears but, being by this time wise in their ways, killed all three and ate part of one.

While he waited at the falls of the Missouri for Clark to come up with the boats, Lewis had almost as close an escape as Field had had. Finding that there was a series of cascades upstream, he pushed on eagerly, his characteristic delight in natural beauty mingled with the satisfaction of success as an explorer, peering down the Missouri's southward meanderings and looking up the course of Medicine River.

His musings had a startling interruption. After killing a fat buffalo with a view of making sure of supper in case he could not get back to camp, he turned just in time to see a large grizzly, which had crept silently to within twenty paces and was now "briskly advancing." Instinctively raising his rifle, he realized too late that he had not reloaded after shooting the buffalo. There was no human help for miles, since he had far outdistanced the whole party.

Lewis decided on a slow and dignified retreat to a tree which stood about 300 yards away down the easy slope of the river bank, his nearest prospect of safety. If worst came to worst, he would have a downhill run, but then, so would the bear. Animals sometimes hesitate when prospective prey retires slowly, showing no fear, but Missouri grizzlies of that day knew nothing of hesitation. Lewis had scarcely turned when the grizzly charged.

Though Captain Lewis broke all known speed records of the expedition, it was nip and tuck for the next 80 or 90 yards, with the grizzly gaining fast. Reaching the tree was hopeless. Lewis thought it over between gasps, then whirled and plunged into the river up to his waist, at which depth the bear would have to swim out to get him. Here he turned and defiantly presented the point of his espontoon.

It was not quite what a Missouri grizzly of the year 1805, normally lord of the prairie, was used to. The bear reached the edge of the water, about twenty feet away, hesitated, wheeled, and then—for no discoverable reason—took fright and ran. Lewis, scrambling out with his powder still dry, hastily reloaded his rifle, which he had "retained in my hand throughout this curious adventure."

Having once decided on retreat, the bear ran across the level plain as hard as he could go for three miles, looking back occasionally as if he feared pursuit, while Lewis watched, feeling "not a little gratifyed that he had declined the combat." Going back along the trail he had left, the captain found the marks of huge claws directly over his own hastily departing footsteps.

He went on for some distance, making up his mind "never again to suffer my peice to be longer empty than the time she necessarily required to charge her," a bit of practical philosophy which the Missouri River grizzlies had been vainly endeavoring to inculcate for the last few hundred miles.

Still studying the river, Lewis rambled on until it was half past six and he found himself twelve miles from camp. He had scarcely turned back when he saw what he at first thought was a wolf. As he looked more closely, he decided it was "of the tiger kind," but there was no time for more zoölogy since the animal, whatever it was, seemed about to spring. This time Lewis's rifle was loaded and ready. The creature, perhaps a wolverene, perhaps a mountain lion, leaped back as he fired. Neither wolverene nor mountain lion would be dangerous under modern conditions but both species were bolder then than they are today.

Lewis reached camp late in the night, almost feeling that he had dreamed the whole thing, except that the prickly pear thorns gave his suffering feet convincing evidence that he was wide awake and that it had all really happened. He found his men just preparing to send out a search party.

His journal for the day closes on a somewhat irrelevant sartorial note. All these adventures had befallen him while wearing a shirt of "yellow flannin," instead of his usual leather. Next morning, he woke to discover a rattlesnake coiled in the tree under which he was lying. Hastily killing it, he seized the occasion to make a few scientific notes on reptilian anatomy.

The grizzlies around the falls of the Missouri proved even more enterprising and fearless than their congeners farther downstream, for these animals, which had never heard a rifle shot and rarely seen even bows and arrows, had no fear of anything alive. Joseph Field, out cruising for timber, had a second narrow escape—which almost duplicated his first adventure, except that this time there was no help at hand—when he met two grizzles at once. Just as he was preparing to fire, he discovered a third, which attacked instantly. Running for his life, he leaped the steep river bank, landing on a "stony bar," which cut his hand and knee and bent his rifle so that he was completely helpless; but the bear, unable to see where he had gone, gave up the chase.

Hunters returning to camp two days later found bear tracks and, first prudently climbing a tree, yelled with all their might. The largest grizzly anyone had yet seen emerged instantly from cover, rushed to the tree, and peering up gave Drouilliard his chance for a perfect shot into the brain. That night still another of the bears came within 30 yards of the camp and boldly carried off buffalo meat. Other grizzlies prowled about the camp by night so often that the whole party had to sleep with their arms; but Lewis's dog Scannon valorously gave the alarm with such tremendous barks when the animals came too close, that none of them actually entered camp.

Other animals made surprisingly little trouble. The big western rattlesnakes, very different from their eastern relatives, caused many alarms but no fatalities. A four-footer struck one man in the leg but did not penetrate his leggin. It was shot before it could strike again. Another man, lying with his head under a bush, idly stretched forth a hand and closed it on the head of a rattler. He, too, escaped injury. A fisherman, looking down one day, saw a rattlesnake between his legs but was able to shoot before it struck.

Lewis heard the whir of a snake's rattle a few inches away as he passed down a trail by night but escaped being bitten, apparently because he passed too swiftly for the snake to coil and strike. There ensued a desperate little battle in the darkness, Lewis slashing and thrusting with his long espontoon, unable to see the snake but guided by the rattle. Eventually he killed it, without being bitten.

There was also one mild adventure with a buffalo bull, which swam the Missouri one night and tried to land on the large bateau, in which the records were stored, the one boat which was the inevitable target of all disasters. The buffalo soon discovered its mistake and in a panic went thundering through the camp in an effort to get away. The men had fallen asleep here and there about the camp, each lying down wherever he could find a comfortable place, so that wherever the buffalo turned it was nearly certain to trample someone. After it had gone thundering past one row of sleeping men, not more than eighteen inches away, the sentry's efforts to drive it away only frightened the bull still more. In panic, the bull turned again and rushed past the lodge where the two captains were sleeping, missing the heads of other soldiers by a few inches. Scannon again saved the day by leaping at the buffalo, barking loud enough to frighten it off for good. No one was hurt, though firearms were damaged.

chapter 14: At the Great Falls

WHILE Lewis waited near the Great Falls, Clark was painfully coaxing the boats upstream, amid constantly increasing difficulties. Keeping a sharp eye out for grizzlies, which were becoming more and more abundant, dodging rattlesnakes, trying to keep the canoes from shipping too much water, cutting their feet on sharp stones and slipping on smooth ones, the river party crawled ahead. One after another, the men fell ill. Two had toothaches, two developed "tumers," another had a carbuncle plus a slight fever. Private Whitehouse was also ill, but no one knew it, for he managed to keep going without mentioning his condition, except in his diary.

The most serious medical problem was Sacagawea, who had been taken ill at the mouth of Maria's River. Clark bled her on two successive days, the approved treatment of the time, though the wonder is it did not kill her, as it is said to have killed George Washington. When she grew worse, he tried "a doste of salts," which did no good at all. Charbonneau, though he had been warned about her diet, foolishly allowed her to gorge on "white apples" and raw fish, after which she became alarmingly ill. Her pulse could hardly be felt; her arm and fingers twitched; she began to refuse medicine. Only her husband could get her to take it, and even he could do so only when she was delirious. Without much hope, Clark tried cataplasms of bark and laudanum: "if she dies it will be the fault of her husband as I am now convinced," he wrote in his journal, gloomily, for he liked the little squaw. He knew, too, that if Sacagawea died, the expedition would find itself left with a four-months-old baby, which would have to be carried across the continent and back with no available milk supply—a unique problem for a military expedition, which even Lewis had never foreseen. They might, perhaps, have tried the expedient of the famous Montana pioneer, Jim Bridger, when his wife, dying in childbirth, left him with a newborn baby girl. The resourceful Bridger is said to have improvised a nursing bottle and brought the baby up on buffalo milk. But that meant killing a cow buffalo every time the baby was hungry, and the expedition was just about to leave the buffalo country.

When Clark caught up with Lewis at the falls on June 16, there was more discouraging news. Lewis reported that they would have to portage sixteen miles around the series of swift rapids and smaller falls above the Great Falls. That would be exhausting enough in itself; but, to make matters worse, they would have to open a road the whole way, before they could start to move the boats and their cargo. There was no firewood—a serious matter when your dinner depends on it; and Charbonneau had begun to whine about going home.

As topographer of the expedition, Clark started over the

portage himself to mark out the best route, while six of the men went out to try to find enough timber for "a parsel of truck wheels." When after much searching they came upon a fair-sized cottonwood, they cut round cross-sections of its trunk for small wheels, made two axles by cutting up the mast of the white pirogue, and pieced out as best they could with soft cottonwood and willow. The two wagons created with such effort were not very good, but they lightened the labor of the portage, which was further reduced by caching such supplies as would not be needed till their return.

Taking Sacagawea's case in hand, Lewis prescribed barks, laudanum, then sulphur water from a neighboring spring. Within a day her fever vanished, her pulse was regular, and she was eager for as much "broiled buffaloe well seasoned with pepper and salt and rich soope of the same meat" as the captain would let her have. Two days later she was able to sit up, walk a little, eat heartily, and down fifteen drops of oil of vitriol, which Lewis now prescribed. How they fed the baby, while his mother was at her worst, must remain a mystery.

While Clark was laying out the portage, the camp at the falls was bustling with activity. The long-awaited moment had come to get out Lewis's pride and joy, the collapsible iron boat, *Experiment*. As it had long since become evident that his original scheme of covering the iron frame with birch bark was hopeless in this country—where, as they discovered too late, there were no birches—hunters went out to kill enough elk to make an elkskin covering. Several men began digging a hole for another cache, while the white pirogue was hauled out of the water and hidden. The other boats were brought as near the falls as possible, to shorten the portage. Two men were nearly killed when one capsized. Any spare time was spent making moccasins for the long land journey across the Rockies, which now could not be far ahead.

When Clark came back on June 20, after finding a "tolerable good road" and marking it out with stakes and flags, all hands set to work to get the canoes and baggage across. They had hardly started when an axle-tree broke and had to be repaired with willow—bad wood but all they could get. Since horses had long since disappeared, the wagons moved by man power only, until some genius thought of rigging sails on them and "Saleing on dry land in everry Sence of the word," before a wind which was as good as "4 men halling at the chord with a harness."

After the weary labor of portaging was nearly completed, a violent storm threatened new disaster. The party with the wagons were working nearly naked in blinding June heat when a violent hailstorm suddenly descended, just as the axle-tree broke. One of the falling lumps of ice weighed three ounces and was seven inches in diameter. Being mostly without hats, largely without clothing, and entirely without shelter on the bare prairie, the men suffered severely during the half hour the ice storm beat upon them. One man was knocked down three times, others were bleeding before they finally reached safety—when the storm cleared. The imperturbable Lewis, who may have been moody at times but who always rose gaily to emergencies, seized this as a unique opportunity for a cold drink. He made a bowl of punch with the largest hailstone.

He would have been a little less calm had he known that Clark was having his one narrow escape of the expedition. With Sacagawea, Charbonneau, York, and the baby, he had gone out to complete his topographical notes, which necessitated keeping to the low ground along the river. Forced to seek shelter by the sudden hailstorm, they found a deep and dry ravine with shelving rocks, which offered apparent safety. None of them realized the speed with which the storm would fill the dry gully above them with water, until a "roling torrent with irrisistable force driving rocks mud and everything before it" was almost on them. Charbonneau clambered up the rocks, dragging Sacagawea, with her baby in her arms, while Clark, with a rifle and shot pouch in his left hand, gave an occasional boost. Suddenly Charbonneau completely lost control of himself, as he so often did at critical moments, and stood perfectly motionless.

The water had already risen to Clark's waist before he could get the terrified fellow moving again and the others safely up the steep bank. Then it came gurgling after him nearly as fast as he could climb. When they had finally scrambled to the top, they looked back to see fifteen feet of water "with a current tremendious to behold" rushing through their late shelter. An instant more and all would have been swept into the Missouri. York, who had gone off to hunt buffalo just before the storm, came dashing back to find his master.

Charbonneau lost his rifle, the baby all his spare clothing, Clark his compass (the only large one the expedition had), and an umbrella which, for some strange reason, he had brought along. Both the baby and its convalescent mother were soaking wet and very cold. Clark hurried them at a dead run back to camp, where he found the portaging party "sorely mawled with the hail."

As a Kentuckian, he had no doubt at all about the next step. York had a canteen with him. Clark "gave the party a dram to console them in some measure for their general defeat." Next day, a search party brought in the all-important compass, which they had fished out of the river mud. They found the ravine filled with rocks, washed down by the torrent, huge enough to have crushed Clark's whole party to death.

Lewis had the rust removed from his iron boat frame, oiled the parts, and put them together, finding to his dismay that the local "drift pine" would not provide the tar on which he had relied to waterproof the elkskin he was using instead of birch bark. He substituted a mixture of charcoal, beeswax, and buffalo tallow, and when the elkskins gave out used buffalo hide. Bark was fitted for a lining inside and wooden thwarts were put in place.

Too late, Lewis discovered that the leather thongs with which the skins were stitched together did not fill the needle holes, and as the drying skin shrank more and more the holes grew bigger and bigger. His only hope now was in his improvised waterproof coating.

Applying two coats of it, he launched the *Experiment* and saw with premature delight that "she lay like a perfect cork on the water," and was so light that five men could handle her with ease. His exultation and all hope vanished together that evening, when he found his tar substitute was cracking and scaling off. He had made a mistake in having the hair, which might have made the composition stick, removed from the skins. There was no time now to go hunting for a new supply and Lewis regretfully ordered the *Experiment* sunk so that the skins would soften and could be removed. The iron framework was broken down and the *Experiment* was abandoned as hopeless. The disconsolate Lewis sought comfort in a little fishing and caught nothing but a few white chub. It was the final blow.

Minor troubles continued to multiply. Clark had difficulty finding timber for the new dugouts that would have to be made to replace the *Experiment*. Ax-handles were always breaking and—as there was nothing but soft wood to make new ones—they kept on breaking. Four woodchoppers broke thirteen in one day and each time work had to stop while a substitute was roughly whittled down.

Not until July 15 were the dugouts made, loaded, and ready to start. The expedition had taken a full month to cover those sixteen miles around the falls of the Missouri. It had been a month of continued disappointments, but the expedition went on. As his schoolmate at Dr. Everitt's had noted in his boyhood, long before, Captain Lewis was an obstinate and determined man, once his mind was made up.

When the Corps of Discovery launched its little fleet of dugouts on July 15, they soon found out how serious the failure of the iron boat was going to be. The dugouts could not possibly carry her whole cargo, and there was nothing for it but to discard all superfluous equipment. Difficulty arose at once. What was superfluous? Marching infantry soon rid themselves of nonessentials, being all too prone to throw away articles they are going to need badly later on. But the Lewis and Clark Expedition's infantry afloat were reluctant to part with any of their treasures, so long as they could cram the canoes with "bulky articles of but little uce or value," which they would never have dreamed of packing on their backs for the last long mile of a hard day's march. Like American soldiers in all wars, they had probably been gathering up souvenirs. Finally forced to discard useless articles wholesale, they were on their way by ten in the morning—"much to my joy," Lewis observed, "and I beleive that of every individual who compose the party."

To lighten the burden on the boats, as he said, but more likely to indulge his inveterate love of the wilderness, Lewis took two men who were temporarily "invalids" and so of no use at the oars, and with Clark pushed ahead overland. It was one of the rare occasions when both captains left the boats at the same time. Finding Smith's River, they named it for the Secretary of the Navy, and wounded a deer, which ran into the water. Scannon once more covered himself with glory by rushing after it, drowning it, and bringing it safely to the shore for supper. Clark found the river so crooked that it was hard to note the courses on his map.

When Clark left to rejoin the boats, Lewis decided to push on with Drouilliard and his two invalids until he reached the foothills of the Rockies, where he would wait for the boats along shore. But he had made the mistake of forgetting his mosquito net and swarms of insects soon forced him to turn back, promising himself "in my wrath that I never will be guil[t]y of a similar piece of negligence while on this voyage." He had also begun to realize that he would need his instruments. There was consolation in the abundance of yellow, purple, and black currants, and service berries, on which the men feasted while Lewis indulged in an ecstasy of botanical note-taking, garnished with much technical jargon.

By the time Lewis had reached the boats, both commanders were beginning to grow anxious over the complete absence of Indians. They had seen none since leaving the Mandans, though they had found traces of 80 leather tepees, a larger leather lodge, and some 40 smaller lodges, which seemed to have been recently abandoned; but there was still not an Indian to be seen. On July 20, both Lewis with the boats and Clark, traveling overland, saw signal smokes suddenly appearing ahead, clear evidence that Indians of some kind had detected their approach and were spreading the alarm. Suspecting that they might get behind him and follow his trail, Clark left clothing, paper, tape, and linen at intervals, with signs indicating that his party were white men and friends. Either Sacagawea or Drouilliard must have drawn the signs for him, though none of the journals definitely say so. It was the squaw who explained why Clark found places where the Indians had peeled off pine bark. They wanted the soft, sap-filled inner bark for food.

Clark was so eager not to frighten the Indians that he personally reconnoitered for three miles ahead of his little group to make sure none were about, before he would let the men with him begin a little essential pot-hunting. When he was sure that there were no Indians near enough to be frightened, the rifles began to pop. Meantime Lewis, to show that the strangers in the canoes were friendly, had hoisted flags, something no Indian war party would ever do.

The four traveling overland having by this time found the going so rough that it was plain they would not be able to

advance much farther, Clark decided to lay in a meat supply
and rest along shore until Lewis and the boats appeared.
His own feet were "blistered and soar" and the men's were
bruised and cut. Yet as soon as the boats came up, he rejected
Lewis's proposal to change places, and pushed on overland
again next morning. He had, however, so completely worn
out his men that only one was able to go on with him, and
he had to choose new companions.

He reached the next puzzle point on the river, the Three
Forks of the Missouri, within two days, after having very
nearly killed both his men and himself. Charbonneau's ankle
gave out and Joseph Field developed sore feet. Leaving them
to rest, Clark, although ill himself, pushed on for another
twelve miles until he came suddenly—parched with thirst and
badly overheated—to a cool spring. Old soldier that he was,
he knew better than to drink immediately and at first merely
wet his head, hands, and feet. Only after this did he drink
any water, but even so, as he pushed on across a hot and
shadeless valley, he soon realized that his strength was going
and that he had made a bad mistake in taking any water at
all. As best he could, he staggered back to his men, reaching
camp so ill that he could barely taste a little of the fawn
which Field, in spite of his own illness, had managed to kill.

Clark was not too far gone, however, to rescue the clumsy
Charbonneau, who seized this inauspicious moment to fall
into the river. Although he had spent most of his life along
the Missouri, the interpreter had never learned to swim, a
fact which had already nearly cost his life once. Ill and exhausted as he was, Clark plunged into the icy stream and
dragged the squaw man out, just as he was being swept away
by the extremely swift current.

After this, Clark felt himself growing worse. Toward evening, he decided that he was so ill he would have to camp on
the spot and try to join Lewis next day. With a high fever,
frequent chills, and "constant aking pains in all his mustles,"

the sick man took to his bed, pausing only to help kill two grizzlies.

In the morning, notwithstanding his pain, he left a note for Lewis at the Three Forks and advanced up the Middle Fork (now Madison's River) for eight miles without finding Indian sign. Returning to the forks he found Lewis, with a badly exhausted party, waiting for him. Lewis had already decided that there would have to be a short halt at the Three Forks, partly to make observations, partly to reconnoiter, and partly to give the worn-out men some rest. The canoes had faced a rapid current all the way, which kept them "in a continual state of their utmost exertion." Oars were useless. The boats had to be poled upstream and the poles they had would not grip the smooth flat stones of the bottom. Lewis got out some gigs he had brought along for spearing fish and solved the problem by attaching them to the ends of the poles. Taking a hand with the poles himself to encourage the men, he won from his sweating command a rather grudging commendation. They thought their captain able to "push a tolerable good pole."

When Clark came back, one look at his physical condition convinced his comrade that they would have to remain in camp for two days at least. Lewis gave him five of Dr. Rush's pills—which the Corps of Discovery had by this time come to regard as a suitable cure for almost anything—and got him to bathe his legs and his bruised and thorn-pierced feet in warm water.

Without being as yet absolutely dangerous, the situation of the Corps of Discovery was rapidly becoming critical. The captains had to make several immediate decisions and the decisions had to be right. When Clark awoke next morning, much improved, he and Lewis went into council while the men began to soak deerskins, preparatory to curing them for clothing.

Lewis and Clark now faced the same problem as at the fork

of Maria's River and the Missouri, only this time there were three forks instead of two between which they must choose. They had to reach the headwaters of the Missouri as soon as possible in order to get across the Rockies before the early snows blocked the passes. As before, it would be fatal to choose the wrong river. Since Clark had already explored the north and middle forks, Lewis hurried a two-man patrol up the southeast fork, while hunters went out to provide meat. The whole expedition was too much concerned with these problems to notice the bits of gold that began to appear here and there in the river sands, as they entered the rich Montana goldfields.

When the patrol came back, there was not really much doubt which way to go. It was reasonably clear that neither the southeast nor the middle fork could lead them very near the Columbia's headwaters, whereas the north fork seemed to lead in about the right direction. When the expedition had halted for its midday dinner on July 22, Sacagawea had suddenly begun to recognize the country through which they were passing. This, she said, was the very river on which her band of Shoshones lived, and the Three Forks were no great distance ahead. As they soon reached the Three Forks, they knew that she was right and that they were in Shoshone country at last. Sacagawea also told them that the upper reaches of the river would be much like what they saw, without waterfalls; and she identified a creek to which her tribe came to collect white earth for paint. All began "to console themselves with the anticipation of shortly seeing the head of the missouri yet unknown to the civilized world." It was one of the few occasions when Sacagawea was able to give accurate geographical information.

A third problem was horses. Clark had seen one "elagant horse," fat and in good condition, but had failed to catch him. He had also seen a horse track, four or five days old, going upstream. That was all, but it proved that Shoshone

Indians with horses must be somewhere about: "we begin to feel considerable anxiety with rispect to the Snake [i.e., Shoshone] Indians," Lewis noted in his journal; "if we do not find them or some other nation who have horses I fear the successfull issue of our voyage will be very doubtfull."

Worse still, the explorers were "without any information with rispect to the country not knowing how far these mountains continue, or wher to direct our course to pass them to advantage or intersept a navigable branch of the Columbia, or even were we on such an one the probability is that we should not find any timber within these mountains large enough for canoes."

This note in Lewis's journal—it is the entry for July 27, 1805—ought to end the legend that the Shoshone squaw "guided Lewis and Clark across the Continent." Sacagawea was an admirable person—brave, patient, faithful, hard-working, uncomplaining—but geography was not her strong point. Five days before, she had recognized the country as her own, yet the expedition was already, for all practical purposes, lost. Although in her own tribal territory, Sacagawea could not tell them anything they really needed to know. She had an Indian child's knowledge of the country around the forks and above them, but any larger geographical question was completely beyond her. She could not tell which fork to take, how to find a pass to the Columbia, or even where to look for canoe timber.

She did, however, identify their camp site at the forks as the very place where her band had been camped on the day in 1800 when the Minnetarees captured her. As well as she could, Sacagawea told the story. When the hostile war party came in sight, the Shoshones fled to hide in the woods, three miles up Jefferson's River. It was useless. The Minnetarees found them and attacked, killing four warriors, four squaws, and some boys. All the other women and four boys were captured. As he watched the busy, cheerful Indian girl, apparently quite unmoved by the tale of terror that she told, the philosophic and moody Lewis (who did not share Clark's amused interest in the squaw and her baby) wrote: "I cannot discover that she shews any immotion of sorrow in recollecting this event, or of joy in being again restored to her native country; if she has enough to eat and a few trinkets to wear I beleive she would be perfectly content anywhere." The impassivity of the Indian deceived him. When emotion became too much for her, Sacagawea was demonstrative enough, a few days later.

Before setting out from the Three Forks, Lewis and Clark paused to name them. Both leaders "corrisponded in opinion with rispect to the impropriety of calling either of these streams the Missouri." They called the southeast fork Gallatin's River, after the Secretary of the Treasury; the middle fork, Madison's River, after the Secretary of State; and the north fork, up which they were going, Jefferson's River, "in honor of that illustrious personage" who was "the author of our enterprize."

Many—probably most—of the geographical names which Lewis and Clark so freely showered on streams and islands as they passed have been forgotten, often because they were so small that they could not be identified by later travelers. The Three Forks, however, were too clearly marked to be forgotten, and the three statesmen for whom they were named were too eminent to be ignored. Jefferson's, Madison's, and Gallatin's Rivers they remain. Among others, Maria's River and Judith's River have retained their names, partly because they were large streams, easily identifiable, partly because their names had that romantic touch which the American so dearly loves.

The names given to the next forks have met a sadder fate. One tributary of Jefferson's River was named Wisdom River, the other Philanthropy River, "in commemoration of two of those cardinal virtues, which have so eminently marked that deservedly selibrated character through life," as the admiring Lewis duly noted. Posterity, alas, transformed Wisdom River into the Big Hole and Philanthropy into Stinking Water.

When the expedition moved again, on July 30, Clark, though now much better, stayed with the boats, while Lewis, taking Charbonneau and Sacagawea together with two "invalid" soldiers, struck out across the river bend. Here, on the spot where the Minnetarees had run down and captured Sacagawea, Lewis's companions got back on board the boats, while Lewis rambled on alone, camping alone that night and meeting the expedition as it came up the river in the morning.

chapter 15: The search for the Shoshones

THE success or failure of the Lewis and Clark Expedition now depended on finding the Shoshone tribe and getting from them a guide—and horses. For more than a year, while the expedition had been traveling up the Missouri, the river itself was the only guide they needed, except at points like the mouth of Maria's River and the Three Forks, where they had to choose between streams of nearly equal size. But, while they could follow the river course without a guide, they could not possibly find their way across the Rockies without an Indian who knew the trails. When they left their boats, as they soon must, horses would be absolutely necessary. Even stripped down to bare essentials, their baggage was far too heavy for the men to carry on their backs across the mountains.

Time was growing short. September was approaching and

they must at all costs get across the Rockies before the early autumn snow came down in their upper reaches, blocking all the passes hopelessly. Within even a few weeks it might be too late—especially if they wasted much more time in a vain search after Indians—for they had no reliable information about the mountains or the passes through them, and only the vaguest idea of the distance between navigable canoe water on the upper Missouri and upper Columbia.

Where were the Shoshones? They had seen enough Indian sign to know that Indians were somewhere about—almost certainly Shoshones, for Sacagawea assured them that this was Shoshone country. It was important to find this particular tribe, for through Sacagawea they would be able to converse easily with them. The smoke signals showed that the Indians had seen the white men. Why, then, did they not appear? Where had they gone? Were they in hiding? If so, did that mean they were hostile, or merely timid?

No one seems to have realized how much afraid the Shoshones were of the armed strangers a few stray Shoshone hunters had seen approaching. The Shoshones were a weak and timid inland tribe, living upon the roof of North America. They knew little of the white men and they had almost none of their priceless goods and weapons. To the East, the savage and well-armed Blackfeet and Minnetarees, whom they called "Pahkees" cut them off from traders and—still worse—usually cut them off also from the abundant meat supplies of the buffalo plains. To the West, the mountain ranges and the steep cañons of the Columbia's upper tributaries cut them off from the trickle of traders' goods and arms from the Pacific coast. To the South, across an endless expanse of mountain and desert, were the Spaniards, with whom it was impossible to trade extensively and who refused to sell arms to the few adventurous Shoshones who braved the dangerous journey.

Armed with only the bow and arrow—there were probably

not half a dozen rifles in the whole tribe—it was difficult for them to kill the fleet antelope and deer of their craggy mountains and they could reach the buffalo hunting grounds at the foot of their mountains only at the risk of their lives. Savage and infinitely better armed, the Blackfeet and Minnetarees lay in wait for them when they ventured out on the plains for buffalo, harrying them back to their crags, or slaughtering them without mercy. Only by taking refuge in the most inaccessible uplands could they escape the occasional war parties which left the great plains and came up into the lower foothills of the Rockies to kill them. It was not worth a war party's time to try to follow them far into the mountains, so little was the plunder, so few the scalps. There was very little food in these bleak hills. The Shoshones had to accept semi-starvation to escape being massacred.

Small wonder, then, that when this forlorn tribe saw a well-armed party advancing up the river, bronzed to the color of Indians and dressed in rough leather, they sought only to disappear. Though the expedition had thus far failed to find the Shoshones, the Indians had detected the white men's presence almost at once, probably because they heard the hunter's rifles. Instantly signal fires rose from the prairies to call Shoshone hunting parties back into their hills, while the expedition wondered at the pillars of smoke.

When Clark had failed to find Indians in July, Lewis had privately decided on "taking a tramp myself in a few days to find these yellow gentlemen if possible"—Indians in those days being frequently described by the whites as "yellow" rather than "red." Toward the end of the month he decided that the time had come and selected Gass and Drouilliard as companions. Then Charbonneau begged to be taken along, and Lewis "indulged" him—a mistake, as he soon found out.

Drouilliard was the only completely healthy man in the group. Lewis himself was recovering from dysentery. Gass had hurt his back falling on the gunwale of a canoe. Charbonneau had a bad leg. In spite of that, starting on August 1, they covered 45 miles in two days, before the pace began to tell. Charbonneau and Gass played out completely. When Lewis tried to push on with Drouilliard alone, the man almost at once had a fall so bad that for fifteen or twenty minutes he had to lie there, unable to walk. As the whole party were now invalids, Lewis decided to return. They reached the boats, which had almost kept up with them, after a two-hour scramble through thorns and prickly pear.

They found the boat party having a hard time of it. The current was so rapid that oars were no use. Even with poles and the tow-rope, the canoes had to be double-manned. Rapids were so bad that their fall was sometimes three feet in the length of a canoe, and to the men who breasted the fierce current, slipping on the stones, they seemed almost perpendicular. "Some places be out in the water where we could Scarsely kick our feet for the rapidity of the current," wrote Sergeant Ordway. Often the men had to grasp the bushes to hold themselves upright as they hauled. Where the river was shallow, the heavy log boats had to be hauled over the rocks. Wet all over from falls in the rushing, icy water, the men were giving out. One had a strained shoulder. Others were suffering from boils. A carbuncle on Clark's ankle had become so large that he could not walk. All their feet were in bad condition.

Clark, however, had discovered that Indians were somewhere close at hand. Before his ankle failed entirely, hobbling ashore, he had found one set of moccasin prints with the unmistakable inturned toe of the redskin. The trail led up a hill from which the camp of the night before was plainly visible. There was no possible doubt now that the Indians knew of their presence and were avoiding them. The evidence of the signal fires was confirmed. August 6 was a day of infuriating minor mishaps. Lewis again went forward on foot until he reached the fork of the Wisdom and Philanthropy Rivers, near which a third small stream further confused matters. Convinced that Philanthropy River was the true course, he left a note to that effect for Clark, and went off himself for a short reconnaissance up Wisdom River.

Unfortunately, Sergeant Gass put Lewis's note on a pole of fresh, green wood. Before Clark arrived, a wandering beaver passed that way and, tempted by the delicious green bark, casually nibbled through the too palatable pole, leaving the all-important message to blow away, while the beaver himself went on about his business.

When Clark arrived, finding nothing to guide him, he turned up the wrong river and was soon in trouble, the stream being so swift and so clogged with bushes as to be almost impassable, though he struggled on determinedly.

Lewis, in the meantime, had crossed over to the true course, Philanthropy River, with Drouilliard hunting some distance on one side of him and Gass on the other, in case Clark should take either one of the two possible wrong streams. After Clark had valiantly forced his way upstream for nine useless miles, Drouilliard found him. On the way back, one of Clark's canoes sank in the rapids and another turned partly over, shipping enough water to wet all the medical supplies that now remained and almost crushing Private Whitehouse, who, jumping out to steady her "when She swang," fell and escaped with a bare two inches of water between him and the heavy dug-out floating over him. Clark's ankle was growing worse. Game was scarce. Food reserves were dwindling. Shannon, out hunting, got lost again—that meant someone would have to go out and try to find him. Worst of all, there was no more Indian sign.

Whipped by a high wind, soaked in rain, the disconsolate Corps of Discovery sought its blankets, cursing—though not before Captain Clark, writhing with the pain in his ankle, had made careful notes on the exact direction of the wind. Next day they dried out their clothes, repaired the airgun so

that "she shot again as well as she ever did," and dropped off
a canoe, no longer needed as their supplies grew less. This
released extra men to hunt as the game became harder to kill.

Still Shannon did not turn up. After Drouilliard had
failed to find him, Reuben Field tried and also failed. Neither
the bugle nor signal guns brought him in. It was three days
before the expedition's perennially wandering boy appeared
at last. He had first lost the party, then gone up the wrong
river—exactly where Field had been unsuccessfully looking
for him at the wrong time, then back to the forks, and finally
up Philanthropy River, till he at length caught up with the
party. He "looked a good deel worried with his march," but
was extremely well fed, for this time he had remembered to
take plenty of ammunition and had killed three deer.

Though there were still no Indians, Sacagawea was encouraging. She recognized a hill that looked like a beaver's
head and felt sure that the explorers would find the Shoshones, if not in this valley, then certainly in the next one
beyond it. The river was now growing so small that it was
clear the height of land between the Missouri and Columbia
could not be very far distant, and somewhere near that great
divide the Shoshones must be camped. Lewis determined to
make another search for them and not return until he had
found them, even if this meant leaving the boats for a full
month.

Since this quest for an unknown and possibly hostile tribe
in wild and unknown country would be one of the most
dangerous parts of a journey on which peril was everywhere,
he wished to make certain notes, in case he did not return.
Mr. Jefferson's instructions had said: "to your own discretion therefore must be left the degree of danger you may
risk." Lewis was going to take several extra risks. Mr. Jefferson had also directed him "to provide, on the accident of
your death, against anarchy, dispersion & the consequent

danger to your party, and total failure of the enterprise."
Certainly the time had now come to make those provisions.

Next morning he walked on ahead of the boats and sat
down by the bank—alone in the wilderness, as he loved to be
—"to accomplish some wrightings which I conceived from
the nature of my instructions necessary lest any accedent
should befall me on the long and reather hazardous rout I
was now about to take." When the boats came up, he stayed
with them until after breakfast on August 9. Then he,
Drouilliard, Shields, and M'Neal slung their packs with the
determination not to come back till they had found Indians
of some kind—and Indians with horses.

Everyone hoped that they would find them before the
stream grew so small that the boats could go no farther. Already Lewis, as he went on ahead, thought it doubtful
"whether the canoes could get on or not, or if they do it
must be with great labour." Dangerous though his journey
was, Clark good-naturedly envied him, lamenting in his journal: "I Should have taken this trip had I been able to march,
from the rageing fury of a tumer on my anckle musle."

Lewis found Indian sign sooner than anyone had expected.
Early next day (August 10), he stumbled on a plainly marked
Indian trail, leading toward the mountains, which he followed rapidly, past a cliff swarming with rattlesnakes, to another fork in the streams. Here Modern Prairie Creek
branches off from what remains of Jefferson's River (at this
point often called Beaverhead River). Lewis was almost exactly on the 45th parallel and not far from the present site of
Grayling, Montana.

The trail branched with the streams. Sending a man up
each stream, Lewis sat down to write a note advising Clark
not to try either fork but to halt at this point until further
word. After the men came back and reported, he decided to
go up the southwest fork (modern Prairie Creek) and added
word to that effect in his note. This time he took good care

to fasten his note to a "dry willow pole" without any green bark which might offer temptation to passing beavers.

As he pushed up Prairie Creek, he soon found first the horse tracks and then the trail itself vanishing under his feet —as wilderness trails often do, almost before the traveler is aware that they are growing fainter. Along the other stream, he remembered, there had also been hoof-marks, though they looked as if they had been left from early spring. Returning and exploring the southeast fork himself, Lewis decided to follow it, and sent Drouilliard back to leave a second note telling Clark of the change in direction.

This stream looked as if the boats could come up it, after all, and Lewis thought that "if the Columbia furnishes us such another example, a communication across the continent by water will be practicable and safe." There would probably, he guessed, be some very swift water on the upper Columbia since it was by this time clear that it must fall from the Rockies to sea level in a much shorter distance than the Missouri.

To Lewis's disgust this second trail also vanished, but as he could now see a pass ahead, he abandoned the trail, sent Drouilliard and Shields out as flankers on each side, and gave orders that the first man who stumbled on anything resembling a trail should silently lift his hat above the underbrush on the muzzle of his rifle. There must be no shouting and no signal shots to alarm the Indians.

They moved ahead in this way, with the least possible noise, for about five miles. Still they saw nothing. Then, suddenly, Lewis gasped. An Indian was approaching on horseback about two miles ahead. Studying the unconscious warrior through his telescope, he saw that the man's dress was different from any Indian costume yet seen. He must therefore belong to a new tribe, which could only be the long-sought Shoshones. Better still, he was riding an "eligant" horse.

The problem was to avoid scaring this wandering scout

away, before they could obtain through him a "friendly introduction" to his tribe. It would be difficult, since Sacagawea, their only Shoshone interpreter, was far behind with the boats; but Drouilliard knew the sign language. The most important thing was to identify themselves as white men. That would not be easy, for the wild dress of the Corps of Discovery and their bronzed faces, baked by months of intense sun, made it hard to see what they were. Even to themselves, they looked like Indians.

When still about a mile distant, the Indian horseman saw the strangers for the first time and halted. Lewis, also halting, pulled a blanket hastily out of his pack and made the friendship sign used by all the western Indians, which he had been careful to learn. Holding the blanket by two corners, he waved it in the air higher than his head, then brought it down to earth, as if spreading it for a guest. This sign he repeated three times.

His eager signals had no effect whatever. The Indian sat still on his horse and watched suspiciously. At this moment, Drouilliard and Shields, advancing on each flank, emerged from the underbrush where the Indian could see them. From where the lone warrior sat, Lewis's movements looked like an attempt to hold his attention with signs of friendship in front while other men slipped around him on each side.

Lewis watched in silent despair. He could see what was happening; he could almost read the distant redskin's mind; but his two men were so far away that they could not hear his voice and he dared not signal them. Drouilliard and Shields either did not see the Indian or else did not realize they were alarming him.

Hastily snatching some beads, a looking glass, and some trinkets out of the pack, Lewis left his rifle and shot-pouch with M'Neal and went forward, alone, holding up the gifts and showing himself ostentatiously unarmed. At 200 paces, the Indian turned his horse and began to move off slowly, while Lewis shouted after him what he believed to be the Shoshone word for "white man"—doubtless carefully rehearsed with Sacagawea—"tab-ba-bone!"

It was the worst thing he could have done. He was trying to say the word which in modern Shoshone is "tai-va-vone." It does not mean "white man" at all, but "stranger, alien, outsider." He must have tried to learn the word from the Shoshone squaw with her stupid husband as interpreter. Either Sacagawea did not understand him or she did not know the right word. She had been only a child when she was captured and had probably never seen a white man at the time or felt the need of a word for "white man." Perhaps Charbonneau bungled the translation as he bungled so many other things.

At any rate, the Shoshone warrior could see well enough that these armed men, who indulged in such extraordinary antics, were strangers, aliens, intruders in Shoshone country. The fact that they shouted to him that they were strangers was not reassuring. In that wild country, every stranger was an enemy.

The Indian kept a wary eye on Drouilliard and Shields, both of whom, meantime, were still plodding stupidly ahead, "neither of them haveing segacity enough to recollect the impropriety of advancing when they saw me thus in parley with the Indian." In desperation, Lewis now risked a signal to halt. Drouilliard obeyed; Shields failed even to see the signal.

Doubtfully, the Indian paused again and made as if to wait for Lewis, who went slowly forward once more for another 50 paces, while the warrior was nervously eying Shields, who, rifle in hand, was still foolishly moving ahead, so that he would soon be in the warrior's rear. From the red horseman's point of view, it looked more than ever like a trap.

Lewis held up the trinkets, continuing his bellows of "Tab-ba-bone!" and pulling up the sleeves of his leather hunting shirt to show the white skin which the sun had not bronzed. The Shoshone watched in growing astonishment. This, to be sure, was not the ordinary behavior of hostile Indians; but neither was it the behavior of any sensible human being the puzzled warrior had ever seen in all his life. It must be some new and devilish trick of the wicked Blackfeet.

The warrior watched Lewis's advance until he was within 100 paces, while the blockhead Shields continued his stolid advance. At 100 paces, the Indian decided the strangers were too close, no matter who they were or what they yelled, whirled his horse, lashed with his whip, and was gone into the willow brush behind him.

It was a heart-breaking moment. For months they had, with increasing anxiety, been looking for Indians and horses. Lewis had found both, and at the last moment Shields's stupidity had driven off the first Indian they saw, who would certainly alarm the rest.

"I now felt quite as much mortification and disappointment as I had pleasure and expectation at the first sight of this indian," wrote Lewis in his diary that night. "I fe[l]t soarly chargrined at the conduct of the men particularly Sheilds to whom I principally attributed this failure in obtaining an introduction to the natives." However much "chargrin" Lewis may have felt, he was himself partly to blame for not having arranged signals between himself and his men, for not having learned a little more Shoshone—and for not having learned it better.

Legends of this meeting lingered long among the mountain Indians and one of them was told some thirty years later to the American traveler, T. J. Farnham. According to this tale, the Shoshone whom Lewis first saw was a mounted scout, moving from place to place outside the camp. At first, on seeing "men with faces as pale as ashes, who were makers of thunder, lightning," he was too astonished to do anything but stare at them. Then he fled to give the alarm to the tribe,

who skeptically replied that "all men were red, and therefore he could not have seen men as pale as ashes." Eventually,
he led them to the spot where they met Lewis, and the scout's
reputation for veracity was re-established.

The story had been much embroidered before it reached
Farnham. Lewis's face was not "pale as ashes"—that was one
of his principal worries. Though he had indeed exhibited
the white skin of his arm, the Indian could hardly see it. The
white men did not at this time display the thunder and lightning of their firearms. There is, however, no doubt, from
Lewis's own account, that a party of warriors did come out
toward the spot soon after, precisely as the Indian account
says.

Calling in his flankers, Lewis in his exasperation and disappointment "could not forbare abraiding them a little for
their want of attention and imprudence on this occasion."
He then found that they had added to their offenses by failing to bring his "spye-glass," which he had dropped with the
blanket when he went forward. Having recovered this irreplaceable article, the disgruntled captain decided to follow
the trail of the retreating Shoshone warrior in the hope that
it would lead to a camp of some kind. After a short distance,
it turned toward the hills about three miles away. The
warrior would certainly give the alarm as soon as he reached
camp, the tribe would be on the alert, and might simply disappear unless Lewis could reassure them quickly.

Fearing to frighten the Indians still more if he followed
the trail too closely, Lewis kindled a fire on an elevation
where it could be seen from all directions and breakfasted
at leisure. No Blackfeet war party would ever do that. He
then prepared an array of gifts—paint, beads, awls for making moccasins, and a looking glass. These he attached to a
pole and left by his fire, hoping that any Indians who might
come out to circle around behind him and scout along his
trail would thus be convinced that this was not an Indian

war party but a friendly group of white men. Only white men would carry such goods and only friends would scatter them about.

A sudden shower having in the meantime obscured the trail, the disconsolate quartet found it difficult to follow when they set out again, but were delighted to find the tracks of eight or ten other horses. To reassure the Indians further, as he advanced, Lewis broke out a small American flag, which M'Neal carried in plain sight as they proceeded, planting it in the ground at each halt. Still without having made contact with the Indians, they finally reached the headwater of the "Missouri"—or what they chose to regard as such. Even without Indians or horses, it was a triumphant moment. M'Neal, remembering their long struggle up that turbulent river, now little more than a brook, put one foot on each bank and "thanked his god that he had lived to bestride the mighty & heretofore deemed endless Missouri." Lewis took special delight in drinking the clear cool water, not muddy as it had been so long, of the "Missouri" on the very hill which they all supposed was its source. Alas for their enthusiasm! Modern geography regards the stream over which they triumphed as a mere tributary creek.

It was only a short distance now to the top of the hill—the great Continental Divide. Ascending and looking westward from it, Lewis could see ahead "immence ranges of high mountains still to the West of us," but he knew that though he was not on the highest point in North America, he was nevertheless looking down the other side, with waters running into the Pacific. Three-quarters of a mile down the mountain, they had their first sight of a stream flowing into the Pacific, a "handsome bold runing Creek of cold Clear water," where Lewis exultantly "first tasted the water of the great Columbia river"—actually the waters of its tributary, the Lemhi.

Heedless of events to come, Lewis plunged on down the

slope in quest of Shoshones. He saw none all that day, but on August 13 he caught a glimpse of two squaws, a man, and a dog about a mile away. He knew that they had seen him, for two of them immediately sat down, as if to await his arrival. Displaying his flag and leaving his pack and rifle behind, Lewis went forward alone. The women soon fled, and when he was within 100 yards the man followed them, in spite of renewed shouts of "Tab-ba-bone!" Indian dogs came so close that Lewis tried to catch them in order to tie beads and trinkets to their necks, hoping that this would convince their owners of his peaceful intentions. But even Shoshone dogs were so suspicious that he could not get near enough.

It was a maddening situation. Somewhere near them was a Shoshone camp—the presence of the squaws showed that. He had seen the long-sought Indians twice but he had totally failed even to speak with them. There was nothing for it but to follow the fugitives along a well-trodden path. The well-marked trail was their only encouragement. It showed that the camp that must be somewhere near was a large one, not easy to move or conceal. One more mile. Then suddenly the white men stumbled on three other squaws, the approach of each group having been masked from the other by a series of small, steep ravines. A young squaw ran away. An old woman with a little girl of about twelve remained. As Lewis walked slowly up to them, both sat down and lowered their heads for the death stroke.

Lewis took the old woman by the hand, repeating "tab-ba-bone," and again stripping up his sleeves to show that he was a white man. Thus reassured, the two "appeared instantly reconciled." Whatever this remarkable creature might be— he said he was a stranger, but anyone could see that—he did not act in the least like a hostile warrior. Even the appearance of Drouilliard, M'Neal, and Shields did not startle the women, especially as Lewis was by this time loading them with beads, moccasin awls, pewter mirrors, paint. Lewis told Drouilliard to tell the old woman in sign language to call back the young squaw who had run away. Summoned by the old squaw, the fugitive soon returned, out of breath from running; and when she too had received some trinkets, Lewis painted all their cheeks with vermilion, emblematic of peace among the Shoshones, though the eastern tribes used it for war paint.

Drouilliard told them in sign language that the mysterious white strangers wished to be taken to the Shoshone camp, being "anxious to become acquainted with the chiefs and warriors of their nation." After the squaws had guided them two miles, the white men met a war party of 60 warriors, hurrying out to the rescue, armed entirely with bows and arrows, except for three cheap traders' rifles. Alarmed by the scout whom Lewis had first seen, the warriors had come out expecting to meet the Minnetarees, who had defeated them in a fight not long before.

The success of the expedition depended on the next few minutes. This time there must be no blunders.

Leaving his rifle behind, Lewis advanced, carrying his flag, while the squaws and soldiers followed at 50 paces. He met a chief and two warriors, riding ahead as advance guard. The chief spoke first to the squaws, who enthusiastically displayed the presents they had received. Thus reassured—no hostile war party ever went about giving presents to squaws—the leaders, somewhat to his dismay, embraced Lewis "very affectionately in their way." Each Indian threw his left arm over the explorer's shoulder, pressing his greasy cheek, bedaubed with paint, against the white man's, exclaiming, "âh-hi-e, âh-hi-e!" This was the Shoshone equivalent of "I am delighted."

Lewis was delighted, too. The friendliness of the band meant horses, and horses meant that the Corps of Discovery could cross the Rockies. But by the time all the other warriors had come up and greeted them, Lewis and his men were far from delighted with the demands of Shoshone etiquette:

"we wer all carressed and besmeared with their grease and paint till I was heartily tired of the national hug." But as Indian good will was essential, there was nothing to do but submit, with a cordial air. After all, as Biddle drily remarks, "the motive was much more agreeable than the manner."

Lewis now had a pipe lit and offered it to the Shoshone braves, who pulled off their moccasins and settled themselves in a circle for a council. Pulling off the moccasins was a sacred act, symbolizing their wish that, if treacherous or insincere, they might ever after go barefoot, "a pretty heavy penalty if they are to march through the plains of their country," Lewis reflected, remembering ruefully the stones and prickly pears through which he had scrambled to find the Shoshones.

After smoking a few pipes, he distributed presents, his beads and vermilion making an especial impression. He told Chief Ca-me-âh-wait, "with his ferce eyes and lank jaws grown meager for the want of food," that he came as a friend, but he would explain who they were, whence they came, and whither they were going after they had reached the Shoshone camp. The sun was very warm. There was no water. The white men would be glad to go to the camp with him. Ca-me-âh-wait made a speech to his warriors, received Lewis's flag as a token of peace, and himself led the way, sending young men ahead to prepare lodges for the white strangers. Exultant, Lewis joined the cavalcade. He had found the Shoshones. He had found horses. He had found the Lemhi Pass.

chapter 16: *Over the*
Great Divide

AT THEIR camp, the Shoshones again pulled off their moccasins, suggesting that their white guests do likewise, and held a formal council to welcome them. Ca-me-âh-wait produced the band's sacred peace pipe, with a bowl of highly polished, semi-transparent stone pointing forward like a cigarette holder, instead of turning upward like an ordinary pipe. After this had made its ceremonial round, Lewis explained in detail the purpose of the expedition. Though his speech was hard for Drouilliard to translate into sign language, Lewis was pleased with results: "it is true that this language is imperfect and liable to error but is much less so than would be expected. the strong parts of the ideas are seldom mistaken."

After the council, the hungry white men, who had had no food at all since the evening before, learned with dismay that there was nothing to eat but berries. The Shoshones shared with their guests the best food they could produce— cakes made of service berries, and choke cherries dried in the sun. After accomplishing the minor miracle of "a hearty meal" on such provender, Lewis went eagerly down to the river to see what prospects there were for travel westward by water. The timber that he found was useless for building more canoes. Though the stream as far as Lewis could see it was navigable enough, the chief told him it became impassable after a short distance. This particular valley offered neither a land nor a water route "to the great lake where the white men lived."

Disappointing though this news might be, Lewis was cheered by the number and excellence of the horses which he saw grazing everywhere, some of them good enough to "make a figure on the South side of the James River"—a Virginian's ultimate praise of horseflesh. Some, with Spanish brands, the Indians blandly explained they had "obtained" from Spaniards far to the South. In those days stolen Spanish horses could be found even on the Saskatchewan.

Knowing that Clark could hardly have reached the rendezvous at the forks of Jefferson's River as yet, Lewis took his time in dealing with the Shoshones. At first they were entirely unwilling to go down the river to meet Clark with their horses. It was dangerous. The Pahkees might be lying in wait. But when they learned that the approaching canoes brought with them a strange being who was neither white nor red but black—all over—their reluctance vanished. To behold such a marvel, they were willing to venture down from the safety of the hills.

As one difficulty vanished, another appeared. Rumors began to circulate that this was all a trap; the white strangers were trying to lure them into an ambush. Lewis reminded them that in the white men's canoes were food and merchandise; and then—knowing the characteristic Indian pride in personal courage—he added that some at least of the Shoshone warriors ought to be brave enough to go and see for themselves. The adroit captain had said exactly the right thing at the right moment. Ca-me-âh-wait instantly replied that "he was not affraid to die."

"I soon found," Lewis gleefully noted in his journal, "that I had touched him on the right string; to doubt the bravery of a savage is at once to put him on his metal." Mounting his horse, the chief made a speech to his warriors, exhorting all who were not afraid, to mount and follow him. Several warriors joined Ca-me-âh-wait and smoked a pipe with Lewis —a ceremony too important to be omitted. Then, amid wails from the old women, imploring the Great Spirit to protect their warriors, Lewis hastily got the little group started before they had time to change their minds. Example was contagious. Ten or twelve more warriors soon came galloping after them. Then the whole village changed its mind and began trailing along behind. The mercurial mood of the volatile redskin had reversed itself, as usual. Indians, as Lewis observed, "never act but from the impulse of the moment. they were now very cheerfull and gay, and two hours ago they looked as sirly as so many imps of satturn."

The trouble was that the Shoshones were likely to change their minds again, so that the trip to meet Clark called for constant diplomacy. Well aware that if they could get enough meat, the hungry Indians would be his enthusiastic friends, he sent Drouilliard hunting and in the meantime supplied the Shoshones with a little tobacco. When Drouilliard failed to bring in game, Lewis's last pound of flour had to be stirred in a little boiling water and divided between four white men and two Indians. When Drouilliard and Shields went out to hunt next day, the Shoshones insisted on sending out two "parties of discovery" to make sure they were really hunting and not leading them into a trap. In spite of the handicap of this uninvited audience, Drouilliard finally succeeded.

Toiling along on foot behind the hunters—he had decided it was better to walk than share a stirrupless, bareback horse with a greasy and odorous Indian—Lewis felt his heart sink as he saw a Shoshone scout whipping his horse back toward him. The man had news of some kind—so much was clear. It would be the last straw if, by disastrous coincidence, a war

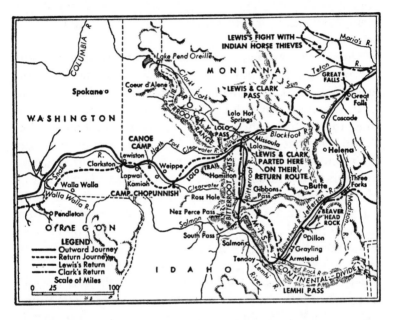

party of Minnetarees really had chosen this crucial moment for a raid. After that, it would never be possible to persuade the Shoshones that it was all coincidence. They would scatter to the hills with their horses and everything would be lost.

He heard the scout shout something in Shoshone, then saw every Indian whip up his horse and dash on ahead. Something had certainly happened—but what? He could only guess, since in Drouilliard's absence he had no way of communicating even in sign language. After he had trudged an anxious mile, he found that all the excitement meant only that Drouilliard had killed a deer. As the hunter, after cleaning the carcass, threw away the offal the half-starved Indians pounced upon it, "tumbling over each other like a parcel of famished dogs each seizing and tearing away a part of the intestens." When Drouilliard killed a second, the Indians ate even the soft part of the hoofs; and before Lewis could give them the venison of a third, he found that all the offal had been eaten already.

Though "they all appeared now to have filled themselves and were in a good humour," the changeable moods of the redskins soon asserted themselves once more. Taking fright again—for no discoverable reason except that they were now emerging from the shelter of the hills—the Shoshones began to slip away one by one. When Lewis was within two miles of the stream, only a small party of 28 men and three squaws were left. Even these became suspicious when they found no white men waiting for them. To quiet their fears, Lewis handed his rifle to Ca-me-âh-wait, telling him to defend himself with that, if enemies should appear, while the other three white men handed over their rifles to other Shoshone warriors. Lewis then sent Drouilliard and an Indian to get the notes that he himself had left for Clark at the forks, which he showed to the Indians, explaining mendaciously that these were messages sent ahead by the approaching white men in the canoes, to announce their early arrival.

It was only by a lucky accident that the messages were still where Lewis had left them. Clark, though out of sight and hearing, was now so close that he had actually seen the forks from a distant hill, and two of his hunters had already been at the forks only a few hours before Drouilliard reached there—without seeing the notes. Though Clark's camp that night was only four miles distant from Lewis's by land, it was ten miles distant traveling with the canoes along the winding river. The question was whether Lewis could persuade the

Indians to stand by with their horses until Clark could arrive.

Unable to read, the Shoshones were satisfied for the moment by seeing the letters. They were white man's magic of some kind. White and red camped together, most of the Indians sleeping in the underbrush, expecting an attack. Lewis, who had no possible way of knowing just where Clark was, spent the night gloomily reflecting that the Indians would certainly disperse in the morning. Nothing he could now do would hold them for more than a few hours after sunrise.

If they decided to go back into the hills, Lewis knew that "we should be disappointed in obtaining horses, which would vastly retard and increase the labour of our voyage and I feared might so discourage the men as to defeat the expedition altogether. my mind was in reallity quite as gloomy all this evening as the most affrighted indian but I affected cheerfullness to keep the Indians so who were about me. we finally laid down and the Chief placed himself by the side of my musquetoe bier. I slept but little as might be well expected, my mind dwelling on the state of the expedition which I have ever held in equal estimation with my own existence, and the fait of which appeared at this moment to depend in a great measure upon the caprice of a few savages who are ever as fickle as the wind."

Rising early, he started Drouilliard down the river to meet Clark, accompanied by one Shoshone warrior who, bribed with a knife and some beads, had plucked up enough courage to make the journey. Drouilliard carried a note imploring Clark to hurry.

It was a needless precaution, for two hours later all Lewis's troubles solved themselves. One Indian, bolder than the rest, had wandered off alone. He now came rushing back, bursting with the news "that the whitemen were coming, that he had seen them just below." The Lewis and Clark Expedition was saved! The only thing to mar Lewis's joy was the regrettable fact that, in their boundless enthusiasm, the Shoshones insisted on embracing him all over again. Soon afterward, Clark, Charbonneau, and Sacagawea came riding up on Shoshone horses. At noon the canoes arrived, their crews wellnigh exhausted. No matter what dangers might lie ahead, the Corps of Discovery knew now that it could get horses and move forward. It was the 17th of August, only eight days since Lewis had left the party. In that short period, he had ensured the success of the expedition that had been his dream since 1792.

Clark had had a hard struggle through swift water so icy that the men's legs ached as they waded, dragging the canoes behind them and occasionally pausing to smash through beaver dams. It was becoming difficult in these cold uplands even to find firewood, though underbrush was thick beside the river; and the only sign of Lewis was four deerskins, found one day hanging beside the bank. There had been a disagreeable incident on August 14, when Charbonneau had given Sacagawea a beating and been severely reprimanded by Clark.

Three days later, apparently on good terms again, Clark, Charbonneau, and Sacagawea set out afoot in the early morning. They had no idea that Lewis and the Indians were near, since the first Shoshone who had seen Clark's canoes in the distance had rushed back to the tribe without hailing them. When Clark had gone about a mile on the morning of August 17, he suddenly saw Sacagawea, 100 yards ahead, begin to dance with every sign of joy. Whirling about, she signed to Clark and pointed to several mounted Indians approaching, at the same time sucking her fingers vigorously. It was sign language: "My native tribe, the people among whom I was suckled. Shoshones!" As the group came closer, Clark recognized Drouilliard, at first indistinguishable from the Indians in his leather clothing. If Drouilliard was with the Indians, Lewis must have succeeded in finding them—and here were horses! The Indians sang delightedly as they rode toward Clark.

The men, tugging their canoes through the chill water that poured down from Rocky Mountain snows, could see nothing whatever through the underbrush on the banks. Then, suddenly, they heard invisible Indians singing not far ahead. This was, of course, the song of the first Shoshones who met Clark. Something was certainly happening. The song could only come from Indians. Had Captain Lewis found them? Or Captain Clark? Were there horses? There was nothing for it but to stay with the boats and get them forward as fast as possible. Then several Shoshones rode through the underbrush and down to the bank with the news that Lewis was just ahead. There must have been a good deal of frantic amateur sign language. After that, there was a perpetual coming and going of horsemen along the river bank, and a flow of orders from the commanders.

"they take us round the neck and Sweze us in token of friendship as they have a practice in Stead of Shakeing hands," wrote Sergeant Ordway dolefully, for the Corps of Discovery never became wholly reconciled to the Shoshone national greeting.

As Sacagawea approached the Shoshones who had come with Lewis, a squaw rushed suddenly out of the throng of curious women and embraced her. She had been one of the young girls whom the Minnetarees had captured. She had escaped, had made her own way back alone, across the plains to her tribe in the Rockies, never dreaming that she would ever see her fellow-captive again. By extraordinary good luck, Lewis and Clark had chanced upon the identical band of Shoshones from whom Sacagawea had been kidnaped. Coincidence would soon go even further, but of that as yet they suspected nothing. While Clark went on, Sacagawea lingered among the squaws.

Received ceremonially by Lewis and Ca-me-âh-wait, Clark

was formally seated upon a white robe. Into his red hair, Ca-me-âh-wait tied six small shells from the Pacific coast, ornaments much valued among the Shoshones. Whites and reds took off their moccasins and the pipe of peace went round again. Having by this time had quite enough of the sign language, Lewis sent at once for three interpreters—Sacagawea to translate from Shoshone into Minnetaree; Charbonneau to translate from Minnetaree into French; Labuiche to translate at last into English for the captains. It was a very bad way to manage translation, but it was the only way there was.

Sacagawea sat down in the council (where normally no woman should appear) and began to translate. Then she sprang up in astonishment. It was, unbelievably, in real life, a "recognition scene" from Greek tragedy. Fact had once again produced one of those incredible, stagy realities that self-respecting fiction abandoned long ago as too improbable. Ca-me-âh-wait, the chief, was Sacagawea's long-lost brother. As Aristotle remarks, it is probable that improbable things will occur.

Running to the chief and throwing her blanket about him, Sacagawea embraced him, weeping profusely. The outward emotional indifference of the Indian, on which Lewis had commented only a few days before, had broken down at last. Even Ca-me-âh-wait forgot the impassivity proper to a chief and warrior sufficiently to be "himself moved, though not in the same degree." After all, a squaw is only a squaw, no matter whose long-lost sister she may be.

This startling reunion broke up the council, though only for a little while. The brother and sister conversed briefly. Ca-me-âh-wait was careful not to let Sacagawea know till after the council that all the rest of their family were now dead, except one other brother and the son of her eldest sister. Sacagawea went back to her place to interpret, occasionally

delaying the council by bursting into tears. It was all a most
un-Indian-like proceeding.

There was one complication in this romantic reunion.
Shoshones often betrothed their daughters before puberty.
When the girls reached the age of thirteen or fourteen, they
were sent around to the lodges of their fiancés, who then
became their husbands. Sacagawea had been thus betrothed
—before her capture and before her sale (or marriage) to
Charbonneau—to a warrior twice her age, now living with
the band, who soon claimed her as his wife. Having two wives
already, however, he gave up his claims when he found that
she had already borne a child to Charbonneau. He did not,
he said, want her after that.

When the canoes came up, the men unloaded and went
into camp on a smooth level bottom near the stream, covered
with green grass. Here they set up a canopy made from one
of the sails, and struck willow boughs in the ground to shade
the visiting chiefs and warriors. It was the immemorial setting for a council in the wilderness. Here, at four that afternoon, the captains in their turn received the Shoshones and
again counciled with them.

The explorers put more than usual eloquence into their
harangue to the Shoshones. Thus far they had made a good
impression on the tribe, which it was vital to maintain. Horses
they must have, and at once. Their main talking-point now
was American trade, which was even more vital to this isolated mountain tribe than to the Missouri Indians. If white
traders came in the wake of the explorers, the Shoshones
would at last be able to get white man's goods, especially the
rifles which would enable them to kill abundant game, thus
ending the constant menace of starvation, and would also
enable them to resist the hostile Blackfeet and hold their
own on the buffalo plains, with their illimitable supply of
meat. Already the Indians were looking longingly at the

white men's rifles, of which the expedition, with its westward journey still incomplete, had absolutely none to spare.

Trade with the Americans would be possible only when the explorers had completed their journey to the Pacific coast and back, Lewis and Clark told the gravely listening Shoshones, haltingly and clumsily through their three interpreters. Therefore: "it was mutually advantageous to them as well as to ourselves that they should render us such aids as they had it in their power to furnish." The white men "did not ask either their horses or their services without giving a satisfactory compensation in return." The more help they gave, the sooner the traders would come and the sooner the Shoshones could get rifles.

Ca-me-âh-wait, in reply, was sorry they could not get firearms at once, but "they could live as they had done heretofore untill we brought them as we had promised." His band did not have enough horses to carry all the baggage, but he would go back over the pass himself and bring back more.

Knowing that "to keep indians in a good humour you must not fatigue them with too much business at one time," Lewis was careful to end the council quickly and display the wonders of the white man and the white man's food. The explorers gave the chief a medal with Mr. Jefferson's portrait, a uniform coat, a shirt, scarlet leggings, and tobacco, while his subordinate chiefs and two young men "much rispected among them" received old medals with George Washington's portrait. Then there was a general distribution of smaller presents and a feast of "lyed corn." York's color, the airgun, and the sagacity of the dog Scannon divided among them the admiration of the astonished tribe.

The Shoshones' description of the country ahead, Clark thought, "if true is alarming," and as he looked at the mountain ranges towering beyond, its accuracy was all too evident. "The account they gave us was verry unfavourable, that the River abounded in emence falls, one perticularly much higher than the falls of the Missouri & at the place the mountains Closed so Close that it was impracticable to pass, & that the ridge Continued on each Side of perpendicular Clifts impenetrable, and that no Deer Elk or any game was to be found in that Countrey."

The two commanders decided that Clark should go ahead to the Shoshone camp, taking with him Charbonneau, Sacagawea, and eleven men. At the camp he would drop off Charbonneau and Sacagawea to hasten the return of Indians with horses. Clark would then himself push on to the Columbia with Gass, Colter, and a few others and see whether he could find timber to build canoes and water to float them. Meantime, Lewis would buy horses, cache the spare baggage and the old canoes and then follow Clark. The men, heartily sick of river travel, were elated at the prospect of getting horses at last.

Of the three animals they were able to buy immediately, Clark took two, so that his men would not have to pack their own baggage over the rough mountain trails ahead. Lewis would need the other to carry meat to camp. As two minor chiefs seemed disgruntled because they had received less than Ca-me-âh-wait, whose uniform coat they greatly admired, Clark gave them two of his own old coats, while Lewis promised further gifts if they helped him over the mountains.

Next day, when Clark set out, Lewis began work. It was August 18, his birthday, which led him to melancholy musings:

"This day I completed my thirty first year, and conceived that I had in all human probability now existed about half the period which I am to remain in this Sublunary world. I reflected that I had as yet done but little, very little, indeed, to further the hapiness of the human race, or to advance the information of the succeeding generation. I viewed with regret the many hours I have spent in indolence, and now soarly feel the want of that information which those hours would have given me had they been judiciously expended. but since they are past and cannot be recalled, I dash from me the gloomy thought, and resolved in future, to redouble my exertions and at least indeavour to promote those two primary objects of human existence, by giving them the aid of that portion of talents which nature and fortune have bestoed on me; or in future, to live *for mankind,* as I have heretofore lived *for myself.*"

If there was a hint here of that melancholia which Mr. Jefferson had sometimes, with misgivings, observed in his secretary, there was also the same note of seriousness and ambition which appears in his family letters. Queer as this passage sounds in an explorer's official journal, there is more in it than the rich, enjoyable gloom of an adolescent's diary.

Untroubled by such musings, Clark, the extrovert, was pushing vigorously down the wild valleys of the Lemhi and Salmon Rivers, on the other side of the Great Divide. Quickly confirming the Indian story of the scarcity of timber, he pushed on until he found an old warrior whom Ca-me-âh-wait had mentioned as knowing the country north of the Columbia. This native geographer had less information than Clark had hoped and what he had was all discouraging. Squatting on the ground, he drew a rough sketch of the river system, depositing handfuls of earth between the streams to show the mountains. Then he lectured: The mountains were rocky, high, snow-covered, "inaccessible to man or horse." The river was swift, filled with sharp rocks, "beat into perfect foam as far as the eye could reach." The country was so bad that no Shoshone ever tried to pass through it. The Nez Percé (Chopunnish) Indians had told him that the river "ran a great way toward the seting sun and finally lost itself in a great lake of water which was illy taisted, and where the white men lived."

Another old man who happened to be visiting from a more

southerly Shoshone band, was equally discouraging in his description of the country to the Southwest, dilating upon "horrors and obstructions scarcely inferior to that just mentioned." The journey was seven days over dangerous mountains followed by ten days of sandy desert, without food of any kind, where the traveler "must suffer if not perish for the want of water." Beyond this was a more fertile country but it was still a great distance to "the great or stinking lake as they call the Ocean." It was a surprisingly accurate description of the American Southwest, but it was of very little use to Clark.

After collecting all the information he could, Clark moved on down what is now called the Salmon River. He soon found that the Indian account of the country had been only too accurate, not only as to the want of timber but in all other respects. Sergeant Gass noted: "The water is so rapid and the bed of the river so rocky, that going by water appeared impracticable; and the mountains so amazingly high, steep and rocky, that it seemed impossible to go along the river by land."

By the 24th, Clark had seen enough. Giving Colter one of his two horses, he sent him back with a letter to Lewis, while he and his men, with one horse for their baggage, followed on foot. As Sergeant Gass's journal says: "We all turned back up the river again, poor and uncomfortable enough, as we had nothing to eat, and there is no game. We proceeded up about 3 miles and supperless went to rest for the night." It was four days before they could find Lewis. Then Sergeant Gass found him in a village, buying horses.

Lewis had remained in the white men's camp at Shoshone Cove long enough to rest his men, make pack-saddles, get his supplies ready for horse transportation, and cache whatever it would not be possible to carry across the mountains. Distrusting the Shoshones in spite of their friendly attitude, he had the cache made secretly about three-quarters of a mile from his camp, while a sentry watched for stray Indians. The men had orders to stop work and pretend to be doing something else if any Indians approached; but none appeared, and the cache was soon finished.

Without any attempt at further concealment, Lewis sank his canoes in the river, filling them with stones to hold them down, so that they were in little danger of being swept away by floods and were safe from prairie fires. Though the Shoshones promised not to disturb them, Lewis relied on normal Indian laziness. There was no telling whether the boats would still be there if they ever came back that way; but diving down, removing the stones, and getting the dugouts afloat again was more work than any Indians were likely to undertake.

The Shoshones remained friendly, though once Drouilliard had to chase a warrior who had snatched his precious rifle and ridden off with it. The thief was so terrified as Drouilliard's horse drew up beside his own that, instead of offering resistance, he knocked the priming out of the rifle to keep Drouilliard from shooting him as he snatched it back. Lewis's main fear was friction with the Indians over their women. He knew well enough that a Shoshone warrior "will for a trifle barter the companion of his bead for a night or longer if he conceives the reward adiquate," though he was glad to see that "they are not so importunate that we should caress their women as the siouxs were." He had no hope at all of keeping his men away from the willing Shoshone squaws: "to prevent this mutual exchange of good officies altogether I know it impossible to effect, particularly on the part of our young men whom some months abstanence have made very polite to those tawney damsels." All he asked of his men was that they should refrain from clandestine affairs, which meant Indian trouble. Inquiry revealed that the Shoshones sometimes suffered from venereal disease and "most usually die with it's effects," but he does not seem to have been alarmed about his men's health.

When Charbonneau, Sacagawea, and Ca-me-âh-wait returned on August 22 with more horses, Lewis held a final council and treated the chief to some of the dried squash they had received from the Mandans and kept for emergencies. It was, Ca-me-âh-wait said, the finest food he had ever tasted—except sugar, of which Sacagawea had given him a small lump. Before starting, the men made a "bush drag" and within two hours had taken 528 fish from the river. To the Shoshones, who had neither hooks, lines, nor nets and had to fish with crude, bone-pointed spears, it seemed like a miraculous draught of fishes. After Lewis had given them most of the catch, he found it much easier to buy horses. A band passing through on its way to the Missouri also contributed horses, in exchange for some of the iron battle-axes that the blacksmiths had made at the Mandan village; as the Shoshones were still using stone ones, the white men's steel was much in demand. One Indian even parted with his mule, an animal much more valuable than a horse on mountain trails.

Lewis's cavalcade now consisted of nine purchased horses, one purchased mule, and two hired horses. He needed 25 pack animals, but as he could not get them, "the Indian women took the ballance of the baggage." The first day's march from Shoshone Cove was only six miles, as Private Wiser developed "a fit of the cholic" and had to be dosed with peppermint and laudanum; and while this was going on, the Indians went into camp for the night, after which there was no moving them. Indians who trailed along, without carrying baggage, had to be invited to go home, as they brought no food of their own and the expedition's supply was barely sufficient.

Early in the afternoon of the second day of their journey toward the Lemhi Pass, the thick-headed Charbonneau casually told Lewis that they would soon meet Indians coming from the other side of the mountain, and that Ca-me-âh-wait's band intended to join them and go east to the buffalo grounds at once. This was the season when the Shoshones joined with their neighbors the Flatheads for defense and in large numbers went on down to the plains in the hope of getting a meat supply before the "Pahkees" could drive them off. The white men would be left in the mountains, on the east side of the Lemhi Pass, with no squaws to carry the half of their baggage for which they had no other transport. Sacagawea had given Charbonneau this warning to pass on to Lewis early in the morning, but with his usual stupidity he had kept the news to himself for half a day. Completely "out of patience with the folly of Charbono who had not sufficient sagacity to see the consequencies," Lewis "could not forbear speaking to him with some degree of asperity on this occasion."

Hastily calling the chiefs together, Lewis reminded them of their promise to see him safely over the divide. They must tell the young men beyond the mountain to remain where they were till Lewis arrived. The two junior chiefs readily agreed but the usually friendly Ca-me-âh-wait was in one of those unpredictable Indian fits of the sulks. Yielding at length, he sent a runner ahead to tell the Indians on the other side of the mountains to stay where they were. Lewis gave the runner a handkerchief, to ensure fidelity, and hastily distributed "billets" entitling the Indians who were helping with the transport to receive merchandise—on the other side of the mountains. As only one deer was killed that day, Lewis gave it all to the Indians and himself went supperless to bed, meditating hungrily on the quantity of wild onions he had seen that day but had not gathered.

As the party reached the spring which Lewis had found earlier and which they all still believed to be the source of the Missouri, "the men drank of the water and consoled themselves with the idea of having at length arrived at this long wished for point." One of the squaws who had been "conducting" two pack horses dropped out of the column and sent the horses forward with "one of her female friends." When Lewis asked what had become of her, Ca-me-âh-wait replied that it was nothing—the squaw had merely stopped to have a baby. An hour later she reappeared, carrying a new Shoshone.

Colter now appeared with Clark's letter, explaining the impossibility of river travel, which meant they would need more horses. Lewis immediately called Ca-me-âh-wait and commenced bargaining, but the chief was evasive. It would be difficult. The Minnetarees had stolen a great many. He hoped the Shoshones could spare some.

Hoping to keep the tribe in a good humor, Lewis "directed the fiddle to be played" and the men to dance—a spectacle which invariably interested all Indians. He also ordered his hunters out next morning, thinking that a meat supply was the best way to keep the Indians faithful. But as he supped on a little parched corn he viewed his men's dance with a jaundiced eye: "I must confess that the state of my own mind at this moment did not well accord with the prevailing mirth as I somewhat feared that the caprice of the indians might suddenly induce them to withhold their horses from us without which my hopes of prosicuting my voyage to advantage was lost."

When Clark reached the Shoshone camp on August 29, everything was ready for departure. A little last-minute trading brought the number of their horses up to 29. On the 30th they parted from their Shoshone hosts, who were eager to be off for buffalo-hunting along the Missouri, but had courteously delayed their departure till the white men were ready. With their guide, whom the men had promptly christened "Old Toby," his four sons, and one other Indian the expedition set off down the Lemhi River as far as what is now Tower Creek. Here they turned in a generally northerly direction over the Bitterroot Mountains, sometimes having to cut a way with axes and struggling with rain, snow, and sleet. All the Indians except Old Toby and one son soon disappeared. By September 4 everything was frozen and they had to delay their morning start to thaw the covers of the baggage. By evening they were coming down Ross's Fork of the Bitterroot River, into the valley now known as Ross's Hole, in the country of the tribe whom they called the Ootlashoots, who are properly known as the Selish, and whom most white men call Flatheads—quite unreasonably, since they have never practiced that flattening of the skull popular among some Pacific coast Indians.

The Selish chief, Three Eagles, was scouting at some distance from his camp that day, since horse thieves were known to be somewhere around. From a distance, in complete astonishment, he saw coming down into the valley a long line of such men as he had never seen before in all his life. They were neither Shoshones nor Flatheads nor did they belong to any of the hostile tribes he knew. Two chiefs rode horses at their head, looking eagerly about the country as they came. Behind them came others on foot, leading pack horses. Strangest of all, not one in all the band wore a blanket. Never had Three Eagles, chief of the Selish, beheld men who wore no blankets. Perhaps hostile warriors had robbed them.

Though they moved openly and did not behave like a war party, the chief slipped off to his camp where he ordered all horses driven in and everything prepared for defense. Then, hidden in the timber, he watched the strangers coming. They still seemed peaceful, yet now he could see that one man was painted black for war. When the two chiefs led the band openly to his camp, he could see that they were white—all except the warrior in black war paint. Returning to his village, the chief greeted them and ordered buffalo robes to replace their stolen blankets. To his amazement he learned that they had blankets in their packs but used them only to sleep in. Strange were the customs of this white tribe.

The ceremonial pipe smoking was not at first a success. Lewis and Clark tried the Indian's tobacco, kinnikinick, dried bark and leaves, or a combination of the two. Finding it too weak, they gave some of their own tobacco to the Indians, who nearly strangled when they puffed it. Finally the explorers mixed the two in a blend which delighted their hosts. Since the Flatheads, who were on the way to the great buffalo-hunt, were extremely friendly, the explorers camped with them for three days. York made his usual impression and had to submit to the inevitable test of his blackness with wet red forefingers. His strength likewise astonished the Flatheads, as did the fact that he could cook.

Leaving the Flatheads, the expedition moved north down the valley of that they named "Clark's River"—the modern Bitterroot—until they went into camp for two nights on what is now the Lolo Fork of the Bitterroot, not far from Missoula, Montana. Having exhausted all their flour and most of their corn, they had had to eat berries. Hunters now brought in venison and Colter came back with three Flatheads, who had been hiding all day within sound of the white men's rifles, fearing they were hostile Indians. Colter, seeing them about to attack him with bows and arrows, had boldly laid down his rifle, made friends, and persuaded them to come back to camp. Like Three Eagles, they were after horse thieves. Two of them, in a great hurry to catch up with the thieves, paused only to eat some boiled venison and receive a few gifts, going on after sunset. A third at first consented to guide them to his tribe, just over the mountains, but he changed his mind next day. Before leaving, however, he described an "old whiteman," who had handkerchiefs like those the expedition carried, and who lived only "five sleeps" ahead. Though the news proved false, it was encouraging for the moment and it was only a few days before Clark picked

up from the Nez Percés more accurate information of white
men ahead of him—or white men who had been there not
long before.

Just as an enforced diet of Lewis's portable soup began to
pall, the hunters brought in two wild horses and a colt, which
Sergeant Gass described as "good eating." Presently they
stumbled on more horse meat, which Clark had left hanging
by the trail for them to pick up.

As they reached the uplands difficulties increased. Lewis
lost his horse twice, once with all his personal baggage. Several horses slipped and rolled down the slopes, one of them
smashing Lewis's little, portable field desk. The cold grew
worse. There was trouble with falling timber. Water failed
and they had to use snow. Lewis, fearing that his feet would
freeze in his thin moccasins, went ahead and had a fire blazing
when the men came straggling into camp, "all wet cold and
hungary." For a time they had nothing to eat but a diet of
wolf and crayfish, ameliorated by three pheasants and a duck.
When things were at their worst, there was nothing to eat
but a little bear's oil and twenty pounds of candles. The men
were glum and weak from lack of food. Again Clark plunged
forward with a small party.

Then level prairie country became visible ahead, and morale bounced upward, though wasps began to sting the horses
as they dropped once more to levels where insects could live.
A note from Clark, left along the trail, said that they would
find him, hunting for food, in the level country ahead. As
they emerged from the worst of the mountains on September
22, Reuben Field came back from Clark's camp with a bag
full of salmon and some Indian bread made of roots. Joyfully, the famished party "halted about one hour and a half
eat hearty of the Sammon and bread, and let our horses feed."
When "groves of handsome tall large pitch pine timber" began to appear, the botanical Lewis was still sufficiently himself to differentiate eight species.

Clark joined them that evening (September 22) with news that he had reached a branch of the Columbia, which seemed navigable and was only fifteen or twenty miles ahead, and that he was in touch with friendly Nez Percés. Pausing at a Flathead village only to bestow medals and presents, they hurried on. The soil, Sergeant Ordway thought, was "verry rich and lays delightful for cultivation." Farm land always interested Ordway. The danger of starvation was over for the time being. Hunters brought in four deer and two salmon. Squaws could be seen digging roots.

They had crossed the Rockies.

chapter 17: Down the Columbia

O N THE south bank of the Clearwater, where the north and south branches meet, Clark found an ideal camp site. Hardship, hunger, strain, anxiety, and danger began to take their toll the moment the excitement and tension ceased. The expedition had hardly reached its rest camp when officers and men alike fell ill. Lewis could hardly stay in the saddle for the last few miles. Some of the men could not reach camp at all. Unable to walk, they sank by the trail and had to be brought in on pack horses, while others, though still able to stagger along, had to lie down beside the trail before they could hobble over the last few miles. Clark, thrown by one of the wild Indian ponies, injured his hip.

With Lewis incapacitated, Clark took over his medical duties, dealing out Dr. Rush's infallible pills lavishly—"to see what effect that would have," according to Sergeant Gass. He also tried salts, jalap, and tartar emetic and in his journal concludes his list of medical experiments with an ominous "&c." that might mean almost anything. However empirical the treatment, the patients all survived, though it was a week before the whole party was on its way to health again, and even then many of the men took a long time recovering from their exhaustion.

During this period of weakness, the expedition was in greater danger than any of its members dreamed. When news of the white men first reached them, the Nez Percés had about decided to kill the strangers on general principles. As they had plenty of warriors, it would have been easy to ambush the various small parties of the expedition while they were straggling down out of the mountains into the Clearwater Valley, and almost equally easy to assemble a large war party and wipe them out in their camp. Long standing tribal tradition, persisting to modern times, says that they were dissuaded by the squaw Wat-ku-ese (Stray Away), who, after being captured by hostile Indians, had escaped with her baby and started back to her own country. After her baby died, the mother, struggling on alone, fell in with white people—the So-yap-po, "crowned ones," who wore hats. One version says that these were a pair of wandering trappers. Whoever they were, they treated the exhausted, solitary, and helpless woman with a kindness she never forgot.

As the Lewis and Clark party straggled into her camp, Wat-ku-ese heard the commotion from the lodge in which she lay ill. "Mans had bows all ready to shoot Lewis and Clark," said an old Nez Percé many years later. Peering out from the lodge door, she saw that these men were of the So-yap-po and, remembering the trappers' kindness, pleaded with the tribe to do no harm to these men: "Do not be afraid of them, go near to them." The Nez Percés tried it. Lewis and Clark shook hands. It was a strange custom but obviously friendly.

"They dandle us!" exclaimed the Nez Percés.

Thereafter, the tribe remained uniformly friendly until Chief Joseph took up the hatchet seventy years later. The westward and eastward journeys of Lewis and Clark remained, for a hundred years, so vivid a part of the tribal lore that even the children knew all about it.

The original hostility was largely due to the panic which their arrival precipitated. The chief Lawyer, famous in the middle nineteenth century as the friend of the white men, was then a child so small that he was still tied up in the usual backboard, or "cradle," on (or in) which squaws carried their children or hung them up to get them out of the way about camp. In after life Lawyer delighted to recount how the Indians of the Nez Percé village near modern Kamiah, Idaho, were terrified when they saw one of the captains, accompanied by Sacagawea, cross the river in a canoe paddled by the first black man they had ever seen. The entire village took to the woods, Lawyer's mother in her fright leaving her baby, strapped in his backboard, leaning against a stump. His father finally ventured back to the deserted village and, finding that these were friendly strangers, picked up the child and took him to his mother.

No hint of possible danger ever reached the exploring party, whose journals never mention any signs of Nez Percé hostility. There was the usual council, at which the captains urged "peace and good understanding" upon the Nez Percés, in speeches which "appeared to Satisfy them much." Gifts satisfied them even more. One medal, wrapped in many thicknesses of buffalo hide, was later dug up at the mouth of Potlatch Creek during excavations for the Northern Pacific Railway. It is supposed to have been the medal that Lewis and Clark gave to the friendly Nez Percé chief, The Twisted Hair. Another medal was later found buried at the mouth of

Ford's Creek, above Orofino, Idaho. Still a third was lost when an Indian canoe capsized in the Clearwater.

An ax which Lewis gave to one of the warriors was so treasured that the proud owner buried it to keep it safe against the day of his death, when he wished to have it buried with him. Unfortunately, the young man to whom he con-

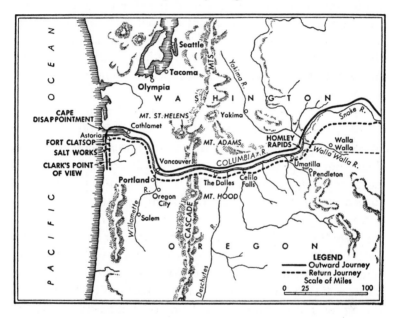

fided his secret could not find the ax when the owner died. As late as 1946, a modern Nez Percé had a vision revealing its whereabouts; but the vision was wrong. He could not find it either. Lewis's gift still lies in its hiding place along the Clearwater.

Another warrior, who exchanged a dog for flint-and-steel, was so pleased with his bargain that he completely wore out the flint with repeated demonstrations of its magic and had to beg a new one when the expedition passed that way again, on its return journey in 1806. Modern Nez Percé legends say that the tribe was chiefly impressed by two things: the ease and speed with which the white men made fire—thanks either to flint-and-steel or to Dr. Saugrain's matches—and the way in which the strange visitors wore hair on their faces.

As word of the new arrivals spread, Nez Percés from all the outlying villages swarmed in to see the white men. Even in 1908, one old squaw still treasured the very cap that she had worn on the day when her mother took her, as a child, to behold these strange people. She was perhaps identical with the squaw Washkin, who used to tell how at the age of four she was strapped to a horse and carried three miles to see the white men.

Once convinced that the strangers were harmless the Nez Percés gave them every possible aid. Though quite as surprised as the Shoshones had been to see human beings eating dogs, they supplied the animals cheerfully enough, the only exception being one squaw, who wept when her pet was consigned to the fleshpots.

The white men, as usual, danced for the Indians, whose modern descendants could still describe the scene in the 1930's. Potts—his monosyllabic name was easy for the redskins to remember—"he boss other mans how to do funny dance and sing songs, and all laugh." Apparently Potts called the figures for a square dance. "Negro York he do lots dance with feet and looks funny."

York enjoyed his customary social success, though Indian children ran to hide at the strange black creature's approach. The Nez Percés dubbed him Tse-mook-tse-mook To-to-kean (Black Indian), a name still used for Negroes. Like a good many of the other members of the expedition, York had a temporary Indian "wife." On the return journey, he found that he had become the father of a little Nez Percé Negro. Occasional modern Nez Percés with kinky hair are perhaps descended from this child. A not very trustworthy Nez Percé legend avers that Lewis himself became enamored of the squaw, Wee-ali-cum.

The usual Indian attempt to rub off York's color with a moistened fingertip led to trouble. York, who had grown rather tired of the experiment after submitting to it in one tribe after another, seized a knife, "make big eyes much white in eyes and look fierce at Chief."

As soon as the men had sufficiently recovered, axes began to ring along the banks of the Clearwater and trees came crashing down to provide a new flotilla of dugouts for the river journey that lay before them. Modern Nez Percés say that the tribe aided in the work and that Lewis himself— though he had by no means completely recovered his strength —swung an ax when the first canoe was made, to make sure it was exactly what he wanted. For the first time, the expedition seems to have used fire to burn out the interior of the logs. Lewis's own efforts were not wholly successful, for the first canoe proved too fragile for the journey, though according to Indian legend it carried six chiefs who accompanied the expedition part way down the Clearwater and then returned to their own country, while two other chiefs went far down the Columbia. Contemporary tradition identifies Lewis's canoe with the dugout now preserved at the Sacajawea Museum at Spalding, Idaho. Stumps of the trees from which the canoes were made were still being pointed out in 1900.

The Twisted Hair, a local chief who was also a *te-wat* or medicine man, made a map for the explorers. Taking a white elkskin, he drew in the course of the river: two sleeps to the large forks; five sleeps to the great falls, where they would find white men. Cannily checking this information with "Several men of note Seperately"—he always kept his informants apart when he could—Clark found it substantially accurate. Though the expedition was not to find white men either at the falls or on the coast, they found abundant traces of their recent presence.

Again caching supplies, including their pack saddles, along
the banks of the Clearwater and branding their horses with
the special branding iron that Captain Lewis had brought
along, the explorers turned the animals over to the Nez
Percés, who obligingly promised to take care of them. On

NEZ PERCÉ WARRIORS by George Catlin. *"Rabbit Skin
Leggings" (at left) and "No Horns on His Head" were two of
the remarkable delegation who went to St. Louis in 1831. According to Nez Percé tradition almost a century later, "they walk
St. Louis to find Lewis and Clark, but when get there Lewis already dead, too bad."*

October 7, the expedition was afloat again in four large
canoes and one small one.

Toward the end of the nineteenth century, one old Nez
Percé was still telling of his father's meeting with one of the
captains, whose canoe turned in to shore at modern Homley
Rapids, to inquire whether there was bad water ahead. Just
as the boat pulled in, the white man, with a loud noise, made

a swan come out of the air. Then he brought fire down out of the sky. In other words, he shot the swan and he lighted his pipe with a burning glass. The journals tell this story of Clark. The Indian who told the story always believed his father had met Lewis.

Gleefully the men of the expedition noted that this part of the voyage would be entirely downstream. No oars, no poling, no labor at the tow-rope, no portages. Their hopes of floating gaily down a broad and pleasant stream were soon rudely destroyed, however, for a new series of troubles began almost at once. On the second day, Sergeant Gass's craft hit a rock, swung in the current, hit another rock, split, filled, and sank. As usual, the men who could not swim were in the boat that had the accident. All they could do was climb out on a rock and hold grimly to their sinking dugout to prevent its being swept downstream and lost. The water was no more than waist deep, but the danger in rapids is not depth. The capsizing canoeist is more likely to die by being swept under and held against a rock by the force of the current, if he is not brained against a rock. In this case there was nothing to do but land, dry out the baggage, and repair the damaged dugout with "Knees & Strong peces."

By next day the old Shoshone warrior and his son who had volunteered to guide them had had quite enough of river travel. Without a word, they disappeared and were never seen again, except for an instant when someone glimpsed them at a distance, running up the river as hard as they could go, several miles above the camp. Finding that they had not even waited for their pay, Clark asked a Nez Percé chief to send them word to come back for it, but the chief shook his head. No use. If the white men paid the recalcitrant guides, the Nez Percés would simply rob them on their way home.

The day closed with a seizure suffered by a Nez Percé squaw, who may have been epileptic. She began to slash her body with a flint "in a horid manner," cutting her arms from wrist to shoulder, sang, gave away her possessions, drank her own blood, made a "hishing noise," ran down to the river, and finally fell senseless. Two days later, another canoe smashed its sides and had to be repaired. Amid these minor distractions, Lewis, though still ill, was recovering.

In spite of these difficulties, the prospects of the expedition grew brighter. Rumors of white men ahead multiplied. Prospects of getting more horses, should they be necessary, seemed better. The numerous Indians all seemed friendly. Two even came up the river in a canoe, volunteering to return with the expedition as far as the falls of the Columbia.

Dog meat was abundant, though this was no comfort to Clark, who never learned to eat it with the enthusiasm of his companions. In the beginning, others had the same misgivings. Sergeant Gass noted with disgust that some of the Frenchmen "prefer dog-flesh to fish." Later, after the expedition had been living for some time on tainted elk meat and pounded dry salmon mixed with sea water, dog became almost a delicacy. Even Gass finally decided that dog meat, "when well cooked tastes very well," providing "strong wholesome diet." Lewis was rather fond of dog because it resembled beaver meat, in which he delighted. While they were wintering on the desolate Pacific coast, he noted: "our party from necessaty having been obliged to subsist some lenth of time on dogs have now become extreemly fond of their flesh; it is worthy of remark that while we lived principally on the flesh of this anamal we were much more healthy strong and more fleshey than we had been since we left the Buffaloe country. for my own part I have become so perfectly reconciled to the dog that I think it an agreeable food and would prefer it vastly to lean Venison or Elk."

By the time the expedition started home, dog meat had become so highly esteemed that it was being bought mainly as a delicacy for the party's invalids. Even Clark unbent sufficiently to admit that it was "a helthy strong diet," but he could not go quite so far as to endorse Lewis's opinion that a diet of dog was "very far superior to the horse in any state." Though Clark once personally bought three dogs from the Indians in Lewis's absence, he bought them only "for the party with me to eate," being careful to buy "some chap-pa-lell" roots for himself.

The palatability of dog was one of the only two subjects on which any disagreement ever rose between Lewis and Clark. The other was salt. The expedition had used up its salt supply on the way across the continent and one of the commanders' first acts on reaching a permanent camp on the Pacific was to send out a salt-making party to boil down sea water. Their crude product was "a great treat" to Lewis when they brought it back to camp. Clark said it was "a mear matter of indifference with him whether he uses it or not."

The canoes met with further disaster as they moved on down the river. On October 14, three struck rocks. One spilled her cargo into the water and the crew had to perch on the rock with roaring water all around them, for an hour, before they could be taken off. The floating baggage was saved, but bedding, shot-pouches, tomahawks, and other irreplaceable articles were lost. One of the Indians boldly swam out into the raging current and saved some of their property, while the men in one of the expedition's own canoes, far ahead, seeing two oars floating past, fished them out and brought them into camp. The precious canisters of powder, lashed fast in the dugout, were still safe when it was finally dragged from the river.

Once again, there was nothing for it but to halt and dry things out; and, in their desperation, the explorers for the first time violated one of the rigid rules of the wilderness: They helped themselves from an Indian cache of firewood. Conscience-striken, Clark noted: "we have made it a point at all times not to take any thing belonging to the Indians even their wood. but at this time we are Compelled to vio-

late that rule." They found some consolation for their troubles in "a good dinner of Blue wing Teel."

Reconnaissance of the river brought new discouragements.
Ahead were rocks, rapids, a crooked channel, shoals that ran
from bank to bank. Sergeant Pryor's canoe was the first to
strike a rock; but, though her cargo was thoroughly wet, she
could be unloaded and pulled off by the others. They reached
the main stream of the Columbia the same day (October 16),
and friendly Indians came down to greet them, singing, beating tom-toms, dancing, then forming a ring and dancing again
about the party. Best of all, these Indians supplied fresh
salmon, dried horse meat, and seven live dogs. There was the
usual council, presentation of medals, speeches, gifts.

When the Indians indicated by signs that the river forked,
not far upstream, Clark went up to see, escorted by three
Indian canoes. He found the mouth of the Tapteel (Yakima)
River and made notes on the Sokulk Indians. Lewis hastened
to take a vocabulary for Mr. Jefferson, while Clark carefully
sketched in river courses and indicated the boundaries of
tribal territories.

On down the Columbia they floated, past Indians who
were uniformly friendly, though occasionally so terrified that
they fled, or hid weeping in their lodges. A little tobacco
smoke wafted their fears away, and Cruzat favored the Indians
with a concert on his violin, "which pleased and astonished
those reches." It would probably have astonished a musician
still more, for Cruzat's fiddle had now been carried several
thousand miles in river damp and across the Rockies in
freezing cold, so that its tone was by no means Stradivarian.

The great chief Yellept, "a bold handsom Indian, with
a dignified countenance about 35 years of age," begged them
to wait until midday so that his tribe could come down and
see these strange creatures. The explorers excused themselves
with a promise to visit Yellept for a day or two on their
return journey, a promise which they in due course fulfilled.

Sacagawea's presence was a great reassurance. At sight of her, the Indians pointed, called others, emerged from hiding, "and appeared to assume new life." No woman ever accompanied a war party—still less a baby!

The high point of the journey was a successful experiment by Private Collins, a resourceful fellow who was beginning to get a little bit thirsty and who now made some excellent beer—at least the uncritical explorers thought it so—on which the journals dilate gratefully. Having nothing else, Collins used bread made from the Indians' quamash roots. His product was really only root beer, but as it was the only beer of any kind for thousands of miles, the expedition quaffed it gratefully.

Signs of the white man ahead increased, showing that the expedition was approaching the Coast. On October 31, they saw Indians wearing scarlet and blue blankets and one with a sailor's jacket. During the next two weeks, they saw a musket, a sword, brass kettles, brass armbands, beads, old clothing of various sorts, and soon afterwards overalls, shirts, pistols, tin powder flasks. Some Indians were wearing seashells in their noses. Sea otter began to appear in the river. It was clear that the long, long trail was nearly at an end, though eager inquiry about white traders and their ships yielded little information. These Indians seemed to be getting white men's goods at second hand, trading with other Indians farther down the Columbia, who were in actual contact with the whites.

New peaks, looming in the distance, helped them get their bearings. On October 19, the party gazed gravely at Mt. Adams under the impression that it was Mt. St. Helen's. Some days later, they identified Mt. Hood, far to the South.

Where the river was too dangerous for the canoes, portages were long and hard. Once Indians, offering assistance with their horses, "repaid" themselves by pilfering from the stores they carried over the portage. Sometimes it was possible to float the canoes downstream crewless, on the ends of long ropes of twisted elkskin. When one rope snapped, Indians farther down obligingly gathered in the canoe with its cargo undamaged. At another point the river had so many "boils swells & whorlpools," that Clark for once took the precaution of setting ashore all men who could not swim, sending the precious firearms and the papers overland with them.

At the Short Narrows of the Columbia River, where the whole tremendous stream rushed through rock walls not more than 45 yards apart, travel grew both dangerous and difficult. To portage around the rapids was impractical, the banks being too difficult. Taking the experienced Cruzat with him, Clark walked along shore to examine the wild water. A good canoe man could shoot it, they both felt sure—and Cruzat brought the canoes down safely, two at a time, "notwithstanding the horrid appearance of this agitated gut swelling, boiling & whorling in every direction." Cruzat was still fresh enough after his perilous day shooting rapids to oblige on the violin, unaccompanied, that evening. Again the men danced, "which delighted the nativs," York's Negro dances making an especial sensation, as they had among the Nez Percés.

The next day's run was nearly as bad, the river passing "through hard rough black rock, from 50 to 100 yards wide, swelling and boiling in a most tremendious maner." When they came to the "Great Shute," now known as the Cascades of the Columbia, where the river dropped 60 feet in two miles, even Clark and Cruzat admitted that canoes could not live. Groaning, the expedition began the portage.

The two Nez Percé chiefs who had accompanied the white men all this distance had been growing uneasy for some time. The river tribes would kill the white men, they felt sure, and as their tribe was at war with the river Indians, their own lives were not safe. Lewis and Clark thought this a good opportunity to make peace and begged them to remain only two days more. The chiefs were evasive—they wanted to go back to the mountains to look after their white friends' horses!—but in the end they stayed, and a dubious kind of peace was patched up before their departure.

Traces of the white man continued to increase as the Corps of Discovery sped on down the river. They saw Indians with various bits of cloth, frying pans, copper articles, a rifle with a brass barrel and cock, sailors' jackets, trousers, hats, shirts, many powder flasks, pistols, a metal bow. Eventually, they met an Indian who spoke a few words of English and knew the name of one of the captains who visited Nootka Sound —"Mr. Haley." The Indian had with him a squaw "who M^r. Haley was fond of &c." Captain Haley, as they later learned, was an especial favorite among the Indians because he gave more presents than the other captains.

As they reached the lower Columbia, they began to find the Indians—perhaps from too much contact with white men —very "assumeing and disagreeable" companions and also inveterate thieves. Once or twice redskins attempted to take rifles and other valuables by violence, but for the most part they simply pilfered when they had a chance. If detected, they usually gave up the stolen articles readily, but once "several of those from below returned down the river in a bad humer, haveing got into this pet by being prevented doeing as they wished with our articles which was then exposed to dry." One ingenious thief stole a great coat and stuffed it quickly under the root of a tree, to be retrieved at leisure. Even the peace pipe was stolen, nor did a search of the Indians' greasy and grimy persons restore it.

Three more English-speaking Indians soon appeared, but as they used their linguistic gifts mainly to cover the theft of a knife, they were not much use. When detected, they returned to their village, and the Corps of Discovery continued to rely upon their own interpreters.

As they approached the sea, the wind grew more violent,

the waves higher, the water first brackish and then salt. Eventually it became so salty that men fell ill from using it to prepare the dried and pounded fish which were now their miserable diet. A Jesuit missionary father later described beaten fish as "a good mortification."

The weather was foggy, cold, and raw. Their bedding was rotting away. Their skin clothing, perpetually wet, was rotting too, and there was no way to replace it. Game was scarce and there was no time to tan leather.

But there was compensation for all this when one day Clark could write in his journal:

"Ocian in view! O! the joy."

The Corps of Discovery felt like Xenophon's Greeks on the day when at last they saw the Euxine and a cry of "Thalassa! Thalassa!" ran down that heroic column.

There is some doubt, however, whether Lewis and Clark really did see the ocean on that blissful day, or merely the wide waters of the lower Columbia; but the moral effect was the same. The expedition was almost right in thinking it had finally reached "this great Pacific Octean which we have been so long anxious to See. and the roreing or noise made by the waves brakeing on the rockey Shores (as I suppose) may be heard disticly." The roar of waves is still distinctly heard at the point where Clark is supposed to have been when he made his note, and that was proof they had reached their goal.

chapter 18: *Fort Clatsop*

"ALL wet and disagreeable" but still "chearfull and anxious to See further into the Ocian," the Corps of Discovery floated down the estuary of the Columbia, jubilant at the thought that they had crossed the continent—one way, at least. The Pacific was just ahead. If they found trading vessels on the coast, all their troubles would be over. If they did not find them, they would have to face a second transcontinental journey.

The shores on each side were steep and rocky, with picturesque castles and pinnacles rising here and there. The unspoiled green forests of Oregon, studded with evergreens immense beyond imagining, the like of which no one of them had ever seen, rose all about them. At one point the canoes even passed over a forest of submerged, gigantic trunks. Along the precipices, one small stream after another leaped out over the sheer edge, then came tumbling down, free of the rock, through the air itself, in exquisite white cascades of frothing water. The north shore was an unbroken battlement of colored rock. It was such country as these easterners had never dreamed of.

They had come to a beautiful land, but its winter weather was another matter. They had never dreamed of that, either. Not cold but raw, with wind and rain and an all-penetrating damp, worse than the savage cold of Fort Mandan. Waves were soon so high that the crude dugouts could hardly ride them, and the men began to get seasick from the violent motion of such small craft. The Pacific tides, which came swelling up the river, added to their troubles.

They went into camp on the night of November 8/9, in what is now Gray's Bay, on the north side of the river—one of the worst camp sites that even the Corps of Discovery had ever known in all their weary journey. Wind, rain, and waves combined against them. The brackish river water was undrinkable. The steep hills came so close to the shore that there was no level ground to lie on. The baggage had to be piled on a tangle of poles to keep it above the tide. Everyone was wet. One of the canoes sank before it could be unloaded. The others filled and sank during the night. It was all the party could do to save their dugouts from complete destruction, for the tide brought in immense trees, 200 feet long, four to seven feet through, dashing them against the beach. It was an unpleasant way to discover the size of the famous Oregon timber.

When, after enduring this wretched state all the next day, they took advantage of a lull in the wind to push on, they could find no land whatever level enough to camp on, and spent a miserable night, huddled together on timber that had drifted against the shore. Here they had to stay throughout the following day, the river splashing under them, their baggage piled on rocks to keep it above the waves that came rolling in, almost smashing the canoes. There was nothing to eat but dried fish, since the precipices along shore were too steep for the hunters to climb and the tangle of woods and under-brush too thick for them to penetrate. The only bright spot in a doleful day was the arrival of a few Indians, willing to barter thirteen fresh fish for fishhooks and other trifles. The Indians near the Columbia's mouth had known for some days that strangers from the East were coming down the river. "Queen Sally," of Cathlamet, about 1850 could still point out from the cliffs the spot where her tribe first sighted the white men's canoes. The expedition's red visitors were understood to indicate by signs that there were white men down the bay, but this was a mistake. The white men watched envi-ously as the Indian canoe, specially built for the Columbia's waters, bobbed away over the waves that were at that mo-ment nearly smashing their own clumsy Rocky Mountain dugouts.

On November 12, thunder, lightning, and hail were added to the expedition's troubles, until, when the rising waves began to threaten their camp, they had to move it half a mile, leaving their baggage on the rocks to take care of itself. The canoes had to be filled with "emence parcels of Stone" and sunk, to protect them from the waves.

Colter, Willard, and Shannon finally went out in a des-perate attempt to find another camp. Colter came back next day on foot, with news that there were Indian camps just below. The redskins had tried to take his gig and knife away and he had had to threaten them with his rifle. Lewis then decided to take out another canoe, in an attempt to find white traders from the ships. Though there were no traders for him to find, it was fortunate that he made the attempt, for he caught up with Shannon and Willard just in time to prevent Indian trouble.

After Colter had left them, the two soldiers had met a band of Indians, whose friendliness was so effusive that it seemed suscipious and who insisted on guiding them to the sea. Un-willing to go with them and equally unwilling to camp alone, for fear of a night attack, the men compromised by tucking their rifles under their heads and boldly going to sleep in the middle of the Indian camp. When they woke in the morning, they found that these expert thieves had adroitly slipped the rifles away without waking them. When Shannon threatened one Indian with a club, another began loading a fowling piece to shoot the white men. Realizing that he was helpless, Shannon took refuge in diplomacy. He explained by signs that a large party of white men would be coming down the river before the sun was so high—indicating the sun's height in the heavens in the usual Indian manner. They would kill every one of this thieving nation.

At that moment, with the precision of a stage entrance, Lewis and his party appeared, well armed. The Indians, properly impressed, gave up the argument and also the stolen rifles. Meantime Clark, at the base camp, was having so much trouble with thieves that he threatened to shoot any Indian who stole a rifle.

After six days of misery, he took advantage of a sudden lull and moved his flotilla about three miles to the present site of Fort Columbia, opposite Astoria, near a Chinook village, where they had a clear view out to sea. Hunting improved, the Indians were willing to sell food, and on the 17th Lewis returned, after rounding Cape Disappointment and traveling a little distance along the Pacific coast north of the bay.

Clark promptly called for volunteers "who wished to see more of the Ocean." Only about a dozen offered to go, the others, as Clark drily remarks, being "well contented with what part of the Ocean & its curiosities which could be seen from the vicinity of our Camp." Clark, too, visited Cape Disappointment and went overland to what Lewis had named "Clark's Point of View" (apparently the modern False Tillamook Head) and then to a headland, which he took "the Liberty of Calling after my particular friend Lewis." This seems to have been what is now called North Head. The men were "much Satisfied with their trip beholding with estonishment the high waves dashing against the rocks & this emence Ocian." The laconic Sergeant Ordway says simply that they had "a handsom view of the ocean." Finding Lewis's name carved on a tree, Clark added his own, and returned overland, meeting numerous Indians, some of whom "appeared to know me & was distant." Their coolness was the result of his recent threat which, Clark was convinced, was "the cause of their conducting themselves with great propriety towards ourselves & Party."

Returning to camp, he watched with amusement while Lewis bargained desperately for an Indian robe made of two very fine sea-otter skins. These animals were hard to get, since when shot they almost invariably sank and were lost; and the party had fired in vain at a number on their way down the river. These particular skins, Sergeant Gass thought, were "the finest fur I ever saw," which "the Commanding Officers wanted very much."

To all offers, the proud owner was adamant. Two blankets? No. Five blankets? No. Beads? He would take blue beads. Lewis now discovered one of the few errors that he had made in planning the expedition's supplies. He had brought a large store of red beads and white beads, but he had not laid in nearly enough blue ones, which to the Pacific coast Indians were "chief beads," the only valuable kind. Clark's offers of his watch, a handkerchief, red beads, and a silver dollar for the sea-otter robe were quite as futile as Lewis's efforts. They persuaded Sacagawea to give up a belt of blue beads she was wearing, and the robe was theirs. To the Shoshone squaw, the beads had no special value, and she was compensated by a coat of blue cloth.

They had hardly gone into this semi-permanent camp when squaws began to arrive in numbers, "I beleave for the purpose of gratifying the passions of our men," Clark noted in the Journals. One meretricious old woman, the wife of

Chief Delashelwilt, arrived with six young squaws—her own daughters or nieces—and deliberately camped where she could "cultivate an intimacy between our men and her fair wards." "The old bawd" insisted on small presents for herself in return for the "indulgencies" of the red-skinned light ladies.

Though better than its predecessors, the camp was uncomfortable, game was scarce, and the perpetual diet of pounded salmon had long since palled. There was also a serious need of salt. It was obvious by this time that there was no hope of starting back across the continent until spring. The party was exhausted. Their clothing was almost falling to pieces. They badly needed a red meat diet. To turn back now was no use—that would only bring them to the Rockies in midwinter, when the passes would be completely blocked.

Another reason for staying on the coast was the hope that one or two trading vessels would come before spring. If even one ship put into the Columbia, its arrival would be "more than an over ballance, for the bad liveing we shall have in liveing on Pore deer & Elk." Since Lewis had a letter of credit from the United States government, there would be no difficulty in dealing with traders, who could easily supply the Indian trinkets necessary for the Indian trade on the way home. Already the expedition began to feel a shortage, for the Pacific coast Indians were charging such high prices for food that the supply of trading goods—after lavish bestowal of presents on the westward journey—was rapidly disappearing.

It is surprising that President Jefferson did not send a naval vessel to wait for the exploring party in the estuary. His reason for not doing so was probably fear of offending Spain. Already much disturbed at the sale of Louisiana, the Spaniards would have found it intolerable to have the United States navy so uncomfortably close to their settlements in California and Mexico. The Spanish government—

correctly enough, as the events of the next half century would show—had forebodings of what the American habit of expansion might lead to.

Hunting was bad along the north bank of the bay, and it was soon apparent that prospects of continuing to buy provisions from the greedy natives of the coast were hopeless. The best the Indians had to offer was a diet of roots and fish, of which the Corps of Discovery had long been heartily tired; and even for this the Indians demanded prices that the expedition could not possibly continue to pay. Already supplied with white men's goods and familiar with white men's ways, these tribes were shrewder bargainers than those of the interior.

The only possible solution was to camp on the coast for the winter. The climate, however disagreeable, would be less severe than that of the mountains. The men could hunt to provide meat—and leather, from which they could make new clothing and moccasins. Everyone would be thoroughly rested by the time spring came. The whole party joined in diligent inquiries as to the best hunting grounds. Deer, the Indians said, were most plentiful farther up the river, but elk abounded on the south shore of the bay. Elk were larger and gave better meat, besides being easier to kill. A camp on the south shore near the sea would offer a good chance of making contact with any trading ship that might pass.

Officers and men went into council together, and a vote was taken, in which even the slave, York, and the squaw, Sacagawea, joined—for Regular Army officers a desperately unorthodox expedient. The expedition was almost unanimous in favor of the plan to cross and look for a site on the southern shore. "Janey," as Clark had begun to call Sacagawea, had an idea all her own. She was "in favour of a place where there is plenty of Pota[toe]s"—by which she probably meant quamash roots. Clark, much amused, soberly set her ideas down in the official journal.

One would like to know more about the nickname, Janey, which the Journals mention only once. Elsewhere Sacagawea is "the Indian woman" or is referred to under her own name, in various frantic spellings. An ingenious guess that "Janey" is really meant for "Jawey"—an abbreviation of Sacagawea—is plausible but quite wrong. The manuscript of the journal has "Janey," very clearly written. Apparently Clark just got tired of long Indian names.

Through more bad weather and high waves, they crept back along the north shore the way they had come, looking for a place where the estuary was narrow enough to cross and again enviously watching the buoyant Indian canoes as they rode easily over the swells. It was hard to get firewood. The bedding had been wet for weeks. The big officers' tent was nearly worn out, so that Lewis and Clark could hardly find a dry place to sleep, while the other tents and the sails were "so full of holes & rotten that they will not keep any thing dry." Squalls were so violent that Clark expected to see the great trees torn up by the roots. Constantly shifting winds blew the smoke of the campfires—"emencely disagreeable, and painfull"—into their eyes. There were no deer, no elk. Swans and geese were too wary for the hunters.

"O! how disagreeable is our Situation dureing this dreadfull weather," wrote Clark at the end of one dismal day and again: "O! how Tremendious is the day." But through all the misery he was quick to note the "butifull pebble of various colours" along the shore, and he kept up his observations of the local birds, as well as "Snakes, Lizards, Small bugs, worms, Spiders, flyes & insects."

When things were at their worst, Sacagawea suddenly produced a piece of bread "made of flour"—not of the Indian roots which everyone had come to loathe. She had been saving it for her baby, but she now presented it to Clark. Though it was by this time an ancient and dubious substance, having "unfortunately got wet, and a little Sour," Clark fell upon the morsel ravenously "with great satisfaction, it being the only mouthfull I had tasted for several months past." It was too bad about the baby, but after all he was always sure of getting his mother's milk.

Then the hunters brought in three hawks, "fat and delicious" and three ducks. They brought no elk, but they had at least seen "sign." Things were distinctly looking up.

Lewis finally managed to get a small canoe across to Tongue Point on the south shore, only to discover that a tangle of swamps, woods, and ponds made travel overland impossible, though the ocean was so close that he could hear the pounding of the waves. Once again they were in more danger than they knew, as they had been among the Nez Percé's. The landing on Tongue Point alarmed the Indians near there, who prepared for trouble by cutting down trees to block the river and hiding their canoes; but, as the white men continued to be friendly, no hostility followed. Turning back to Meriwether Bay, now called Young's Bay, Lewis found a site along a little river, within hearing of the Pacific breakers. Here they determined to settle for the winter.

Selecting high ground to be out of the swamps, Lewis began work on shelter and fortifications, while Clark plunged off toward the coast, often in mud and water to his hips, through "bogs which the wate of a man would Shake for ½ an Acre." Killing an elk for food, he finally reached the coast, under the guidance of some chance Indian acquaintances. It was encouraging to find one Indian who knew enough English to remark that "Sturgion was verry good," though he let the white men find out for themselves that sturgeon was also very scarce.

Asked by the Indians to fire at a duck, Clark, by pure chance, shot off its head—a feat which led to loud comments of "Clouch Musket, wake, com ma-tax, Musket!" (Good musket. Do not understand this kind of musket.)

Racked with dysentery, colds, boils, colic, and aching muscles, the party toiled in the constant rain to get their cabins up. There were grim jokes about the Pacific. "I have not," Clark noted, "seen one pacific day Since my arrival in its vicinity." "There is more wet weather on this coast than I ever knew in any other place," wrote Sergeant Gass in disgust; "during the month, we have had but three fair days." It was just ordinary Oregon winter weather, consisting mainly of rain with occasional fogs to give variety.

There was some compensation in the excellence and the abundance of timber provided by the magnificent conifers for which Oregon is still famous, which yielded "the streightest & most butifullest logs," splitting readily into boards for the roofs. They made "the finest puncheons I have ever seen," said Gass, with a carpenter's appreciation of sound wood. "They can be split ten feet long and two broad, not more than an inch and a half thick." Better still, the men even found some boards ready made, in an abandoned Indian shelter. Food improved as the hunters suddenly began to find elk, sixteen of which they killed in a single day. The Clatsop Indians living in the neighborhood gave every outward evidence of being friendly.

By December 17, work was so far advanced that the men were already chinking and daubing the cabins and cutting doors. By Christmas Day the fort was nearly done and the party were "Snugly fixed in their huts." Though all the work was not yet complete, by the end of the year 1805 the expedition was living in the most luxurious quarters thus far erected in Oregon. The cabins were sixteen by 30 feet—at least those were the measurements of the two which survived in ruins until 1853. In the "south cabin" was a huge tree trunk that could not be removed. Someone had the idea of smoothing off its top and making a table, and since the table was literally rooted to the earth, the hut had to be built around it. The table survived until the middle of the nine-

teenth century. There were eight cabins in all, one for stor-
age, the other seven for living quarters, their doors facing in,
their outer walls joined by a stockade, able to resist any possible Indian attack.

The attack never came, but Lewis and Clark, who had kept
their arms repaired and inspected and their camps guarded
all the way, still believed in taking as few chances as possible.
No sooner were they established in the fort than the captains
issued orders for regular tours of guard duty. Fort Clatsop
that winter was going to be a regular military post of the
United States army—even if no one else in the army dreamed
that it existed. One sergeant and three privates constituted
the guard, which changed daily at sunrise; and, as at Fort
Mandan, the sentry walked his post in a military manner in
front of the officers' quarters, leaving it only as duty might
require.

Although the Indians continued to show every sign of
friendship, this vigilance was maintained throughout the
winter. The guard was always alert, and all natives were
bluntly invited to leave at sundown except in special cases,
as when a small party was caught barefoot in a snowstorm.
Large groups of Indians were put out, no matter what the
weather, and the two officers constantly struggled against the
men's tendency to relax their distrust as the winter wore on
and relations continued to be amicable. The men were cau-
tioned against striking Indians if they could possibly help it,
though they were authorized to expel troublesome redskins
from the fort if they had to. "we well know," say the Journals, "that the treachery of the aborigenes of America and
the too great confidence of our countrymen in their sincerity
and friendship, has caused the distruction of many hundreds
of us."

They never learned that at least once the Klatskanin Indians did discuss an attack, but were dissuaded by the Clatsop
chief whom Lewis and Clark knew as Cómowool, though his

real name was Yanakasac Coboway. Treacherous attacks on
white men visiting the Pacific coast were not uncommon.

A salt-making party searched the coast five days before,
near a Killamuck village just north of Tillamook head, they
found a suitable site, marked today by a pile of the very
stones they used for their fireplace. Here a magnificent beach
made it easy to get at the sea water. They were soon producing from three quarts to a gallon a day of "excellent, fine,
strong, & white" salt, which delighted men who had tasted
nothing of the sort for many a long day. Indian tradition
says that the local redskins all moved up and lived near the
saltworks, lending the salt makers an old canoe, in which to
let the sea water clear a little, before boiling. The site was
identified in 1900 by a Clatsop squaw whose mother remembered the white men's making salt at that spot. It was also
identified by Silas B. Smith, grandson of Coboway. By the
end of February, the party had boiled down twenty gallons
of salt, twelve iron-bound kegs of which had been carefully
stored for the homeward journey. Only Clark was indifferent
to this achievement, being convinced, like a true Kentuckian,
that it was not nearly so good as salt from the Kentucky
springs.

The Indians gave the salt makers some blubber from a
stranded whale, which proved "pallitable and tender." When
Clark hurried off to see whether he could get any more of
this welcome addition to their monotonous diet, Sacagawea
begged to go along: "She observed that She had traveled a
long way with us to See the great waters, and that now that
monstrous fish was also to be Seen, She thought it verry hard
that She could not be permiteed to See either (She had never
yet been to the Ocian)."

Clark's party arrived too late, for the Indians had already
stripped off everything that could either be eaten or boiled
down for oil. Only the skeleton remained. Though the Indians were still there, storing whale oil in bladders and the

whale's own entrails, Clark was able to buy only 300 pounds
of blubber and a few gallons of oil. He consoled himself
with the reflection that Providence had been "more kind to
us than he was to jonah, having Sent this Monster to be *Swallowed by us* in Sted of *Swallowing of us* as jonah's did."

On the way back to the fort, Private M'Neal struck up acquaintance with an obtrusively friendly Killamuck, who
locked arms with him and took him into one of the lodges
to get some blubber. When he invited M'Neal to come to
another lodge "to get Something better," a Chinook squaw
seized him and tried to hold him back. She was "an old
friend of McNeals"—probably the same girl who had infected
him with venereal disease—but as their previous acquaintance
had not included much conversation, M'Neal could not understand the warning she was trying to convey. Shaking her
off, he set out gaily with his new-found warrior friend. Knowing that the Killamuck meant to kill him and seeing no other
way to save the stupid fellow's life, the girl rushed outside
and began to shriek, followed by another friendly squaw who
added to the noise.

Clark, who sat smoking with some braves a short distance
away, heard the sudden uproar and saw most of the Indians
around him jump up and rush for the village, while one began to make signs that somebody's throat was being cut. He
sent Sergeant Pryor hurrying to the rescue with several men.
They met M'Neal, hastily retreating but still more puzzled
than alarmed. He could say only "that the people were
alarmed on the oppsit side at Something but what he could
not tell." Investigation showed that the over-friendly Killamuck meant to knife him quietly and get his blanket. Clark,
caustic for once, named the neighboring creek M'Neal's Folly;
a more kindly posterity calls it the Nehalem River.

Plied with eager inquires about the trading vessels, the
Indians gave the names of various sea captains, of which
Lewis and Clark compiled neat tables. Some of the news was

hopeful. Captain Youin was expected in "1 moon" in a "large ship." He never came. A long list of captains were expected in two or three moons. They never came either. Probably they were among the numerous mariners then anchored far up the coast in Nootka Sound, where Lewis and Clark knew nothing of them. Another captain, "1 Ey^d Skellie," who also had a large ship, was a "long time gorn." Captain Haley, of whom they had heard a good deal as they came down the Columbia, had left some months earlier.

The Indians told them nothing of the one trading vessel, already on the coast, that might have helped them. This was the brig *Lydia,* Captain Samuel Hill commanding, which had left Boston on a voyage around Cape Horn on August 31, 1804, while Lewis and Clark were counciling with the Sioux on the Missouri. Arriving off the Pacific coast in early 1805, she had actually entered the Columbia River April 5, just as Lewis and Clark were preparing to leave Fort Mandan. She had remained in the estuary for a month, and Captain Hill had taken a small boat 100 miles eastward up the Columbia while Lewis and Clark were toiling westward up the Missouri. It was probably his visit which the Rocky Mountain and Columbia River Indians had been trying to describe in answer to the expedition's questions.

Sailing farther north, Captain Hill received a letter smuggled to the coast by two white captives who had survived a massacre of sailors in 1803. By kidnaping an Indian chief and holding him for exchange, he was able to rescue both the white men before turning back to the Columbia. He entered the river again in November, 1805, after Lewis and Clark had passed downstream, and probably while they were still encamped along the bank.

John R. Jewitt, one of the rescued captives aboard the *Lydia,* later wrote: "We proceeded about ten miles up the river, to a small Indian village, where we heard from the inhabitants that Captains Clark and Lewis, from the United

States of America, had been there about a fortnight before, on their journey over-land, and had left several medals with them, which they showed us."

Though Captain Hill had made great efforts to rescue the captives, a feat which other trading captains thought impossible, he was so little concerned about the Lewis and Clark Expedition that he did not even mention it in his manuscript autobiography.

The Indians seem to have been either too stupid or too spiteful to guide the captain to Fort Clatsop. They were, perhaps, taking revenge for the severity with which Clark had repressed their thefts. The *Lydia* stood on and off the coast until August 12, 1806, by which time the expedition was well on its way home. Captain Hill mentions meeting other trading vessels, and the Indians reported that their friend Haley and three other skippers were trading farther north along the coast, but none of them appeared in the Columbia.

It was encouraging to find that the names of the sea captains known to the Indians were all either British or American, showing that neither the Russians in the North nor the Spanish in the South had been breaking into the Columbia River trade, which Mr. Jefferson coveted for the United States. The Indians, who had learned to say "damned rascal," "Sun of a pitch," and "maney blackguard phrasses," had also learned some reputable English. They could say "heave the lead," "knife," "file," "musket," "powder," and "shot"; but they seemed to know nothing of any other European language. None of them had any clear idea where the traders came from or where they went. Asked which way they sailed when departing, they invariably pointed southwest—correctly, since both whalers and trading vessels of that day usually sailed home by way of Hawaii and China.

It was deadly dull at Fort Clatsop. The rain kept all but the hunters, the solitary sentry, and the salt makers inside their cabins, and Indian girls provided the only amusement. "The young females are fond of the attention of our men," Clark noted, and again: "The young women sport openly with our men, and appear to receve the approbation of theer friends & relations for so doing maney of the women are hansom."

The men's patronage of the young squaws offered by the wife of the Chinook chief, Delashelwilt, on the north bank of the Columbia, had already resulted in an outbreak of venereal disease. Having come prepared for just such an emergency, Lewis gave the men mercury treatment and by January optimistically supposed that they were cured. Just as he was congratulating himself that the epidemic was under control, the same group appeared, paddling up the river to Fort Clatsop in a huge canoe more than four feet from beam to beam. This time Chief Delashelwilt himself accompanied the floating Indian brothel and the young squaws, "which the Old Boud his wife had brought for Market." They seemed, as Lewis observed with dismay, "determined to lay close sege to us," settling down near the fort, so that the redskinned whores were readily available all the time. Nothing discouraged Chief and Mrs. Delashelwilt in their promotion of organized vice. Sergeant Gass remarks that the old woman "frequently visited our quarters with nine girls which she kept as prostitutes," having apparently added three more squaws to her original stock in trade.

Lewis hastened to warn the men of the special danger of infection from these particular women, and all promised to have nothing to do with them, however free they might make with the other Indian girls. The meretricious nine finally departed, together with the "Old Bawd" and Chief Delashelwilt—the latter carrying with him "a certificate of his good deportment," in spite of his interest in the local red-light district. When the expedition started for home, the very first Indians they met were the persistent "old baud and hir

Six Girls," the other three having apparently given up a life of sin in despair at its unprofitable nature.

There were plenty of other young squaws, for the coast Indians had been corrupted by association with white sailors from the trading vessels. Previous amours of the expedition, though there had been some outright prostitution, had been partly a matter of fertility rites, partly a matter of Indian notions of hospitality. Most of the Pacific coast squaws were plain commercial prostitutes who, as Sergeant Gass remarked, were "much inclined to venery" and were "sold to prostitution at an easy rate."

Though scabs and ulcers made it only too clear that venereal disease was common among the coastal Indians, anxious inquiry by Lewis and Clark showed that the Indians had no cure for it. They could only endure it and die prematurely, though the use of a few native simples was supposed to give some relief. These coastal Indians seemed to suffer more than those of the Rockies, as was natural, since they were in frequent contact with the trading vessels which sailed around the world, gathering up infection in every continent.

In spite of the danger, the officers had no hope of controlling the love-life of their group of ardent young men during this period of enforced idleness. All they hoped for was to keep them away from dangerously infected women. Lewis had enough confidence in his men to feel sure they would let "the old baud" and her group alone, "notwithstanding every effort of their wining graces." As for other squaws, the officers finally "divided some ribin between the men of our party to bestow on their favourite Lasses." This was a little scheme on the part of the anxious commanders "to save the knives & more valuable articles," which would otherwise certainly have been appropriated by the men and would have vanished into the greedy hands of complaisant Indian damsels.

Lewis's observation on the "wining graces" of the squaws

was rather heavy-handed satire, for bad as was the impression which most of the coastal Indians made on Lewis and Clark personally, the squaws in particular filled them with disgust. Both remark in their journals, which at this period they frequently copied from each other: "the most disgusting sight I have ever beheld is these dirty naked wenches."

In spite of this pronounced distaste, the captains were plagued by eager and willing squaws. One young Indian, who had received medical treatment, came back to the fort bringing his sister, whose favors he gratefully offered to Lewis and Clark as a medical fee. When the embarrassed officers declined the aboriginal beauty as gracefully as possible, the poor girl, who was herself "anxious to join in this expression of her brother's gratitude," was "mortified that we did not avail ourselves of it." She hung about Fort Clatsop for two or three days, hoping that this unxepectedly adamantine virtue would melt and sharing quarters with Sacagawea in the room immediately adjoining the officers' quarters. Obstinately declining the eager solicitations of the enlisted men, she was always underfoot and in the way when the officers were about, until she went away at last, "regretting that her brother's obligations were unpaid."

When the captains sent a gift of food to the village chief, Cuscalah, that dignitary appeared with two squaws, offering one to each officer. "This being declined, Cuscalah as well as the whole party of Indians were highly offended; the females seemed particularly to be much incensed at our indifference about their favours."

Clark noted with some amusement that the frailty of many young squaws was of long standing. One bore tattooed on her arm the name of a former admirer, "J. Bowman." A Chinook warrior with violently red hair and a much-freckled, fair skin, bore his name—or his father's—tattooed on his arm: "Jack Ramsay." His father, a deserter from a British trading vessel, had lived for years among the Indians and, when his son was born, had forbidden his squaw to flatten the child's soft skull between boards, after the local custom. He himself had tattooed the name on the boy's arm.

In spite of the abundance of Indian girls, Fort Clatsop was never popular with its garrison. The expedition had achieved its object, and—having reached their goal—the soldiers began to think of home. Clark notes on February 2, 1806: "all are pleased, that one month of the time which binds us to fort *Clatsop*, and which seperates us from our friends, has now alapsed." Life was dull. Rain fell perpetually. Several of the men sickened and their recovery was always slow, partly because it was impossible to feed them properly and partly because they were so nearly exhausted by all they had endured. It looked for a time as if Private Gibson might die, and the expedition had to carry Private Bratton halfway into the Rockies before he finally recovered of a lumbar ailment.

Game was scarce. The black bear were hibernating. Deer and beaver were rarely found. Even elk were usually none too plentiful and all were lean. Hunters sometimes had to go so far to find game that they could hardly get the carcasses back to camp. When the hunters were nearer, men working in camp listened for their shots, hungrily hoping that each distant bang meant meat. For some reason there was no effort to kill seals, though when Indians gave them seal meat they found it "a great improvement to the poor Elk." Sacagawea was never quite convinced that the seals were not a strange race of Indians, living in the sea, who, when she tried to talk to them, always slipped away to their home under water. It was one of her tales which the Shoshones never quite believed, when she told it in her old age.

Food was not the only lack. Scarcity of meat meant scarcity of leather, and tanning such skins as they had was difficult. They had not enough elk brains for the usual frontier tanning process, and the pine ashes of their campfires did not yield lye. Worst of all, in March tobacco gave out entirely, a serious matter, since 30 of the party either smoked or chewed it. As substitutes, they fell back on crabtree bark for chewing, saccacomis and the inner bark of red willow for smoking. The men who chewed tobacco thought the bitter crab bark a good substitute, but eventually cut up the wood in the tobacco-soaked handles of their pipe-tomahawks and chewed that.

Still, there were compensations. Excellent appetites made up for the badness of the food. Fresh-killed elk meat, even though lean, never completely palled. Lewis comments enthusiastically on an "excellent supper" in early February—elk marrow bone and a brisket of boiled elk with "the appearance of a little fat," which he says, "for Fort Clatsop is living in high stile." Next day it was elks' tongues and marrow bones, which even the ascetic Clark called "a great Luxury for Fort Clatsop." Lewis found "my ordinary meals not uninteresting to me, for I find myself sometimes enquiring of the cook whether dinner or breakfast is ready." Nevertheless, he did not "feel strong." Nor, it is probable, did anyone else, though matters improved when the Indians began to bring in the eluchon, or Columbia River smelt, a fish which Lewis and David Starr Jordan, a century apart, agreed in thinking the best in the Pacific.

Delighted with the exquisite workmanship of the conical hats which the coast natives wove of cedar bark and grass, the captains bought a quantity and distributed them to the men. Their own they had made to measure and were pleased to find that "they fit us very well, and are in the form we desired them."

Lewis labored mightily over the botany of the region. Evergreens, shrubs, ferns, even the grasses were minutely described in the most elaborately technical language. Shellfish, reptiles, birds, and mammals were less technically described, since Lewis knew more botany than zoölogy. The Journals also contain detailed reports on Indian costume, canoe-building, domestic animals, and every minute detail of tribal life on which the explorers could get information.

During this and some other parts of the expedition, Clark kept his diary up mainly by copying Lewis's. Sometimes where Lewis describes something "I" had done, Clark changes this to "Capt. Lewis," but more often he merely copies it, "I" and all. More important than Clark's share of the Journals is the map which he finally put together, from the field notes he had so laboriously taken after leaving Fort Mandan. The trail across the Rockies was located by a series of celestial observations. No such map of the West had ever been produced before, and Clark must have experienced a real thrill of satisfaction as he sat back from his rough drafting table—probably the big tree stump that no one could move— and showed the finished result to his partner.

Examining their new map, the two explorers felt sure that they had found "the most practicable and navigable passage across the Continent." Studying the map of their journeying from Fort Mandan to the coast—on which Clark had been working most of the winter—they now realized that they could save much time by traveling directly overland to the vicinity of the Falls from "Travelers' Rest," at the beginning of the Lolo Trail, thus escaping the laborious canoe travel along the upper waters of the Missouri. Being without horses, they could not have used this route on their way westward; but as they listened to Indian accounts of the overland trails, they determined to test them on the way home.

chapter 19: *Homeward bound*

DECIDING the date of the return journey—once they had given up hope of
of a ship—called for a great deal of careful thought. The
expedition would have to reach the foothills of the Rockies
the moment the passes were open, or a little earlier. Otherwise the Nez Percés, who had all the horses, might take them
along to the buffalo hunting grounds on the other side of
the mountains and there would be no transportation for the
baggage during the brief but crucial period when they were
crossing the Rockies. An early start was also advisable to
avoid being caught, late in 1806, by the Missouri River ice,
which would force them to spend another winter at Fort
Mandan. Still another reason was the health and morale of
the men, both of which were always better on the march. It
was regrettable that they had to start before the spawning

salmon came crowding into the Columbia, providing an abundant supply of fresh food; but they would have to rely on the salmon to move up the rivers fast enough to catch up with the expedition.

A plan to leave a few men behind on the Pacific coast, to return by any trading vessel which might possibly still arrive, was considered and abandoned. If all went well, the expedition would get home, now that it knew the way, faster than any trading vessel could cross the Pacific and Atlantic, rounding both Asia and Africa en route, especially if her captain first spent several months trading with the Indians.

It began to look rather doubtful whether any of them would survive the return journey overland, but they had to choose between that risk and the risk of waiting in vain for a ship. Though they had had a long rest at Fort Clatsop, the constant dampness had had a bad effect on the men's health and all were weak from their bad and monotonous diet. There were several stubborn cases of venereal disease, and some of the men were ill from other causes. Private Bratton's obscure lumbar ailment was still so serious that he could not walk. It would be impossible to get enough horses in the Columbia Valley to take them across the Rockies at a single trip and no one had any idea what had become of the horses they had left with the Nez Percés. Even if The Twisted Hair had cared for them, as promised, the white men were not sure of finding his band again. Food would be a problem till they reached the buffalo country beyond the Rockies. Buying from the Columbia Valley Indians had always been difficult. It would be harder now that their trading goods were so nearly exhausted.

Determined that some record of what they had done should survive, if they themselves did not, the captains made a list of the entire party, in several copies, to which they added a map of their route and a "preamble" explaining that "The Object of this list is, that through the medium of some civil-

ized person who may see the same, it may be made known
to the informed world, that the party consisting of the persons whose names are hereunto annexed; and who were sent
out by the Government of the United States in May 1804,
to explore the interior of the Continent of North America,
did penetrate the same by way of the Missouri and Columbia
rivers, to the discharge of the latter into the Pacific Ocian,
where they arrived on the 14th. of November 1805, and from
whence they departed the . . . day of March 1806 on their
return to the United States by the same rout they had come
out." The expedition started for home on March 23, and
this date was filled in at the last moment.

With the irony that attaches to all Lewis and Clark's efforts
to find a trading vessel, one of these papers fell into the hands
of Captain Samuel Hill, of the *Lydia,* almost as soon as they
had left. Carried to Canton, where he arrived November 2,
1806, it fell into the hands of a gentleman there, probably an
American, who sent a copy to a friend in Philadelphia, under
date of January, 1807, with a message: "From the natives
Captain Hill learned that they were all in good health and
spirits; had met many difficulties on their progress, from
various tribes of Indians, but had found them about the
sources of the Missouri very friendly, as were those on the
Columbia river and the coast." The *Lydia* reached Boston
May 12, 1807.

As March wore on, the bustle of preparation increased at
Fort Clatsop. Two canoes had been damaged. An Indian
dog had gnawed the leather moorings of another, setting it
adrift. The Indians were reluctant to sell even one canoe
—a valuable article, which brought the same price as a wife;
and Lewis and Clark's stock of trading goods was now so low
that it was difficult to buy anything: "two handkerchiefs
would now contain all the small articles of merchandize
which we possess." In addition, they had a few larger items
intended for barter, including red and blue robes made by

cutting up a flag, some old clothing trimmed with ribbon, and an artilleryman's coat and hat. The artillery uniform of that period was gay enough to delight any savage heart; but there was only one. The anxious commanders thought this a "scant dependence indeed, for a tour of the distance of that before us."

Lewis finally sacrificed his own infantry officer's gold-laced uniform coat and this, plus tobacco and some skillful bargaining by Sergeant Pryor, finally secured the canoe.

"I think the U'States are indebted to me another Uniform coat," Lewis wrote ruefully, "for that of which I have disposed on this occasion was but little woarn."

When it proved impossible to buy an additional canoe, which seemed absolutely necessary if they were to travel at all, they broke their usual rule of respecting all Indian property and simply took one, salving their consciences with the reflection that the Indians, some time before, had stolen a quantity of their elk meat. When complaint was made, the Indians had brought in a number of live dogs to replace it, but the Indian dogs, not liking the look of the white men's camp kettles, had absconded. By a very strained morality, the canoe could be regarded as reparations on the elk-and-dog-meat account, but it had to be kept hidden when Indians visited camp, and it was embarrassing to have the legitimate owner turn up and recognize it, later, after they had started up the river.

There was a thorough overhauling of the party's arms. Drouilliard's rifle needed a new lock. Sergeant Pryor's had a broken "cock screw." The far-sighted Lewis got out the spare parts that he had purchased two years before against just such a contingency, and that ingenious tinker, John Shields, gunsmith to the expedition, put them in place with the few tools that had not been cached. When the expedition started homeward, not only were all its arms in good order but it had nearly 300 pounds of lead and 140 pounds of powder, still dry, though it had been under water many times. The lead canisters in which the powder was sealed had proved perfectly watertight and could themselves be melted down into bullets when empty. There was enough ammunition to get the party home, even if their caches of powder along the Missouri should have been robbed.

As they turned over their little fort to the Clatsop chief, Coboway, the Corps of Discovery looked back on it with a certain affection. They had been half-starved, flea-bitten, rain-soaked, weak, and thoroughly uncomfortable most of the winter, but the fort had provided them with warmth, safety, and shelter. It was rather like leaving the old family home: "at this place we had wintered and remained from the 7th. of Decr. 1805 to this day and have lived as well as we had any right to expect, and we can say that we were never one day without 3 meals of some kind a day either pore Elk meat or roots."

In spite of occasional friction, the Lewis and Clark Expedition left a good reputation among the Indians. In countless talks by sleepy campfires, the white chiefs were remembered until a legend grew up about them to be handed down from one generation to another. Long, long afterward, an old chief told a settler that the white captains were "real chiefs" not like the Americans who came after them, who were nothing but "tilikum," common people. For nearly half a century, Ske-ma-kwe-up, one of the last survivors of the Wak-kiakum Chinooks, treasured the medal that the captains had given him, until, to the old man's distress, it was lost.

Chief Coboway used the fort as a fall and winter hunting lodge for ten or fifteen years, though he had two other residences. He proudly kept the "Indian Commission" Lewis and Clark had given him until a Canadian traveler—scenting the possibility of American claims to Oregon—persuaded him to give it up and burned it, supplying British papers in exchange. Coboway's three daughters, who had grown used to white men's cabins at Fort Clatsop, all married white men; and his grandson, Silas B. Smith, after a New Hampshire education, became a member of the Oregon bar. Coboway himself lived until about 1825.

Always, even to the third generation, the chief's descendants and his tribe remembered the white captains and their wonderful marksmanship. Twiltch, a hunter, boasted to the end of his days that he hunted so well because the white captains taught him. A relative, Ka-ta-ta, remembered that he had hunted elk with them. The family tradition, half Indian, half white, always had it that old Coboway alone prevented an Indian attack upon Fort Clatsop, though of this the Lewis and Clark Journals give not the least hint.

Fort Clatsop was still standing when the Canadian explorer, Alexander Henry, visited it in 1831, but it was then rapidly going to pieces. The naturalist, Townsend, in 1836 found the logs still sound but the roofs gone and the whole fort "overgrown with thorn and wild currant bushes." By about 1850 only two cabins and some ruins were left, but the old stump table was still in its place in the south cabin. The site is now only a clearing in the woods, with the battered remains of what was once a marker.

Lead bullets presumably fired by the explorers during target practice were dug out of one tree, under eight inches of wood, late in the nineteenth century, and the bones of the animals on which the explorers feasted also remained for a long time. The trail which Lewis and Clark opened to the sea was kept open by Indians and elk as late as the 1860's.

It was raining as the expedition prepared to leave Fort Clatsop. That seemed natural—it had rained during most of their stay. But "it became fair about Meridian, at which time we loaded our canoes & at 1 P.M. left Fort Clatsop on our homeward bound journey." Sixteen miles farther on, they reached an advance camp, where Drouilliard and two others had already killed two elk. Hunting remained fairly good as they went up-river, but a new difficulty developed. Vultures were now so abundant that they often ate the game before carrying parties could find it and bring it back to camp.

From the sea to the Falls of the Columbia, they passed through Indian tribes whom they had long ago condemned as a bad lot. Never really hostile, the Indians were occasionally insolent, usually surly, always light-fingered, and never co-operative. The costume of the river squaws disgusted even these hardened travelers. It consisted mainly of a leather breach clout, drawn tight enough to display the ladies' anatomy in full detail. The flimsy bark fringes which the coastal ladies had worn had been bad enough, but this the travelers regarded as "a much more indesant article."

They paused for one last exploration of an unknown part of the Columbia watershed. Study of topography during the winter had convinced both leaders that they must have overlooked a large southern tributary of the great river. With the guidance of two young braves, Clark soon found the Willamette River, whose mouth was in those days so masked with islands that they had failed to see it.

While on this side journey, Clark contrived to terrify one village into giving him a little help, by the judicious use of "magic." Landing to buy food, he found the Indians surly and unwilling to let him have anything at all. He happened to have with him a bit of artillery fuse—"a small pece of port fire match," a paper case filled with slow-burning composition, used by the artillery of that day. Slyly dropping an inch of this into the fire, Clark began making his compass needle follow the movements of a small magnet, while the astonished Indians watched. Suddenly the fuse blazed up into colored flames. The terrified redskins, convinced that this was very big medicine, hurriedly produced some food and begged the white magician to "take out the bad fire." This was quite impossible. Not even water would quench port fire match; but, knowing about how long the thing would burn, Clark graciously consented just as the right moment came. At the magician's will, the dreadful fire flickered and died down.

Here clearly was a medicine man with whom it was dangerous to trifle. Women and children fled to take shelter in their beds or behind the warriors. The food he had requested was instantly produced. Clark paid for it and departed in triumph, rejoining Lewis after a trip of less than two days with a map of the Willamette River, which an old Indian had made for him. Seeking confirmation, as usual, Clark found another old Indian who made a similar map in sand.

The hunters' rifles blazed busily, while their companions dried the meat they killed as fast as it came into camp. By April 7 there seemed to be enough meat, supplemented by their store of dried salmon, to carry the expedition safely through to the Nez Percé country, where they could be sure of game.

Indian thievery became a worse nuisance than ever as they reached the first portages. The white men's property was safe enough in canoes in the open river, but the confusion of unloading, carrying, and reloading at the portages made pilfering easy. One persevering old thief, detected creeping toward the baggage in the darkness and driven off with a switch, seems to have been the same man who was caught almost immediately afterward stealing a spoon. Thompson had to use force to recover a stolen ax. John Colter found an Indian openly using a tomahawk stolen the preceding November. He, too, had to use force. Shields had to draw his knife to keep Indians from robbing him of an honestly purchased dog.

The last straw was the theft of Lewis's Newfoundland dog. Scannon was the mascot of the expedition. He had traveled with Lewis all the way from Pittsburgh to the Pacific, had caught squirrels, waterfowl, and a deer for his master's dinner, had saved several lives when he drove buffalo out of camp, had been a gallant sentry when grizzlies came too close in the darkness. No matter how many Indian dogs they bought and ate, no soldier had ever cast a hungry eye at Scannon's bulky figure. They shared their rations with him, though like all Newfoundlands he must have eaten very nearly as much as a man.

And now the Indians had the captain's dog on the road that would speedily end in a camp kettle. An armed rescue party went rushing out, found the trail, and after a chase of half a mile, caught up with the miscreants. There was no fighting. The redskins discreetly yielded, and Scannon was returned in triumph to his master. The enlisted men soon became "well disposed to kill a few of them," and Lewis and Clark themselves once more had to threaten the Indians with death if the thefts continued.

On the other hand, there were instances of surprising honesty. A forgotten beaver trap was brought promptly into camp and so was some lost powder and shot—a practically priceless commodity. When a canoe went adrift, the Indians brought it back to camp.

Canoe travel was easy on the lower waters of the Columbia; but somewhere Lewis and Clark would have to find at least a dozen pack horses to carry the baggage—plus Private Bratton, who still could not walk—when swift water, not very far ahead, forced them to abandon the canoes. On April 15, as they approached the Narrows and Celilo Falls, Clark set off on a horse-trading expedition, leaving Lewis to bring the canoes as far upstream as he could. Trading was difficult, since the expedition had so little to offer. The Indians at first wanted "eye dags," a kind of war hatchet. The white men had none of these; and, as all the blacksmithing tools were on the other side of the Rockies, it was impossible to make any.

Clark had to go from one village to another, spending chill and wretched nights in vermin-ridden, mouse-infested native huts, without blankets, without firewood, and often without anything to eat except roots for himself and dogs for his men. Every night they slept with their arms, ready for attack by their surly Indian hosts. Dickering with the greedy native horse-traders was difficult. They would "tanterlise" Clark for a day at a time with promises of horses and then refuse to sell. One Indian, who did sell two horses, almost immediately demanded their return. Another, having sold a horse and taken goods in exchange, promptly lost the horse—which he had already sold!—gambling. Clark had to give up the horse and ruefully gather up the trading goods he had given in exchange. He finally managed to buy three himself while Charbonneau got a "verry fine mare" in exchange for ermine, elks' teeth, a belt, and some small goods. A few blue beads would have ended their difficulties, but they were all gone.

When Lewis, coming up from the river to see what he could do, managed to exchange a kettle for a fifth horse, Willard carelessly let one of the precious animals get away. Willard's blunder was too much for Lewis who "repremanded him more severely for this piece of negligence than had been usual with me." Charbonneau managed to get a horse by giving (literally) his shirt with some other articles, and then a day or two later, finding another horse and having another shirt available for barter, managed to buy a second. However, he lost one horse permanently and one temporarily by failing to picket them properly, so that the expedition was not much better off.

Clark, meantime, was using "every artifice decent & even false statements to enduce those pore devils to sell me horses." Finding that one of the chiefs was afflicted with sores and his wife with pains in the back, he treated them both, though he privately described the lady as "a sulky Bitch." The grateful patients promptly sold him two horses. It took nearly a week to get nine or ten horses, each at an "extravigant price." Then, just as the prospects of getting more seemed hopeless, a Nez Percé traveler came along on his way up the Columbia with a number of horses, which he offered either to rent or sell. Many of the animals were in bad condition and almost all were stallions, wild, vicious, and especially hard to handle because it was spring. Though closely guarded and hobbled, some mysteriously strayed away; and there was strong suspicion that the original owners were quietly stealing them back.

While Clark had been busy horse-trading, Lewis had been bringing the canoes up the Columbia and around the Long and Short Narrows, meantime keeping the men at work on pack saddles and elkskin harness, so that the moment Clark sent a horse it could be put to work. Spring floods having made the Falls, the Narrows, and the smaller rapids more formidable than ever, Lewis decided to get rid of canoes as fast as possible, starting with the larger ones which were difficult to portage. When Clark sent the first four horses, Lewis had the two largest dugouts cut up for firewood. Two days later, when he had eight horses, he got rid of another canoe, chopping it also up for firewood when the Indians—who hoped to get it for nothing—refused to give anything for it. By the end of April, when they had enough pack horses to carry all their baggage they finally exchanged their last canoes for a few beads, which would be useful in further trading. This unusual purchase was possible only because Drouilliard, tomahawk in hand, had ostentatiously prepared to cut up the canoes for firewood.

As his procession of wretched nags struggled along the Columbia, Clark viewed with astonishment the abundance and excellence of the horses owned by the tribes farther up the river. In spite of bad care, bad riding, and a diet of nothing but winter grass, his expert Kentucky eye "did not see a single horse which could be deemed pore, and maney of them was verry fat." But the explorers could buy only two.

When, on April 27, they met once more the band of the Walla-walla chief, Yellept, who had tried to detain them as guests the autumn before and whom they had promised to visit on the way home, they were again among friends. Yellept was cordiality itself, providing an armful of firewood and three roasted mullets from his own stores, while other Indians brought additional fuel—a precious gift on the treeless uplands through which they were now passing. After a two-day shortage of food, four dogs now provided a feast for the party —except, of course, Clark.

Yellept appeared next morning with "a very eligant white horse," which he offered for a single kettle. As there was no spare kettle, Clark gave the chief his sword, "for which he had expressed a great desire," together with 100 bullets and some powder and other small articles. Yellept's sword is probably identical with the one bearing the name "Clark" on the scabbard, which was found between two Indian graves at Cathlamet, Oregon, in 1904. Following Yellept's example, two minor chiefs presently gave a horse apiece in return for medals, pistols, and ammunition.

There was an exquisitely polite dispute with the hospitable Yellept about the expedition's departure. Lewis and Clark wanted to borrow canoes just long enough to get across the river. Yellept, hospitably insistent on their remaining with him, "would not let us have canoes to leave him this day." Their amicable dispute ended in a courteous compromise. There was no wind at the moment and the river was calm. If Yellept would provide canoes to get the horses across while it was so easy, his white friends would remain in camp with him for the night.

Agreed! The kindly chief took his own canoe across the river himself, and another Indian lent his in exchange for some medicine which his squaw needed. One would like to know how anyone ever got a horse into a dugout canoe or ever kept him quiet after getting him there, but it is a matter on which the Journals are silent.

Word had by this time spread that the white strangers were mighty healers, the result of a little successful medical treatment that they had given on their way to the coast the autumn before. Sick and injured Walla-wallas now swarmed about

them from all directions. One man had a knee contracted
from rheumatism, another an arm broken above the wrist,
which had no dressing but a piece of leather. Sore eyes were
almost universal and one squaw had "violent coalds."

Clark did the best he could, again replacing Lewis as medical officer. He put rough splints on the broken arm, made
a sling, and gave the sufferer some lint bandages for future
self-treatment. There was a general distribution of "eye
water," which seems to have been a solution of lead and zinc
salts. He gave the squaw with the cold a little medicine and
"raped her in flannel." Her husband was so grateful that he
presented Clark with a horse, as fee.

A neighboring village arrived en masse to see the strangers. Cruzat, the Paganini of the expedition, once more played
the violin. The white men danced for the Indians; the Indians danced for the white men; then they all danced together.

In the morning Yellept, ever a man of his word, provided
canoes to take the baggage across the river after the horses,
and the expedition took leave of "those honest friendly people the Wallahwallahs," whom they had found "the most
hospitable, honist and sincere people that we have met with
on our Voyage." After their experiences among the river Indians, the men were particularly impressed by the honesty of
the Walla-wallas, as they parted from them once more, this
time for good. Their friend Yellept died "of great sorrow"
some years later. A well-attested legend says that the old
chief's sons died one by one, and that when his last son died,
he caused himself to be buried with him, alive.

chapter 20: Over the Rockies again

A S THEY approached Nez Percé country in early May, the Corps of Discovery could see for themselves that Twisted Hair and his band must still be somewhere on the west side of the Rockies, for even the spurs of the mountains were "perfectly covered with snow." It was what they had expected, since various Indians had told them that no one would be able to get through the passes until after the next full moon—that is, about the 1st of June.

When they reached the chief's camp on the Clearwater, they were dismayed to find him very cool, and still more dismayed when he broke, almost at once, into a violent altercation with another chief, The Cut Nose (Neeshneeparkeook). They still did not know what had become of the horses they had left in the care of Twisted Hair, and there seemed little hope of finding out, for the two angry chiefs spat Nez Percé at each other much faster than anyone could understand. Finding sign language useless in such a situation, they appealed to a Shoshone prisoner, who knew the Nez Percé language and who, through Sacagawea, could interpret for them. The captive, unfortunately, was a stickler for etiquette. It would be most improper, he explained, for him to interpret a private quarrel between two chiefs, nor would he take any part in Lewis and Clark's effort to pacify them. All they could do was sit and listen disconsolately to a quarrel which they could not understand, gloomily certain that whatever else the dispute meant, it meant trouble for them.

When they finally gave up and went into camp, they noted with increased concern that the two chiefs with their followers had ostentatiously pitched their own camps at a distance from each other and that "all appeared sulkey."

At this crisis, Drouilliard, coming in from a hunt at just the right moment, was sent to smoke with The Twisted Hair and then invite him to smoke with the white chiefs. By this bit of diplomacy, the captains soon found out what the trouble was. The Twisted Hair arrived, in response to their invitation, with his good nature restored, but with bad news. He had taken charge of their horses, as he had promised; but, during the winter, two other chiefs, The Cut Nose and Broken Arm (Tunnachemooltoolt), had grown jealous. To conciliate them, The Twisted Hair had allowed them to help care for the white men's horses—in other words, he had allowed them the free use of some valuable mounts. Though the horses were safe, somewhere in the neighborhood, they were scattered and it would take time to gather them up.

What had happened to their pack saddles? Again the news was bad. The Twisted Hair explained that the cache had been badly made. Earth had fallen in, exposing the saddles. Some had probably been lost. As soon as The Twisted Hair had learned what was happening, he had taken out all that were left and had buried them again in a new cache which he had made himself.

The Cut Nose presently appeared to explain malevolently that The Twisted Hair was a bad old man who wore two faces. He had not really taken care of the white men's horses. He had let his young men spoil them. Only from the highest, most altruistic, most disinterested motives, had the white men's friends, The Cut Nose and The Broken Arm, intervened to save the horses from the carelessness of that very dubious character, The Twisted Hair.

The Twisted Hair said nothing in reply to these accusations, but—having been reminded that he would receive the promised "two guns and ammunition" when the horses were returned—he redeemed his reputation as soon as the captains visited his lodge. The Nez Percé chief, though hot-tempered, was perfectly honest and so was his tribe. He took Lewis and Clark at once to the new cache where their saddles were stored and that afternoon brought them about half the saddles, together with the ammunition that had been buried at the same place. Soon afterward, 21 of the horses were brought in, most of them in good condition, though a few showed signs of the bad handling common among all Indians. The honest Nez Percés continued to bring in horses until, by the end of May, all but two had been returned. These, they said, had been taken by the Shoshone guides who had led the expedition across the Rockies the autumn before.

Including the horses Lewis and Clark brought with them from the Columbia, this gave them more than 60, "in excellent order and fine strong active horses," except one that proved so wild they got tired of struggling with him and ate him. When some of the stallions proved hard to control, they were gelded, with Indian assistance. Watching their men racing with the Indians, even these natives of horsey Virginia and Kentucky admitted that some of the Indian nags would have been thought fast back home.

They moved, on May 10, as far as Commearp Creek, where stood the village of The Broken Arm, who received them formally under the flag they had given him in the autumn. Refusing any payment, this hospitable band gave them two fat young horses to use for meat, besides a quantity of roots and a salmon trout, and set up a special lodge for the white chiefs.

As neighboring Indians came pouring into the village, the explorers discovered that curiosity over their arrival had accidentally brought together the four principal Nez Percé chiefs and some of the lesser chiefs. Seizing this opportunity, they assembled both chiefs and warriors and explained "the nature and power of the American nation" from a roughly drawn charcoal map, making the usual promises that traders would come to supply the tribe with the white man's goods, and urging the tribe to keep the peace.

It took half a day to convey these simple ideas, for the speeches all had to go through a long series of interpretations. The captains spoke in English to one of their Frenchmen, who in turn translated to Charbonneau. He then translated in Minnetaree to Sacagawea, who translated to the Shoshone prisoner. From his lips, the Nez Percés finally received the speech in their own language.

Seven chiefs, according to Nez Percé tradition, were present at this council. The Nez Percé leaders, who agreed with the views of the white captains and wanted to get them approved by the tribe, understood political methods thoroughly. When the council was over, they had kettles of food prepared. Those warriors who wished to vote "Ah" (yes) to the white men's proposals were invited to approach the kettles and signify their approval by helping themselves. Those who wished to vote no could signify their disapproval by staying away from the kettles. The "Ahs" had it by an overwhelming majority!

Friendship was further cemented by the white men's medi-

cal aid. On the way westward, Clark had given some treatment to a Nez Percé warrior, whose knee and thigh were so
badly affected that he could not walk. During the winter,
this man had recovered completely, and thanks to this lucky
cure, Clark's medical reputation now overshadowed Lewis's.
Realizing that, as they no longer had enough trading goods
to buy provisions, medical fees were the expedition's only
hope, Clark treated all who came, sometimes 50 patients at
a time. In many cases he flatly refused treatment "unless they
would let us have some dogs or horses to eat," a matter of no
great difficulty, since the Nez Percés had plenty of dogs, which
they never ate themselves, and were quite accustomed to paying fees to their own medicine men.

The treatments were a great success. When Clark opened
an abscess on a squaw's back, the woman declared next morning she had never slept so well since the infection began, and
her grateful husband presented the explorers with a horse.
A phial of the magic "eye water," plus a handkerchief and a
few small articles, produced a "very eligant Gray mare." The
treatment of a little girl's rheumatism was good for another
horse. Doses of sulphur and cream of tartar, to be taken each
morning, were an immense sensation. When Clark dressed a
tumor on a warrior's thigh, the grateful patient exclaimed
that the white men had restored the use of his leg.

Slightly ashamed of the element of quackery inherent in
these treatments, Clark notes in the journal: "I think it par-
donable to continue this deception for they will not give us
any provisions without compensation in merchendize, and
our stock is now reduced to a mear handfull. We take care
to give them no article which can possibly injure them, and
in maney cases can administer & give such medicine & sirgical
aid as will effectually restore in simple cases." Sad to say,
some of the dogs received as medical fees were too thin to be
edible and there was no time to fatten them.

Since they did not eat dog, the Nez Percés were always

rather scornful of white men who did, and this fact led to the only friction that marred the friendly atmosphere. One young warrior who thought the canine diet of the Americans ridiculous, to emphasize his point, "very impertinently threw a half starved puppy nearly into the plate of Capt. Lewis," laughing loudly as he did so. Threatening the man with his tomahawk, Lewis threw the puppy back in his face, whereupon the offending brave withdrew, "apparently much mortified." It was rather hard on the puppy, though no one seems to have thought of that.

Clark's medical practice had grown so unexpectedly extensive that when the chiefs returned for the customary second council, he was too busy with his patients to attend, and Lewis had to receive them alone. The chiefs agreed to make peace with the Shoshones and to send emissaries with the white men, to make peace with the Blackfeet and "Pahkees." As to sending a chief to visit the Great White Father, they never quite made up their minds.

The explorers, like most other white men, did not realize what a serious thing it is for an Indian to leave his own territory. To the whites, he seems to wander endlessly so that a little additional travel ought not to matter. Actually, he wanders only in a definitely restricted area. Take him out of that and he is, literally, lost. Even in the latter nineteenth century, the Carlisle Indian School had constant difficulty in persuading chiefs to let their children journey to the strange and unknown land of Pennsylvania. It is no wonder, then, that so few chiefs were willing to visit the Great White Father in 1806; and, as experience later showed, the lot of those who did was not particularly enviable.

When it became clear that there was no hope of crossing the Bitterroot Range until the snow had melted, the exploring party moved down the Commearp Valley to the Clearwater, where they went into camp in an excellent site pointed out to them by their Nez Percé friends. Here the floods that came pouring down the mountains offered a kind of index to the rate at which the snow was melting. There was plenty of food, for though the hunting did not equal that in the buffalo country, there were bear, deer, and pheasant; and the salmon, coming up the rivers from the Pacific, finally caught up with the expedition. The friendly chief of the Salmon River Nez Percés, Hahats-Ilp-Ilp, told them to kill any horses they wanted. They all belonged either to him personally or to warriors of his band, who were glad to have their white friends eat them.

Clark's medical practice continued to grow as his reputation spread. He practiced as oculist, pediatrician, orthopedist, surgeon, psychiatrist, and in half a dozen other specialties. Eventually he acquired so many patients with sore eyes that he gave a bottle of the expedition's "eye water," famous by this time from the coast to the mountains, to his friend The Broken Arm, suggesting that he use it on any Indians who might need it and come back for more when his supply was gone. Delighted, the chief set up as an oculist himself.

Laxatives and volatile external liniment worked wonders. So did the red men's faith. All the red patients declared that every day in every way they felt better and better. Clark was rapidly becoming the most famous medicine man in all the Bitterroot range.

The embarrassing thing was that, though Lewis and Clark had cured half the ailing redskins in the Clearwater Valley (or at least persuaded them to believe they were cured), they couldn't cure their own ailing soldier. Private Bratton remained so weak that they had to carry him, by canoe and on horseback, for nearly two months. He had been under constant treatment—and still he was barely able to sit up.

Finally Private Shields remarked that he had seen similar maladies cured by sweating. Where everything else had failed, the sweat bath seemed worth trying. The men sank a hole four feet deep in the earth, built a fire in it, and after the coals had been pulled out, popped poor Bratton in, stark naked. He was given water to sprinkle on the bottom and sides of the hole, creating "as much steam or vapor as he could possibly bear," meantime taking huge draughts of strong horse-mint tea. He was plunged twice in cold water, sweated again for another three-quarters of an hour, then wrapped in blankets and allowed to cool gradually. He began to improve the next day and was soon able to walk about.

The Indians then brought in a chief whose arms and legs had been paralyzed for three years and whom Clark had previously given up as hopeless. This was probably the Walla-walla, or Cayuse, chief, Tom-a-tap-po, whose daughter, Petow-ya, remembered all her life how the white men had cured her father with a sweat bath and how the chief had repaid them in dog meat. Lewis thought the disabled chief "an excellent subject for electricity," but in that time and place it was not a very practical suggestion. Given the same treatment as Bratton, the chief promptly recovered the use of both hands and both arms, vowing that he felt better than he had for months. A day or two later he began to wiggle the toes of one foot and move the leg, while the other leg showed some improvement. Lewis and Clark almost began to believe in their own medical skill.

They needed all the confidence they could get, for they were now called upon to treat Sacagawea's baby. This sturdy papoose, now fifteen months old, had already lived through enough to kill any ordinary child. Almost from birth it had been traveling with the expedition, sometimes on horseback, sometimes in damp and leaky canoes, sometimes slung over its mother's back, in the usual Indian "cradle" or a fold of her blanket. It had escaped drowning twice. It had shared the cold, rain, and semi-starvation that had laid one after another of Lewis and Clark's especially chosen soldiers low. At last, when it began teething, even the indestructible baby fell ill.

Clark, who was devoted to little "Pomp" and his mother,

"Janey," was much exercised. What Sacagawea thought and felt during her baby's illness, no one ever wrote down in the Journals. The child's neck and throat were swollen and he was feverish. The two captains first dosed the little thing and then poulticed his neck with wild onions, "as warm as he could well bear it." When this failed to produce results, Clark tried a salve of pine resin, beeswax, and bear's oil. However crude the pediatric methods of the two infantry officers, they were successful. The papoose got well, lived to receive a white man's education, visited Europe, and returned at last to the western lands of his mother's people.

Remembering the hardships of their first Rocky Mountain crossing, the leaders were determined to have plenty of supplies this time, though the first attempts to secure them were dismayingly unsuccessful. Charbonneau and LePage, loading a horse with such odds and ends of trading goods as they could scrape together, set off for the village. They managed to let their horse fall into the river, losing some of the goods, wetting the rest, and ruining the vermilion paint they carried. It was too bad Charbonneau had to be sent on such an errand, but he knew better than the other men how to deal with Indians. When the Indians themselves tried to cross the river with a raft-load of roots and bread for their white friends, the raft upset. Shannon, Collins, and Potts, on a similar mission also upset, losing their blankets, some clothing, and the canoe itself. They very nearly lost Potts, too. After thousands of miles of river travel, he still had learned to swim only a little.

Sergeant Gass lamented the loss of the blankets as "the greatest which hath happened to any individual since we began our voyage." The icy foothills of the Rockies were no place to lose blankets, since by this time there were only three men in the whole group who had one to spare.

With so much of their already scanty stock of trading goods gone, the captains made eye water and "basilicon" for sale, and cut the buttons off their coats. The enlisted men, who seem to have given all their buttons to ardent Indian girls long before, devised "a number of little *notions,* useing the Yanke phrase," by combining their meager stores with a vast ingenuity. They also dug out of the baggage old pieces of seine, fish gigs, bits of iron, bullets, and old files. By the first week of June, such commodities had purchased enough roots and root-bread for the mountain journey.

They also managed to recover two tomahawks which had vanished the autumn before. One had simply been picked up by the Nez Percés after Clark had lost it. The other, which had been stolen, had belonged to Sergeant Floyd, and Clark was determined to take it back to the United States as a memento for Floyd's friends. The most recent Nez Percé owner, who had bought it of the original thief, had just died, and his heirs wished to bury it with the owner, after the usual Indian custom. They finally changed their minds when Drouilliard gave them a handkerchief and some beads, while the chiefs Neeshneparkeeook and Hahats-Ilp-Ilp each contributed a horse to be killed over the grave.

The captains had been watching their men anxiously during this idle period. They had seen the effects of idleness and bad diet at Fort Clatsop; again morale seemed to be going to pieces. To give the men something to do while they waited here at the foot of the mountains, they set them to running foot races with the Indians, pitching quoits, playing prisoner's base. This, with the prospect of home before them, had a tonic effect, and soon all were again "allirt." Even Private Bratton seemed completely well, at last.

On June 10 they moved a little nearer the mountains, to let the hunters lay in a supply of meat. It was disappointing to have vultures devour four deer before the men could carry them to camp, but the hunters killed enough other game to replace the loss. On June 15 they started their swift forced march over the mountains, having for the first time enough horses to carry all their men and all their baggage.

Though the trip back over the Lolo Trail, through the Bitterroot range, was a desperate, difficult, and dangerous part of the journey—on which success or failure depended— it was not a very long one. The total distance from Nez Percé country to Travelers' Rest camp of the year before, on the Bitterroot River, east of the mountains, was only about 150 miles. The Lolo Trail, at its highest point, is about 6,000 feet above sea level; but the Corps of Discovery had been climbing gradually ever since they left Fort Clatsop and they were already more than 2,000 feet above the sea in their temporary base camp among the Nez Percés. A short climb up the steep sides of the Clearwater Valley would bring them up to about 5,000 feet. The crisis would come in the last 1,000 feet and in the endless rise and fall of an almost invisible trail in mountains so wild that they might lose their way at any moment. Even though they had crossed it the year before, the Lolo Trail would look very different buried under the heavy snow which would obscure or cover many landmarks. Game would be scarce. There would be little food for the men and, for many miles, absolutely no food for the horses. They would have to cross in a single swift rush of a few days only; or they would not cross it at all till the summer was well advanced—and that would be too late.

They soon found that the Indians had been right in warning that there would be no forage for their animals during several days' travel on the upper passes, unless they waited until July 1. Still, that was just one of the chances they would have to take and everyone was "anxious to be in motion, convinced that we have not now any time to delay if the calculation is to reach the United States this season." Let the horses do without forage for a bit. Passing the memorable point where Clark had left meat from a slaughtered horse to feed the men behind him in 1805, they pushed on until, by evening, they had reach snow eight or ten feet deep; but as it was packed hard, the snow was more of a help than a hindrance, since it buried the rocks and tangled timber that had caused so much difficulty on the outward journey across the Lolo Trail. With hands and feet numb with cold, they went grimly on next morning; but it was not long before they began to hesitate. Drouilliard, their "principal dependance as a woodman and guide," doubted that they could reach Colt Creek without Indians to guide them; and short of that point there would be nothing for the horses, not even brushwood, while there was danger that even the veteran Drouilliard might become "bewildered in these mountains." It was Daniel Boone's old and famous phrase. A pioneer was never lost, but occasionally "bewildered."

If that happened, they might in their bewilderment lose horses, baggage, instruments, and the records of all the expedition had accomplished. More and more the commanders were concerned about the safety of those journals of theirs, which by this time told so long a story of so much achievement. No one mentioned their lives. Lewis and Clark could see "from the appearance of the snows that if we remained untill it had desolved sufficiently for us to follow the road that we should not be enabled to return to the United States within this season." There was nothing for it but to turn back and see whether the Nez Percés would help them. They had promised to send two warriors after them, who might even go along to Washington. That—as must have been expected from the start—was only a polite evasion; but perhaps the friendly chiefs would at least supply guides to get them over the mountains.

Storing baggage, reserve food, instruments, and papers, "beleiving them safer here than to wrisk them on horseback over the roads and creeks which we had passed," they turned back—"melancholy and disappointed," according to Sergeant Gass. Drouilliard and Shannon hurried to the villages to remind the Indians of their unfulfilled promise to send peace emissaries and to ask for a diplomat who knew the Bitterroot trails. They were authorized to promise a rifle to any Indian who could get them as far as Traveler's Rest, and two rifles plus ten horses to any Indian who would guide them as far as the falls of the Missouri. They could be generous with horses once they had reached the falls, where they would no longer need them.

Disaster dogged their retreat. They lost four horses and a mule. Potts cut a vein in his leg; it was all Lewis could do to stop the bleeding. Colter and his horse tumbled together in fording Hungry Creek, rolling over one another in the rocks and water, Colter clinging to his rifle as his equally precious blanket went whirling down the stream. By one o'clock they were back at the camp of the day before. The hunters killed only two deer. Nets, gigs, spears, and bullets failed to kill any salmon, producing only one small, thin trout. They eked out their supplies that night with some morels discovered by Cruzat, fungi which most epicures consider a delicacy but which Lewis thought "truly an insippid taistless food."

Later, as the thought of fat salmon fresh from a well-fed winter in the sea became irresistible, the men fell back on the infantryman's last resort. They learned to bayonet salmon and, as the hunters began to bring in game, their diet temporarily improved. At least there was grass enough to keep the horses strong for the next attempt to cross the mountains.

Deciding on the 20th to move back to the camp from which they had started, the captains began to discuss what they should do if they could get no guides. As Indians frequently crossed the Bitterroot Range in summer, the trees were marked by scars and gashes, where Indian pack horses had bumped against them. Perhaps a party of the best woodsmen, sent ahead, could find the trail from these and could then blaze it clearly for the rest of the expedition to follow.

When, however, on the way back they met two Indians,

Lewis and Clark persuaded them to camp on the spot and wait a few days. If Drouilliard and Shannon failed to get guides, perhaps these warriors could be pressed into service. Leaving them camped by the trail, the expedition moved on down the mountains and by the 22nd was in the camp from which it had set out. Here Clark found some beads, forgotten in a pocket, and sent Whitehouse to the Nez Percé camp to buy salmon.

Drouilliard, Whitehouse, and Shannon returned together, bringing the brother of Cut Nose and two other young warriors—"young men of good character and much rispected by their nation"—who had volunteered to serve as guides for a fee of two rifles. How three Indians could divide two rifles, nobody bothered to inquire.

Since they had already wasted an entire week and there was no time to lose, they set out on June 24, the morning after the guides arrived, "nooned it as usual" at their former camp, found that the two warriors they had left had gotten tired of waiting and gone ahead, but caught them during the afternoon, together with two of the men who had gone ahead with them to make sure they did not disappear entirely. That night, as they camped in the chill of the mountains, the Indians set fire to the lower branches of fir trees, transforming whole trees into towering columns of flame in the lonely mountain night, as the upper branches kindled. This was a spell to bring fair weather for the journey—also a magnificent spectacle, which is still remembered in modern Nez Percé tradition and duly recorded in the Lewis and Clark Journals.

There was trepidation next day when one of the Indians announced that he felt ill—the red man's usual prelude to abandoning an enterprise of which he has grown tired. The three guides fell behind the expedition, which pushed on with the other two Indians, never expecting to see the guides again and with no idea how long the remaining Nez Percés would stay with them. To everyone's delight, it turned out that the guide really was ill, though he soon took the trail once more, caught up with the column, and pushed on hero-ically with them while he was recovering.

By the 26th they were back at the point where they had stored their baggage and the records nine days before. Noth-ing had been damaged. Warned by the guides that there was a long way to go before they would find any more grass for the gaunt and hungry horses, they managed to get the bag-gage back on the horses and eat a little food within two hours. That night one more Nez Percé overtook them.

Next day they came to a lofty eminence where Indians had built a stone mound and erected a pole, and here the guides insisted on halting to smoke, probably because the spot was sacred. Looking about, the explorers realized both the dan-ger and the grandeur of the savage country they were travers-ing: "we were entirely surrounded by those mountains from which to one unacquainted with them it would have seemed impossible ever to have escaped; in short without the assist-ance of our guides I doubt much whether we who had once passed them could find our way." Both Lewis and Clark made the same entry in their diaries, noting also that their earlier hope of following marked trees to find the trail would have been difficult or impossible.

No matter, now. The three Nez Percés were "admireable pilots," following the snow-covered path so accurately that, wherever the snow grew thin enough to see the trail, the cavalcade invariably found itself on exactly the right spot. By the 28th, the Indians were promising grass, just ahead—a vital necessity by this time, for the horses had had nothing what-ever to eat for several days. True to their promise, they brought the column to abundant forage early in the day.

By the 29th, they were out of the snow and coming down the northeast side of the mountains, into modern Montana, beyond what is now called Glade (Quamash) Creek. Meat, oil, and salt were all gone. Roots were the only food left, but as

the hungry column plodded down the trail, they saw a wonderful and blissful sight. Their hunters, preceding them, had
killed a deer. The carcass, ready to eat, lay there beside the
trail. Better yet, they had come to a hot spring. Meat and
hot baths together were almost too much luxury.

When the Indians dammed the brook running from the
hot spring, Lewis luxuriated in a nineteen-minute soak,
though Clark was content with ten minutes. Next day Lewis
and his horse rolled 40 feet downhill, but neither was injured, and that night they were back in their old camp,
"Traveler's Rest," not far from Missoula, Montana, where
they had paused September 9 and 10 the year before. In spite
of all their hardships and adventures since they had passed
that way, not one man was missing.

chapter 2I: *The Captains*

separate

THE time had come for the Corps of Discovery to separate. There were still large areas of unknown country north and south of the route of their westward journey, and Mr. Jefferson would want to know all about them. After discussing for some time the best division of their forces, the captains decided that Lewis would travel overland north of the Missouri, exploring the basin of Maria's River as far as he could, while Clark would go south to the Yellowstone and float down its current into the Missouri. From the headwaters of Jefferson's River he would start Sergeant Ordway downstream, with the canoes they had left there the year before.

Lewis would be pretty certain to meet two tribes which were likely to be hostile, the Blackfeet and the Minnetarees of the Prairie—the latter entirely distinct from the friendly

Missouri Minnetarees. Though Clark could hope for better luck among the Indians on the other side of the Missouri, both parties would be dangerously small, especially when they had to subdivide to handle both horses and canoes. Both were carrying weapons and equipment that would be priceless to any raiding Indians they might chance to encounter. Bobbing down the rivers on canoes, rafts, and improvised buffalo-hide "bull boats," on horseback and wearily afoot, the little groups would be scattered over hundreds of miles of wilderness. Reassembling the party would not be easy.

Lewis noted in his journal that he "hoped this seperation was only momentary," but he was not optimistic. Still, the Missouri River was a landmark that not even the clumsiest woodsman could miss. If any members of the two parties reached it alive, they were sure to find each other again, sooner or later, simply by following the stream.

Since both men and horses, exhausted after crossing the Rockies, needed a rest, the captains were in no hurry about starting. They decided to stay in camp two days, which were, however, by no means days of idleness. Hunters went out at once and by noon were back with twelve deer. "This is like once more returning to the land of liveing," wrote Clark, "a plenty of meat and that very good." Shields tinkered so industriously with two rifles which had blown off their muzzles that he had both in working order before the time came for the new start. Both, when tested, shot "tolerable well," but Shields had had to cut the muzzle of one rifle off so short that the captains exchanged it for a longer rifle that they had already given the Nez Percé guides. The Indians also received a second rifle, as promised, with ammunition. The white men's own arms were put in prime order, all powder horns were filled, and every man received a supply of bullets.

The Indian guides, at first eager to start for home, were finally persuaded to travel a day or two more with Lewis's party. The Nez Percé chief's son was so grateful for a small medal that he insisted on exchanging names with Lewis, who thus became White Bearskin Folded (Yol-me-kol-lick). The Shoshone chief, Ca-me-âh-wait, had long since given his name to Clark.

A little scouting around the hot spring increased the Indians' uneasiness. A few days earlier they had seen the print

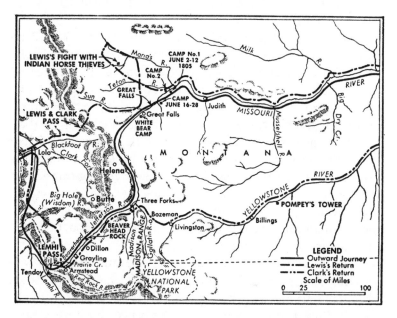

of bare feet. There were no moccasin prints whatever. This, they feared, meant that hostile "Pahkees" had been raiding the local tribes, reducing them to such poverty that they lacked even moccasins. The complete absence of local Indians strongly suggested that they had been driven entirely away, since there was now no "sign" at all. When further scouting eventually revealed further Indian sign, it was not reassuring. They found the fresh track of a horse. The Nez Percés shook their heads: Minnetarees!

The two groups set out in opposite directions from Travelers' Rest on July 3. Lewis rode down Clark's River (the modern Bitterroot), with nine white men and the Indians, while Clark and his group turned up the stream, retracing the route of 1805. With Lewis were Sergeant Gass, Drouilliard, the Field brothers, Werner, Frazer, M'Neal, Thompson, and Goodrich—and probably the dog Scannon. Clark had the rest of the party, including Charbonneau, Sacagawea, and the baby.

Reluctantly setting out with Lewis's party, the Nez Percé guides grew more and more fearful as they went along, though there was no more sign of Indians of any tribe at all. By the end of the second day, the Nez Percés were in such utter terror of possible Pahkees that nothing would induce them to go farther, their one thought now being to get back to their own country as soon as possible. They stayed long enough to show Lewis two routes to the falls, though they were pessimistic about his chances of ever getting there alive: "these affectionate people our guides betrayed every emmotion of unfeigned regret at seperating from us; they said they were confidint that the Pahkees, (the appellation they give the Minnetares) would cut us off."

The Nez Percés had reason for their pessimism. They were leaving Lewis somewhere near the site of modern Missoula, Montana, from which his route ran through a narrow cañon, which French trappers of later years called the Porte l'Enfer and which is still known as Hellgate. Since all travelers from the West to the buffalo country had to come this way, it was the constant resort of Blackfeet war parties. Legend says they slaughtered so many that skulls and bones lay all about the cañon.

Lewis soon came upon an abandoned Indian camp, and, since the fires had been carefully concealed, knew that a war party had camped there. Expecting attack at any moment, he followed the trail up the Big Blackfoot River (Cokalahishkit), noting that though the camp seemed about two months old, the trail was growing fresher. He met no Indians, however, as he crossed the headwaters of Dearborn's River and came down the Sun River to the falls. The pass which he used to cross the Continental watershed has ever since been known as the "Lewis and Clark" Pass, though in fact Clark never even saw it.

With rested men and horses, guides for the first two days, a direct overland route, and a plentiful supply of buffalo meat most of the way, Lewis and his men made a quick and easy trip, reaching the Great Falls July 13. Their only adventure came at the very start—the crossing of the Bitterroot. Lewis himself undertook to cross on a raft with two of the men who still "could scarcely swim." When the swift current carried them a mile and a half downstream and the raft showed signs of sinking, Lewis lightened the burden by swimming for the shore, while the feebler swimmers clung to their raft till it reached land.

As they came in sight of White Bear Island, above the rapids leading to the Great Falls, buffalo were so abundant that they frightened the horses—mountain nags not used to life on the plains. "The bulls keep a tremendous roaring," Lewis noted, "we could hear them for many miles and there are such numbers of them that there is one continual roar." He estimated that there were 10,000 buffalo within a two-mile circle of the Island. Since the buffalo were so abundant, it was easy to get enough hides to make bull-boats and cross the Missouri; and the men, who had starved on roots in the Pacific valleys, were delighted to find that they now had more "fine beef" than they could eat.

The wolves that hung on the flanks of the enormous buffalo herds howled constantly around the camp by night. Grizzlies were no longer dangerous, since mounted men could easily keep out of their reach; but it was dangerous to hunt them on the gun-shy Indian ponies—accustomed only to hunting with bow-and-arrow—which were likely to buck and throw their riders at the first shot. Gass and Thompson had no trouble escaping one large grizzly which chased them, but they did not dare fire at it.

Opening the cache at the falls was a melancholy business. The Missouri had flooded so high during the winter that all of Lewis's bearskins and botanical specimens had been destroyed. The stopper had come out of a phial of laudanum, ruining most of the reserve medical stores. His papers, though damp, could be dried out, and the carefully made chart of the Missouri had escaped damage entirely, while the pressed plants could be partly replaced on the homeward journey. The iron boat, *Experiment,* had proved practically indestructible, though of no earthly use.

Indians immediately stole ten of the best horses. Drouilliard trailed the thieves to their recently abandoned camp, so cleverly hidden in a tiny valley that not a hoofmark was to be seen a quarter mile away, though the grass in the camp itself was eaten down to the roots. As the Indians had a two-day start and as he began to have doubts of his ability to overtake and fight the whole band single-handed, Drouilliard gave up the pursuit. Lewis, who had "already settled it in my mind that a white-bear had killed him," was so glad to get his invaluable woodsman back that he ceased to worry about the stolen horses, even though they included "seven of the best I had"—you could always trust an Indian horse thief to take the best.

Private M'Neal, who had almost gotten himself murdered in an Indian village near Fort Clatsop, now had a fight with a grizzly bear, almost hand-to-paw. Approaching the great brute while it was hidden in the underbrush, M'Neal and his mount discovered the bear at the same time. It was only a few feet away. The horse whirled and bolted, throwing M'Neal flat on the ground just under the grizzly, as it reared on its hind legs. Leaping to his feet with no chance to fire, M'Neal hit the bear such a resounding thwack over the head with his rifle butt that he knocked it to the ground, while the breech went flying off the rifle.

Beyond a cut from the trigger guard, the indignant bear was not much injured by this unceremonious treatment, but it was distinctly not the kind of thing grizzlies of 1806 were used to. The astonished bear, somewhat dazed, sat scratching

M'NEAL TREED BY A BEAR from Sergeant Gass's Diary
"The horse whirled and bolted, throwing M'Neal flat on the ground just under the grizzly . . . Leaping to his feet with no chance to fire, M'Neal hit the bear . . . a resounding whack over head with his rifle . . . The astonished bear, somewhat dazed, sat scratching his aching head . . . just long enough to give M'Neal time to reach the highest branches of the biggest tree he could find."

his aching head with his enormous claws and meditating the next move, just long enough to give M'Neal time to reach the highest branches of the biggest tree he could find. Sergeant Ordway's diary says that the blow "Stonded" the bear, and there has been some debate whether he meant "stunned" or "astounded." The disgruntled grizzly, with a very sore head, was probably a little of both, but two other diaries say "stunned."

Sufficiently taken aback to ignore the horse, which was M'Neal's best hope of getting back to the party, the bear simply sat down at the foot of the tree and waited hopefully for M'Neal to descend, while the horse headed for the horizon. When evening came, and M'Neal showed every sign of clinging to his perch for dear life, the grizzly got tired waiting and wandered off. Making sure it had really gone, M'Neal looked around for his horse, found that it had stopped at a safe distance, chased it for two miles, caught it at last, and made for camp as fast as he could go.

Incredible as M'Neal's story sounds, the same thing happened some years later to two white hunters on the Laramie River. One man was armed with a "double trigger" rifle, the other with a "single trigger." A grizzly charged them while the two rifles were leaning against a tree, and in the ensuing scramble each man got the other's rifle. The double trigger would not fire, the single trigger fired too soon. Both men belabored the bear with the butts until it fled, having done no injury beyond a bitten hand and a torn sleeve.

On the 17th, leaving Sergeant Gass and four men to get the supplies that had been cached in 1805 over the long portage and around the falls, Lewis set off across country for Maria's River, taking only the indispensable Drouilliard and the Field brothers.

Gass had orders to clear out the cache, take everything over the portage and, when Sergeant Ordway arrived with the canoes, to drop down the Missouri to the mouth of Maria's River. Here he was to wait for Lewis. "Should his life and health be preserved," Lewis promised to meet him there on August 5. However, as the Maria's River trip was definitely dangerous, if Lewis failed to appear, Gass was to wait only until September 1. After that, he was to give his captain up for dead and go on down the river. Lewis and his trio had barely departed when, on the 19th, Sergeant Ordway and nine men from Clark's party came floating down the river with the canoes and supplies from Jefferson's River, which had been found in good condition.

Lewis was by that time already on Maria's River, where he found the hunting so bad that, within a week, he and his men had nothing to eat but grease, rendered from tainted meat and mixed with mush made from roots. The whole mess had to be cooked over buffalo dung fires, since there was no wood.

As the absence of game and the track of a wounded buffalo strongly suggested the presence of Indian hunters, Lewis kept a guard awake all night, taking his turn as sentinel with the rest.

If they met any Indians at all, they would be either Minnetarees of Fort de Prairie or Blackfeet, "a vicious lawless and reather abandoned set of wretches," with whom Lewis wished to "avoid an interview," if possible.

For a time, it looked as if they would not be disturbed, for, though Indian sign continued to appear, the Indians themselves did not. On July 23, Drouilliard found the lodge poles of eleven tepees, which seemed to have been abandoned for about ten days. By the 25th, having explored a good deal of the river valley, Lewis was beginning to think of turning back, since if he delayed much longer the expedition would have to spend another winter at the Mandan Village instead of reaching St. Louis that year. As the weather had been too cloudy for celestial observations, he decided to wait one more day; but when the 26th came and the weather was still cloudy, he gave up. About noon he sent Drouilliard down the river, hunting, while he and the other two ascended a "high plain" to get a panoramic view of the country. He had hardly done so, when he beheld 30 horses. Getting out his telescope, he soon found their owners. From a hillock, just above the horses, a band of Indians were looking intently down the stream. They had not yet seen Lewis and the Field brothers, but were watching Drouilliard. Lewis thought he could make out approximately fifteen saddles, which seemed to indicate fifteen Indians—more, if some of them were riding bareback.

"This was a very unpleasant sight." It was impossible to warn Drouilliard without revealing his own presence. If he and his men slipped away silently, Drouilliard would probably be killed. If they joined Drouilliard and tried to run for it, the Indians would see the weakness of the party and they would all be killed. The white men's horses were so bad that they could hardly hope to outride the Indians.

Boldness was the best, in fact the only, possible policy. Putting the best face on the situation that he could, Lewis unfurled an American flag and with Joseph Field carrying it, advanced openly toward the Indians, looking a great deal more fearless than he really felt. Only then did the band— all of whose attention had been concentrated on Drouilliard —discover the other three white men. Since neither side knew how strong the other might be, the Indians were very nearly as fearful as the whites. They began to "run about in a very confused manner as if much allarmed." A few rushed down the hillock and drove their horses up toward the band, returning to the hilltop as if to defend themselves. Lewis suddenly realized that the Indians were "more allarmed at this accedental interview than we were," and by this time he felt sure there were only eight of them. Seven of the saddles he thought he had seen through his telescope were probably nothing but pack saddles.

Telling the Field brothers that he expected trouble and would "resist to the last extremity prefering death to that of being deprived of my papers instruments and gun," he warned them to "be allert and on their guard." If he could get Drouilliard back, the odds would be only two to one.

When the Indians were still a quarter of a mile away, one

GRIZZLY BEARS by Charles Bodmer. *After a number of hair-raising escapes from fearless bears, which weighed up to half a ton, the Expedition developed a healthy respect for the brutes, which varied in color from yellowish to very light gray. Lewis noted, "these bear being so hard to die reather intimedates us all: I must confess I . . . had reather fight two Indians than one bear."*

THE ROCKY MOUNTAINS IN THE EARLY NINETEENTH
CENTURY by Charles Bodmer. *"As they reached the uplands difficulties increased. Lewis lost his horse twice, once with all his personal
luggage . . . For a time they had nothing to eat but a diet of wolf
and crayfish, ameliorated by three pheasants and a duck. When
things were at their worst, there was nothing to eat but a little bear's
oil and twenty pounds of candles. The men were glum . . ."*

warrior galloped toward the white men. Lewis instantly halted and dismounted. The warrior rode up to within 100 paces, halted, and looked the strangers over. Holding out his hand, Lewis beckoned him to approach, but the Indian, paying no attention, galloped back, after which the whole band began to move forward. At 100 yards all but one stopped, while Lewis, hastily halting his own men, himself went forward to meet the one advancing Indian and shook hands. The Indian went on past him to greet the Field brothers, while Lewis approached the seven other Indians.

When the Indians, in a friendly way, asked to smoke with the white men, Lewis adroitly replied that the man who had gone down the river had the pipe and suggested that one of the Indians go with Reuben Field to bring him back. While the search party was out, Lewis, conversing in sign language, learned that these were Minnetarees of the Prairie. This was not quite true, as one of the younger Indians was a Blackfoot, Wolf Calf, who was still able to tell a surprisingly accurate story of the meeting in 1895, and there was at least one other Blackfoot, Side Hill Calf. Lewis had met both the tribes he most feared. To gain time for Drouilliard's return, Lewis asked if there were any chiefs among them. When the Indians pointed out three, which seemed a large proportion for a group of eight men, Lewis, though skeptical, presented one with a medal, one with a flag, and one with a handkerchief.

As even presents did not bring out more Indians, Lewis, who had at first believed that part of the band was in hiding, finally concluded that there really were only eight, especially as the agitation which the Indians had showed suggested a small band, fearful that they might be outnumbered. Their friendly attitude may have been due to fear that the white men, too, had reinforcements within call.

Lewis now felt more cheerful, "convinced that we could mannage that number should they attempt any hostile measures." Still in sign language, he suggested that, as it was growing late, they should all move down to the river to camp for the night; and as they approached the stream, they met Drouilliard, Field, and their Indian escort. The Indians set up a large semicircular shelter of skins and invited the white men to join them under it. Drouilliard and Lewis accepted. The Field brothers lay near the fire.

With Drouilliard to interpret, conversation went more easily. The Indians said that they were part of a larger band about half a day's march away. A white man, probably a wandering trapper, was with the band. Another large band of buffalo hunters would probably reach the mouth of Maria's River within a few days—distinctly bad news.

Lewis in turn told them that he had come from the East, "up the large river which runs toward the rising sun"; that he had "been to the great waters where the sun sets"; that he had met many nations whom he had persuaded to make peace; and that he had sought out his present friends to persuade them, too, to keep the peace and to trade with the Americans at the mouth of Maria's River. If the eight Indians would come with him to Maria's River, he would give them ten horses and some tobacco; and he further wished them to send a message to their chiefs to come and council with him there. To this there was no reply. Everyone went to sleep, while Lewis took the first turn of guard duty.

At half past eleven, he woke Reuben Field, with orders to rouse everyone if a single Indian left camp, as he rather expected an effort to steal his horses, and then rolled into his blankets at last, glad to get some sleep after a long, hard day.

"Damn you, let go my gun!"

A lusty yell from Drouilliard woke him about dawn. He saw Drouilliard twisting a rifle from an Indian's grasp while the redskin still held Drouilliard's shot-pouch. The Field brothers were gone, though he could hear a vigorous scuffle 50 or 60 yards from the tent. A moment later there was a screech from the Blackfoot, Side Hill Calf, as Reuben Field drove a knife into his side, striking the heart. Side Hill Calf ran, as men with fatal stab wounds sometimes do, about fifteen paces before he fell dead.

Lewis woke, yelling to ask what the trouble was—"which I quickly learned when I saw drewyer [Drouilliard] in a scuffle with the indian for his gun." Reaching for his own rifle, the captain "found her gone," and whirled around with a drawn pistol just in time to see the Indian who had stolen "her."

Catching the thief after a 50-yard chase and covering him with the pistol, Lewis ordered him to lay down the rifle. As he complied, the Field brothers rushed up and covered the Indian with their rifles as well. Just as they were about to fire, Lewis stopped them, since the thief did not seem inclined to offer any resistance. Dropping the rifle, the warrior turned, walked slowly off, and disappeared. Drouilliard, who by this time had regained both his rifle and his shot-pouch, asked permission to kill his own thief, but Lewis forbade it, "as the indian did not appear to wish to kill us."

Since the white men, much better armed than they, were now fully alert, the Indians tried to escape, with the horses. The three enlisted men rushed off after five who were driving horses up the river, while Lewis on foot gave chase to the pair who had gotten away with his own mount. Out of breath after a run of 300 yards, Lewis yelled to the Indians that he would fire if they did not give up his horse. Though they can hardly have understood his words, they could not possibly mistake his intentions. One jumped behind a rock and shouted to his companion who turned, facing Lewis at 30 paces. There was no time to argue. Lewis shot him through the belly and the Indian, falling on his knees and right elbow, returned the fire, the bullet coming so close that Lewis distinctly felt its wind on his bare head.

As the wounded redskin crawled behind a rock to reload, Lewis suddenly realized that, being without his shot-pouch, he himself could not fire again. Giving up the horse, he scrambled for camp. On his way, he met Drouilliard, who had heard the firing and was coming back to help, while the two Field brothers continued the chase after the horses. At the camp, the two rounded up as many Indian horses as possible, while Drouilliard bellowed after the Fields to return. Too far away to hear him, they soon returned of their own accord, bringing four horses.

Joseph Field's carelessness had been responsible for the whole affray. Though he had faithfully stayed awake while on guard, he had stupidly left his rifle lying behind him, near his sleeping brother. One Indian, slipping silently out of the tent, had grasped both rifles before either of the brothers knew what was happening, while at the same instant other Indians seized Drouilliard's and Lewis's rifles. Joseph Field, the sentry, did not even reach for his rifle till he saw the Indians snatching up the other pair, and by that time it had vanished. A yell roused his brother, and they both dashed boldly off into the darkness after the thieves, armed only with their knives.

It had not been a very profitable venture for the Indians. Two were dead, and they had lost several horses, much better than those they had stolen from Lewis, besides their tent, their baggage, some buffalo meat, which was a welcome addition to Lewis's larder, four shields, two bows, some quivers full of arrows, and one of their two rifles. Lewis burned the shields, bows, and arrows, taking the extra rifle with him. Being a soldier, he was careful to rescue the American flag he had given the chief.

When he examined the chief, Side Hill Calf, he found that he was still wearing the medal he had been given and left it on the body "that they might be informed who we were." Walking back to the scene of his own combat, Lewis found the man he had shot, lying there dead. Looking over the mounts, he took four of the Indian horses and turned the other nine loose, together with one of his own.

It was high time to be heading back for the mouth of Maria's River and reinforcements. They had killed two warriors. Six had escaped and would probably return with one, or both, of the two large bands they had described. There was grave danger that the Indians would pursue to take revenge for the two dead braves. The Indians would have every chance to intercept the four white men before they reached the rendezvous where Sergeant Gass was waiting. Even there, Lewis expected to have only nine men, since he did not know that Sergeant Ordway's party had arrived.

They rode without pause until three that afternoon, when they halted to get some food and to let the exhausted horses graze. On the way, Lewis was delighted to find that his new Indian horse was rather better than the mount the Indians had stolen. Covering another seventeen miles before dark, they killed a buffalo cow, cooked a hearty meal of beef, and pushed ahead in the moonlight. At two in the morning, "very much fatiegued as may be readily conceived," they halted somewhere near modern Fort Benton, Montana, and camped for the rest of the night.

Waking at daybreak, so saddle-sore that he could hardly stand, Lewis roused the others, equally saddle-sore. It was essential that they should cover the few remaining miles to the Missouri at once, since not only were their own lives in danger, but there was equal danger that the avenging Indians would go directly overland to the mouth of the river and destroy the whole party, together with the journals of the expedition. If they were attacked in the plain, as was still entirely possible, Lewis gave orders to tie their bridles together, stand behind the horses, and fight it out to the end.

Riding hard for the next twelve miles, they heard something that sounded like a rifle shot. Eight miles farther on, they heard several rifles distinctly. There was no mistaking the sound now. These were army rifles fired by white men. Indians loaded their rifles with very small charges which produced only a feeble pop. Somewhere just ahead, their own canoes were coming down the river. If Lewis and his men could reach the steep clay bluffs along the Missouri and could attract the attention of the men in the dugouts before the swiftly moving craft swept down the current and out of sight, they were safe.

Clark's party had in the meantime been moving up the Bitterroot (Clark's River) for some days, then down Jefferson's River, then by way of Wisdom River to the Yellowstone, and down its course with nothing worse than the minor mishaps incidental to wilderness travel. There was a series of accidents. Charbonneau had a bad fall from his horse while chasing a buffalo. Gibson fell on a sharp snag, which ran nearly two inches into his thigh, laming him so badly that he had to be carried in a litter.

Rattlesnakes were large and aggressive but no one was bitten. Mosquitoes were a much more serious matter, for both Clark's and Lewis's groups. They penetrated Clark's net and bit Lewis's dog Scannon so badly that the poor beast howled with the pain. Sergeant Ordway's face and eyes swelled, and the baby's face puffed out with the poison like a little red balloon. Clark thought that the reason the deer were so thin was that the ravenous insects sucked away so much of their blood.

In spite of difficulties, Clark and his men made rapid progress, especially as they soon came into Shoshone country that Sacagawea had known as a young girl. Her brother's band of Shoshones they never found again. Though the story that Sacagawea "guided Lewis and Clark across the Continent" is the purest nonsense, she was now the first of the party to orient herself. Clark himself notes in his journal that she was "of great service to me as a pilot through this country." As they approached Shoshone Cove, where they had hidden their canoes the year before, she was soon able to assure Clark that he was on the right road. She also recognized the plain through which they were going as she had traveled it often in her childhood, when the tribe went to gather roots and to trap beaver. A gap in the mountains would soon appear, she predicted, through which they would reach the canoes. She was right.

On July 8, 1806, a few days after leaving Lewis, Clark was back in the expedition's camp of the year before, where he found the canoes still safe where they had sunk them in the river, and the cache of reserve supplies intact. Tobacco was the first and most important matter, for the devotees of chewing tobacco had been deprived of the real thing for months and had by this time used up even their stock of bark substitutes for nicotine. There was a great rush to get the cache open. As Clark noted: "the most of the Party with me being Chewers of Tobacco become so impatient to be chewing it that they scercely gave themselves time to take their saddles off their horses before they were off to the deposit."

Luck favored them—everything in the cache, though a little damp, was still usable. Clark hastily handed out to each of the tobacco-famished men two feet of tobacco, cut off the long rolls, or "carrots," that the expedition carried, took one-third of the remainder for possible Indian trading, and packed up what was left to be taken down the river to Lewis and his men. Additional stores of tobacco which Lewis had hidden in a separate cache could not be found, despite much anxious and ardent excavation. It was a tragic loss.

Finding all but one of their canoes safe, Clark's men had completed repairs and were off down Jefferson's River by July 10. When Clark found that the canoes could "go as farst as the horses," he left Pryor behind to take charge of the animals and himself traveled with the flotilla. Covering in three days the distance that had taken more than a week on the way upstream the year before, Clark met Pryor on July

13 at their camp of July 27, 1805. Early in the afternoon, Sergeant Ordway started downstream on his way to the Great Falls with six canoes, ten men, and a letter to Lewis, while Clark set out overland with 49 horses and a colt. When the horses, unshod like all Indian nags, wore their unprotected hoofs down to the quick on the sharp rocks, the resourceful Clark made moccasins of green buffalo hide. This protective device seemed to "releve them very much in passing over the stoney plains."

As they went on, Sacagawea again proved her value as a guide. Of the three possible passes, Clark found only the modern Bridger Pass and the modern Bozeman Pass. When Sacagawea recommended the latter, Clark took her advice, and so, a great many years later, did the Northern Pacific Railroad. This brought them over into the Yellowstone Valley not far from the modern town of Livingston, Montana.

Unable to find timber suitable for large canoes here, they moved down the valley on horseback, soaked by the rain, since they now had no covering but buffalo skins. Eventually they came to timber that could be made to serve their purpose.

Though they had seen only one Indian—of whom Charbonneau caught a remote glimpse—distant smoke suggested that there were more Indians about somewhere. Their horses began to disappear. The losses were always small. Now one would vanish in the night. Then two or three. No one could be sure whether they had been stolen or had simply wandered off. No one found any Indian sign, but it was strange that only the best horses were missing when morning came. When half their horses vanished in a single night, doubt was no longer possible.

The guard, going out to protect what the Indian horse thieves had left, found the remaining animals so nervous that they stampeded. When a searching party had finally rounded them up, Sergeant Pryor brought back with him a bit of an

Indian robe and a moccasin, still wet about the sole, which seemed to have been worn only a few hours earlier. A scout, swinging in a wide circle around the camp, finally found the tracks of the stolen herd, which had been driven at full speed down the valley. Indians were around somewhere, though to the very end no one ever saw them.

The sooner Clark got his last horses out of this country the better. Canoe travel was now the best way for the main party to move, for the Yellowstone was a fairly large stream, but it was desirable to keep the herd as long as possible, if only for trading purposes. Sergeant Pryor received orders to take two men, Windsor and Shannon, and drive the horses directly overland to the Mandan villages. From the Mandans he was to go north to the Assiniboine, find Haney, the friendly Canadian trader whom they had met in 1804, and deliver a letter asking him to persuade Sioux chiefs to visit Washington. Clark's canoes would pick them up on the way down the Missouri.

The plan failed when the Indians stole every horse that Pryor had, the second day after he set out. Desperately Pryor tried to follow the trail of the thieves. No use. He and his two companions were left afoot on the merciless prairie, uncomfortably aware that the Indians, whose invisibility was the most disquieting aspect of the situation, might still be hanging about with a view to securing scalps as well as horses.

In the midst of their troubles, the night after their loss, a wolf came into camp, bit the sleeping Pryor's hand, and was about to attack Windsor when Shannon killed it. Such an incident could not happen today, but the wild animals of 1806 had very little fear of man. One of Loisel's companions, similarly attacked, seized the wolf by the jaw and dragged it over to the nearest rifle. Then, finding he could not fire with one hand, he clubbed it to death while an obliging friend assisted with an ax.

Though their only hope now was to find Clark, Pryor had

no idea of the captain's whereabouts, except that he must be somewhere well down the Yellowstone, probably a couple of hundred miles away, since the two parties had been traveling for three days. There was nothing for it but to shoulder their packs and start for the river, hoping to intercept the canoes. If they failed—

They did fail.

When they reached the river at Pompey's Tower, Clark had already passed, leaving a neat new inscription in the rocks by way of record. Having now no hope of any help whatsoever, the isolated trio started shooting buffalo to get enough hides to make bull-boats more or less like those of the Mandans. None of them had ever made a bull-boat but they had all seen plenty of them—round, tub-like affairs with a framework of flexible sticks lashed together and covered with skin, their gunwales bound with sinew, and the whole coated with tallow after drying. They were cranky craft, desperately hard to handle. The Mandans never used them for journeys—just for paddling about camp. However, for Pryor and his men it was bull-boats or nothing, and bull-boats would have to do.

Serenely unaware of his sergeant's predicament, Clark ran his canoes swiftly down the Yellowstone, pausing only when he caught sight of Pompey's Tower, which is still one of the sights of the West, a great, flat-topped mass of rock, rising almost sheer above the broad, flat plain of the Yellowstone valley. Across the river other rocky cliffs rose almost directly from the stream. The Tower, when Clark saw it, was about 250 paces from the river as it is today, though at one time in the nineteenth century the Yellowstone moved far enough out of its bed to lap against the perpendicular rock. Clark examined the Indian carvings, now very obscure, carved his name about two-thirds of the way up, and then scrambled to the flat top for a wider view of the country, as the explorers always did when they had a chance. He never guessed that the Canadian, Larocque, whom he had met at the Mandan

Village, having passed that way September 15, 1805, had almost certainly been the first white man to visit the rocky mass.

W.m Clark
July 25.th 1806

After Clark's visit, practically every white man passing that way paused at Pompey's Tower. Lieutenant Henry E. Maynadier, exploring the prairies with the Raynolds Yellowstone Expedition in 1860 and halting there to observe a solar eclipse, found Clark's signature still sharply cut in the rocks. A party from Montana, passing down the river five years later and reading the Lewis and Clark Journals as they went, paused to find the carving too. Forsyth's troops, passing in 1875, included a stonecutter who found that the lines of the signature were being weathered away and deepened its lines with a chisel. Today, though again somewhat weathered, the inscription that Clark left nearly a century and a half ago is still clearly legible through the modern iron grating that protects it from vandalism.

There is no real doubt that Clark named the Tower for Sacagawea's baby, whom he habitually called "Pomp," a nickname he later used for one of his own baby boys. "Pomp" was a Shoshone word for "first born," though it was also, of course, a name much used in the Old South for slaves. The neighboring creek he named "Baptiste's Creek," obviously for the baby, whose Christian name was Jean Baptiste. Efforts to show that the captain was really thinking of an Old World monument are very doubtful, as are efforts to show that the creek was named for Baptiste LePage. Many creeks were named for men of the party, but in every case the Lewis and Clark Expedition used the men's surnames, not their Christian names.

Various odd stories have grown up to explain the name, however. One legend avers that the Tower is named for a steamboat hand named Pompey, who was buried there. As there were no steamboats on the Yellowstone for many a long year, this tale is demonstrably false. So is the story that Clark named it for his slave, Pompey. York was the only Negro on the expedition. By the twentieth century a still more ridiculous legend had developed. A casual traveler at the modern village of Pompey's Pillar, Montana, was told that Lewis and Clark had a "Negro cook and his name was Pompey and he died here and was buried across the river on that butte and they called this town after him."

As Clark's little command approached the Bad Lands, grizzlies began to appear again. The first grizzly they met disappeared in the dusk, taking four bullets with him, for the expedition had, by this time, lost its fear of the huge brutes and had learned how to handle them. A few days later a curious grizzly reared on its hind legs to get a better view of the strange objects passing down the river. Clark brought it down with a single shot in the head—something only he and Drouilliard had been able to do.

After they reached the Missouri on August 3, another grizzly, seeing the canoes and apparently mistaking them for swimming buffalo, plunged into the water in pursuit. Clark kept the men quiet until the bear was within 40 yards. Then the whole party blazed away without killing him. Still another bear escaped the next day because no one could get a shot.

On August 8, Clark and his men were astonished to behold

Sergeant Pryor, Windsor, and Shannon, whom they supposed to be traveling overland with the horses, floating down the Missouri in their buffalo-skin tubs. They had found, and in a moment of incredible folly had tampered with, the note to Lewis which Clark had left at the mouth of the Yellowstone—the one place where Lewis was sure to look for a message. Pryor's loss of the horses meant that Clark's appeal to Haney for help with the Sioux would have to be given up. Otherwise, the horses did not matter very much. The expedition would be traveling on the Missouri for the rest of the way home.

The problem now was to find Lewis. As he had left no message at the Yellowstone, he was probably still somewhere up the Missouri, if he was alive at all. Clark could only hope that his partner's half of the expedition would soon be following him down the river.

On August 11, Clark had his first contact with civilization —two white or half-breed trappers, adventuring much farther up the river than trappers usually went. These men had little news, since they had left the Illinois country in 1804, about the same time as Lewis and Clark themselves, and had wintered with the Teton Sioux. They had, however, met Corporal Warfington's party on its way home from Fort Mandan in 1805, and they had seen some Yankton Sioux chiefs on their way to Washington with Dorion. It was a relief to know that Mr. Jefferson had received at least some word from his expedition through these two parties.

The problem now was to re-establish contact with Lewis.

chapter 22: *A rifle shot in the underbrush*

A S LEWIS'S men reached the bluffs overhanging the Missouri, they could see Ordway's canoes coming down the river. It was true: they really had heard white men's rifles. Ordway was so delighted to see them that, not content with a salute from the swivel, he added a volley of small arms. Lewis's horsemen raced for a low spot, where they could scramble down the bluff and reach the water's edge below, while the canoes were turning hastily in to pick them up.

No Indians had appeared as yet, but there might be no time to lose. Hastily releasing all their horses and tossing the saddles into the river, Lewis and his men scrambled into the canoes. Though they had covered about 120 miles of wild prairie in a little more than twenty-four hours, there was still danger. Sergeant Gass had gone ahead overland with other horses, to the mouth of Maria's River. Lewis had told the Indians white men would be camping there. Gass might be surprised and killed at any moment. The flotilla moved swiftly down the Missouri until it found him—safe.

There was now very little danger of an Indian attack. The two sergeants' parties totaled fifteen men, and Lewis's party added four more rifles. The Indians of that day were not nearly so well armed as their sons and grandsons of fifty years later. Such rifles as they had were few and bad, and their ammunition scanty. Most warriors still used the bow. Lewis and his men—alert, well armed with the swivel, blunderbusses, the airgun, their rifles, and abundant ammunition, afloat well out in the river or barricaded in their camp—could stand off almost anything the Blackfeet and Minnetarees could send against them. In such a fight, arms mattered a great deal more than numbers.

Not until the end of the nineteenth century was the Indian side of the story told, revealing the odd fact that each side was running away from the other as hard as it could go. The Piegan Blackfoot warrior, Wolf Calf, had been a very young boy in the band that met Lewis. In his old age he told the story to George Bird Grinnell, a noted student of Indian lore, who wrote it down: "he was with a war party to the south when they met the first white men that had ever come into the lower country. They met these people in a friendly fashion, but the chief directed his young men to try to steal some of their things. They did so, and the white men killed the first man with the 'big knives.' This was the man killed, I suppose, by Fields. Afterwards the Indians ran off some of the horses of the white men."

Listening to the aged warrior, then supposed to be one hundred and two years old, Grinnell had little doubt that the Indians "flew north about as fast as Lewis flew south and east." However, Lewis had done the right thing in getting away as fast as possible, for when the Indians had recovered from their fright some of them began to seek revenge. In 1807 the Canadian explorer, David Thompson, found the Piegans still watching the Missouri in the hope of avenging "the murder of two Peagan Indians [i.e., Piegan Blackfeet] by Captain Lewis." But these were probably only a few hot-headed young braves. There was certainly no immediate pursuit of Lewis. The six surviving redskins had had quite enough of fighting the United States army, and their chiefs probably felt they deserved what they got. It is a very wicked thing to attack a man after you have smoked the peace pipe with him.

Knowing nothing of this and still fearing an attack, Lewis lost no time in putting as much river as possible between himself and any Indian raiders that might be following him. Hastily inspecting the supplies that had been taken out of the cache, he found most of his foodstuffs and all his powder in fairly good condition, though furs, buffalo robes, and other baggage had been damaged. The red pirogue had gone to pieces so badly that he broke her up to save the nails and iron. He still had a small fleet—the big white pirogue and the five canoes, in which he dropped on down the river fifteen miles the same day, noting with satisfaction that he was now getting into country where the buffalo were both fat and abundant. Best of all, the salt in the cache had been undamaged. There would be plenty of it for the meat they could now kill. The party could feast all the way to St. Louis and there would be plenty of new skins to make tents. It was too bad the river water was so muddy as to be nearly undrinkable. They drank it.

At a good seven miles an hour, the explorers slipped on downstream with a strong current to help the oarsmen, killing a stray bear or two, working to preserve skins and skeletons for Mr. Jefferson, keeping a few hunters out along shore to supply fresh meat. Once an incautious female grizzly came within 50 yards of camp before anyone saw her. Much interested in the strange sight, the confiding creature rose on her hind legs and "looked at us with much apparent unconcern." Several rifles cracked. The bear was soon providing badly needed oil.

From some such casual encounter must have come the two grizzly bear cubs which Lewis presented to Mr. Jefferson on his return. The Journals say nothing whatever about them; but there is no doubt that Lewis did present the President with some very young grizzlies and that for a time they lived in a stone bear-pit on the White House lawn, to the malicious amusement of the President's Federalist enemies.

As they passed the mouth of the Yellowstone on August 7, they stopped to examine the bank for a message from Clark. Knowing that Lewis would look for a note at this point, Clark had stopped to leave one, carefully secured so that it could not blow away and prominently displayed where there would be no trouble finding it. Thanks to Pryor's foolish interference when he came down the Yellowstone trying to catch up with Clark, there was now nothing left for Lewis to find except a piece of paper with his name on it and fragments of the note that had been attached to some elk horns. Someone had traced in the sand the words: "W.C. a few miles farther down on right hand side."

Why a conscientious and intelligent man like Pryor presumed to interfere with a note left by one commander for the other remains an incomprehensible mystery. Since he was himself trying to find Clark, he naturally stopped to read the note; but it was obviously his duty to put it back where Lewis in his turn could also find it. Perhaps Pryor assumed that Lewis had already passed—though it was none of his business to make assumptions of that kind. Perhaps he failed to fasten it securely. Perhaps an animal disturbed it after he had left. He must have had a good explanation, for he was not disciplined for his meddlesome blunder.

Since the message in the sand and the fragments of the

note showed that Clark had already passed, Lewis and his
men hurried on. Downstream they soon found some meat
hanging on a pole. It was still fresh; Clark could not be far
ahead. Sergeant Ordway, going ashore, found the tracks of
two men and a fire still burning, apparently "mended up
afresh" not more than an hour before. Part of an old Chinook
hat, lying near, was recognizable as having belonged to Private Gibson.

Urged on by Lewis, the men bent to their oars, but, however near Clark may have been, he was going as fast as they
were and it seemed impossible to catch up with him. Reasonably sure of finding him soon, Lewis finally halted for the
better part of two days to repair the canoes, to let his ragged
crew make themselves some new leather garments, and to
give time for Colter and Collins, who had gone hunting on
August 3, to rejoin him.

As there was no sign of the two men on the 11th and as
elk were plentiful, Lewis decided to wait a little longer and
in the meantime to replenish his larder. Taking Peter Cruzat
—an extremely skillful riverman, though blind in one eye
and near-sighted in the other—he went ashore and soon killed
an elk, while his companion wounded a second. Reloading,
they started off after the wounded animal, taking separate
paths through a thick growth of willows. Lewis had just
caught up with the elk and was taking aim, when a rifle
cracked somewhere near him in the underbrush and a bullet
drove through his buttocks.

"Damn you," yelled Lewis, "you have shot me."

There was no reply, no sound, not even a rustle in the
thickets. Looking around for Cruzat, Lewis could see nothing. By this time "the stroke was very severe." He yelled
again. It seemed inconceivable that Cruzat was not somewhere close at hand. Still no reply. More shouts produced
only silence, though the two hunters had parted only a little
while before.

Had Cruzat been silently stabbed by a lurking Indian? No other men of the expedition were ashore. The report of the rifle had sounded only about 40 yards distant. If Cruzat had fired at that range, he could not possibly fail to hear Lewis now and, if alive, should have answered.

If Cruzat had not fired, an Indian had. Where there was one Indian, there were likely to be more. There was only one thing to do. Lewis hobbled toward the boats, every step costing him agony, as the leg muscles pulled against his wound. For the first 100 yards he kept shouting to Cruzat to make for the boats. Still there was no reply.

Reaching his men at last, Lewis got them under arms and started back with them to rescue Cruzat, but by the time he had gone 100 yards, he was in such pain he knew that he could go no farther. He ordered the men to advance without him. If outnumbered by Indians, they were to fall back on the boats, firing as they retreated.

Hobbling back as best he could, Lewis armed himself with rifle, pistol, and the famous airgun. For twenty minutes he waited there alone, expecting Indians at any moment and, since there was no chance of escape, prepared to sell his life dearly. He could hear no sound of combat ashore. No shots. No outcry of any sort. Silence.

Taking over the command, Sergeant Gass went forward with a patrol of three men and reconnoitered cautiously. He saw neither Indians nor Indian sign, but at last he found Cruzat, quite unhurt and much astonished at the news that Captain Lewis had been shot.

When the men came back, bringing a badly scared Cruzat with them, he still asserted vigorously that he had shot an elk but certainly not his commander. He could prove the truth of part of his assertion by producing the carcass. Finally he admitted that *if* he had shot Lewis, "it was not his intention," and he absolutely denied having heard his shouts for aid. Ordway's diary says that, when it was finally proved there

were no Indians anywhere in the vicinity, "then Peter knew
that it must have been him tho an exidant." It was obvious
that Cruzat, peering through the underbrush with his one
bad eye, had mistaken the leather-clad Lewis for the wounded
elk they were both looking for.

Sergeant Gass helped the commander strip off his blood-
covered leather breeches. The spent ball had lodged in them
—an army bullet which no Indian could possibly have fired
and which fitted the short-barreled rifle that Cruzat carried.
On this ballistic evidence, Lewis reached the only possible
conclusion: "I do not beleive that the fellow did it intentionally but after finding that he had shot me was anxious to conceal his knowledge of having done so." The matter rested
there. When Lewis submitted his final roster of the expedition to the War Department, he placed no comment whatever, good or bad, after Cruzat's name, though he had praised
him in the Journals.

When all is said, Cruzat deserves a tiny niche in military
history. He is the only soldier in all the world's armies ever
known to have shot his commanding officer in the seat of the
pants with impunity.

As well as he could, twisting round to reach them, Lewis
dressed his own wounds. Though they were bleeding badly
and though he soon developed a high fever, the ball had
missed bones and arteries. Lewis himself filled the bullet
holes with patent lint from the medical stores and had himself laid in the pirogue. The men brought in the elk meat
produced by this disastrous hunt, and the boats pushed off
with the commander flat on his back and suffering a good
deal of pain.

They soon had the satisfaction of finding a new note from
Clark, saying that Sergeant Pryor's party had joined him, and
on August 12 they met the two white trappers who had just
passed Clark's party. While they were still chatting, Colter
and Collins, safe and sound, caught up with them at last.

Scanning the shore line about noon next day, they saw several canoes drawn up and a party of what seemed to be white men moving about. It was Clark and his party, who had barely gotten started that morning when Shannon discovered that he had forgotten his tomahawk and went back with a comrade to retrieve it. Being in no great hurry now, Clark kept his whole group waiting for Shannon's return—probably with the private hope that this delay might enable Lewis to overtake him.

There was a joyful crackle of small arms and blunderbusses as the two parties saluted, but Clark, looking across the open water for his friend, missed a familiar figure. He must have known at once that something was wrong and there must have been one horrified instant when he wondered whether Lewis had been killed—now, of all times, when they were approaching the journey's end. Then he could see that Lewis, though prostrate, was alive and, as the boats came splashing in to shore, he could listen to his cheerful insistence that the wound would be healed in twenty to thirty days. Unconvinced by this optimism, the cautious Clark made a careful examination. The wound, still fresh, was so painful that Lewis fainted as his friend cleansed and dressed it.

Soon after this final reunion of the Corps of Discovery, the two white trappers came down the river, too. They had made up their minds to accompany the expedition back to the Mandan country.

With his wounds so stiff and sore that he could not leave the pirogue, Lewis had to sleep uncomfortably aboard. Though both captains had kept separate journals all the way, he now allowed Clark to keep the only journal for the last few weeks. Characteristically, before closing his personal record of the expedition, he still found strength for one last extensive botanical note, lengthy and highly technical, on "a singular Cherry which is found on the Missouri in the bottom lands." It was Meriwether Lewis's last contribution to the famous Journals.

Running swiftly down the current, they soon came to the camp of their old friends, the Minnetarees. Charbonneau went over to his former home to invite all chiefs to a final council, while Clark smoked with a local chief. The council failed in its main purpose, to persuade the tribe to send chiefs to Washington. They were at war again, the Minnetarees explained, and could not come.

In council at the neighboring Mandan village, next day, Chief Black Cat, after making the same excuse, finally agreed to send one of his young men. As the proposed emissary had just been caught stealing Private Gibson's knife, which he relinquished "with a very faint apology," Clark indignantly rebuked the chief "for wishing to send such a man to See and hear the words of So great a man as their great father."

Their own powers of persuasion exhausted, the explorers in despair asked Jussome to see what he could do. She-he-ke, "The Big White," at length agreed to make the journey if he could take his wife, Yellow Corn, and their son, plus Jussome, his wife, and their children—which, says Clark wryly, they were "obliged to agree to do."

Dispersal of the Corps of Discovery began at the Mandan villages. Most of the enlisted men were just soldiers who wanted to go home. Not so John Colter, who found in wilderness adventure the very breath of life and who, after two years of the loneliest parts of North America, feared that he "would be lonely in St. Louis." The two white trappers had been talking to Colter. Presently Colter was talking to his commanders. He had been offered a share in the trappers' venture if he would return to the Yellowstone with them, where they would stay until they could "make a fortune."

Lewis and Clark finally agreed to let him go, "as we were disposed to be of service to any one of our party who had performed their duty as well as Colter had done." Still, it would not do to have all their men dropping out to make their fortunes. The commanders called their whole force together and explained why they could not grant this special privilege to Colter unless the others agreed to finish the journey. Everyone agreed—everyone but Colter wanted to go home.

Charbonneau, Sacagawea, and the baby also stayed behind when the expedition started once more. They were home already. Charbonneau would have gone on to St. Louis if the Minnetaree chiefs had been willing to make the journey. Without them, he was no longer needed as interpreter "and he was therefore discharged and paid up," receiving $500.33⅓ for his services on the expedition and for a horse and lodge which he had supplied. Sacagawea, who had made none of his blunders and been ten times as useful, was a squaw. She received nothing—an injustice which Clark realized clearly enough and for which he made amends as soon as he could, though it does not seem to have troubled Lewis in the least. To Clark's offer to take the squaw man and his family to St. Louis at once, Charbonneau replied "that he had no acquaintance or prospects of makeing a liveing below, and must continue to live in the way that he had done."

Clark—who had grown very fond of little "Pomp," or Baptiste—offered to take him along to St. Louis and educate him, but both Charbonneau and Sacagawea thought the child was still too young to leave his mother. Though nineteen months old, he had still not yet been weaned. They offered to bring the child to St. Louis for Clark to rear and educate, when he was older.

As the expedition would no longer need the swivel, Clark with much ceremony presented it to the Minnetaree chief, Le Borgne, bidding him "when he fired this gun to remember the words of his great father which we had given him."

She-he-ke almost lost courage when the time came to embark for the white men's distant and mysterious country. Clark found him in his lodge, surrounded by friends, the warriors smoking, the squaws weeping. After one more pipe, She-he-ke announced that he was ready, and the whole village swarmed down to the boats to see him go.

As Clark offered his hand in farewell, the Mandan chiefs begged him to stay with them only one minute longer. Solemnly, the council pipe was lit once more, while the chiefs solemnly declared that though they had not at first believed all that Clark told them, they knew now that he had spoken the truth. Except in self-defense they would never go to war again. With a final saluting volley from the boats, the red chiefs and the white chiefs parted forever.

At their old winter quarters, Fort Mandan, a little way downstream, Clark halted the boats long enough to go ashore and look around. All was in ruins. Every cabin but one had been burned, though a few pickets still stood where the stockade had been. What his private thoughts were as he glanced about, no man will ever know. Though he kept brisk, impersonal diaries for years, William Clark was never one to set down his private emotions in black and white.

Here they had fought it out through the winter of 1804–1805. Here was the real starting point of the hard and desperate part of the expedition. Well, they had done it. They had crossed the continent, braved the Rockies, endured starvation, struggled with lice, fleas, wounds, disease, wild beasts, evaded the red man's wiles. They had come back safe, alive, and healthy—all except poor Floyd. Snugly secured from damp in their tin cases in the boats that waited impatiently for him on the shore, were the records that told the whole story. Mr. Jefferson would be pleased.

No one in America could share these pleasantly triumphant musings. The whole United States had given the Lewis and Clark Expedition up for lost. There had been no real word since Corporal Warfington and his men returned from Fort Mandan, more than a year before. Silently, the expedition had vanished into the mysterious wilderness on the roof of North America, and out of that silence only vague rumor had returned. Dividing his time between Washington and Monticello, Mr. Jefferson pondered sadly the fate of the daring young men whom he had sent off to death in the wilderness. No one knew what had become of them; no one would ever know. He had failed with Ledyard. He had failed with Michaux. Lewis must be dead. Clark must be dead. Shot? Knifed? Tomahawked? Scalped? Tortured to death? Killed by animals? Dead of starvation? Frozen? Where? No one knew. Somewhere between Fort Mandan and the Pacific—which no one dreamed that they had reached—their bodies must be moldering.

Somewhere on the ocean tossed the brig *Lydia,* bringing from China the letter that told Lewis and Clark's story. But the *Lydia* was too slow.

The sensitive conscience of Mr. Jefferson must have known numerous twinges. Had he done wrong to send young Lewis on that desperate journey? It was hard to face the old mother on the old plantation house on the banks of Ivy Creek, though both of them could still hope—a little.

Looking out from Locust Hill across the sweet Virginia countryside, day after anxious day, Lucy Marks could see west to the Blue Ridge. Beyond that last blue mountain, somewhere, illimitably west, was Meriwether—or Meriwether's bones. Did she, too, despair? Or did she still feel sure that nothing could stop her daring, darling, brilliant, stubborn soldier son? She knew well enough by this time, if she had not known before, that those two letters—one as he set out, one as he left Fort Mandan, so artfully designed to be consoling—were not true, were at any rate very far from the whole truth. There had been no word, now, for so long. It had been a longer, harder job than Meriwether had thought.

In January of 1806 Mr. Jefferson had received, through

some Osage chiefs, "a pretty direct account" of how Lewis and Clark had struggled across the Rockies the autumn before. This was exclusively Indian news, spreading from tribe to tribe until it reached the Otoes, who brought word to the Osages. The rumor averred "that Capt. Lewis & his party had reached that part of the Missouri near the mountains where the Indian tract [track] leads across (in 8 days march) to the Columbia, that he had there procured horses and had, with his whole party entered the tract."

Mr. Jefferson sent word promptly to Reuben Lewis, but he warned that there was little hope of any more news until the expedition actually returned. Once they started down the Missouri, the returning explorers would travel faster than rumor itself. He was right. Word that Lewis and Clark had reached the Columbia safely had come back to the Mandan villages by July, 1806, but the travelers reached the Mandan country and St. Louis itself before the news could travel farther.

Did Clark, as he looked at those shattered palisades and blackened cabins, think of the safe and peaceful plantation life to which he was returning? And the little Hancock girl, back in Virginia? He would soon be home. Judy had been getting into her 'teens when he left. It was three years since he had seen her. Judy was a big girl now, about sixteen. Not a very big girl—only five feet four and a half inches, blue-eyed, with hair that some thought blonde, some a very light brown, some faintly auburn. It was light hair, anyhow. He had given Judy's name to a river. Perhaps he had better give his own name to Judy.

Clark jumped aboard. The wounded Lewis settled himself in the white pirogue. The oars splashed. Judy had been called the most beautiful girl in Virginia. Captain Billy Clark agreed with that. The current caught the boats. Only about 1,600 miles to go, now. Blue eyes, light hair, a little thing. Downstream they swept at 80 miles a day. From grizzly bears and wolves and rattlesnakes, from hostile Sioux and Blackfeet, from a diet of roots and pounded salmon, dog and horse, from prairie heat and mountain cold, from prickly pears and labor at the tow-rope and endless Indian councils, the Corps of Discovery was going home.

Home!

chapter 23: *Last long miles*

THE last leg of their journey, long though it was, seemed a mere pleasure excursion to the sturdy Corps of Discovery, who knew now what hardship really could be. The daily run had increased enormously, but the Missouri's current did most of the oarsmen's work. No more struggling against it with poles and oars and ropes. Fat game and fresh fruit were plentiful. No more quamash roots, dog meat, horse meat, or half-starved elk and lean mountain deer. The big waves "flacked" into their little dugouts, so that one man had to be kept constantly bailing, but that was a small matter.

She-he-ke was not even yet quite done with his prolonged tribal farewells. The day after they left the Mandan Village, they saw an Indian on shore who seemed eager to be taken on board. Stopping to pick him up, they found that he was She-he-ke's brother, come to say one more good-by. After the brothers had taken "an effectunate leave" of each other, the canoes swept onward, while She-he-ke beguiled the tedium of the journey with tales from Mandan history and tradition.

White men now began to appear with some frequency, since all traveled the river route and there was little chance of missing each other. On August 21, they met three Frenchmen coming upstream from the Arikara villages. Two of them were old friends, engagés who had accompanied Lewis and Clark as far as Fort Mandan in 1804. The Frenchmen had little news, except that the Arikara chief, who had gone down-river with Gravelines and Warfington in 1805, to visit the United States, had died on his way home, and 700 Sioux were about to fight the Mandans and Minnetarees. The death of this chief caused the relentless hostility to white men that the Arikaras soon developed; but the three Frenchmen had been discreetly silent, and the tribe were as friendly as ever when Lewis and Clark arrived.

After supplying the Frenchmen with ammunition, of which, since opening the last caches, the expedition had plenty, they came sweeping into the Arikara village in grand style, firing four guns in salute, while Indian rifles crackled a friendly welcome from the bank. The farewell council was not quite so cordial, mainly because a visiting Cheyenne chief, Grey Eyes, was present. This man was always distrustful of the whites, fearing that their medals were bad medicine. He was still dubious and still troublesome three years later when Sergeant Pryor was trying to get She-he-ke home to the Mandans. Though they still wanted traders to come, the Arikaras refused to send anyone else to see the Great White Father until the chief who had already gone returned safely. Since Lewis and Clark now knew that he was already dead, this was discouraging, especially as the Arikaras were one of the only three tribes who had thus far been willing to send anyone at all.

After several days of uneventful travel, Clark saw a group of mounted men on the shore. Peering through his telescope he saw that they were Indians, except one who looked like a white man. When they fired a volley in greeting, the expedition returned a salute of two rounds. Still uncertain who they were, Clark went over with the Frenchmen—who knew some Maha, Pawnee, and Sioux—to meet the Indians on a sand bar in midstream. A little halting conversation revealed that these were the old enemies of the Corps of Discovery, the Teton Sioux, but that the friendly chief, Black Buffalo, was somewhere near. The presence of the white man, if such he was, never was explained.

The mere name of the Teton Sioux was enough for Clark. He told the Indians roundly that he regarded them as "bad people." They must not cross the river, and if they came near the camp, the white men "Should kill them certainly." In stiff unfriendliness, the conference broke up. Too late, the old chief, Black Buffalo, who had accompanied the expedition a little way up the Missouri in 1805, appeared pacifically on the bank and rubbed his rifle three times, the oath of a warrior upon his weapon that he would not harm them. His peaceful assurances were offset by seven warriors who perched upon a hilltop near the river, bawling down defiance and inviting the white men to come across and be killed. Paying no more attention to any of them, the expedition went on downstream, prudently sticking to the far side of the gratifyingly wide Missouri.

When next day nine Indians ran down to the bank about two miles below the mouth of the Niobrara River, beckoning the flotilla to land, they were treated coldly. After an interpreter had shouted over to ask what tribe the Indians belonged to and had received no answer, Clark went on until he was out of sight, picked a place where he had a good field of fire, and landed. He was alarmed about the last canoe, which was well behind the rest of the party and out of sight. A quarter of an hour passed silently. Then, sure enough, there was a burst of fire upstream. With ten or fifteen men,

Clark went to the rescue overland, while Lewis able by this time to hobble about, formed the rest of the party for defense.

Clark soon saw his canoe, almost a mile away and well out of rifle range. Finding that the Indians were still where he had left them, he walked out openly on a sand beach. The Indians came down to meet him in a friendly way and they all shook hands. The firing had been only target practice. They had been shooting at an old keg thrown overboard from the canoes. They were Yankton, not Teton Sioux, and one was the brother-in-law of the younger Dorion. Clark and the Yanktons walked back to the white men's camp together and held a friendly council, the Mandan chief assisting, until the lagging canoe caught up and they took a friendly leave.

Two days later, on September 2, the explorers received their first real news from home. As they passed the mouth of the Vermilion River, they saw two boats drawn up on shore with several men moving about. They had reached the camp of James Aird, a Scot from Prairie du Chien, on his way to trade with the Sioux. A few years later, he would be arrayed against General William Clark in the War of 1812, but he was friendly enough now, though he had "a chill of the agu on him," in other words, malaria. The voyagers learned that Aaron Burr had killed Alexander Hamilton; that General James Wilkinson, Clark's friend from the days of Wayne's campaign, was now Governor of Louisiana Territory; that British naval vessels had fired on an American ship "in the port of New York," killing one man; and that the Spaniards had captured an American frigate in the Mediterranean. The two last bits of news probably referred to the firing on the U.S.S. *Richard* by H.M.S. *Leander,* off Sandy Hook, April 25, 1806; and to the firing on the U.S.S. *President,* by Spanish gunboats off Algeciras in the autumn of 1804. Aird also informed them that Robert M'Clelan, whom Clark had known as a scout under Wayne, was not far downstream. They would soon meet him.

Though Aird either had no whisky or could spare none, he generously sold Lewis and Clark tobacco for Indian trading and presented each of the men with enough to last until St. Louis. He also exchanged flour, a luxury which none of the expedition had tasted for about a year, for corn.

Taking leave of the generous Scot, they ran down-river as far as Floyd's Bluff, where they paused long enough for a reverent visit to the grave of Sergeant Floyd. Finding that Indians had opened and only half refilled it, they covered it with earth. The grave remained lonely and undisturbed thereafter, until in 1856 and 1857, the Missouri began to cut into the bluff, when the bones were reverently reburied in a safer part of the bluff, where they still lie, beneath a modern monument.

Keeping a sharp eye out for M'Clelan's boats, they met next day a trading craft belonging to Auguste Chouteau, the St. Louis merchant, under one Henry Delaunay, drawn up ashore to dry out goods. To the rapturous delight of the Corps of Discovery, Delaunay had whisky and was willing to part with a whole gallon. Then and there the Lewis and Clark expedition had a dram apiece, "the first spiritious licquor which had been tasted by any of them since the 4 of July 1805"—a drought of fourteen months.

The general joy of the day was marred only by She-he-ke and his squaw, weary with so much travel, and the children, who relieved their discomfort by squalling. Lewis was now practically well. He could walk easily and even run, and it was evident that he would have entirely recovered by the time they reached St. Louis.

On September 10, they met a group of Frenchmen on their way to the Platte River, from whom the Corps of Discovery eagerly "axcepted of a bottle of whisky," something they accepted from anybody who had so much as a drop all the rest of the way down the Missouri. The chief news was that "Mr. Pike" (Captain Zebulon Pike, another of Wayne's officers)

MANDAN BULL-BOATS by Charles Bodmer. *Bull-boats were "round, tub-like affairs with a framework of flexible sticks lashed together and covered with skin, their gunwales bound with sinew, and the whole coated with tallow after drying. They were cranky craft, desperately hard to handle. The Mandans never used them for journeys — just for paddling about camp."*

JUNCTION OF THE MISSOURI AND YELLOWSTONE by Charles Bodmer. *On their return trip in 1806, Lewis and Clark planned to split the Expedition in order to cover as much ground as possible. Lewis was to go overland north of the Missouri, exploring Maria's River. Clark was to go south to the Yellowstone and float down its current into the Missouri.*

had set out on an expedition up the Arkansas, traveling up the Missouri some time before Lewis and Clark came down.

Two days later, they met another of their former engagés, who told them M'Clelan was only a few miles below, and a little farther on they met one of his party. As they "proceeded on," they soon met M'Clelan himself, together with their friends Gravelines and Dorion, both on their way back to the Arikaras with presents and a message from the President. Gravelines confirmed the news of the Arikara chief's death. He was on his way back with an official present of muskets which the government vainly hoped would "cover the dead" and placate the furious Arikaras.

M'Clelan gave the officers the unimaginable luxury of wine and the men, according to Sergeant Ordway, "as much whiskey as we all could drink"—which must have been a good deal after their long drought. There was much talk by the campfire that night. M'Clelan told them the expedition had been given up for lost in the United States. One story was they had all been killed; another that the Spaniards had captured them and they were all toiling as slaves in Mexican mines. Dorion had been sent back, partly to persuade more chiefs to come to Washington and partly to get news of Lewis and Clark.

They parted next morning, the captains cherishing the princely gift of three more bottles of wine from their old army friend, and the enlisted men cherishing a warm glow from a second chance at "as much whiskey as they would drink." The canoes made only a short distance that day.

Next day they met another party of French traders, and again the party feasted, this time on biscuits, cheese, onions, and spirits. Small wonder that they "Sung Songs untill 11 oClock at night in the greatest harmoney," or that the official journal gravely records that the men did very little rowing the next day and saw a great number of rattlesnakes. They had a snakeskin to prove that at least one of the snakes was real.

There was a somewhat less friendly meeting on September 16 with a very youthful scion of the prominent Robidoux family, whose trading license the officers inspected skeptically, since it bore no seal, lacked the Governor's signature, and was signed by an official whose name they did not know. Though Robidoux's brother had been suspected of "attempting to degrade the American Charector in the eyes of the Indians," Lewis and Clark finally let him proceed with a warning not to try anything of the sort himself.

On the 17th the captains met another army friend, with almost the same name as M'Clelan. This was Captain John McClallan, a former artillery officer and an acquaintance of Lewis's, who was on his way to visit the wilderness frontiers of Mexico to open trade—another scheme of General Wilkinson's. Astonished to see Lewis alive, he told them that the expedition "had been long since given out by the people of the U S Generaly and almost forgotton." Only Mr. Jefferson "had yet hopes of us." McClallan had biscuits, chocolate, sugar, and whisky which, after the manner of old soldiers, he was glad to share with his comrades, and for which they "made return of a barrel of corn & much obliged to him."

At the very end there was an outburst of minor illnesses, mostly sore eyes and—strange malady for these hardened explorers at the very end of the journey—sunburn! The sun on the plains was one thing. Sun plus reflection from the water was too much for them. Three men were unable even to pull the oars that sped them home. But there were still enough good eyes aboard to keep a sharp look-out, and on September 20 they saw a strange and wonderful thing on the banks. A herd of cows were grazing. The peaceful bossies, calmly chewing their cuds, were "a joyfull Sight to the party and caused a Shout to be raised for joy." Not even Homer, smiting his blooming lyre in the courts of classic kings, ever achieved a line more eloquent than Clark's simple entry in the day's journal.

Soon afterward they came in sight of La Charrette. Again "the men raised a Shout and Sprung upon their ores." La Charrette was only a squalid, struggling settlement of 30 houses, but they knew what flag flew rightly over that village. They were in the United States again; they were home; they were alive—facts which rather surprised everyone in the United States, including the Corps of Discovery themselves.

Overjoyed, the men asked their officers' permission to fire a salute and, when this was promptly granted, let go three rounds with a tremendous cheer, while five Missouri trading boats, lying off the village, blazed away in reply with such arms as they had aboard.

Two young Scots traders supplied beef, pork, and flour for the men and invited Lewis and Clark to "a very agreeable supper." That night they laid their weary bones in a real bed in a thoroughly watertight tent, after purchasing two gallons of whisky for the men, who scattered to the settlers' hospitable cabins for the night. Once more they heard, with amusement, that they had been given up for lost.

Next day was still more exciting. As they approached the village of St. Charles, they saw, on the bank, ladies—real ladies, white ladies, walking with gentlemen, since it was Sunday. It was over two years since any of them had seen a white woman. With a burst of energy, the men "plyed thear ores with great dexterity" until, firing three joyful rounds, they came ashore to be surrounded by villagers, including ladies, eager to welcome them.

On September 22, the bows of the canoes turned in at Fort Bellefontaine, the garrison flag, with its seventeen white stars on the blue field, its red and white stripes, aflutter on the staff, the artillery booming a welcome, and a surprised group of fellow-soldiers gathering to greet them. Lewis had already begun to compose a report. Clark had begun writing to "my friends in Kentucky."

Pausing at Fort Bellefontaine to get some clothing for their Mandan chief, they went on next day to their old camp at Rivière du Bois, where Sergeant Ordway was gratified to find "a widdow woman who we left here & has a plantation under tollarable good way."

Though the susceptible Ordway was soon contemplating both matrimony and agriculture, the expedition wasted no time on widows, however attractive. By noon that day, September 23, they reached St. Louis, landing in the center of the village, while "the people gathred on the Shore and Hizzared three cheers," and rifle fire crackled their last salute, all of which the Corps of Discovery modestly felt they thoroughly deserved.

Out of the water came the canoes for the last time, and the party scattered to look for lodgings and new clothes, "much rejoiced that we have the Expedition completed," according to Sergeant Ordway. "They really have the appearance of Robinson Crusoes—dressed entirely in buckskins," mused an observer on the bank. But that could be remedied. The officers hurried out to buy cloth and send it to a tailor, though they commenced at once to pay formal calls, still dressed in their rough leather garments.

There was a dinner for the two captains, where some very dull French verses were sung in their honor:

> Le Capitaine Louis pour combler sa gloire
> Aux source du Missouri s'en est allé boire,
> Du mont ou ce fleuve sort,
> Il a pris sa course au nord.

There must have been a stanza in this ditty glorifying Clark too, but it has disappeared. Better than either homemade verse or dinners, there was a ball. The expedition had danced without partners all the way across North America. Here

were ladies, beautiful ladies, white ladies, who danced di-
vinely, who wore gowns, who showed a flattering interest in
the adventures of this band of heroes returned as from the
dead.

A messenger went hurrying up the Mississippi to the
United States postal agent at Cahokia. The postal riders must
wait. Hold the United States mails. News was coming, news
for Mr. Jefferson, the President of the United States.

chapter 24: *Heroes in love*

"**I** SLEPED but little last night," Clark noted in the journal next morning; "however we rose early and commencd wrighting our letters." Lewis scrawled a hasty summary for Mr. Jefferson on sheets slashed from the blank pages of the journal:

"In obedience to your orders we have penetrated the Continent of North America to the Pacific Ocean and suficiently explored the interior of the country to affirm that we have discovered the most practicable communication which dose exist across the continent."

A word in favor of "this estimable man Capt. W^m. Clark": "If sir, any credit be due to the success of the arduous enterprize on which we have been engaged he is equally with myself entitled to the consideration of yourself and that of our common Country." Last of all, a final, pathetic, personal note: "I am very anxious to learn the state of my friends in Albemarle particularly whether my mother is yet living." Mr.

Jefferson was requested to reply to Louisville, whither both the captains were going.

Post-riders galloped their forest ways. News of the expedition's safe return traveled slowly through the United States, though everyone in St. Louis tried to send it east as fast as possible. The St. Louis correspondent of the *Federal Gazette* got the equivalent of a modern "flash" off to his editors one hour after the explorers arrived, though his hastily written story was some weeks on its way to his paper:

"Concerning the safe arrival of Messrs. Lewis and Clark, who went 2 years and 4 months ago to explore the Missouri, to be anxiously wished for by everyone, I have the pleasure to mention that they arrived here about one hour ago, in good health, with only the loss of one man who died." Private individuals sat down and wrote the news to all their friends. Other correspondents scribbled busily. News stories and private letters were eagerly copied from paper to paper throughout the country.

"Wrighting" occupied both Lewis and Clark for several days. Both captains plied their pens somewhat impatiently, for like their men they were eager to be off to the East. Having no official report to make, Clark wrote a long letter to his brother, George Rogers Clark, giving a concise summary of the expedition. Lewis found time during his first week in St. Louis to write a very detailed account of the whole expedition to some unknown friend, the only known copy of which is a manuscript in one of David Thompson's notebooks, now in the Vancouver Public Library. As usual, the two friends borrowed from each other's writing.

The men had to be paid off, a task which Lewis, the former infantry paymaster, undertook himself. Since money had been no use on the way across the continent, no one had been paid, and every man now had a fairly large lump sum coming to him, most of which went as quickly and as foolishly as any other soldier's pay.

Most of the men were eager to turn their land claims into cash at once, even though Congress had not yet formally authorized the claims. Sergeant Ordway, thrifty Yankee that he was, bought up the claims of Baptiste LePage, William Warner, and Silas Goodrich, paying $200 for the first two and $250 for the third, and thereby acquiring 960 acres in addition to his own 320. Shannon bought Howard's claim. Drouilliard bought Whitehouse's and Collins's claims through Lewis, acting with power of attorney. Lewis later sold this for him. Gibson, in the same way, bought up the claims of M'Neal and Thompson, which he sold to Frederick Bates, Secretary of Louisiana, who in the spring bought Gass's claim for $300. One of the Field brothers bought Frazer's claim for $250. Most of these sales were rushed through on September 29, just after their return, and all carried a proviso that if Congress failed to make the land grants, the sellers need not return the money they had received!

Preliminary settlements being soon over, the captains were off for the East with York and She-he-ke, in October. In that month Clark coldly and formally returned to the Secretary of War the second lieutenant's commission which had been little less than an insult when he received it: "The inclosed Commission haveing answered the purpose for which it was intended, I take the liberty of returning it to you." His promotion to first lieutenant while he was at Fort Clatsop, January 31, 1806, had been purely a matter of routine.

Rejoicing in new clothing which they had hastily ordered in St. Louis—a welcome change from rotted elkskin—the two friends reached Louisville in November. On the 5th, Jonathan Clark entered in the diary which had recorded their departure: "Captains Lewis & Clark arrived at the Falls on their return from the Pacific Ocean after an absence of a little more than three years."

Leaving Clark to visit his relatives and then go to Virginia to woo Judy, Lewis started eastward. He was at Frankfort,

Kentucky, about the middle of November, accompanied by She-he-ke and a band of Osage Indians whom Chouteau had brought down the river. Chouteau took his Osages to Washington, while Lewis and She-he-ke went on together. The explorer had hardly reached Virginia soil when there was new work for him. The government of Virginia had grave doubts about "Walker's Line," the boundary with North Carolina. Here was the celebrated Captain Lewis, who had just surveyed a continent. Would he pause long enough to make a celestial observation and see whether the Tar Heels were in illicit possession of several square miles that really belonged to the Old Dominion?

At a point about two miles from the Cumberland Gap and 200 yards south of Walker's Line, he took out his sextant about November 23. Sure enough! The point of observation was 36° 38′ 12.1″ North latitude. Officially, the boundary was 36° 30′. The line as Walker had run it was nine miles and 1,077 yards too far north. Virginia was entitled to the land. Having thus extended the boundaries of his country some 2,000 miles and the boundaries of his state nearly ten miles, Lewis pursued his way to Ivy Creek and Monticello. It would be interesting to know what She-he-ke thought of the curious ways of white men and the fuss they made about a little strip of land.

At Charlottesville, Lewis found a letter from Mr. Jefferson, dated October 20: "I recieved, my dear Sir, with unspeakable joy your letter of Sep. 23 announcing the return of yourself, Capt Clarke & your party in good health to S^t. Louis. The unknown scenes in which you were engaged & the length of time without hearing of you had begun to be felt awfully." Mr. Jefferson also sent greetings to She-he-ke: "Tell my friend of Mandane also that I have already opened my arms to recieve him." They were both invited to visit Monticello to see Mr. Jefferson's "kind of Indian hall," in which his Indian curiosities were displayed. It did not occur to Mr. Jefferson, in his enthusiasm, that nothing Indian was much of a curiosity to either Lewis or She-he-ke.

Lewis was in Washington by early January. On the 10th he attended a gala reception at the White House for the "King and Queen of the Mandans." On the 14th, he himself was guest of honor at a dinner given for him alone, after the hosts had waited several days for Clark, who had not the least intention of leaving Judy for ceremonial dinners. An excruciatingly bad poem by Joel Barlow "On the Discoveries of Captain Lewis," read at the dinner, suggested changing the name of the Columbia River:

> Then hear the loud voice of the nation proclaim
> And all ages resound the decree:
> *Let our Occident stream bear the young hero's name*
> *Who taught him his path to the sea.*

Lewis submitted to the War Department an official list of all members of the expedition, with a final commendation of "the ample support which they gave me under every difficulty; the manly firmness which they evinced on every necessary occasion; and the patience and fortitude with which they submitted to, and bore, the fatigues and painful sufferings incident to my late tour to the Pacific Ocean." The phrasing shows clearly that though Lewis personally regarded Clark as his equal on the expedition, official Washington regarded Lewis as the commander.

He added special notes on some of the men who had especially distinguished themselves. There was a long note on the dead Floyd, "a young man of much merit," and a suggestion that some kind of payment ought to be made to his father, "a man much respected, though possessed of but moderate wealth." There was warm commendation for that trio who had done so many difficult and dangerous things, Drouilliard and the Fields. The brothers were bracketed as "two of the most active and enterprising young men who accompanied us. It was their peculiar fate to have been engaged in all the most dangerous and difficult scenes of the voyage, in which they uniformly acquitted themselves with much honor." Drouilliard: "a man of much merit," had been "peculiarly useful" for his languages and his skill as a woodsman. Lewis thought he had not been paid enough—a most unusual opinion for an army paymaster. Shields, an "artist" as a gunsmith, had saved the day repeatedly by his "skill and ingenuity." Charbonneau was described briefly as "a man of no peculiar merit," which was only too true, though Clark took a somewhat more charitable view.

As news of the Lewis and Clark Expedition's return spread, Americans everywhere were stirred. The magnitude of Mr. Jefferson's purchase was revealed. An American Corps of Discovery had moved across it to the Pacific, returning—after they were all supposed to be dead—with news of strange and wonderful things in that vast, unknown expanse. New prospects were open to the new nation. When Clark reached Fincastle to make love to Judy, the citizens presented an "address," which shows how the country as a whole must have felt: "The rewards which a grateful country may think proper to bestow, ought not to be apportioned to common merit or services." Mr. Jefferson had always agreed with that. So did Congress. The House of Representatives set up a committee. Secretary of War Dearborn, called upon for suggestions, proposed that each enlisted man should have 320 acres of land, Clark, 1,000, Lewis 1,600. But Lewis would have none of that. He had promised Clark emoluments equal to his own. The powers in Washington yielded. With exemplary speed a bill went through, giving each captain 1,600 acres and 320 to the others. All were to receive double pay, and a surviving receipt shows that this meant $1,228 for Clark and presumably the same amount for Lewis.

The governorship of Louisiana was vacant. The Indian problem there was pressing. The British would be certain to attack there if war broke out. Who was so well fitted to govern and protect the territory as the men who knew it best. Lewis was made Governor early in 1807, resigning his commission in the Regular Army in March. Clark was made Brigadier-General of Louisiana Militia. Mr. Jefferson had at first wished to make him Lieutenant-Colonel in the Second Infantry; but, on the ground that such a promotion would violate a principle, the Senate rejected it, 20 to 9, at the same time offering to approve any other nomination in the gift of the government.

Equally interesting to that botanical enthusiast, Meriwether Lewis, was the distribution of the seeds and specimens he had brought home. A special packet of seeds went to Mr. Jefferson, with some of which he must soon have been puttering eagerly in the garden at Monticello, while others went to the Philadelphia horticulturists, Bernard McMahon and William Hamilton. By April 5, 1807, McMahon had seven species of the new plants "up and in a growing state" and was eagerly asking for more. Pursh, the German botanist, whom McMahon was entertaining, met Lewis about this time and began to make botanical drawings from his dried specimens. In spite of the curiosity of eager botanists, the plants were grown in strictest secrecy for several years, so that Lewis might have full scientific credit when his book should appear.

Though the extensive collections made on the first part of the journey had been destroyed or badly damaged in the cache on the Missouri, Pursh saw about 150 specimens, collected beyond the Rockies and on the return journey, not more than a dozen of which he thought had yet been recorded as native to North America. Later botanists have modified this a little, but the genera Lewisia and Clarkia still stand as botanical memorials to the expedition and several of the plants they brought back are still grown in American gardens. Pursh took some, perhaps all, of Lewis's specimens with him to England, where he used them in writing his *Flora Americae Septentrionalis,* published in 1814, while Great Britain and the United States were at war. Some of the specimens found their way back to Philadelphia and are now in the Academy of Natural Sciences there.

Safely home from the wilderness—somewhat surprised to be still alive—young, famous, successful, the new Governor of Louisiana Territory and the new Brigadier-General promptly fell in love—Lewis tepidly, unhappily, as always; Clark tempestuously and successfully. "I have become quite a galant and somewhat taken with the fair creatures," Clark wrote his brother Edmund from Washington, but his real interest was in Judy Hancock, whom he soon persuaded to marry him.

Like all young lovers, Clark was as eager to encourage his friend's love affairs as he was to talk about his own. He was somewhat dismayed to discover Federalist leanings in his prospective father-in-law, but after all, politics had nothing to do with marrying Judy. He poured out the whole story of his engagement to Lewis early in 1807: "I have made an attacked most vigorously. we have come to terms, and a delivery is to be made first of January P when I shall be in possession highly pleasing to myself." Judy had set January, 1808, as the date of their marriage.

As for her father's regrettably Federalist inclinations, Clark hoped "to introduce some substantiall sincere republicanism into some branch of the family about January." When Clark confided his engagement to Mr. Jefferson, that constant friend presented him with jewelry for Judy—a necklace, two bracelets, earrings, a pin and a ring, of pearls and topaz.

Lewis himself, though dallying with several trivial sentimental affairs of his own, was mildly amused by his friend's ardor. In the months between the return of the expedition and his departure for St. Louis, as Governor, in 1808, Lewis fancied himself in love several times, though he had returned

to find that Maria Wood, that "lovely fair one" for whom
he had named Maria's River, would soon be marrying someone else. The sting of disappointment, if there was one, must
have been very slight, for he was soon writing his friend
Clark romantic letters about other beauties of the moment.

About the time of Clark's betrothal, Lewis had definitely
decided to ask a mysterious, and still unidentified, girl to
marry him. He confided in Clark in a letter long since lost,
though Clark's reply tells the story clearly enough: "My
F[riend,] you[r] choice is one I highly approve, but Should
the thing not take to your wish I have discovered a most lovly
girl Butifule rich possessing those accomplishments which is
calculated to make a man hapy—inferior to you—but to few
others the Daugh[ter] of C——. his politicks is in opposition
to yours." Surely, if Clark could swallow the Federalism of
his fiancée's family, Lewis could do the same.

Lewis did not marry the rich and beautiful Miss C——,
either, but he was for a little while desperately in earnest
over the beautiful unknown about whom he had confided in
Clark. "For god's sake," he wrote his friend, "do not whisper
my attachment to Miſs —— or I am undone."

Pausing at the home of Clark's future father-in-law, George
Hancock, Lewis almost found another lovely fair one in Miss
Letitia Brackenridge. "His Excellency," as people had begun
to call him, had shown himself so plainly interested in the
girl that his family were agog. Reuben Lewis was enthusiastic
about the lady—"accomplished & beautifull," indeed "one
of the most beautifull Women I have ever seen both as to
form & features." The Lewises and Markses were fully prepared to welcome a new sister-in-law.

But the beautiful Miss Brackenridge in the end became
just one more of the girls that Lewis never quite married, for
"he was disappointed in his design of addressing her." This
very proper young lady had heard from some busybody "of
the Governours intention of Coarting her." The great ex-

plorer, the dashing soldier, the President's friend, the new Governor of Louisiana Territory, the man everyone was talking about, was coming to the Hancock estate just for her. Modestly, Miss Brackenridge concluded that "if she remained it would look too mutch like a challange," and set off with her father for Richmond. If this was mere coquetry, if the lady was trying the ancient feminine ruse of fleeing in order to be pursued, it did not work. Lewis finished his visit in Fincastle and placidly pursued his way toward St. Louis to take up his post as Governor.

"Be that as it may," wrote his brother Reuben, "she is [a] verry sweet looking Girl & I should like to have her as a Sister." His Excellency the Governor of Louisiana Territory was much interested in sweet-looking girls. He always had been. But his interest did not prompt him to delay his journey in order to pursue this one to Richmond. It is doubtful if they ever met again. In due course, like all of Lewis's other rather lukewarm flames, she probably married someone else.

The truth is that Meriwether Lewis was no ladies' man, and—moody, solitary fellow that he was, more in love with wilderness adventure than with anything else—would probably have made a very bad husband for any of the conventionally elegant young ladies of his class and period. Besides, what mere girl could approach the grace, the charm, the intelligence, and the tremendous vigor of his fascinating mother? His disappointments in affairs of the heart were nothing new. It had always been so. As a boy, he had been enthusiastic about the girls of Albemarle. But he had gone off to the wars, sending back in his letters gay messages "to all the girls" as a gallant young officer should—but never messages to any girl in particular. When he came home, the girls were mostly wed.

There was always a new crop of girls, and doubtless a new crop of infatuations. But then he went off to Rivière du Bois.

When he came back at last, the new crop were mostly married, too. He found "fair friends" at St. Louis; but soon he
was saying ardent farewells, as he set out for the far Pacific.
The St. Louis ladies could hardly be expected to wait for
this dilatory lover, who was very likely to be killed in the
wilderness. There were new Virginia girls to greet the heroic
explorer on his return. But from them, too, he turned away,
back to St. Louis, the Mississippi, and the edge of civilization.

Milly Maury, the schoolmaster's daughter, who asked for
"Mirwether's" portrait as she lay dying; the "insurgent girl"
in Pittsburgh; the fair Maria, she of the exquisite complexion; the charming but timid Miss Brackenridge; the rich
and beautiful Miss C——, whom Clark had chosen for him;
the mysterious Miss ——, of whom nothing whatever is known
—all these love affairs were failures.

What, after all, is a woman, compared to solitude in the
wilderness, Indians, the bright face of danger, the high adventure of the Rockies, canoes in foaming rapids, a grizzly
hunt, or sword blades flashing in the sun, a flag that flutters
over steel-tipped columns, the cadenced tramp of doughboys
at your back, and polished brass and bugles, calling, calling,
and rifles crashing smartly to "Present"?

chapter 25: His Excellency, Governor Lewis

TO THIS day, no one knows what wild schemes had been brewing in the eager, restless, unscrupulous mind of Aaron Burr. Armed seizure of American territory in the lower Mississippi? A grandiose scheme to make himself Emperor of Mexico? Seizure of Spanish territory? Whatever it was, it was certainly treason; and Lewis and Clark returned from the wilderness in the midst of the excitement, just in time to assist their friend Mr. Jefferson. Four days after they landed in St. Louis, the President issued his proclamation against his former Vice-President, who was by this time safely in jail, awaiting trial.

Lewis and Clark were men that Mr. Jefferson could trust, and he turned to them immediately. It was not long before a third member of the expedition, Robert Frazier, was also busy in Louisiana, ferreting out the schemes of the "Burrists" who still remained at large. Lewis remained in the East as Mr. Jefferson's personal representative at Burr's trial, while Clark was sent hurrying back to St. Louis, where Private Robert Frazer, late of the Corps of Discovery, was uncovering alarming evidence "with rispect to Burrism in Louisiana." Clark paused on his way through Virginia long enough to say good-by to Judy, though he was being urged westward by a friendly admonition from Governor Lewis to "make your disertations on the subject of —— to Mifs —— as short as is consonant with your amorous desires." Both the Governor and the President wanted their trusty Brigadier-General at the scene of a possible armed outbreak as soon as he could get there.

Organizing the Louisiana Militia and suppressing Burr's sympathizers—if the plot had gone so far that suppression became necessary—were not the only tasks with which Clark had been charged. Now as always, both he and Lewis were scrupulously looking after the interests of the enlisted men who had followed them so loyally. Clark took with him money and land grants for most of the party; but, since the Corps of Discovery was by this time scattered, he was given a year in which to find the men and turn over the extra pay and the papers entitling them to their land. He was also to begin the long, vexatious, and expensive effort to send She-he-ke and his family safely home to the Mandan country.

His principal worry at the moment was that, as a Brigadier-General in what might prove a very critical post, he might find it hard to get enough leave to go back to Virginia and be married. "You can hint a little on that Subject if you think proper, and let me know," he wrote Lewis, who must have hinted to good effect, for there was no difficulty about Clark's leave when the happy day arrived.

One delightfully human and totally unconscious revelation of the new general's love for his Judy had survived from this period of enforced separation. Clark must have forgotten that it ever existed or he would certainly have torn it up. At first sight the paper does not look romantic at all, for it is just the draft of a very dull and very formal letter to Secretary of War Dearborn about a bill of exchange. Alone in his office, Clark's thoughts strayed from official correspondence in St. Louis, back to Virginia, where Judy was waiting to marry him. He had a pen in his hand. Like many another, he fell to "doodling." Idly the quill pen slipped over the paper.

Julia Hancock

is what he wrote—he was a little clearer about his Judy's name now than he had been when he named that river. If she was far away, where he could not see his lady love, at least he could write her name. He scribbled her initials, too. He found it all so pleasant that he wrote it again, three times:

Julia

Julia   Julia

He had made a mistake about her first name when he named Judith's River. Never mind. He was going to change her name for good, very soon. Greatly daring, at the very bottom of the paper, he wrote for his own eyes alone what that name would be:

Julia Clark

Then he forgot to tear it up!

Lewis could not leave for his territorial capital until Aaron Burr's treason trial was over; and Frazer had collected so much information about the conspiracy that he was bound over as a witness against persons apprehended as the associates of Burr "in his treasonable practices, and who are to be tried about the beginning of May next." As one of the acts alleged against Burr had been committed in Virginia, the old state capitol of Richmond was selected for the treason trial.

Thither went Captain Lewis to represent Mr. Jefferson. But Burr had concealed his steps cleverly. The evidence against him was too slight for conviction. His schemes had collapsed but so did the case against him. He walked out of the trial, a free but ruined man. Lewis watched it all and returned to Washington. Though there is not the slightest evidence that they ever exchanged a word, it is possible that, at the trial, he caught a glimpse of Theodosia Burr Alston, who was with her accused father.

Starting for St. Louis in the late winter of 1808, Lewis paused with his brother Reuben in Kentucky to struggle once more over the land claims there. The family's claims, he wrote from Louisville, were secure, but he could find no trace of his own. Going on overland, he reached St. Louis on March 8, 1808, while Reuben, traveling down the Ohio and up the Mississippi, arrived about two weeks earlier. Even on this trifling journey, the Governor was careful to reassure his mother as to Reuben's safety.

Clark, who had returned to the East some months before Lewis arrived, had been married January 5, 1808, had spent his honeymoon in Virginia, and was now busy with happy plans to bring his "family," that is, his bride and a niece, to St. Louis. Marriage was not to separate the heroic friends. Lewis went into the raptures of a real estate agent as he described a house he had found for them—four rooms on the ground floor, an attic for slaves, a garden already planted. If there was not room for a bachelor like himself, he would find an office elsewhere "and still consider myself your mesmate." Eventually he is said to have found lodgings with the wealthy Chouteau family.

The Governor went to endless pains to ensure his friend's bride a pleasant voyage on the Mississippi. Clark needed two boats, since he was bringing not only furniture for his new household but also heavy equipment for the Indians—running gear for a horse-power mill, blacksmith's tools, and other bulky articles. To Colonel Thomas Hunt, now commanding his old regiment, the First Infantry, the Governor specially applied for the services of his and Clark's old friend, Nathaniel Pryor, to command the escort.

Pryor, now a Regular Army ensign, was to meet Clark and his bride with two large keelboats and a military guard, either at Fort Massac or at the mouth of the Ohio. This was to be no ordinary Mississippi journey. Lewis had seen to it that the ladies would be comfortable, even on a keelboat.

The ever jovial Clark had written that he would arrive in St. Louis with "goods" or "merchandize." Lewis replied in the same jocular vein: "I must halt here in the middle of my communications and ask you if the matrimonial dictionary affords no term more appropriate than that of *goods,* alias *merchandize,* for that dear and interesting part of the creation? it is very well Genl., I shall tell madam of your want of Gallantry; and the triumph too of detection will be more compleat when it is recollected what a musty, fusty, rusty old bachelor I am."

"I trust," the Governor added, "you do not mean merely to tantalize us by the promise you have made of bringing with you some of your Neices, I have already flattered the community of S Louis with this valuable acquisition to our female society."

Clark and his bride left Louisville June 2, 1808, but they brought only one niece, "the beautiful and accomplished Miss Anderson," daughter of his sister, Elizabeth. All young ladies of the early nineteenth century were "beautiful and accomplished," but Clark's niece really was such a pretty girl that she caused a quite adequate flutter in the overwhelmingly masculine society of old St. Louis. A friend wrote to the crabbèd Frederick Bates, soon to be Lewis's bitterest enemy: "Great agitation in S^t. Louis among the bachelors, to prevent fatal consequences a Town meeting has been proposed for the purpose of disposing of her by lot."

The agitation among St. Louis bachelors did not extend to the bachelor Governor, nor did he resume his attentions to the other "fair friends" in St. Louis to whom he had been so eager to say farewell in 1804. Miss Letitia Brackenridge, for whose sake he would not even trouble with a trip to Richmond, was the last girl in whom he showed even a casual interest.

From bright anticipation of his friend's arrival, Lewis turned to the tangled affairs of the Governor's office. Political tasks were new to the explorer, who had never been either a politician or a civilian executive and who now had to be both. Meriwether Lewis had been a woodsman or a soldier all his life. Give him troops to move, a mutiny to suppress, a surly Indian chief to cajole, an unknown mountain range to cross, a grizzly to kill, or any kind of danger to overcome, and he was in his element. But there were none of these in the Governor's office. An occasional grizzly would have been a relief compared to what he had to face. His enemy, Frederick Bates, was not far wrong when he wrote: "How unfortunate for this man that he resigned his commission in the army: His habits are altogether military & he never can I think succeed in any other profession."

The situation Lewis inherited was complex and infinitely vexatious. There was trouble with the original French population and the American newcomers, who failed to get along together. There was trouble with land titles—French, Spanish, and American—which were in hopeless confusion, especially titles to lead mining claims. There was trouble with white squatters and white hunters, intruding upon government and Indian lands with cheerful indifference to titles. There was trouble with traders, who joined with squatters and hunters to make trouble with the Indians. There was trouble with the British, who deliberately stirred up both the traders and the Indians. It was not an unusual situation for a newly settled American territory. Michigan was just as bad.

Lewis's territory was riven between two violently opposed political factions, each of which tried to attach the new and inexperienced Governor to itself. "Burrism," too, had left a deep division. The former Governor of Louisiana—Clark's old friend, General Wilkinson, who had probably been involved in Burr's schemes and who had certainly committed treason enough on his own account—was facing trial. He was acquitted mainly because the abundant written evidence of his guilt had been carried off to Cuba, with the rest of their archives, by the departing Spaniards. When, some ninety years later, the American army arrived in Cuba, it was too late again—the archives had been taken to Seville. There, in the twentieth century, American historians found clear evidence of Wilkinson's guilt at last—a hundred years too late. No one knew how many of Burr's and Wilkinson's adherents were traitors too and how many were innocent dupes. In dealing with suspected Burrists, Lewis had to make wholesale removals from office, which meant more enemies. He made a series of new appointments, though confirming some old ones. Daniel Boone became once more Justice of the Femme Osage, where he had settled long before, under the Spaniards. Lewis also offered a justiceship to the explorer, James Mackay, who had helped prepare the expedition, but Mackay declined.

From the start, the new Governor proposed to take a friendly but firm course with the Indians. Early traders had pretended to offer the redskins "protection," which they had neither power nor authority to give. When Indians got killed in the petty tribal forays which were always going on, the white men bought their way out of their difficulties by "covering the dead," that is, making payment for murders they had no way of preventing.

In Washington, the Secretary of War, Lewis, Clark and the veteran Indian agent, Nicholas Boilvin, had worked out a new policy. Traders would be kept under control. White and Indian alike must hereafter look to the United States for protection. Save in extreme cases, there would be no more "covering the dead" for, as Lewis put it: "we cannot with complacency, think of paying for disobedience to our will." Murderers, red or white, would be tried and executed. For Indian control, Governor Lewis now relied mainly on his power to stop trading and take away the government blacksmiths that were being sent to the Indians—Alexander Willard, of the Corps of Discovery, among them. That, he hoped, would cut the Indians off from their supplies, their weapons, their ammunition, and their repair facilities. He was right, but his measures infuriated traders and Indians alike, and increased the opposition to him in Louisiana.

Clark took some troops up the Missouri, built a fort, and negotiated a treaty designed to keep the Osages quiet. Promptly the Indians complained to Lewis that they had not understood the treaty and only part of the tribe had agreed to it. Patiently, Lewis negotiated another.

At least Clark had established control of the Missouri River by building Fort Osage at a point where all passing craft had to run under its guns—the two friends had noted the advantages of that site during the long winter at Fort Mandan. Nevertheless, rumors of Indian danger—a danger that had been imminent in 1807—multiplied again, as 1808 wore on into 1809. Settlers at Boone's Lick had to leave their farms when Lewis found that he could not protect them so far from St. Louis.

Undeclared naval war with Great Britain already existed, and 1812 was rapidly approaching. Communications with Washington were so slow that Lewis never knew whether war might not have been declared without his knowledge, in which case the British would become still more active in stirring up the Indians against him. Meantime, there was no doubt about the unfriendly machinations of British traders, who—moving about among the Indians in wild country, where there was no way to control them—did their best to keep the redskins attached to the British Crown and the British trading posts.

Alertness and precaution had been Wayne's safeguards against the Indians. They had saved the Corps of Discovery. Lewis and Clark did not intend to be caught napping now. As rumors increased, Lewis began to use troops in small detachments. At first he sent out scouts and fairly large patrols from the First Infantry, but there were not enough Regular troops—there never are. Orders to call a special force of Clark's Militia went out on November 28, 1808. In April, two companies of mounted riflemen, "The Louisiana Spies" were organized. In May, 1809, five companies were called out, and Fort Madison was reinforced. It was a busy time for Brigadier-General Clark, but the Indians knew what was good for them and stayed quiet.

The series of alarming reports that poured in on Washington from Missouri and Indiana about this time show how grave the situation really was; but like most successful military precautions, Lewis's were not appreciated because of their very success. They prevented danger from developing, but when the danger did not come, they seemed useless. Though the Militia were returned to civil life in July, 1809, the civilian population were still much dissatisfied with a Governor who took no chances in safeguarding their scalps and property. Calling citizens away from their ordinary lives to active duty is never popular, and Secretary Bates sneered heartily at the whole business, though he had himself been as much alarmed as anyone over the Indian danger only a year or two before.

Lewis's white population was nearly as unruly as the redskins. Dueling and plain murder were common. Spanish justice had never run very far beyond the boundaries of the villages, where Daniel Boone and other justices administered a rough and ready law of their own devising. Murder often

went unpunished because escape was so easy. One Moses
Kenny, originally from Bourbon County, Kentucky, finding
an enemy sleeping, poured boiling water over him, and then
beat him almost to death. When the man finally died, Kenny,
fearing that he, too, might soon be in hot water, simply
vanished. Murders of Indians by whites were almost impossible either to detect or punish. Murders of whites by Indians
were hard to handle, because punishment of the murderers
always roused the tribes. The white men, they thought, made
a dreadful fuss over an occasional scalping.

On the other hand, justice was sometimes a little too hasty.
After a white murderer had been duly tried and hanged, it
was discovered that one of the jurors had not understood any
of the evidence. He did not know a word of English!

The long-drawn quarrel with Frederick Bates, which both
Lewis and Clark struggled to allay, did more to prevent
Lewis's success as Governor than any other single factor. Its
virulence is especially strange since Lewis, Clark, and Bates
were all linked by Masonic bonds. Bates was a self-educated
Virginia lawyer of literary tastes, bad temper, and intolerable
magniloquence, who, after a period as assistant and deputy
county clerk in Virginia, had combined small government
posts with the management of a store in Detroit. Having lost
his business in the fire that destroyed the town, he turned to
politics, holding various minor offices until he rose to be
territorial judge. After toying with Federalist ideas, he had
returned to staunch Jeffersonian "republicanism"; and this,
together with his administrative experience, seemed to make
him a suitable successor to Browne, the suspected "Burrist,"
as Secretary of Louisiana Territory, the equivalent of a Lieutenant Governor.

Bates had met Lewis—whom he had known in Detroit and
who had been a close friend of his brother Tarleton Bates in
Pittsburgh—on amicable terms in Washington. He there
received "many friendly assurances" which convinced him

that their "mutual friendship would plant itself on rocky foundations." Preceding Lewis to Louisiana Territory, he served as Acting Governor until the Governor himself arrived. At first he was almost obsequious. "No one feels the want of your superintending presence so much as I do," he wrote the new Governor early in 1808, while to Madison he wrote that Lewis would be able to take over the administration "without one embarrassment which can be imputed to me." In February, 1808, he was eagerly expecting Lewis's arrival—"every day" on the 23rd; "every hour" on the 24th; "every moment" on the 26th. As late as March 20, 1808, he was still praising Lewis, "whose great and only object, I am convinced will be, the promotion of our best interests."

Four days later he had begun to change. Affairs, he wrote his brother, looked "somewhat squally since the arrival of Gov Lewis." Friends of the numerous officials whom Bates had removed were bringing pressure on the new and inexperienced Governor. Their first effort, a friend wrote to Bates (in somewhat scrambled grammar), was to "create a breach between the Gov. and Secretary which, is, said, & impressed on the minds of the people has already taken place, & that Gov. Lewis has expressed his disattisfaction of the Secretarys conduct." It was a situation in which Lewis was certain to antagonize either a good many influential citizens or the even more influential Secretary. In the end, he antagonized both.

Bates's confidence in the new Governor soon evaporated completely. He thought Lewis's measures "harsh and mistaken" and Lewis himself "inflexible in error." In other words, he wouldn't listen to Bates.

Some months later, while Bates was still meditating an appeal to Washington, "a circumstance"—no one knows what it was—roused "the overflowings of a heated resentment, burst the barriers which Prudence and Principle had prescribed." (Bates always wrote like that.)

He took his "wrongs with an extreme freedom to the Governor." Since Lewis was conciliatory, they patched up a temporary truce. Bates went away feeling that "We now understand each other much better. We differ in every thing; but we will be honest and frank in our intercourse." He continued to "lament the unpopularity of the Governor; but he has brought it on himself." He also continued to scoff at the "mighty stir & bustle about Indian War," though no one who knew Indians as Lewis and Clark did could mistake the danger, which was to burst on the territory a few years later.

But the breach between the Governor and Secretary soon grew beyond hope of reconciliation. The envious Bates thought Lewis had been "spoiled by the elegant praises of Mitchell & Barlow, and overwhelmed by so many flattering caresses of the high & mighty, that. like an overgrown baby, he began to think every body about the House must regulate their conduct by his caprices." He is alluding to the enthusiasm which Dr. Samuel Latham Mitchill, one of the leading scientific men of the day, had shown for the expedition's discoveries and to the poem which Joel Barlow had written about them. The "high and mighty" can only be Mr. Jefferson.

Bates attributed "alienation and unmerited distrust" of himself to the unpopular Governor's jealousy of the popularity which Bates believed himself to possess. "He had not generosity of soul to forgive me for it."

The popularity on which Bates plumed himself must have been strictly limited, for his own letters show that he was quarreling venomously with everyone in sight except Clark, a tactful person who is never known to have quarreled with anybody. Bates had the bad taste to indulge in an altercation with one of his fellow land-commissioners, Judge John B. Lucas, in the very presence of the land claimants appearing before them.

He waited till after the commission's adjournment one day to assail the other commissioner, Clement B. Penrose "in concise and angry terms."

"I have said that you were the enemy of Gov Lewis and would willingly be the Governor yourself," Penrose admitted.

"If you ever again bark at my heels, I will spurn you like a Puppy from my Path," screamed Bates.

Gossip about replacing Lewis as Governor soon began to spread. Lewis believed—or Bates thought he believed—that the Secretary was leading a group who intended to "denounce him to the President and procure his dismission." With Mr. Jefferson in the White House, the intrigue would have failed; with Mr. Madison, Lewis was not quite so certain. Many an eager politico was casting sheep's eyes at the Governorship.

When Lewis called on Bates for an explanation, the latter exhibited "that independance which I am determined shall mark my conduct on all occasions."

"Well," said the sensible Lewis at length, "do not suffer yourself to be separated from me in the public opinion; When we meet in public, let us, at least address each other with cordiality."

If Bates had been willing to remain outwardly civil, the quarrel might have been smoothed over. Being Bates, he was not willing. There were soon other squabbles. Once Clark was called in. Again there was a quarrel over certain statements which Bates said he had made on orders from Lewis. When Lewis denied it, Bates told him the public would believe Bates. Lewis told him to take his own course.

"I shall, Sir," said the magniloquent Secretary, "and I shall come, in future to the Executive Office when I have *business* at it."

This gave Bates a chance for another of the childish public scenes to which he was addicted. He was conversing with some gentleman at a ball when the Governor entered and drew up a chair close to his Secretary. It was a public effort on Lewis's part to be tactful. There was an abrupt pause in the conversation. Bates had said he would meet his chief officially only—never socially. Everyone waited to see what would happen. They saw Bates rise ostentatiously and walk to the other side of the room.

In a towering passion, Lewis stalked out and, from an adjoining room, sent a servant for Clark. He told his old friend that Bates "had treated him with contempt & insult in the Ball-Room and that he could not suffer it to pass." Clark did what he could to smooth matters over, but dared not ask Bates to meet the Governor "as he foresaw that a Battle must have been the consequence of our meeting." After a few weeks Clark called on Bates, with whom he seems to have remained on good terms, and suggested that he make amicable advances to Lewis.

"*NO,*" replied the atrabilious Secretary (the capitals and italics are all his own), "the Governor has told me to take my own course and I shall step a *high* and a *proud* Path. He has *injured* me, and he must *undo* that injury or I shall succeed in fixing the stigma where it *ought* to *rest.* You come as *my* friend, but I cannot separate you from Gov Lewis— You have trodden the *Ups* & the *Downs* of life with him and it appears to me that these proposals are made solely for *his* convenience."

The time came when this pompous and verbose ass really did have business on which he had no choice but to meet the Governor. Lewis, still conciliatory, "pressed" him to be seated and offered "very handsome explanations." Bates owlishly replied that "they *sounded* well," but there could be no reconciliation till he had consulted their common friend, William C. Carr, a locally prominent lawyer. God knows why, since he was soon abusing Carr as virulently as anyone else. When Carr and some others were called in, Bates finally expressed "entire satisfaction." Outwardly the breach was closed. Privately, Bates continued his diatribes.

To Lewis's official trials, private financial difficulties were added. Early in his brief career as Governor, he had plunged into extensive land purchases. By December, 1808, he had bought 5,700 acres near St. Louis, "in situations which I concieve the most elligible in the country in many points of view." This included three small farms, bought of Pierre Chouteau, for which he had also bought a small herd of cattle. He was a careful landlord who, when he rented maple sugar rights specified that the lessee was "not to tap the trees but with an auger and not to bore more than two holes in a tree in the same season."

He had high hopes of bringing his mother out to live in Louisiana and had selected the healthiest part of the country for her residence. He hoped also to bring his half-sister Mary, always an especial favorite, and her husband. All of this would cost money. Having already paid, or obligated himself to pay, two or three times his annual salary for Missouri lands, he proposed to sell the old home on Ivy Creek to meet the cost.

His land purchases and the expenses of the Governorship strained his private finances so badly that in November he had to borrow $49 from Clark to pay for medical attention to his servant, John Pernia. He grumbled at the amount, "which I conceive exorbitant, but which my situation in life compells me to pay." Another personal loan from Clark, recorded in Lewis's personal account book, is merely amusing:

> January 25th [1809]
> Borrowed of Genl. Clark
> this sum at a card party in my room $1

The clouds were gathering. It would not be long before all his creditors were down on him at once, while Washington's red tape snared him in its fatal tangles. Yet amid it all, Lewis was willing to accept the responsibility of rearing and educating Jussome's thirteen year-old boy, Toussaint, at his own expense.

One vexing problem, which for two years had looked as if it were going to be eternal, was settled in the spring of 1809; but since its solution did not satisfy the bureaucrats in Washington, his success merely involved him in fresh troubles. She-he-ke, the Mandan chief, had been on the Governor's hands all this time, for though he had been promised safe return to the Mandan country, every effort to send him there had failed. Robert M'Clelan, the trader, who had already taken some other Indians home, had hoped to take him back early in 1807, but the scheme fell through.

In the autumn of 1807, Clark finally arranged to send Ensign Nathaniel Pryor, with two N.C.O.'s and eleven soldiers as an escort for She-he-ke, while Lieutenant Joseph Kimball and additional troops escorted Pierre Dorion's Sioux chiefs. She-he-ke himself had asked to be sent with the Sioux. A trading party of 32 men under "young Chouteau"—that is, Auguste Pierre Chouteau—accompanied them. All went well until Pryor and Chouteau reached the Arikara country, Lieutenant Kimball and the Sioux chiefs having dropped off at their destination, farther down the river, without trouble. Since Lewis and Clark had passed down the Missouri in 1806, however, the peace that they had so laboriously patched up between the Arikaras and Mandans had collapsed, and the tribes were again at war as usual. The Arikaras, having learned of the death of their chief who had gone to Washington, were now hostile to white men.

Pryor was not to find matters so easy. When the boats reached the lower Arikara village, September 9, 1807, they were immediately greeted with several shots, the bullets whizzing uncomfortably close to the white men. Nevertheless, when "young" Dorion indignantly asked what this reception meant, they were blandly invited to put in to shore for corn and oil. Deciding that it was better to show confidence, the party approached the shore, to be immediately surrounded by several hundred Indians, many of them with rifles. Manuel Lisa, the trader, had already gone up the river, after foolishly telling the Arikaras that Pryor and Kimball were coming. The Arikaras had robbed Lisa of half his goods and were only waiting for his return to kill him.

Watching her chance, a Mandan woman prisoner whispered warning to Pryor: His party was in the greatest danger; the Arikaras meant to attack.

Pryor promptly put She-he-ke in the cabin, built a hasty breastwork of baggage on the boat, and prepared to fight it out. Seeing what was happening, the Indians began "chewing" bullets and sending their women and children to a safe distance. Since this meant that hostilities were imminent, Pryor's interpreter—probably René Jussome, though Pryor describes him merely as an "old Spaniard," in whom he had no confidence—gathered some chiefs together so that Pryor could hold a hasty council. After reminding them that "on a former occasion you extended to Louis [sic] and Clark the hand of friendship," he presented a medal to Grey Eyes, the Comanche chief who had hesitated to accept a medal from the Corps of Discovery the year before and who was extremely surly about accepting it now.

Though the Indians made no reply, they allowed the boats to proceed upstream, followed along the shore by a mob of savages, "using threats and menaces," without actual attack. Dorion and Jussome went overland at the risk of their lives, hoping to smooth things over; but when the boats reached the upper Arikara village, the Indians appeared on the beach "in a violent rage."

As he wanted to see the chief of this village and had to get his two interpreters away at all costs, Pryor put boldly in to shore, regardless of danger. He could, he thought, meet an attack, if there was going to be one, as readily on the beach as in the river, which was so shallow that the Indians could wade in after him and in which he was pretty certain to get stuck on a sand bar. Again feigning friendliness, the Indians tried to persuade him to enter a narrow channel leading inland, where his retreat could be cut off; but Pryor, seeing the obvious trap, told them he would go no farther. Dorion, meantime, was still frantically conferring with any chief that would listen to him.

Not wholly liking the appearance of the two military craft, bristling with rifles far better than their own, the Indians first went after Chouteau's trading barge with its valuable stores of goods. Seizing the cable, as the Teton Sioux had seized Lewis and Clark's three years before, they waved the soldiers to proceed upstream with the other boats. Chouteau, who had incautiously gone ashore with some of his men, shouted in alarm to Pryor that he "hoped he was not to be abandoned in so dangerous a situation."

"Make them an offer!" yelled Pryor.

Chouteau hastily proposed to leave the Arikaras half of his goods. The village chief promptly demanded that the Mandan chief also be turned over to him. When Pryor refused in no uncertain terms, the Arikara chief hastily retired. Grey Eyes —who continued to make trouble until American troops killed him in 1823—threw his medal on the ground, whence Jussome retrieved it. An Indian whacked a white man with the butt of his rifle.

The crisis had been reached. Raising the war whoop, the warriors scrambled for the shelter of the willows along the bank and opened fire. Chouteau and his men tumbled into their boat, while Dorion and Jussome, by some private miracle of their own, managed to reach the white party. Pryor's infantry opened with swivels, blunderbusses, and small arms before the Arikaras could cover the 60 yards to shelter.

As the boats began to withdraw, after fifteen minutes of combat, Chouteau's struck on a sand bar, so that his men had to leap overboard and drag their barge through the sand,

with Indian bullets splashing all about them. Once out of
the bars and shallows, the boats found a clear channel and
slipped swiftly downstream in the current, carrying on a
running fight with Indians racing along the bank, for an
hour.

The fight ended when a Sioux chief, who had visited
aboard the boats before the firing started, ran out on a point
with about 40 warriors. Easily recognizable because he was
indiscreet enough to wear a white band around his head, he
was hit by a shot "which was aimed particularly at him," and
"appeared to expire in a moment on the Beach." After that,
the Indians had had enough.

When pursuit ceased, the white men lashed their boats
together and took stock of casualties. Chouteau had three
men killed and seven wounded, one of whom died in a few
days. Two soldiers had been wounded and a "hunter" had
a broken leg. This must have been Shannon, who had a leg
wound so serious that he was eighteen months in military
hospital, until the surgeons, despairing of his life, amputated
the leg. Lewis and Clark saw to it that their old friend was
well cared for.

To make matters worse, Jussome, after years of acquaintance with She-he-ke, had chosen this moment of crisis to
quarrel with him and had gone over to Chouteau's boat,
where he was now among the wounded, with bullets in thigh
and shoulder almost completely disabling him.

In spite of everything, Pryor was so eager to carry out
his mission that he proposed going overland to the Mandan
country. She-he-ke very sensibly refused. It would have
meant taking women and children on a three days' journey
in hostile country, depending on a wounded interpreter who
was already on bad terms with the chief. Going on was hopeless. There was nothing to do but return to St. Louis where
Pryor reported that at least 400 men would be needed to

force the river passage, and that even 1,000 might not get through.

Governor Lewis and General Clark now had She-he-ke on their hands again, and, having begun to get exaggerated ideas of his own importance, the Mandan chief began to be rather a troublesome guest. Though entertained in the officers' mess near the town, "with every kind and hospitable indulgence," he demanded quarters in St. Louis. When his friend Clark was there, She-he-ke complained, he had not been sent off to live with mere "little chiefs." As Clark had gone east to get married, while Lewis had not yet arrived, it was difficult to make the change and She-he-ke's dignity was affronted. He now regarded himself as the "brother," rather than the "son," of the Great White Father. On that theory, the Mandan chief was as important a figure as the President of the United States, and he wanted to be treated accordingly.

Governor Lewis and General Clark struggled with the problem of getting him home until 1809. Then Lewis entered into an agreement with the Missouri Fur Company to return the chief, his squaw, and his baby, together with the Jussome family, to the Mandan country, for $7,000. The company was to provide a force of 125, led by Pierre Chouteau, of whom 40 were to be "Americans and expert riflemen," enlisted in General Clark's Missouri Militia for the expedition only. Leaving St. Louis about the middle of May, the party—which included Reuben Lewis—overawed the Sioux, who were at first inclined to make trouble, and found the Arikaras friendly. She-he-ke was safely home by autumn.

The results of his sojourn among the white men were not very happy. The purpose of bringing chiefs east was to impress them with the marvels and the power of the white men. She-he-ke had been far too profoundly impressed—that was just the trouble. Although he had been a chief since 1797 at least, he had always been rather despised by the Mandans as lacking the immense reserve and complete impassivity proper to a warrior. When he told the Mandans of the wonders he had seen, they shook their heads. She-he-ke had always talked too much. Now they knew he was a liar also. Such things could not be. His reputation was completely ruined, especially as he made things worse by his boasting and his affected airs. He often wished, he confided to a white visitor, that he could go and live permanently among the white men.

After all the trouble that it caused, She-he-ke's Washington excursion led to very little good. He introduced poultry to the Mandans—the English traveler, Bradbury, was much surprised by the rooster he saw outside the chief's lodge. He learned a good deal of English—Bradbury was almost equally surprised by an invitation to "Come in house." He remained a firm friend of the Americans, but as he was killed by a raiding party in 1812, his friendship had little practical effect. The medal Lewis and Clark had given him passed from his son, White Painted Horse, to his grandson, Tobacco, and to his great-grandson, Gun-that-Guards-the-House, who in 1910 still possessed it. It is now owned (1947) by Mr. Burr Crows Breast, Elbowoods, North Dakota, She-he-ke's great-great-great-grandson.

chapter 26: Tragedy in Tennessee

DURING the summer and early autumn of 1809, the difficulties Lewis had encountered from the start were growing worse and more irritating. His personal popularity was decreasing. Even if his enemy Bates exaggerated in saying that the Governor had "fallen from the Public Esteem & almost into the public contempt," there is no doubt Bates was right when he wrote shortly afterward: "Our Gov: Lewis, with the best intentions in the world, is, I am fearful, losing ground."

His friend, Mr. Jefferson, had joyfully retired to private life and Lewis could not rely on President Madison for sympathy or support. His term as Governor would soon expire and his reappointment was doubtful. Bates was quick to suggest that Lewis had been "too unfortunate to expect a second nomination—such, at least is the prevailing opinion."

Administrative difficulties continued. Lewis remained hopelessly at odds with Secretary Bates, who privately did everything he could to undermine the Governor's position. His personal difficulties were quite as grave as his official ones. He feared his health was failing, and was always dosing himself with medicines of some kind. In his eagerness to establish his private fortunes, he had very much overextended his private financial ventures. In his discouragement he had, for nearly a year, been talking dolefully about leaving Louisiana forever.

The wire-drawn ingenuity of Washington's official bumbledom, which in mid-summer contrived to find fault with his drafts for official expenditures, was the last straw. Early in July, finding that a draft for eighteen dollars had been rejected, Lewis prepared for the worst, knowing "the fate of other bills drawn for similar purposes to a considerable amount cannot be mistaken." Out of his scanty private purse, he paid off one or two of the first protested drafts, as they came drifting back from Washington; but he knew that larger ones were coming and that his personal funds would be "entirely incompetant to meet those bills if protested."

His worst fears were soon realized. On July 15 the Secretary of War wrote, refusing to honor a draft of $500, which Lewis had drawn to provide Chouteau with tobacco and powder for Indian presents to be used by the expedition that was taking She-he-ke home. It had already cost $7,000 to send out this expedition. As for the extra $500, the Secretary wrote with bitter official irony, "it is thought the Government might, without injury to the public interests, have been consulted." Appeal to President Madison was cut off: "The President has been consulted and the observations herein contained have his approval—and your Excellency may be assured that they are dictated by a sense of public duty and are perfectly consistent with the great respect and regard with which I have the honor to remain, etc etc." The sardonic courtesy of the

close was the most cutting thing about the letter. One further
draft was rejected by the War Department, and the Treasury
also rejected drafts.

News of the protest, as it spread, brought all Lewis's creditors down on him at once. These gentry were numerous and
the sums they demanded large. Lewis himself wrote: "Those
protested Bills from the Department of War and Treasury
have effectually sunk my Credit; brought in all my private
debts, amounting to about $4,000, which has compelled me,
in order to do justice to my Creditors, to deposit with them,
the landed property which I had purchased in this Country,
as Security." As the $500 protested draft for trading goods
alone equaled a quarter of his annual salary, it is no wonder
the creditors were alarmed.

Dismayed at the prospect of complete financial ruin, Lewis
gathered up his vouchers, determined to go to Washington
and prove his case there. Once he had brought Washington
to see reason, his personal finances would straighten themselves out easily enough. Official correspondence with the
War Department and the Treasury would be useless, since
the mail one way took from one to two months. Nothing but
personal interviews would be effective. There was nothing
unusual in Lewis's difficulties. Clark, too, had had to go to
Washington not long before to straighten out a similar question.

Meantime, the anxious Governor made such arrangements
in St. Louis as were necessary. On August 30, 1809, he attended his last meeting with the Governor's Council. He returned to the sellers some of the lands he had bought, where
possible retaining the privilege of redeeming them later. He
was careful to leave a note of John Colter's claim for payment
for services on the expedition, since Colter was still somewhere in the Yellowstone, and no one knew at what moment
his canoe might come bobbing down the Missouri. Money
for the faithful Colter must be ready and waiting, no matter

when he came. Lewis also sent a land warrant to be sold in New Orleans, the proceeds to be placed in bank for the payment of his debts. It was bitter to part with it.

By the time Lewis had finished, he had stripped his resources so completely that he could not pay his doctor's bill. He had to sign a note to Dr. Anthony Saugrain for medicine received, which was later paid by Lewis's attorneys from the sale of his land, though not before payment had been so long delayed that the thrifty physician added $7.20 for interest!

The size of his bill for medicine shows that Lewis was in poor health, or thought he was; and there is no doubt that he was taken genuinely ill on the journey. Jottings in his account book indicate either a variety of maladies or pure hypochondria—or perhaps only that interest in everything medical that characterized Lucy Marks and all her sons. His jottings include: "billious fever," "Pills of opium and tartar," "Receipt for the best Stomachic," and "antibillious pills." They sound alarming, but you can find the same sort of notes in the Journals of the expedition.

He appointed Clark and two other intimate friends as his attorneys, with full power to dispose of his property, and on September 11 he made a will, leaving everything to his mother. There was nothing unusual in this. Lewis was merely taking the ordinary legal measures of a prudent man whose affairs were in some confusion, who would not be able for some time to attend to them himself, and who was setting out on a dangerous journey. If, as his enemy Bates gleefully hoped, he was not reappointed Governor, he might not return to St. Louis at all.

There is no doubt that when the Governor left he had every expectation of going to Washington, visiting Ivy Creek, and returning to his territory. He wrote his friend Amos Stoddard to forward mail to Washington "untill the last of December after which I expect I shall be on my return to St. Louis." In his private notebook he entered: "Directed my letters to be returned to the City of Washington." His letters to his mother were buoyant with the hope of seeing her soon. He even undertook, while in New Orleans, to find out what had become of the bones of a mammoth which Clark had sent Mr. Jefferson and which had not yet arrived.

Though Lewis was certainly unwell, the wild rumors of his illness that spread need not be taken too seriously. The *Missouri Gazette* specifically says that he "set off in good health for New Orleans on his way to the Federal City," though the emphasis of the statement faintly suggests official propaganda.

His original intention, when he left St. Louis on September 4, 1809, was to travel down the Mississippi to New Orleans and there take a ship up the coast. On his way downstream, however, the Governor learned of danger from British warships, then hovering off the American coast. Though war had not yet been declared, no one knew when it would break out; and there was a fair chance that some British naval officer would make the Governor of Louisiana a prisoner, seizing the papers on which he relied to clear his reputation, as well as the Journals of the expedition. Already suffering from the heat, which would grow worse as he went on south, Lewis decided to give up the sea trip and go overland through Tennessee, thus escaping both the hot weather and the British navy. He halted at Chickasaw Bluffs (Memphis) for about two weeks and here, on September 16, he wrote President Madison.

The form of the letter, with its sprawling and uncertain hand and the constant striking out of words and interlineation of others, to no particular purpose, show clearly that—no matter how well Lewis may have appeared at New Madrid—he was very far from being his usual bold and decisive self by the time he reached Chickasaw Bluffs. On September 22 he wrote another letter to his friend Stoddard, in which he said that illness forced him to go by way of Tenneessee.

At Fort Pickering, the army post at Chickasaw Bluffs (Memphis) which he had once commanded, he met old army friends and drank more than he was accustomed to. It is the only mention of intemperance of any kind in his whole career. His entire behavior was odd enough to alarm his friends. September 28, about the time Lewis was starting overland, the news had spread as far as Nashville that the Governor, after arriving at Chickasaw Bluffs "in a state of mental derangement," had there "attempted to put an end to his own existence." Captain Russell, the commander, "had taken him into his own quarters where he was obliged to keep a strict watch over him to prevent his committing violence on himself." This may have been merely the result of too much liquor combined with worry; but it certainly adds strength to the view that Lewis committed suicide. On the other hand, Lewis's notebook entries at this very time are eminently clear and sensible. The best explanation of his odd conduct is probably malaria, as it is well known that fever of any kind invariably made him light-headed.

When he finally started across Tennessee, Major Alexander Neeley, a former army officer now in the Indian service, decided to go with him, in spite of the fact that Lewis was already accompanied by his servant, John Pernia, and by Reuben's Negro servant, "Captain Tom." The little party struck out on horseback with a few pack horses, through Indian country to the Natchez Trace, which they probably reached at the point where it crossed the Tennessee River.

Somewhere along the way, they encountered a casual traveler who left a record of the meeting: "He travelled with Capt Lewis on his way to Nashville one whole day but a short time before that meritorious but unfortunate man put an end to his existence—Lewis had been overnight at Perrys & gave him one of his little Books & had promised to send him one of his large ones when Printed but he never lived to accomplish it." The "little book" was undoubtedly a copy of the prospectus for the edition of the Lewis and Clark Journals which Lewis hoped to publish.

Where and what Perry's may have been, no one knows—probably another wilderness "stand." The story has a certain importance, since it shows Lewis's state of mind to have been quite normal at this time. There is no mention of eccentricity of any sort, and Lewis is cheerfully intent on the publication of his new book, notes for which he carried with him.

The Natchez Trace, along which he traveled, was a narrow wilderness road, not wide enough for wagons but passable either on foot or on horse. It ran from Natchez to the Tennessee River and then on through modern Lawrence and Lewis Counties in Tennessee, passing directly through the present Meriwether Lewis National Monument, and on to Nashville. Its passage through Chickasaw and Choctaw territory was permitted by an Indian treaty negotiated by General Wilkinson in 1801, primarily to enable official post riders to carry the scanty mail—a few letters and newspapers and official dispatches—to the American post at Natchez. It was also much used by merchants and traders, who, after traveling down the Ohio and Mississippi by boats, avoided the difficult journey upstream by returning overland. The Trace was only a series of old Indian trails, from which trees and underbrush had been partly cleared to allow the passage of saddle horses. It ran through wild country, infested by outlaws, where one might travel more than 100 miles without seeing a house or an Indian wigwam.

The first halt of Lewis's party within United States territory was to be at Grinder's Stand, only a few yards beyond the Indian boundary line, where a certain Robert Grinder, or Griner, had squatted the year before, building two cabins and a stable. His chief source of income seems to have been the food, liquor, and shelter he dispensed to benighted travelers, though he may have done some farming and perhaps some Indian trading. According to tradition, he was on excellent terms with the Indians, whose lands came almost to his cabin door. His establishment was so close to the Trace that no traveler passing that way could possibly miss it. The place had a rather doubtful reputation, but it cannot have been very sinister since the local justice of the peace used to drop in for coffee regularly.

Robbery was frequent all along the Natchez Trace since, in the absence of banks, travelers had to carry their currency with them; and many who passed that way were returning from profitable trading voyages along the Mississippi, carrying the proceeds home with them. Travelers habitually carried their gold and silver sewn in rawhide belts or cases, which they buried in the woods at night before lighting their campfires, to escape robbery. Dark tales were afloat of purses that disappeared along the way, and there is no doubt whatever that Lewis's purse did vanish on the night of his death, never to be recovered.

The accepted—and very dubious—version of what happened next is well known from three letters which Captain John Brahan, 2nd Infantry, wrote from Nashville to the Secretary of War, to Mr. Jefferson, and to Major Amos Stoddard a week after the tragedy; from the account based on this which Mr. Jefferson himself contributed to the published edition of the Lewis and Clark Journals a few years later; and from information which the ornithologist, Alexander Wilson, collected on the spot. These are partly, but only partly, confirmed by newspaper accounts; by the stories of a white and a Negro servant girl years afterward, when they were both old women; and by an oral tradition which to this day is very much alive in rural Tennessee.

Captain Brahan got his information from Major Neeley, who was not present at Lewis's death and who simply repeated what he heard. The entire suicide story, therefore, depends entirely on what the people at Grinder's Stand that night told Neeley the next day, with some possible confirmation from Lewis's two servants, who were sleeping in the stable. It was, to say the least, embarrassing to have the Governor of Louisiana die violently and mysteriously at your cabin. If the Grinders really had anything to conceal, their suicide story was the easiest defense to offer. If Lewis really did commit suicide, Mrs. Grinder's own story shows her behaving in a remarkably callous fashion.

According to Neeley, the party left Chickasaw Bluffs "the last of Sept." They traveled slowly, since it took them about ten days to reach Grinder's Stand. "The Governor appeared some days thereafter while on their Journey to be some what deranged in mind." One day beyond the Tennessee River, they camped for the night. Here, two of their horses got loose in the woods and wandered off. Lewis suggested that Neeley remain behind and round up the horses, while he went on with Pernia and the Negro, promising to wait for him at the first white settlement, in other words, Grinder's Stand.

It was natural enough for a sick man, caught in the wilderness, to push on for shelter. It is not so clear why Neeley, if he really thought Lewis was deranged, went after the horses himself, instead of sending the two servants. It is probable, however, that the horses were pack animals carrying important baggage, perhaps the vouchers and the notes of the expedition. The notes eventually reached Philadelphia; nothing further is heard of the vouchers.

Whatever his motives—and they were doubtless excellent —Neeley assented, and Lewis rode on until he reached Grinder's Stand—"no person being at home but the wife of Mr. Grinder," according to Brahan. This, incidentally, is not true. The Grinder children, a little slave, Lindy, the white maidservant, Polly Spencer, and probably a Negro boy were all present; and there is a local legend that Grinder himself was not nearly so absent as he seemed.

The various accounts of Lewis's death that have survived are contradictory in minor details; but it is only too easy to construct with fair accuracy the general story of what happened in the isolated forest clearing that night. Lewis rode up alone late in the afternoon of October 10, 1809, "dressed in a loose gown, striped with blue"—a queer costume for a ride in the wilderness. It was about sunset. He requested lodging and, when asked if he was alone, said that two servants were a little way behind and "would soon be up." He asked for spirits but drank only a little. When Pernia and Reuben's slave, Captain Tom, rode into the clearing, Lewis asked for his canister of gunpowder.

While he waited for supper he walked up and down in the yard, muttering to himself. Someone caught the words: "They have told lies on me and want to ruin me." When supper was served, he ate only a few mouthfuls before jumping up with his face flushed "as if it had come on him in a fit," but calmed down enough to light his pipe, draw a chair to the cabin door, and remark quietly to his hostess, "Madam, this is a very pleasant evening." He fell to pacing again, then once more "sat down to his pipe," and again commented, "what a sweet evening it was."

When Mrs. Grinder commenced to get a bed ready for him, he said he would sleep on the floor and sent a servant for bearskins and a buffalo robe. Soldier and explorer, he had slept that way often enough and probably preferred it to the rather dubious beds of such an establishment. Just after supper, he found that he had lost his pocketbook—not an unusual occurrence at frontier taverns, but something which his hostess never mentions in any of her statements. While he was looking for his money, Mrs. Grinder came in, looked under the robes herself, and said it was not there. No one ever found it afterward.

During the evening, Lewis examined his pistols, talking to himself meanwhile. Much needless fuss has been made over this last fact. The pistols of that day were very different from the modern automatic with its metallic cartridges, always

ready to fire. Nothing was easier than to knock out the priming secretly, thus rendering a pistol quite useless. Any sensible person would examine his weapons before going to sleep
in such surroundings, especially Lewis, an infantry officer who
was meticulous about small arms. The fact that he talked to
himself means nothing—it is a common habit among people
who have lived much alone in the woods.

After everyone had gone to bed, a first shot was heard from
the cabin where Lewis lay alone, followed by a second, and
perhaps later by a third. After the final shot, the wounded
man came reeling out of the cabin and struggled to the
kitchen door, some twelve feet away, asking Mrs. Grinder,
who was by this time locked up in the other cabin and peering fearfully through the cracks, to give him water and dress
his wounds. When she refused to give aid of any kind or even
to leave her cabin, Lewis managed to reach a tree across the
road, where he fell. Gathering himself up, he came back and
again asked for water, which was once more refused.

Just what the two men servants were doing all this time,
no one has ever explained except a newspaper writer who
says Mrs. Grinder "called to the servants without effect." It
is hard to suppose that if they were sleeping in a barn 200
yards away they failed to hear the pistol shots; but it is true
that in those surroundings a few shots were no great matter.
When questioned in later life, Captain Tom used to shake
his woolly head and say that the whole affair was better not
discussed.

Lewis was left alone in agony all night or at least most of
the night. About daylight, according to Aunt Lindy, the
"furriner," Pernia, came to the kitchen and told Mrs. Grinder
that Lewis was cutting the veins in his throat. If Mrs. Grinder
would give him water, he would give up his razor. Going
over to his cabin, they found, according to one account, that
he had crawled to the door and was asking for water; accord-

ing to another, he was lying on the bed. Again he muttered: "They are telling lies and trying to ruin me."

He was horribly wounded in the side and in the forehead, where the skull had been blown open, exposing the frontal lobe of the brain, a kind of wound which rarely causes immediate death. A piece of his skull had been blown into the mantel and there were wounds in his side. It seems clear that he also had knife or razor wounds, either at the throat or the wrist. He begged them to take his rifle and shoot him, exclaiming: "I am no coward; but I am *so* strong, *so hard to die.*" The last few words must be exact quotation—they are the very words Lewis applies to a wounded grizzly in the Journals.

When they had given him a little water, they asked why he had shot himself. "If I had not done it, some one else would," the dying man said.

In his agony he must again have struggled out of the cabin, for when, during the morning of October 11, the government post-rider on the Natchez Trace reached Grinder's Stand, he found Lewis's body lying near the road, 100 or 150 yards from the Grinder cabins—somewhere near the present grave, since there is a tradition that Lewis was buried where he fell. Examining the body, he thought a bullet had entered the body *in the back* and, looking further, found a bit of wadding that looked as if it had come from a musket, lying between Lewis's body and the stable. This suggests that an assassin, standing near the stable, fired at Lewis from behind. The wadding would then either drop somewhere between the muzzle and the target or would be carried into the wound. It could not possibly be carried clear through the body. Smith does not seem to have observed knife wounds.

A coroner's jury was called together, an inquest was held, and a verdict was rendered. The records of Maury County for this period have disappeared, including the inquest record, but the various jurors often discussed the case, and the oral

tradition of their views has come down in several of their
families with surprising agreement as to the main facts. The
jurors were Samuel Whiteside (foreman), R. M. Cooper,
George Vincent, a certain Sharpe (or Shipp), a certain Car-
roll, and a certain Johnson.

Since every coroner's jury is given an opportunity to view
the body, this one presumably did so, as tradition among their
descendants clearly indicates. Descendants of both Vincent
and Sharpe say that Lewis was shot "from behind slightly"—
exactly what the post-rider said. There were apparently two
wounds in the side and one in the head. There were no powder stains on the clothing or on the flesh, as there certainly
would have been if Lewis himself had held the pistol.

The late William J. Webster, an attorney of Columbia,
Tennessee, who devoted a great deal of study to the death of
Lewis, who lived near the scene, and who interviewed many
descendants of the coroner's jury, is supposed to have seen
papers showing exactly what the verdict of the coroner's jury
was. These were "among the old papers of the Maury County
Historical Society," all of which have long since disappeared.
Though the papers are lost, one version is that the verdict
said: "He might have committed suicide." Descendants' stories leave little doubt that the jurymen really believed it was
murder—and after all the jury had a better chance to find the
truth than anyone else.

Why did the jury believe one thing and report another?
Their statements to their families explain that, too. The
plain truth is that they were afraid. The foreman himself
is reported by the late F. C. Frierson to have told his friends:
"that the Jury were Cowards and were afraid to bring in a
verdict of murder, which they all knew was what they should
have done. I could not imagine what they were afraid of!
But some one said that the murderers had Indian Blood in
their Veins, and they were afraid they would meet a similar
fate." People who do not live defenseless in isolated farms on

the Indian border will find it easy to scoff at their timidity.

The Grinders naturally came under suspicion. Grinder is said to have been arrested and brought to trial or before a Hardin County grand jury in Savannah, Tennessee, the charge being dismissed for lack of evidence. Why the case should be tried at such a distance, no one knows. It is doubtful if there is any truth in the story. The criminal records of both Hardin and Maury Counties for this period have also disappeared, but the son of the Maury County justice in office at the time of Lewis's death was positive Grinder never appeared in his father's court, though Lewis died within that jurisdiction. The justice himself frequently passed the cabin of the Grinders, with whom he was well acquainted, one bit of evidence in favor of their good character.

Suspicious neighbors thought they noted a sudden increase in the family's prosperity within the next few years. In 1814, Robert Grinder paid $250, a large sum on the frontier in those days, for a farm of 100 acres, more or less, on Duck River in neighboring Hickman County, from which he had originally come. It was good hill land, with a stretch of fertile bottom land which is known as "Grinder's Island" to this day. Legend also avers that he bought several Negro slaves, though there is no evidence for this beyond the obvious fact that the farm was too big for one man to work.

When the question naturally arose whence Grinder got his money—since the profits from his "stand" must have been exiguous in the extreme—the local populace were quick to recall the mysterious death of five years before. The niece of Grinder's daughter-in-law long afterward accepted the theory that Lewis was murdered—a theory still much resented by Grinder's modern descendants. She averred that Grinder's son kept buried in a chimney corner "the old man's pants," the legs of which were filled with gold "and it was said and believed in the family that this was Merriwether [sic] Lewis gold." She insisted that Aunt Malinda "saw the old man have a lap full of gold," but Malinda herself never said so. It was not the kind of thing a slave discussed.

Though this is fantasy rather than evidence—there is no reason to suppose that Lewis carried much gold—it is hard to find anyone in Maury County who today accepts the suicide theory; and this was true even during the investigations of William J. Webster, who worked at a period fairly close to the time of the death. The contemporary Tennesseeans who believe Lewis was murdered can at least base their views on a consistent and continuous oral tradition, which is itself based on the private opinions of the jury who saw the body.

Though the jurors dared not put their true opinion into their verdict, at least two of the six privately, in their family circles, declared that Lewis had been murdered. There is no record that any of them ever expressed any belief in the official verdict which they had themselves rendered. The murder question is still so ticklish in twentieth-century Tennessee that a Hickman County antiquarian absolutely refused even to meet the writer to discuss it in February, 1946!

There is some rather dubious ground for believing that Mr. Jefferson later gave up the idea of suicide and asserted that Lewis had been murdered. The letter in which he stated his revised opinion is said to have been in a volume of Jefferson *MSS.* compiled by Jefferson Randolph which came into the possession of Dr. Wilson Randolph, by whom it was unfortunately "loaned out." Jefferson is said to have written that "*subsequent evidence* tended to prove Meriwether Lewis did not kill himself but was murdered."

The strong suspicions of murder merely circulated orally in the sparsely settled backwoods of Tennessee, where the coroner's jury lived. When they were finally collected and written down, it was long after the event, they had no written authority behind them, and at first they attracted little attention. Lewis lay in an almost forgotten wilderness grave, where the forest came crowding in, even after the symbolic broken column, which still stands over his body, had been erected to his memory.

The evidence for murder is not very strong, and the stories from Fort Pickering strongly suggest suicide, but none of the evidence is really conclusive. It is impossible to make a positive statement, either way. Mrs. Grinder's story, if true, shows a perfectly incredible callousness. According to her own account, she watched the sufferings of the dying Lewis for a long time, yet refused to give him the water which men with gunshot wounds invariably crave. It is sometimes said that she was too timid to come out of her cabin. Such timidity is not characteristic of frontier women; and she was not too timid, according to her own story, to live alone with a slave, a servant girl, and a few children on the edge of the Indian country. However timid she may have been, it was perfectly possible for the three women to make enough noise to waken the servants in the stable, assuming that they really had slept through two or three pistol shots.

One of the chief mysteries in the whole affair is what the two servants were doing while Lewis was stumbling and crawling about the clearing, trying to get some water. If the post-rider told the truth—and he had no conceivable motive for doing anything else—the dying man had made his way 100 to 150 yards along the trail toward the woods. Was he trying to escape from danger? The accepted story sounds very much like a narrative concocted to conceal a crime.

Such a theory by no means implies that the Grinders were necessarily involved. There is no real reason to doubt that Grinder actually was away from home that night. It is well known that the Natchez Trace was haunted by armed robbers. Is it possible that Indian or white outlaws swept down on the lonely stand, attacked the Governor of Louisiana—the only man there who was likely to have any money—and got safely away, with or without connivance? Pure hypothesis, of course, but not by any means an impossibility.

However implausible, one motive for crime cannot be quite ignored. There is a tale that on the expedition, which included some rough geological and mineralogical reconnaissance, Lewis had found a gold mine. He had told his friends that he was keeping this a secret, but that he had papers showing how to find the mine, in the event of his death. Gilmer hazarded the guess that Lewis might have been killed by persons "in search of his account of the place where gold was to be found." This at best unlikely story is weakened by the fact that no papers were reported missing after his death—only money. But robbers would not have known that Lewis's papers were on the pack horses that had gone astray.

The fact that no one saw powder burns on the body is strong evidence against suicide. If Lewis was really shot in the back, the suicide theory collapses at once. Here, however, we must reckon with the possibility that the wound in his back may have been an exit wound, made by a ball passing through the body. On the other hand, it is equally possible that the wound in front of the body was an exit wound made by a bullet fired from behind. The evidence balances.

Most suspicious of all are the facts that Lewis's body was left lying along the Trace until the middle of the morning; and that, when it was finally examined, there was only 25 cents in the pockets. He had borrowed a check for $99.50 only a few days before and since then had been traveling through the wilderness where he could not cash it. Where was the check? And where was the other money that he must have carried? He is said, of course, to have lost his purse at Grinder's, but under the circumstances, it was a very queer time and place to lose a purse!

The Lewis family has always held firmly to the theory that the Governor was murdered by his servant Pernia, though there is no real case against him. On the morning after the death, Pernia was discovered wearing his master's clothing, but there is nothing really suspicious in that. Gentlemen in those days often gave cast-off garments to their body servants. Lewis's body was roughly dressed—there is no further mention of the loose striped gown—but that is not suspicious either. Any woodsman wears his roughest clothing for a wilderness journey. Long afterward, William Moore, the husband of Lewis's half-sister, Mary Marks, encountered Pernia by chance on the streets of a southern city—either Mobile or New Orleans—and forced him to give up property which had belonged to Lewis. Family tradition says this included a gold watch, papers, and a rifle, though one would hardly expect Pernia to be carrying the last two about with him. Even the watch is doubtful. There is no doubt that Clark took possession of *a* watch belonging to Lewis, though he may have owned two.

Pernia seems to have been entirely innocent. Lewis trusted him enough to make him a witness to his will and to list his debts "in a small minute book deposited with Pernia my Servant." Pernia's name appears in the will now in the Albemarle Court Records, which was recorded March, 1810.

He was sent on to Virginia by Neeley, who provided money for the journey, to which Captain Brahan added a small sum. That is not the way army officers deal with suspicious characters. Aunt Malinda asserted that after his arrival in Virginia, Pernia was accused by Mrs. Marks (whom she called Mrs. Lewis) of killing her son. Exclaiming "I'll see Gov L before dark," he "cut his throat from ear to ear in Mrs. L's yard." Nobody in Albemarle, where tradition is treasured, ever heard this tale.

The story that Lewis was mentally deranged must also be treated with reserve. He was certainly ill. He had had difficulties with Bates, a singularly irritating individual. His personal finances were in a bad way. He had been drinking heavily. His reappointment was in doubt. His accounts were disputed by Washington auditors. But though the government's financial methods drive men to distraction, they rarely drive them to suicide. If they did, the streets of Washington would be littered with corpses.

When Neeley was suddenly confronted with his friend's corpse and heard Mrs. Grinder's story, his mind went back over the episodes at Fort Pickering and Lewis's state of mind during the wilderness journey, and he may have exaggerated his natural exasperation into "derangement." Mr. Jefferson, remembering Lewis's melancholia, accepted the theory. After all, neither was a psychiatrist. But Bates, who hated Lewis and never failed to speak ill of him, never mentioned anything of the sort until after his enemy was dead. No one in St. Louis had mentioned it. Lewis had seemed normal enough at New Madrid. People who think that the hardships of his wilderness expedition unhinged his mind three years later have simply never traveled in the wilderness.

Bates had the news in a friend's letter of October 31: "This moment the Secretary at War has mentioned to me his having by this days Mail received an account of the extraordinary death of Governor Lewis: which no one here undertakes to account for—& certainly the short acquaintance I had with him at St. Louis in June last wholly precludes my having any reason to offer for his committing an act so very extraordinary & unexpected."

Bates shed a flood of crocodile tears: "Indeed I had no personal regard for him and a great deal of political contempt; Yet I cannot but lament, that after all his toils and dangers he should die in *such a manner.*" His brother, J. W. Bates, is frankly bitter: "Our papers have lately resounded with the death of Gov: Lewis:—His panegyrists have almost chaunted his apotheosis. From the slight knowledge which I had of the man, I thought they might have given to his character intrepidity & bravery; but without detracting from his merits might have spared the affirmation that he was a 'scientific & classical scholar—a gentleman equally fitted for the Cabinet & the field.' It has indeed become but too common of late

(& perhaps it was always so) to bestow on departed characters, qualifications which had they themselves aspired to while living, scorn & derision must inevitably have overtaken them."

Their sister Nancy was much gentler: "We heard of the death of Meriwether Lewis about 3 or 4 week[s] since; he was a particular friend of our brother Tarleton's. poor unhappy man, how wretched he must have been. And I lament his death on you[r] account, thinking it might involve you in difficulties."

News of the death was not immediately announced when received by the War Department, but the Philadelphia firm of Bryan & Schlatter secured advance information from "our friend at Washington." In the preceding April, they had forwarded Lewis's obligations to this agent to secure collection, and were now, on November 12, much alarmed about their cash. They wrote to Pierre Chouteau: "We therefore think it our duty to give you this timely information for your safety &c that your Father may take the necessary steps to secure Himself by an attatchment of his property &c in that country if he pleases *provided* he is not *already secured*—we conceive should this be the fact his Governor Lewis's obligation will not be Honor'd here—we therefore have to request your Father will be pleased to make us as early a remittance as possible, having been *kept out of our money far beyond our usual credit already.*" The letter is further evidence of the confusion in Lewis's financial affairs.

The efforts of Edward Hempstead, administrator, to untangle the estate brought out more claims. Hempstead soon had eight cases against the estate, including a claim by John Colter, who had not received the Congressional rewards paid at the end of the expedition because he was off exploring in the Yellowstone. Lewis had received for him, from the War Department, $380 for pay plus commutation of clothing and rations and a further $179 for extra pay awarded by Congress. During Colter's wanderings, Lewis had not been able to pay the money over, though he had carefully listed the obligation in his account book. Clark was called as a witness.

John Hastings Marks, Lewis's step-brother, finally went out to St. Louis in 1811 to help settle the estate and, returning, tried to find Neeley. Mrs. Neeley turned over Lewis's horse and rifle to him, but said that Neeley, then away from home, habitually carried Lewis's dirk and pistols with him.

Hempstead was in and out of court with the estate for some years. In 1814, he reported that additional assets had come to light but not enough to satisfy claims. His report as executor, filed February 8, 1815, shows a total of $4,557.75. Among the assets were cattle, of which three cows and a calf were bought by William Clark, grotesque conclusion to one of the great friendships of history.

chapter 27: His Excellency, Governor Clark

C LARK was in Kentucky when the news of the Tennessee tragedy arrived. Leaving Missouri after Lewis, he had taken the more usual and direct eastward route up the Ohio to Louisville, where he paused at his brother Jonathan's. He had just reached Shelbyville, Kentucky, on October 28, when he picked up the Frankfort *Argus* and read a news story which declared that Lewis had cut his own throat. At once he remembered the anxieties with which his friend had been struggling.

"I fear O! I fear the weight of his mind has overcome him," he wrote Jonathan.

Hoping against hope, he tried to persuade himself the news might be false: "I fear this report has too much truth, tho' it may have no foundation." In the first shock of horror, he was ready to accept the idea of suicide; but when, much later, the possibility of murder was suggested, he caught at it eagerly. It cleared Lewis's reputation and Clark, in his later years, seems to have accepted it as true. "Uncle had a great love for Lewis," wrote a niece, "& he never spoke of him without the tears coming into his eyes. he never believed he committed suicide, and he had great love & respect for him."

When he found, as he soon did, that Lewis was really dead, Clark took charge of his friend's affairs as well as he could— Reuben Lewis being at this time far up the Missouri, where he did not even learn of his brother's death until 1811. Lewis's papers and baggage were sent on from Nashville and Chickasaw Bluffs. Clark went through them, finding the will dated September 11, 1809, which left everything to Lucy Marks. He sent the papers to Mr. Jefferson to be turned over to the family, and with a friend prepared to take Lewis's watch to Albemarle in person.

Lewis's death left Clark wholly responsible for the publication of the expedition's Journals. Like all beginning authors, the explorers had at first entertained visions of fame and fortune from their book. Lewis had issued two prospectuses in 1807, had tried to get a ghost writer to return to St. Louis and work with him, and had begun arrangements for illustrations. After Lewis's death, Clark worked for some time to get all the journals together, and then invited Nicholas Biddle, later President of the Bank of the United States, who had agreed to edit them, to visit him at his father-in-law's home. They spent several days together going over the Journals, which Biddle then took back to Philadelphia with him. Clark sent George Shannon to assist the editor in the intervals of his Philadelphia law studies. Clark was much interested in the work. "Dear George," he wrote Shannon April 20, 1811, "write me all about my Book."

The venture turned out to be a complete failure. The scientific notes, which were to have been prepared by Dr.

Benjamin Smith Barton, a Philadelphia botanist, never appeared, since Barton died with the work barely begun; and, in spite of Mr. Jefferson's impatience, publication of the Journals was long delayed. Biddle finally had to turn over the last editorial work to another hand. After the book finally appeared in 1814, the publishers failed and sales were negligible. Two years later Clark, in St. Louis, was still trying to get a copy of his own Journals.

The question of Lewis's successor was difficult. It was believed at the time, probably correctly, that Clark was offered the post, since he had already shown competence as an administrator and had been suggested for the Governorship of Illinois Territory. Clark himself was so little interested in becoming Governor that he used his influence to secure the office for another man. President Madison consulted Mr. Jefferson, who, from the slippered ease of his retirement at Monticello, cast a speculative eye across the valley toward Ashlawn, home of his friend James Monroe. Toward the end of November, Mr. Jefferson rode over to call and—after observing "how much the death of Merewᴴ. Lewis was to be regretted, by the loss the publick had sustained in so deserving an officer"—suggested that Monroe take his place, whereat Monroe was mildly disgusted. If he accepted office at all, he intimated, it would have to be something better than an obscure territorial Governorship, practically in the shadow of the Rockies. Eventually, Benjamin Howard, Congressman from Kentucky, was appointed April 17, 1809, holding office until 1813, when Clark replaced him, as both Governor and Superintendent of Indian Affairs. Louisiana had become Missouri Territory in 1812.

Clark may have refused the Governorship because, with Lewis's experience in mind, he felt his own political inexperience. More probably it was because he hoped for active service in the War of 1812, then rapidly approaching. When there was talk in 1813 of giving him a command, William

Henry Harrison remarked: "In the kind of warfare in which
we are engaged I had rather have him with me than any
other man in the United States." His appointment as Governor, in 1813, however, ended his hope of a command; and
he continued to be reappointed for one three-year term after
another, until Missouri became a state in 1820.

Missouri's escape from anything worse than Indian raids
during the war was largely due to Clark's skill in handling
Indians. Whenever the British had the Sioux of the upper
Mississippi ready for the warpath, friendly tribes under control of Clark's agents made hostile demonstrations just sufficient to call the Sioux warriors back to their villages. Clark
headed off most of the possible Indian trouble at the start,
when he took a large delegation of chiefs to Washington and
adroitly won them over to the American side. It was an anxious trip, for American feeling was bitter against all Indians
and there was always danger that some eastern super-patriot
would murder a few of the visiting chiefs. Clark's diplomacy
convinced them of American power and kept them safely
on the American side.

In 1814, the war began to take a more serious turn in Missouri Territory. The British had pushed down the Mississippi
as far as Prairie du Chien. "God only knows what our fate
is to be," Mrs. Clark wrote her brother, and for a time Clark
contemplated sending his family either to Kentucky or Tennessee for safety. Thanks to Clark, the danger was soon over.
When four river gunboats were authorized, he shrewdly had
one of them built in St. Louis—so that "the hostile Indians
should hear of it, and magnify its size and importance (which
I understand they have)."

In May, 1814, he took personal command of an expedition
to Prairie du Chien, in the very heart of the pro-British Indian country. After driving the British off easily, he was very
nearly killed in council with ostensibly friendly Indians. A
warrior, pledged to kill the Red Head, approached him in

the council. As he did so, Clark significantly shifted his huge saber to a handy position across his knees. The British were loud in their charges of "horrible cruelties" by Clark's "relentless Assassins," and described Clark himself as "this Ruffian."

They were alarmed because Prairie du Chien gave the Americans control of the upper Mississippi. One anxious British officer insisted that unless the place was retaken, "there was an end to our connexion with the Indians." Clark had hardly returned to St. Louis when they returned with a large force of Indians and militia which compelled the American garrison to surrender; but the war was nearly over and Missouri was safe from anything worse than Indian raids.

These grew more serious after the Treaty of Ghent had nominally ended hostilities. The advantage then was all with the Indians. The Treaty forbade military operations pending treaties with Britain's Indian allies—a proviso which checkmated the Americans while it did not worry the hostile tribes in the least. The worst Indian attacks came between the signing of the Treaty of Ghent and Clark's own treaties with the red men.

Early in 1815, together with Auguste Chouteau and Ninian Edwards (Lincoln's friend), Clark was appointed to the commission which made peace with nineteen tribes at Portage des Sioux. Here he met once more the friendly Sioux chief, Black Buffalo, who had traveled aboard his boat in 1804 and who died at Portage des Sioux during the council. In the following year he made peace with ten other tribes who had not attended the first conference.

Thereafter, Clark's Indian problems consisted mainly in keeping peace between the tribes, preventing or punishing murder, purchasing tribal lands and moving the Indians slowly west, driving white squatters off Indian lands, keeping the Indians from returning to land they had already sold, recovering stolen horses and kidnaped children, punishing robbery and murder both by whites and Indians, keeping whisky from the ever-thirsty redskins, and persuading Indians in American territory to look to the "Red Head Chief" in St. Louis, rather than to the British Indian agents along the Lakes. From St. Louis he worked through a network of Indian agents, many of them former army officers, who actually lived on their agencies with the tribes, among them his old friend Nathaniel Pryor.

One legendary incident illustrates his adroitness in dealing with Indians. The newly discovered lands were a paradise for early naturalists, many of whom began collecting there. The Indians were amazed one day to behold a grown man dashing about the prairie, catching insects with a net. Young warriors, sent out to capture him, brought the terrified entomologist into camp, where it was gravely decided he had better be killed. Before doing so, however, the chiefs sent down to St. Louis to get the approval of the Red Head Chief. By no means sure what might happen to the unlucky scientist if he ordered his release, Clark sent back instructions to send him as a prisoner to St. Louis, so that he might kill him himself. The tribe, so the story goes, solemnly granted this privilege to their friend.

In general, Clark had the co-operation of the leading chiefs, most of whom loved and trusted him. His name, according to certain white admirers, carried a "reverential awe" among the tribes, but neither awe of their own chiefs nor the Red Head Chief could control the younger warriors, really wild young people, always eager for a scalp or a foray or a little simple robbery. "We know," said two chiefs in 1815, "that among all nations the young men are foolish and will not be advised by their chiefs." Since much of the trouble was started by white men, the Fox chief Tiomay (the Strawberry) had a clear case when he asked: "How can we stop our men when your white men cannot stop the whites from committing crimes. Both of our cases are hard;—Our young men will not do what we wish—and yours act the same way."

Clark's conference at Prairie du Chien in 1825 finally ended the war—nominally ended in 1823—between the Chippewas, Sacs, and Foxes on one side, and the Sioux on the other. Iowas, Menominees, Winnebago, Pottawatomies, and Ottawas also attended, being more or less concerned in land disputes as well as in the war itself.

The President's negotiators finally had to persuade the Sioux to meet the Sacs and Foxes in one conference, and then to meet the Chippewas separately. After days of speeches, tribal boundaries were set up at last, the Sacs and Foxes relinquished to the whites all lands east of the Mississippi, the treaty was signed, and a thousand Indians feasted at government expense.

Trouble broke out again in 1830, when the Sioux and Menominees massacred Sacs and Foxes, who fled to Rock Island in terror. Clark set out for Prairie du Chien in the steamboat *Planet,* taking some Missouri Indians along. At first the Sacs and Foxes refused to meet their enemies at all. Clark applied his favorite formula—"time and a little smoking"—plus a plentiful distribution of presents. When the boat reached Galena, she was swarming with Sacs, Foxes, Iowas, Otos, Missouri, Sioux, and Winnebagoes. By July 15, the Sacs and Foxes on one side and the Sioux on the other had agreed to mark off a neutral strip 40 miles wide across northern Iowa and southern Minnesota. The Indians returned to their homes aboard a steamboat appropriately named *Red Rover.*

Much of Clark's trouble in his work with the Indians, during the period after the war, was due to British traders, illegally operating on American soil and doing their best to keep the redskins attached to the British Crown and trading at the Canadian posts along the border. "If the Indian is our Enemy it is the Trader who has made him so," he had been warned as early as 1807. The British used some very queer arguments to persuade the Indians. Certain Hudson's Bay men explained "that Lewis and Clark were not Americans but children of the Pope, and that therefore the country did not belong to the Americans"! Other British traders told the Indians that their American Father, the President, was "so poor that he Could not furnish turnips to his dinners," and that "none of his children know how to make blankets."

The British intruders could easily undersell their legitimate American competitors. The best Indian goods, being British made, passed duty-free through Canada, while they had to pay a 60 per cent duty at American ports. When British traders were caught, their goods could be confiscated, but in that wild country it was almost impossible to catch them. It was also difficult to tell who was really Canadian and who was American. Ostensibly "American" traders had an odd way of turning up in Montreal and settling down there after they had made their fortunes.

Even the legitimate Indian trade often attracted rascals of the worst sort. Traders could make from one to 200 per cent profit trading in beaver skins, and sometimes the profits were several hundred per cent higher than that. When one of Clark's agents made government Indian payments of $3,000, he found that a single trader had his hands on $2,300 of it by three o'clock the next afternoon!

Such profits were perennially tempting—if you lived to enjoy them. Adventurous men accepted the danger for the money there was in it, though for their enormous profits the traders, hunters, and trappers had to run enormous risks. The Arikaras alone killed nearly 30 white men in a few years of nominal peace. One party of white hunters were wiped out simply because the Osage warrior, Mad Buffalo, "had came for scalps and white mens Scalps were as good as Red Mens." With refreshing absence of race prejudice, he scalped all but a half-breed, whom he defiantly spared to carry the news back to the white men. The bleeding heads he then cut off and left stuck on poles.

Whisky was at the root of much of the trouble. One of Clark's agents averred that every outrage during a twelve year period was due to firewater. Being useful in cheating the Indians, it was often "secretly administered to some of the principal Men, previous to & pending the Negotiations, by interested Individuals." The earlier sobriety of the Missouri River Indians had long since broken down and, as Clark said: "Not an Indian could be found among a thousand, who would not (after a first drink) sell his horse, his gun, or his last blanket, for an other drink."

Control was almost impossible, since traders could legally take a gallon a month into Indian country for each of their engagés. However thirsty, the engagés got very little of this and the Indians a great deal—well watered, since in the upper Missouri whisky was worth $24 to $32 a gallon.

Even a scrupulous man like David Thompson was compelled by his partners to take liquor to the Indians, though Thompson, to dispose of it, deliberately "placed the Kegs of Alcohol on a vicious horse; and by noon the Kegs were empty, and in pieces, the Horse rubbing his load against the Rocks to get rid of it."

Clark thought he might be able to control abuses if he were given a special corps of about 1,000 men. Needless to say, he did not get them, though he did manage to suppress the distillery which one group of enterprising traders set up inside Indian country.

The long and weary effort to civilize and educate the Indian was already beginning. Clark exerted himself to the utmost to overcome the redskins' improvidence and make good farmers of them. Blacksmiths went out to the agencies to repair firearms and tools. Practical farmers went out to teach agriculture. But such a program went against Indian nature. Hoeing, digging, plowing, reaping were squaws' work. Warriors were not interested. When white agricultural teachers were sent out to them, the Indians expected the teachers to do the farm work themselves, and even to put up the fences. Efforts at grammar school education were nearly as futile. There were no local schools, and the Indians hesitated to send their children to the distant East. His sons would learn to despise him, one father explained, if they went to a white man's school.

Clark was able, however, to provide education for two, perhaps three, of Charbonneau's half-breed children, and he also cared for René Jussome's daughter. In 1810 old Charbonneau, almost certainly accompanied by Sacagawea, came to St. Louis, bought land, and tried to settle down. It was no use. The call of the prairies was too strong. Clark took his property off his hands and Charbonneau was off again to the wilds, where he lived a long, unedifying life, still marrying a squaw or two every now and then until he was an old, old man.

The children, and perhaps for a time Sacagawea, stayed in St. Louis. Clark's accounts show that he paid a Baptist minister for the education of "J. B. Charbonneau"—Baptiste, the little redskin "Pomp" who had traveled across the continent with the Lewis and Clark Expedition. A priest, Father Neil, took charge of another son, Toussaint; and Clark became guardian of the little girl, Lizette, the daughter of a Shoshone squaw of Charbonneau's who died in 1812, and who may have been Sacagawea. One of Baptiste's schoolmates at the Rev. Mr. Welch's school says specifically that "the boy was under the guardianship of Gov. William Clark." He used to like to point out in Clark's Indian Museum the bark canoe "in which he had been born"—mere boyish romancing, since there had been no bark canoes at Fort Mandan and Sacagawea did not bear her papoose in a canoe. Baptiste and Toussaint were provided with a Roman history, "Scott's lessons," a dictionary, shoes, paper, quill pens, fuel, board, laundry, and ink. William Clark Kennerly, nephew of the explorer, used to tell in after life how he had personally known the boy Baptiste while he was at school in St. Louis.

When Prince Paul of Wuertemberg visited the West, he became interested in the lad and took him to Europe, later bringing him back to the United States, apparently on his own second visit in 1829. Baptiste afterward served as guide and interpreter to many white travelers in the West, including Clark's son, Jefferson Clark.

In 1831, a remarkable delegation arrived from the closely associated Nez Percé and Flathead tribes. It has never been quite clear what they really wanted, mainly because no one in St. Louis could speak their language. Nez Percé tradition says that Lewis had spoken to them of religion. If so, it is his only recorded religious utterance, for though his mother was an active Methodist, he himself seems to have had little religious feeling. Protestant tradition has it that they were seeking the Bible. Catholic tradition says they sought a Black Robe. Skeptical historians have suggested that all they really wanted was the "big medicine" which gave the white man so much power.

It seems certain that, weary of their own primitive religion, they had learned something of Christianity from Canadian Indian converts who had settled among the Flatheads. According to Nez Percé tradition more than a century later, "they walk St. Louis to find Lewis and Clark, but when get there Lewis already dead, too bad."

Both Clark and the Catholic Bishop Rosati found it all very difficult. No one spoke Nez Percé. The subtleties of theology were a little obscure in sign language. As a layman of the Protestant Episcopal Church, Clark did the best he could. He summarized the Bible story from the Garden of Eden to the coming of the Saviour, the doctrine of salvation, the Crucifixion, explained the Ten Commandments and Christian morality. The Indians found it hard to understand but they knew they wanted this medicine.

Alas for them, there was no missionary to send. Bishop

Rosati had only a few priests. No Black Robe could go. The
Protestants failed likewise. The two older Nez Percés, converts to Catholicism, died, in or near St. Louis. Disconsolately, the young men set out on the long way home in March
of 1832, accompanied by the artist Catlin, who seized the
chance to paint their portraits. One of the young men died
on the way home. The only survivor, Rabbit-Skin Leggings,
met and talked with Nez Percés but never returned to Nez
Percé country. A second delegation is said to have been sent
to St. Louis. Another, probably the third, set out in 1837,
including representatives of both Flatheads and Nez Percés,
and perhaps an Iroquois. They were all killed on the way.
In 1839 another delegation came. This time a Black Robe
was ready. The famous Father de Smet went out to convert
various Rocky Mountain tribes, but Methodist and Presbyterian missionaries had already gone to convert the Nez Percés
and Oregon tribes. It was one result of the Lewis and Clark
Expedition which no one had quite foreseen.

As territorial Governor, Clark was a great success. Universally admired and respected, he had a gift for handling
people that might have carried him far, if he had cared for
politics. Even Frederick Bates never had a word to say against
him—which was almost unique. "Supprizing to think how
well we get along," he wrote his brother Edmund of his relations with the legislature; but it was not really surprising, for
in his seven years as Governor Clark never vetoed a single
bill, always contriving to have doubtful measures modified
before they were passed.

When Missouri became a state, he helped establish the
new constitution and became an unenthusiastic candidate for
Governor. At first he refused to run at all, for his Judy was
in her last illness. Eventually he told the voters that choosing
a Governor was their business not his, and on that unpromis-
ing platform became a candidate. Defeated two to one by
Alexander McNair, Register of the Land Office, he placidly

continued his work as Superintendent of Indian Affairs until June 30, 1821, when he closed down his office. The next year he became "Superintendent of Indian Affairs at St. Louis," dealing with northern and western tribes outside the state, an office which he held the rest of his life.

Where Lewis had failed, he succeeded—smoothing over the fierce political passions of Missouri Territory, helping his obstreperous white charges develop toward statehood, restraining his savage red charges. He is credited with some 30 Indian treaties. When he could, he prevented tribal wars. When he failed, he struggled to end them. He bought old tribal lands and assigned new ones. Greedy white men thought him a great deal too fond of the Indians, for Clark in those years of change wanted to secure some kind of justice for his red children.

It was a good life, there by the Mississippi, in Clark's last peaceful years, a life with an incomparable ease and grace, yet with the rough vigor and adventure of the prairies at its very door. French gaiety and formal courtesy relieved the starkness of other American frontiers. There was much doffing of hats. Even when a Frenchman wore only a handkerchief on his head, he lifted it politely to all acquaintances, male and female, and then stood composedly in the street rearranging it. The poorer French *habitants* owned almost nothing, but "surrounded with wretchedness they dance and sing; and if they have their relations within sound of their violin, they have nothing more to ask of the Virgin." The gentry had their own farms and gardens, well stocked with "froot trees," which Clark brought from the East. Persimmons were native. Flowers were everywhere. No one ever sent flowers because everyone had so many of his own.

The intellectual life was, perhaps, a little limited, but there was always Dr. Saugrain, still amusing himself with scientific experiments, as he had been doing when the expedition started. Visiting Indians thronged to see these marvels. The doctor asked them to open a door—the knob was electrified. The doctor dropped a coin in water and told them they could have it. As eager copper fingers reached for it, the doctor slyly turned on the current. The terrified Indians ran. Big medicine, but it hurt.

Their friend Clark, the Red Head Chief, played them no such tricks. Always the big Indian council room adjoining his house was filled with them. They could feel quite at home there for it also served as a museum for displaying his Indian collections. Although Clark never became an Indian linguist, an interpreter was always at hand, and it was easy to talk to the Red Head Chief. The sights of St. Louis and his hospitality impressed his Indian visitors about equally. "I have been to the town of the Red Head," said Tarrarecaweho, a Pawnee chief, "and saw there all that a red skin could see."

"When I go to St. Louis I go to see Choteau or Clark," said another Indian; "—he says hello—and negro comes in with great plate of cake, wine, &c—he say 'eat, drink.' If he want anything else he say 'hello'—three—four five six negro come in and do what he want—that I call happy—he no plough—he no work—he no cut wood." Slaves were, in fact, so numerous about the Governor's house that a jocular friend suggested they "must be in each other's way."

Only York was missing. He had gone back to Louisville with Clark and was hired out in the vicinity, so that he could be near his wife, the slave of a local family. For a time he seems to have fallen under Clark's displeasure, but eventually his master freed him and set him up in business with a wagon and team of six horses, hauling freight between Nashville and Richmond. As an independent businessman, you could scarcely call York a success. It was hard to get up in the morning when nobody made you. He did not take very good care of his horses. Two of them died. When he sold the others, he drove a bad bargain. He became a free servant and was ill treated.

"Damn this freedom," he said, "I have never had a happy day since I got it," and started back to Clark. On the way, as Clark later told Washington Irving, he died of cholera in Tennessee.

It is just possible that Clark was misinformed about his death. In 1832, the very year in which Clark chatted with Irving, the trapper Zenas Leonard found a Negro chief among the Crow Indians. He spoke the language fluently, was a distinguished warrior, and had married four wives. He told his white visitors that "he first came to this country with Lewis and Clark—with whom he also returned to the State of Missouri, and in a few years returned with a Mr. Mackinney, a trader on the Missouri river, and has remained here ever since, which is about ten years." It is just possible that York enjoyed freedom more than his old master thought and had preferred to disappear. Was it not better to be a chief, with four wives, a victorious warrior among the Crows, than a slave in Kentucky or a struggling freedman in Tennessee?

Clark could afford to live well in his later years, and his home was as luxurious as it could be made, so far from manufactures. The loss of the Governorship with its $2,000 salary, meant a serious loss of income, for as Indian Superintendent his salary was only $1,500. The Missouri Fur Company, later the American Fur Company, in which he was associated with Reuben Lewis and others, was not a success, partly because the promoters refused to let John Jacob Astor have a share. But the eventual success of Clark's handling of the family land claims made up for all this, though he did not fare so well as Lewis's friend, Amos Stoddard, whose speculation in western lands netted his family three-quarters of a million dollars. William Clark was a fairly wealthy man by any reckoning before he died, able to leave his four surviving sons $32,000 each.

Full of life, even in his old age, Clark delighted in entertaining, whether at his three cherry dining tables or at his

"Plain Breakfast table" in town, or *al fresco* at his farm. To the end he was a jovial soul. Catlin describes "the venerable Governor Clark, whose whitened locks are still shaken in roars of laughter, and good jests among the numerous citizens, who all love him." Washington Irving, who visited him on the farm, has left a description of the life there in his notes:

"Drive out to Gov. Clark's—cross prairie—flowering & fragrant shrubs—the Gov farm—small cottage—orchard bending & breaking with loads of fruit—negroes with tables under trees preparing meal—fine sitting room in open air—little negroes whispering & laughing—civil negro major domo who asks to take horses out—invites us to walk in the orchard & spreads table with additional covers—citting-room—rifle & game bad & c. in corners—Indian calumet over fireplace—remains of fire on hearth, showing that morng has been cool—lovely day—golden sunshine—transparent atmosphere—pure breeze.

"Fine nut trees, peach trees, grape vines, catalpas &c. &c. about the house—look out over rich, level plain or prairie—green near at hand—blue line at the horizon—universal chirp and spinning of insects—fertility of country—grove of walnuts in rear of the house—beehives—dove cote—canoe—Genl arrives on horseback with dogs—guns. His grandson on a calico poney hallowing & laughing—Genl on horseback—gun on his shoulder—cur—house dog—bullying setter. . . .

"Dinner plentiful—good—but rustic—fried chicken, bacon and grouse, roast beef, roastes potatoes, tomatoes, excellent cakes, bread, butter &c."

The cooking of the Clark household had a reputation. An English traveler expatiates happily on "some wild ducks very nicely dressed and which I thought as tender and high flavoured as the famous canvass-back ducks of the Susquehanna." Since there was for a long time no hotel in St. Louis, the Clarks kept up the usual southern hospitality. Even when there was a hotel, Mrs. Harriet Clark practically kidnaped a French visitor because he had been taken ill and she thought the hotel accommodations bad. While she took the Frenchman for a drive, his baggage was surreptitiously transferred to Clark's house, where he remained until he had recovered.

Americans of every kind visited the Governor or corresponded with him. Mr. Astor inquired about a site for fur-trading. There is a message from a "Mr. Roosevelt." Mr. Jefferson, Clark's "best loved Friend," desired curiosities for his new University of Virginia. Old Daniel Boone and his family came calling from their village. The Boones knew Clark simply as "Will." Mr. James Audubon was grateful for his "kind disposition evinced to be of service." Mr. Audubon shared General Clark's interest in birds. Mr. George Catlin was even more congenial—he liked to paint Indians.

An obscure young lieutenant of engineers, assigned to works on the Mississippi, inquired about getting a house. The lieutenant's name was Robert E. Lee. He had been at West Point with Meriwether Lewis Clark. Lieutenant Lee seemed like a promising young officer who might have a future as a soldier.

In his old age, Clark learned one thing about the Lewis and Clark Expedition that was new, even to him. John Tanner called. He was the man who had been living with the Ojibways when the expedition passed and who had delayed too long in calling at Fort Mandan. He now wanted Clark's help in getting his family away from the Indians. "Governor Clark showed his wonted kindness," according to Tanner, by providing a boat and equipment.

Foreign visitors came too, among them a series of three German princelings, Paul Wilhelm of Wuertemberg, Maximilian of Wied, and the Duke of Saxe-Weimar. The Prince of Wuertemberg was delighted to meet aboard a river steamer with "der General Sir Williams Clarke." With some hesitation—was the man trying to found a German colony?—Clark granted a passport for travel in Indian country "as a Botanier" to "this Gentleman (or Prince as he may be termed.)" Lafayette, visiting St. Louis on his American tour, had to be entertained by Clark and Chouteau, since Bates, now Governor but churlish as ever, retired to his house on the ground that the legislature had given no authority for entertaining the distinguished visitor. Clark's gift of a live grizzly bear cub was not wholly fortunate. Lafayette wrote him later that he had hoped to make a pet of the little creature; but, the effort proving less and less successful as the bear grew bigger and bigger, the marquis had to turn his grizzly over to the Jardin des Plantes.

William Clark in his later years looked every inch the governor—tall, erect, dignified, ever with the air of the old soldier about him, "on the whole the same style of man as Washington—perhaps a trifle taller." At first the hair for which the Indians named him—"very red in those days"—flowed long about his head. Then, as it grew grayer and scantier, it was bound up in the conventional eelskin queue. When the Indians could no longer call him Red Head, he became the "Sand-haired Father."

Never much interested in dress,—he had lived too long in elkskin and field service uniform for that—Clark usually gave the impression of being very well dressed. An admiring niece thought it was because he was "a very fine looking man" to start with. An English visitor thought him "a most agreeable old gentleman." Even as late as 1901, a small boy's memories of General Clark—and the Indian curios that he brought as presents—lingered in an old man's mind. Clark, he remembered was "dressed in the style fashionable in that early day, of the civilian, with nothing to indicate the frontiersman. As I remember him, he was quite robust, of fine physique and a grace and ease of manner which greatly impressed me."

Clark's family life was supremely happy, marred by no more tragedy than falls to the lot of many another. His little daughter Mary and his wife Judy died in 1820, in Virginia, far from the turmoil of the electoral campaign, and on November 28, 1821, he married Mrs. Harriet Kennerly Radford, the other girl whom he had helped with that balky horse so many years before. This, too, was a happy marriage. The Clark children, who had always known her, accepted the stepmother affectionately. Clark calls her "your ma" in letters to Judy's children. Judy had borne him five children, two of whom—Mary, his only daughter, and his deformed son Julius —died in childhood.

By his second wife he had two children. The first seems to have been originally named Thomas Jefferson Kennerly Clark, though he was known in after life as Jefferson Kennerly Clark, and always known in the family by the same name as Sacagawea's papoose—"Pomp." Clark remarks happily in one of his letters: "Pomp is a noisy wild fellow." The second son, Edmund, died when he was less than a year old.

Ever an indefatigable filer, Clark treasured every scrap of paper relating to his children. A document still survives, carefully endorsed, "Miss Mary M. Clark's letter recd. 13th July 1821 answered by all the boys." All the letter said was:

Dear Papa
 I hope you are well. I want to see you, and my Brothers. kiss them for me. I am a good Girl, and will learn my Book.

Clark treasured the simple, childlike message. His little daughter died three months later.

His letters to his sons show him as a sympathetic, understanding father, anxious lest he had not provided enough money, carefully choosing gifts, warning sagely about loaning or borrowing money and the evils of "Disipation," bursting with paternal pride when his son Meriwether is made colorbearer at West Point, praising the cadet's drawings but urging him: "be caucous of your eyes, drawing Strains them very much." His own eyes were beginning to fail. Had all that drawing in the wild, wild West weakened them? He worried about his other sons, but Meriwether Lewis Clark was his pride and joy: "on you my son our greatest hopes rest, only percevere my boy and you will come out an orniment to the country which gave you burth nearly any thing can be effected by purseverance."

Yet even Meriwether caused occasional anxiety. As he approached the end of his cadet days, young Meriwether showed signs of falling in love with Mary Radford, his step-sister, who was also a second cousin. He hinted as much to his father, who replied from Washington in February, 1829:

"If it is Love which requires council let me advise you to devert your reflections on that subject, at least untill you Complete your education."

Finding that it was indeed love, the anxious father let his stepdaughter read part of one letter, and then wrote Meri-wether: "I have no doubt of her having a very correct opinion of your feelings; in relation to which she acts very prudently."

Mary was not quite so prudent as her stepfather thought. While Meriwether was away, she became engaged to Major Stephen Watts Kearny, a relative of the Civil War general, who rose to be a major-general himself. There was no diffi-culty about parental consent. The wedding party had assem-bled, the wedding dinner was waiting, the wedding guests had come, and the ceremony was just about to take place when young Meriwether Lewis Clark burst in impetuously from nowhere, demanding the bride for himself. That young lady promptly fainted, then suddenly discovered that she was not quite certain which gentleman she really did wish to marry.

It was all very embarrassing. There was a scene of much confusion, many parental head-shakings, much hush-hushing, some muttering, and a vast curiosity among the guests, who were finally persuaded to leave without the wedding they had come to see. A suggestion that they all take some refreshments was not a conspicuous success.

Mary, who still could not quite make up her mind between her two suitors, was spirited out of town for a few days. What happened afterward, no one quite knows. She married her major in a private ceremony a few days later. Young Meriwether vanished from the scene completely. He was not too blighted to marry afterwards—twice; and his rival Kearny died in his house some eighteen years later.

1831 was a year of doubled tragedy for Clark. His son Julius, deformed, growing deaf, and breathing with difficulty, finally died on September 5. Mrs. Clark died on Christmas Day. "My afflictions are as much as I can bear at present," he wrote to Meriwether, the only note of complaint in all his massive correspondence.

The aging Clark struggled on, alone except for his children, finding continual reason for pride in the career of his son Meriwether, a keen soldier who saw much service against the Indians and rose rapidly in the army. The boy was worthy of his father, the old man thought, he was even worthy of his namesake. Clark dipped his goose quill and scrawled some more advice: "Your fair is rough, recollect that your father has met with bad far and you are more Stout than he was, take Care of yourself and do not unnecessarily [yield?] either to Climate or the enemy."

Yes, the fare had been rough, up there in the Rockies. Bad on the Columbia, too. At least, young Meriwether Lewis Clark wouldn't have to eat dog. Ugh! how Clark had hated the stuff, though Lewis had actually come to like it. Just as well to give the boy a hint about needless danger. Plenty of danger on the expedition, but they never ran unnecessary risks. That's why they had succeeded. Black Hawk's warriors, fighting General Atkinson, could not well be fiercer than Little Turtle's, fighting Wayne back there in '94. How long ago it was—almost four decades. There had been a lot of living in those four decades. . . .

Eventually Meriwether gave up the service and settled in St. Louis. A few months before his death his father, now nearing sixty-eight, left his own lonely house and moved in with his son. The climate of St. Louis, unwholesome in those days, was worse than usual that year. The sturdy old man, vigorous almost to the end, was beginning to weaken. He died at Meriwether's home, September 1.

"Uncle Clarks death was an easy peaceful one he was not sick long & not much changed," wrote his niece, Mary Kennerly Taylor, who saw him die. "Father Mother & me were by him he spoke to the last. & told Mother to take care of Pompy as he always called his son Jefferson K. Clark."

One curious irony attended his death. In London, the Royal Geographical Society failed to note his passing. Henry Schoolcraft called their attention to their lapse. Then a final tribute was paid to William Clark in 1852—fourteen years late!

chapter 28: *More undiscovered country*

ONE by one, as the years passed, the Corps of Discovery began to slip away into country which even they had never yet explored. Sergeant Floyd had died at the very start of the expedition. Far to the west, among the Blackfeet, Potts died under a shower of arrows in 1808, a year before Lewis. Colter, captured with Potts, escaped death by an incredible feat. Stripped naked and told to run for his life, pursued by a mob of warriors, he killed —with the man's own spear—the only Indian fleet enough to catch him; hid under a floating mass of timber all day long, while searching Blackfeet prowled about above him; swam away in the darkness; and then walked for seven days, stark naked, keeping alive with such roots as he could find, until he reached Manuel Lisa's fort. Wearying of the wilderness at last, he returned to Missouri, married a girl named Sally, commenced farming, and died in 1813.

Drouilliard, who had gone back up the Missouri with Lisa, was brought back in 1808 to stand his trial for murder. It was embarrassing for Governor Lewis for Drouillard was being tried for having carried out, under Lisa, exactly the same orders that Lewis had given him when Reed deserted in 1804. Lisa, too, had directed Drouilliard to bring in a deserter, dead or alive. Drouilliard had wounded the man so badly that he died, but the court in St. Louis acquitted him on the ground that he was obeying orders. Two years later, he was killed by the Blackfeet near the Three Forks—so near his camp that he could have been rescued easily if the wind, blowing in the wrong direction, had not carried the sound of the shots away. His comrades read the story in the dust where they found his body. He had fought it out to the end, maneuvering constantly to keep his horse between him and the Indians, until at last a circling Blackfoot shot him from behind.

Pryor after an adventurous career in the army, rising to a captaincy in the War of 1812, became an Indian trader, then one of Clark's sub-agents, married an Osage squaw, and died among her kinsmen in 1831. Shannon became a judge, then U.S. District Attorney, and fell dead in the court room at Palmyra, Mo., in 1836. Bratton fought in the War of 1812, then settled at Waynetown, Indiana, on land which his family still hold, became a justice of the peace, and died in 1841. Willard, after serving in 1812 and in the Black Hawk War, died in California in 1865—still eagerly discussing the adventures of the Corps of Discovery. Ordway went to farming in Missouri and died there.

Most of the others simply vanish. Gibson settled in St. Louis and probably died there in 1809. Reuben Field returned to Kentucky. Werner became one of Clark's sub-agents. Windsor was still in the army in 1819. Frazer had to appeal to Clark for help in legal difficulties, first when he beat the sheriff sent to arrest him for debt, again when he attacked an Arikara Indian in the streets. He was still in St. Louis in 1815. He got out the prospectus for an edition of his journal but it never appeared and even the manuscript is now lost. He is perhaps identical with the Robert Windsor Frazier who was living near Brattleboro, Vermont, in 1834.

Last white survivor of the Corps of Discovery was Paddy Gass, who—after fighting in 1812 and losing an eye at Lundy's Lane—returned to West Virginia, where he lived on a small pension, became an inveterate tippler, married when he was about sixty and with amazing speed produced a family of seven children. Reforming suddenly in 1858, he became a convert to the Campbellite faith, and was duly baptized in the Ohio River, hundreds of people gathering to see the old sinner dipped.

Though he detested Negroes, Gass was a staunch Union man when the Civil War broke out. His Fourth of July speech to departing Union soldiers in 1861 impressed a boy-ish by-stander, who wrote out later how old Paddy "told the new soldiers that they must not go out with the intention of expecting they was going to have a Picnic but O far from it and they would not see so much spread before them of a table to eat as they could look now and see no no for if you go through and see what I have seen of war and starvea-tion you will think of what I tell you for I have been three days without one Bite to eat of any thing at all then when I did get it be the dievel it was nothing but cracked corn mixed with clear water and roasted in hot ashes but it tasted good my boys it was good to us if we only had enough of that but we got it by running out a lot of red dievels in to the Booshes and takeing all they had left but little did we care what be-came of them so we got a wee bite to eat." It was a fiery speech amid weeping mothers and "many apploses"—after .which Paddy refreshed himself "where a Brewry man had a wagon load of beer and Porter." He was proud of his journal of the expedition, the first full account of it published and kept a copy for his children to read. He died April 3, 1870, aged 99.

Only two of the Corps of Discovery were left. On the Wind River Reservation in Wyoming, still dwelt the old squaw, Sacagawea and her son Baptiste, the baby "Pomp" that Clark had loved. Charbonneau had vanished, somewhere on the prairies, years before, after a long and unedifying career. When the expedition was still somewhere between the Mandan Village and St. Louis, Clark had written the squaw-man a long letter, offering to educate "my little dancing boy Baptiest," and either to set Charbonneau himself up as a farmer, to become his partner in the Indian trade, or to secure him an official position as Indian interpreter. Charbonneau and Sacagawea tried to settle down in Missouri, but it was no use. They were soon "weary of a civilized life." In April, 1811, "a Frenchman named Charbonet and his Indian wife, both of whom had accompanied Lewis and Clark to the Pacific," joined the party of Henry M. Brackenridge to go back up the Missouri to the only life they really cared for. Charbonneau became a government interpreter under Clark. His reputation was never very savory. One acquaintance calls him "the old Knave." Another suggests that both he and Jussome "ought to be hung," but he did good service as an interpreter for Prince Maximilian of Wied on his tour of the prairies, and his cooking—especially his coffee, mince pies, and puddings—were universally esteemed.

He was indefatigable in matrimony. In 1833 he had two "lovely" wives, but one of them ran away. At eighty, he married an Assiniboine girl prisoner, only fourteen years old, the occasion being celebrated with "a splendid Chàrivèree, the Drums, pans, Kittles &c. Beating; guns fireing &c." The old rascal is said to have offered his bride to the rest of the men in camp.

The last news of him is in a letter by Joshua Pilcher, Clark's successor as Superintendent of Indian Affairs. In August, 1839, he arrived in St. Louis, "tottering under the infirmities of 80 winters, without a dollar to Support him." He had been discharged as interpreter but, the notice having failed to reach him, had worked six extra months, for which he wanted pay. Pilcher gave it to him, for "this man had been a faithful servant of the Government—though in a humble capacity." With that, the old man disappears into the wilds again, to die as he had lived among the Indians—and certainly to marry a few more squaws.

There are three separate stories of Sacagawea's later life, though—in spite of much dispute—there is not much doubt of her identity with the squaw who died at Wind River in 1884. There was, it is true, a Shoshone (i.e., Snake) wife of Charbonneau's who died Dec. 20, 1812, at Lisa's fort far up the Missouri. John Luttig entered in his journal there: "this Evening the Wife of Charbonneau a Snake Squaw, died of a putrid fever she was a good and the best Woman in the fort, aged abt 25 years she left a fine infant Girl." This would fix the date of Sacagawea's death—except that Charbonneau had two Shoshone wives.

There is also a queer story told by the Minnetaree warrior, Bull's Eye, in open council where other Indians could hear and correct his story. He claimed to be the grandson of Sacagawea, wife of "Sharbonish," with whom she "went far away somewhere." She was killed, said Bull's Eye, by hostile Indians near Glasgow, Montana, when he himself was four years old, i.e., in 1869.

Far to the West, however, among the Shoshones, there flourished an old squaw who was certainly named "Sacajawea," who had an uncanny knowledge of minute details of the expedition, who insisted that she had been part of it, who was devoted to Clark's, rather than to Lewis's, memory, and whom Baptiste Charbonneau recognized as his mother. Long

before her death, she was being pointed out as the real Sacagawea.

She separated from Charbonneau when that tireless polyg-
amist married just once too often—this time a young and
beautiful Ute damsel. When the wives quarreled, Charbonneau, siding with his bride, whipped Sacagawea. Indignantly
abandoning him at last, she wandered off to the Comanches, a
tribe closely related to the Shoshones, and married a Comanche warrior euphoniously named "Jerk Meat." Nez Percé
tradition says that after his death in battle she lived with
them for a time before settling down with her son Baptiste
and her foster-son, Bazil, in the Shoshone band of the great
chief Washakie. Here she ended her days, enjoying free rides
on the white men's stage coaches, well supplied with U. S.
government rations, treasuring the papers given her by "some
great white chiefs," never happy unless she could see the
mountains, thanking the spirits every morning for the new
day, worshipping the little white flowers that grew at the
snow line, which she thought must be the spirits of little
children. They found her lying dead in her blankets on the
morning of April 9, 1884. The papers buried with her would
have established her identity beyond dispute; but when the
wallet containing them was at last exhumed, the papers had
rotted away. Her son Baptiste, the baby "Pomp," died the
next year, last survivor of the Corps of Discovery.

Around their graves pulsed the life of the expanding nation, for which the captains and their men had opened the
way. Americans had been quick to follow them. Within a
few months of their return, Manuel Lisa was sending the first
of many fur-trading parties to the Forks of the Missouri and
beyond, with experienced Lewis and Clark men to guide it
with their acquired knowledge, perilously won, of the new
country. John Jacob Astor pondered reports of the expedition; it was not long till the "Astorians" were on their way to
the Pacific to set up a permanent post. One ardent youngster,

hearing Ordway's stories of adventure, rushed off, joined the first exploring party that would take him, and was off to Oregon. There were hundreds like him. Far up the muddy Missouri and on to the Shining Mountains went those amazing adventurers, the "Mountain Men," sometimes in bands, sometimes in fearless, scattered parties of two or three or four. Many of them died in the mysterious new lands that drew them; but those that returned brought marvelous tales as well as their furs. John Colter's reports of the wonders he had seen on the upper Yellowstone—which Clark had missed—began to be believed. "Colter's Hell," the skeptics called the reported area of boiling springs and flowing steam and spurting geysers.

Other military parties went out to explore unknown rivers whose mouths Lewis and Clark had passed. Pike and his men were off into the unknown before the Corps of Discovery returned, and other explorers followed swiftly, expanding the discoveries of the Corps.

Behind them came the settlers. The American frontier was beginning its march beyond the banks of the Mississippi, which entered its last stage with the rush to Oregon. First a handful of missionaries, responding to the plea of the mountain Indians who had journeyed to St. Louis to see the Red Head Chief and ask about the white man's faith. Then Marcus Whitman's thousand settlers. Then two thousand more. Then thousands upon thousands, creaking in their bullock-drawn wagons across the Plains. They followed the Oregon Trail, not the river route of the two captains; but there would never have been wagons going westward without the first perilous adventures of the Corps of Discovery.

Who owned Oregon? No one quite knew; but when the suave diplomats gathered to discuss sovereignty and territorial rights, there was no disputing that the American, Gray, had first found the Columbia's mouth; that the Americans, Lewis and Clark, had first explored the broad stretches of its middle waters. Because of the Corps of Discovery, Oregon is American to-day. And ten white stars in the blue field of Old Glory stand for states of the Union that one by one grew up in farms and mills, cities and homesteads, along the trail where weary men in tattered elk-skin cursed the rocks that tore their feet, sweated at the tow rope, poled against the savage current of the muddy Missouri, stumbled in the chill streams of the Rockies, and staggered down the western end of the Lolo Trail.

So they lie today—white, red, half-breed, and Negro—under the flag with the new stars they added, scattered over the land they served, the land they explored: Lewis under his broken column in Tennessee, still solitary in the wild woods he loved; Clark on the knoll at Bellefontaine; Charbonneau God knows where upon the lonely prairie; Sacagawea and her child still among the tribe.

But suppose the Angel Gabriel should prove just a little fallible. Suppose he should make just one mistake. If he were to forget the trump of doom and blow instead the battered "sounden horn" of the expedition, would they not all rise, pack the miraculous airgun once again among the molding leather tents and the battered (but water-tight) leaden canisters of powder, whistle for the dog Scannon, and—with sharp eyes alert for grizzlies, game, and Indians—run the rough dug-outs into the muddy Missouri current, once again to go exploring, and to wonder at the changes in the vast land they gave the Nation.

APPENDIX

Acknowledgments

THE writer of a work of this sort, most of the research for which is done in the field or in small, highly specialized, and widely scattered local archives, inevitably receives a great deal more friendly aid than he can possibly acknowledge. Interest in Lewis and Clark is almost universal among the modern inhabitants of the country they traversed nearly a century and a half ago; and it is pleasant to remember that—except for one case of flat refusal to let me see some unimportant secondary sources—I have met with nothing but friendly interest and willing co-operation from Virginia to Oregon and from Canada to Tennessee.

Certain obligations, however, are too great to be ignored. The Yale, Columbia, and Congressional Libraries have generously granted stack privileges; and I am deeply indebted to a large group of archivists and librarians, especially Miss Anne S. Pratt, Reference Librarian at Yale; Dr. Elizabeth B. Drewry, Dr. Edward F. Rowse, Mr. Charles A. Moreland, Mr. William J. Bottomley, and Miss Sara R. Dunlap, of the National Archives; Dr. Clarence E. Carter, of the State Department; Mr. Archibald P. DeWeese, of the Information Division, Mr. Gerald D. McDonald, Chief of the American History and Genealogy Division, Mr. Lewis N. Stark, Chief of the Reserve Division; Mr. F. Ivor D. Avellino, Assistant in the American History Division; Mr. Gerard L. Alexander and Mr. Theodore Ryder, Assistants in the Map Division, of the New York Public Library; Mr. Julian P. Boyd,

Librarian of Princeton University and editor of the Papers of
Thomas Jefferson, and Mr. Lyman H. Butterfield of the Jefferson
Papers staff; Mr. Harry Clemons, Librarian, Mr. Jack Dalton,
Reference Librarian, Mr. John Cook Wyllie, Curator of Rare
Books, Mr. Francis L. Berkeley, Jr., Curator of Manuscripts, Miss
Evelyn Dollens and Miss Jane Carson, of the Alderman Library,
University of Virginia; Mr. Nelson W. McCombs, Librarian, and
Mr. Alfred B. Lindsay, Assistant Librarian, of the Washington
Square Library, and Mr. Mulford Martin, Librarian of the Commerce Library, New York University; Mr. William J. Van Schreeven, Head Archivist of the Virginia State Library; Rev. Joseph
P. Donnelly, S.J., Librarian of St. Louis University; Rev. W. L.
Davis, S.J., Head of the Department of History, Gonzaga University, and Archivist of the Oregon Province, Society of Jesus, and
Mr. Robert I. Burns, S.J., formerly his assistant; Miss Alice Reynolds, of the Harvard College Library; Mrs. John Trotwood
Moore, State Librarian and Archivist of Tennessee; Miss Helen
M. McFarland, Librarian of the Kansas State Historical Society;
Mr. Ora Williams, Curator, and Miss Clara Zimmerman, Manuscript and Accessions Clerk of the Iowa Department of History
and Archives; Mr. Emory H. English, editor of the *Annals of
Iowa;* Miss Rose Demorest, of the Carnegie Library, Pittsburgh;
Miss Ludie J. Kinkead, of the Filson Club; Mr. Lancaster Pollard, Superintendent, Mr. Howard M. Corning, Reference Librarian, and Mrs. Lewis A. McArthur, former Librarian, of the
Oregon State Historical Society; Mr. Charles van Ravenswaay,
Director, Mrs. Brenda R. Gieseker, Librarian, and Miss Caroline
Crutcher, Assistant, of the Missouri Historical Society; Mr. Russell Reid, Superintendent, and Mrs. Florence H. Davis, Librarian,
of the State Historical Society of North Dakota; Mr. Will G.
Robinson, Secretary, and Mr. Lawrence K. Fox, former Secretary, of the South Dakota State Historical Society; Miss Lucinda
B. Scott, Librarian, and Mrs. Anne McDonnell, Assistant Librarian, of the State Historical Society of Montana; and Mr. E. S.
Robinson, of the Public Library, Vancouver, B.C.

On difficult questions of military history I have had invaluable
assistance from Colonel William A. Ganoe, Colonel Ellwood W.
Sargent, Lt. Colonel Hoffman Nickerson, Lt. Colonel Calvin

Goddard, Colonel Leo A. Codd, and Major B. R. Lewis. Mr. R. S. Thomas, military historian of the War Department Special Staff, has solved a whole series of special puzzles.

In the collection of portraits, I have been greatly assisted by Miss Helen C. Frick, Director, and Miss Ethelwyn Manning, Librarian, of the Frick Art Museum; Mr. Jeremiah O'Connor, Curator of the Corcoran Gallery; Mr. Warren A. McCullough, Custodian of Independence Hall; and Miss Marjory Douglas, of the Missouri Historical Society. Mr. Perry T. Rathbone, Director of the City Art Museum, St. Louis, has graciously permitted reproduction of the unique silhouette of Meriwether Lewis in his private collection.

The drawings by George Catlin are from his "North American Indians" courtesy of the Yale Library; the paintings by Charles Bodmer are from "Travels in the Interior of North America" by Prince Maximilian von Wied-Neuwied, courtesy of the New York Public Library.

Mr. Claude G. Bowers, Ambassador to Chile; Professor Isaac J. Cox, of Northwestern University; Mr. Charles Morrow Wilson, Mr. Jacob H. Lowrey, Mr. Meade Minnigerode, Mr. Holmes Alexander, Mrs. Anya Seaton Chase, and Mrs. Elizabeth Meriwether Gilmer ("Dorothy Dix") have assisted in my seven year search for the truth about Meriwether Lewis and Theodosia Burr.

Mr. Hugh Lee Webster, of Columbia, Tenn., like his father a lifelong student of the tragic mystery of Lewis's death, has provided a great deal of information and has also been kind enough to read the chapter dealing with it. Judge Samuel C. Williams, of the Tennessee Historical Commission, has supplied various details on Lewis's early command in Tennessee and also on his death.

Miss Alice E. Smith and Mr. Ernest St. Aubin, of the Wisconsin State Historical Society, have continued the valuable aid that I formerly received from the late Dr. Louise Phelps Kellogg and the late Miss Annie A. Nunns.

On Indian languages and customs I have had the benefit of advice from Mr. M. W. Stirling, Chief of the Bureau of Ethnology; Dr. John P. Harrington, of the Bureau of Ethnology; Mr.

John C. Ewers, Associate Curator of Ethnology in the National Museum; Professor E. Adamson Hoebel, of New York University; Dr. C. F. Voegelin, Indiana University; Mr. Archie Phinney, Superintendent of the Northern Idaho Indian Agency; Mr. L. W. Shotwell, Superintendent of the Yakima Indian Agency; Mr. George F. Will, President of the State Historical Society of North Dakota; Mr. J. A. Medaris, Chief Clerk of the Fort Berthold Agency; and Mr. C. T. Stranahan, of Lewiston, Idaho. Mrs. Joe Evans, Sr., of the Sacajawea Museum, Spalding, Idaho, gave me the privilege of examining her collection of Nez Percé Indian accounts of Lewis and Clark.

Mrs. George Gordon, of Stafford, Va., and Mrs. Howell Carr Lewis, of Charlottesville, Va., permitted me to examine family records relating to Meriwether Lewis. Mrs. John C. Doolan, of Louisville, allowed me to examine the Jonathan Clark Papers. Mrs. Elizabeth M. Story, of Oswego, Ore., a descendant of George Shannon, and Mrs. Maud J. Bratton-Chesterson, of Waynetown, Ind., a descendant of William Bratton, also supplied family records. Miss Anna Kruger, of Waynetown, furnished an unpublished MS.

Mr. Donald Culross Peattie, Mr. Victor H. Paltsits, and Mrs. Elvira M. Davis lent me material from their private collections. The Rev. J. Neilson Barry, of Portland, a veteran student of the expedition, kindly criticized portions of the MS., made numerous suggestions as to maps, lent materials, and answered a series of questions extending over eight years.

The National Park Service has opened its historical files and has given me every possible assistance. I am especially indebted to Mr. Hillory A. Tolson, Acting Director, Chicago; Mr. Charles E. Peterson and Mr. John Albury Bryan, of St. Louis; and Mr. Clyde B. King, formerly stationed at the Meriwether Lewis National Monument.

A number of librarians and others have helped in running down obscure bits of special information. Mr. Milton Edward Lord, Director of the Boston Public Library; Mr. Stephen T. Riley, Assistant Librarian of the Massachusetts Historical Society; Mr. W. Kaye Lamb, Librarian of the University of British Columbia; Mr. Lawrence Waters Jenkins, Director of the Peabody

Museum, Salem, Mass., helped to clear up the movements of the brig *Lydia*. Mr. Robert Hunt Land, Associate Librarian of the College of William and Mary, and Mrs. Mary R. M. Goodwin, of Colonial Williamsburg, helped to trace Lewis's early education. The Hon. G. Lanctot, Deputy Minister in charge of the Public Archives of Canada, and Mr. J. B. Tyrrell, of Toronto, supplied Canadian materials. Dr. Milo M. Quaife, Secretary, and Mrs. Elleine H. Stones, of the Burton Historical Collection, Detroit Public Library, helped to trace the Bates family. I am indebted to Miss May Morris, Librarian of Dickinson College, for information on the Rev. James Waddel; to Mr. Boies Penrose for information on Clement Biddle Penrose; to the late Dr. John Eric Hill, of the American Museum of Natural History, and Mr. Lee S. Crandall, General Curator of the Bronx Zoological Park, for zoological data on grizzly bears; to Miss Mary C. Sherrard, of the Coyle Free Public Library, Chambersburg, Pa., for information on Patrick Gass; to the Hon. Claude G. Tarleton, Presiding Judge of the Marion County Court, Palmyra, Mo., for tracing the true story of George Shannon's death; to Mrs. Edward S. Boyd, of the Public Library, Woodbury, Conn., for information on Amos Stoddard; to Miss Ethel L. Williams, Assistant Reference Librarian of Howard University, for information on York; to Mrs. Gertrude Henderson, of Sioux City, Mrs. Lillian R. Smith, Curator of the Sioux City Public Museum, and Miss Doris Rockafellow, formerly of the Public Library, for help with Sergeant Floyd's story; to Dr. Francis Haines, of the State Teachers College, Lewiston, Idaho, for information on Indian horses; to Mrs. Richard Hogshead, Moffat's Creek, Va., for locating the Bratton homestead; to Miss Ruth Lapham Butler, Custodian of the Ayer Collection, Newberry Library, for certain MSS.; to Miss Dorothy Drake, of the Sacremento City Library, and Miss Mabel R. Gillis, California State Librarian, for tracing Alexander Willard; to Miss Alice M. Sterling, of the Newcastle Free Public Library, Newcastle, Pa., for helping to trace Private Gibson; to Miss Roemol Henry, Librarian of Transylvania College, for information on George Shannon's life there; to Mr. Russell F. Barnes, Librarian of the Minnesota State Historical Society for aid in the search for illustrations; to Miss M. Whitcomb Hess for information on Dr. Saugrain; to Miss Gertrude D. Hess, Assistant Librarian of the American Philosophical Society for aid with Lewis and Clark MSS.; to Miss Hilda Hammer, Reference Librarian of the Omaha Public Library, for local source material; to Miss Dolores Cadell, Reference Librarian of the San Francisco Public Library, Miss Grace Berger, of the Kansas City Public Library, and Miss Louise G. Pritchard, of the Portland Public Library, for guidance to early local newspapers; to Professor Thomas M. Raysor, University of Nebraska, Dean Frank Cotner, Professor Merrill G. Burlingame, and Mrs. Lois B. Payson, Librarian, of Montana State College, for local information; to Mr. Arthur Styron, for help with Monroe's correspondence; to Mr. Lyle Wright, of the Huntington Library, and Mr. P. G. Morrison, Curator of the Rare Book Room, University of Chicago Library for help in locating MSS.; to Mr. Harry R. Burke, of the St. Louis *Globe-Democrat,* for suggestions as to Frederick Bates; to Justice Raymond L. Givens, Idaho Supreme Court, for help with the Lewis and Clark route through Idaho; to Mr. George R. Shields, of Washington, for information on John Shields; to Professor Donald Scott, Director of the Peabody Museum, Harvard University, for information on the Lewis and Clark collections there; to Mr. Rawson C. Myrick, Secretary of State of Vermont, Miss Dora E. Hodgdon, of the Vital Records Department, Miss Clara E. Follette, of the Vermont Historical Society, and Miss Marion Humble, of the Rutland Free Library, for information regarding Robert Frazer; to Mrs. Gladys Smith Puckett, Miss Elizabeth Showacre, Reference Librarian, and Miss Mary Johnson, First Assistant, of the Spokane Public Library, for assistance in using their superb western collection.

It should be useless, though it is customary, for me to add that I am alone responsible for such errors or omissions as may have found their way into the book.

Notes

ABBREVIATIONS

Am. Phil. Soc.—American Philosophical Society, Philadelphia.

Biddle—Nicholas Biddle (ed.): *History of the expedition under the command of Captains Lewis and Clark.* New York: Allerton, 1922. 3 vols.

Carter—Clarence E. Carter (Ed.): *Territorial Papers of the United States.* Washington: Government Printing Office, 1934.

Craig Papers—Papers of Major Isaac Craig, Carnegie Library, Pittsburgh.

DAB—*Dictionary of American Biography.* New York: Scribner, 1928-1937.

Draper MSS.—MSS. in the Draper Collection, Wisconsin State Historical Society.

Dye MSS.—MSS. collected by Eva Emory Dye, Oregon State Historical Society.

Enc.—Enclosure.

Evans MSS.—Nez Percé Indian statements collected by Mrs. Joe Evans, Sr., Sacajawea Museum, Spalding, Idaho.

EWT—Reuben Gold Thwaites: *Early Western Travelers.* Cleveland: A. H. Clark Co., 1904-1907. 32 vols.

Filson—Library of the Filson Club, Louisville, Ky.

GAO—General Accounting Office, Washington, D.C.

Gass—Journal of Patrick Gass, in various editions.

Glimpses—*Glimpses of the Past,* issued by the Missouri Historical Society, St. Louis, Mo.

Hodge—Frederick Webb Hodge: *Handbook of American Indians North of Mexico.* Washington: Government Printing Office, 1912. 2 vols.

Jacob—John G. Jacob: *Life and Times of Patrick Gass.* Wellsburgh, Va. [now W. Va.]: Jacob and Smith, 1859.

James—Thomas James: *Three Years among the Indians and Mexicans.* (Ed. Walter B. Douglas). St. Louis: Missouri Historical Society, 1916. [Original edition, 1846.]

LC—Library of Congress.

Marshall—Thomas Maitland Marshall (Ed.): *Life and Papers of Frederick Bates.* St. Louis: Missouri Historical Society, 1926. 2 vols.

Masson—Louis François Rodrigue Masson: *Bourgeois de la Compaignie du Nord-Ouest.* Quebec: A. Coté, 1889-90. 2 vols.

MLNM—Meriwether Lewis National Monument.

Mich.—*Michigan Pioneer and Historical Collections,* issued by the Michigan Historical Commission.

MinnSHS—Minnesota Historical Society.

MontSHS—Historical Society of Montana.

MoHS—Missouri Historical Society, St. Louis.

MVHR—*Mississippi Valley Historical Review,* issued by the Mississippi Valley Historical Association, Cedar Rapids, Iowa.

NA—National Archives, Washington.

NYPL—New York Public Library.

OreHS—Oregon State Historical Society.

SW—Secretary of War.

SWDF—Secretary of War's Document File.

Thwaites—Reuben Gold Thwaites (Ed.): *Original Journals of Lewis and Clark.* New York: Dodd Mead, 1905.

UVaLib—Alderman Library, University of Virginia.

VaSLib—Virginia State Library.

WD—War Department.

WR—War Records, National Archives.

WSHP—Publications of the State Historical Society of Wisconsin.

WSHS—State Historical Society of Wisconsin.

In the following pages, no references are given for quotations from the Journals kept by Lewis and Clark themselves or by the enlisted men of the expedition, the purpose being to avoid a needless mass of notes which are not necessary where chronology is an adequate guide. On the same principle, no references are given for the Lewis and Clark letters in the Missouri Historical Society, the one great collection, since they too are chronologically arranged.

Other sources are indicated in the usual way, though I have not listed the less important documents in the National Archives. It has not always been possible to give page references for Dr. Clarence E. Carter's series of *Territorial Papers,* since several of the most useful volumes are still either in MS. or in galley.

Quotations from the Lewis and Clark Journals are from Thwaites's edition, Biddle's much re-written version being used only when it seems to add new material.

The first figure in each pair below is a page reference, the second a paragraph reference.

4.4. Jefferson Papers, fol. 18767 (LC).
5.3. Ibid., fol. 18766.
6.4. Lewis's receipt to Isaac Craig, Mar. 22, 1801. Receipt Book, Craig Papers. There are various references to Lewis in these papers. See Craig's note of Sept. 15, 1800, AA/Craig/VII.: Abstract of Forage, Sept. 9, 1800, AA/Craig/V.c.; credit to Peter Audrain, AA/Craig/VII.a, no folio.
9.4. The DAB is wrong in stating that Frances Clark had red hair. See G. R. C. Ballard Thruston's MS. annotation in the Filson Club's copy. On the Clark genealogy, see Draper MSS. 2 J 102; 10 J 27-28; 7 J 32-33; 10 J 29, 32, 38 (2), 40, 164-165, 183, 186, 200-203, 258, 259; 34 J 89; Coues, I, lxiii-lxv; G. R. C. Ballard Thruston in *History Quarterly,* 9:1-34 (1935). On Frances Clark's marriage, see Jones to Dye, Aug. 28, 1901, fols. 5-6, Dye MSS.
10.1. The cabin site is modern Buena Vista Farm, about a mile north of the point where Route 250 crosses the Rivanna. See Mary Rawlings: *Ante-Bellum Albemarle,* p. 61.
10.2. Goochland Deed Book 2, p. 222.
11.4. S. T. L. Anderson: *Lewises, Meriwethers, and their kin,* pp. 22-26; Louise Pecquet du Bellet: *Some prominent Virginia families,* II, 631; John Meriwether McAllister and Lura Boulton Tandy: *Genealogies of the Lewis and kindred families,* pp. 40-48; correspondence of Mrs. Anderson in the Dye MSS.

12.3. Will of Robert Lewis, Albemarle Will Book 2, pp. 204-209; Albemarle Deed Book 6, pp. 245-246.

13.1. Documents in LEW-1835-Bounty Warrants, VaSLib.; *Cal. Va. S.P.* VIII, 222; Edgar Woods: *Albemarle County in Virginia*, pp. 364-365, 368; *Va. Hist. Reg.*, 5:24 (1852). Thomas Porter, Quartermaster, certifies that Lt. Lewis bore his own expenses, in a certificate of July 17, 1776, of which there is an eighteenth century copy in the Lewis Papers. MoHS, and a modern copy in the Dye MSS.

Date of death is established by his widow's certificate in LEW-1835-Bounty Warrants. See also Albemarle Order Book, Aug. 3, 1835 and Aug. 2, 1841; MS. 1135, Report No. 114, UVaLib.

13.2. Albemarle Will Books 2, p. 384; 3, p. 12; 12, pp. 479-483; 13, pp. 36-38; *Journ. Committee of Public Safety*, June 25, 1776, I, 43, 84; Va. State Land Office, *Revolutionary Military Certificate Book* 3, p. 499; 25th Congress, Rep. No. 940, HR; Hening, X, 374; Louis A. Burgess: *Va. Soldiers of 1776*, 738-740; S. T. L. Anderson, *op. cit.*, p. 115; H. J. Eckenrode: *Special Report of the Department of Archives*, p. 44.

13.4. On Marks, see Lewis Papers, MoHS; Edgar Woods, *op. cit.*, pp. 263, 364; John H. Gwathmey: *Hist. Reg. of the Virginians in the Revolution*, p. 500; *Journ. Council of State of Va.*, I, 133, Aug. 24, 1776; I, 250, Nov. 23, 1776.

14.1. G. R. Gilmer: *Sketches of some of the first settlers of Upper Georgia*, *passim*, and map, p. 9; S. T. L. Anderson, *op. cit.*, p. 182; Mary Rawlings: *Albemarle of other days*, p. 81, thinks the wagon incident occurred while leaving Georgia, but Marks was dead by that time.

14.3. Gilmer, *op. cit.*, pp. 104-105; *Va. Hist. Reg.* 5:48-49 (1852); Wheeler, I, 60.

16.1. Gilmer, *op. cit.*, p. 104; Mary Rawlings, *op. cit.*, p. 59.

16.2. Edmund Bacon, Mr. Jefferson's overseer, in appendix to Hamilton W. Pierson: *Jefferson at Monticello* (1862).

16.4. Gilmer, *op. cit.*, p. 104.

17.2. S. T. L. Anderson, *op. cit.*, p. 182; Mary Rawlings, *op. cit.*, p. 59; *Jefferson's Albemarle* (Am. Guide Ser.), pp. 129-130.

17.3. M. L. Anderson, MS. address in MoHS.

18.2. S. T. L. Anderson, *op. cit.*, pp. 504-505; plan in possession of Mrs. George Gordon, Stafford, Va., copies of which are in MoHS and author's collection.

18.4. Albemarle Will Book 3, pp. 48, 78, 95, 130-131. Mr. Jefferson in his "Memoir" of Lewis describes Nicholas Meriwether as guardian, but the court records show this must have been unofficial.

19.2. Lewis to Mrs. Marks, n.d. (copy); Anderson to Dye, Nov. 8, 19, 1901, Jan. 9, 1902, Dye MSS.

20.2. Richard Beale Davis: *Francis Walker-Gilmer*, pp. 360-361. The original MS. is in Wm. J. Robertson Papers, UVaLib.

20.3. On Dr. Waddel, see James Waddel Alexander: *Memoir of the Rev. James Waddel;* Philip Vickers Fithian: *Journ. and Letters*, p. 118; Dickinson College Alumni Records; William Wirt: *British Spy* (9th ed.), pp. 133-143; John H. Gwathmey: *Twelve Virginia Counties*, pp. 287-288; William Henry Foote: *Sketches of Virginia*, pp. 348-354; Edgar Woods: *Hist. Albemarle County*, p. 334; William Meade: *Old churches, ministers, and families of Virginia*, I, 216-220; II, 44.

21.1. Lewis's letters quoted in this chapter are in MoHS. There are photostatic copies in VaSLib.

21.3. Albemarle Will Book 3, p. 95.

23.1. Draper MS. 2 L 29.

24.3. Albemarle Will Book 3, pp. 48, 78, 95, 130-132.

25.1. Formerly Battery F, Fourth Field Artillery. See W. A. Ganoe: *Hist. U.S. Army*, p. 91; O. W. Spaulding: *U.S. Army in War and Peace*, p. 116.

27.1. Ganoe, *op. cit.*, p. 93; *Jonathan Heart's Journal* (1885), p. 30-n; *Military Journal of Ebenezer Denny*, pp. 257-258; *Life and Correspondence of Rufus King*, I, 197.

27.3. Deposition of John Leith, Oct. 17, 1785, William Henry Smith: *St. Clair Papers*, II, 633; *Simcoe Papers*, I, 101.

29.1. *Maryland Journal*, Jan. 30, 1787; Draper MS. 11 J 133-137.

29.3. Clark to Governor, May ? 1786, *Cal.Va.S.P.*, IV, 122; Innes to Randolph, July 21, 1787, Ibid., 322.

29.4. Logan to Governor, Dec. 17, 1786, *Cal.Va.S.P.*, IV, 204-205; *Mil. Hist. Ky.*, p. 42; Draper MS. 11 J 108; *Cal.Va.S.P.*, IV, 213; John H. Gwathmey: *Twelve Virginia Counties*, p. 188; Marshall Wingfield: *Hist. Caroline County*, p. 178.

30.1. *St. Louis Enquirer*, Aug. 5, 1820; Gwathmey, *op. cit.*, p. 188; Wingfield, *op. cit.*, p. 178; DAB, IV, 142; *Journal of Col. John Hardin's Campaign*, in MoHS.

30.4. *Mil. Hist. Ky.*, p. 58; Draper MS. 2 L 28. There are references to the rank of cadet in *Journ. Council of State of Va.*, I, 84, 181; II, 515.

31.1. *Writings of Washington* (1939), 31:511.

32.1. Winthrop Sargent's Diary, *O. Arch. & Hist. Qy.*, 33:242 (1924).

32.2. ASP V (Mil. Aff. I), Nos. 5, 8, 9, pp. 37, 40-43.

32.4. John M. Oskison: *Tecumseh and his times*, p. 59; Draper MS. 8 J 295-296, 317-318.

33.2. Sargent's Diary, *loc. cit.*, p. 268. For incidents, see J. Pritt: *Mirror of Olden Time Border Life* (1849), pp. 541-544.

35.1. Draper MS. 16 U 5.

35.2. Stephen Decatur, Jr.: *Private Affairs of George Washington*, p. 324; S. D. Fess: *Ohio*, I, 104.

35.3. Draper MS. 16 U 5.

36.2. Heitman (1903), I, 306; Charles K. Gardner: *Dict. of . . . Army* (1860), p. 115; Monthly Return of the Legion, 1793 (NA); Clark to Biddle, Aug. 15, 1811 (LC).

37.2. The flour allowance is for the Revolutionary War. See Ganoe, *op. cit.*, p. 83. The portrait in Independence Hall confirms the family tradition that Lewis had fair hair and blue eyes. See Anderson to Dye, Mar. 18, 1902, Dye MSS. The statement that he had black hair is apparently due to an over-developed photograph of this painting. On double scalps, see Draper MS. 16 U 12.

37.3. Draper MS. 9 J 320. The original of the second quotation (11 CC 124) reads: "1 Indian: to 4 Regulars, and 2 Indians: to one Kentuckian."

38.2. Calvin M. Thomas: *Little Turtle*, p. 180; John McDonald: *Biographical sketches*, pp. 183-196; James B. Finley: *Autobiography*, pp. 54-83; H. C. Knapp: *Hist. Maumee Valley*, pp. 95-96; M. M. Quaife: *Chicago and the Old Northwest*, p. 224; O. M. Spencer: *Indian captivities, passim*.

38.3. The spelling M'Clelan is based on his letter to Lewis, Apr. 5, 1807, MoHS.

39.2. Diary, MoHS; Draper MS. 33 S 180; *Kentucky Gazette*, May 11, 1793.

41.2. Draper MS. 41 J 105; *Am. Hist. Assn. Rept. 1896*, Pt. I, p. 1091.

41.3. Draper MS. 34 J 5.

42.1. George Will in *Am. Pioneer*, 2:291-292 (1843); Isaac Weld: *Travels* (4th ed., 1807), II, 205; *Simcoe Papers*, III, 9.

42.2. Oskison, *op. cit.*, p. 64; Draper MS. 16 U 16; O'Hara to Craig, Craig Papers, AA/Craig/I.B. Oct. 14, 1793; Draper MS. 30 S 191-192.

43.2. Draper MS. 33 S 218. For the attack on Fort Recovery, see Wayne to O'Hara, July 4, 1794, and O'Hara to Craig, July 5, 1794, Craig Papers, AA/Craig/I.B.

43.4. Diary, *passim*; Draper MS. 42 AJ 76, 2 L 33-37, 5 U 33.

44.1. Draper MS. 2 L 33.

44.2-3. Diary, May 13, 1794; Draper MSS. 33 S 228, 2 L 33.

45.3. Lt. Boyer's Journal, p. 3.

46.3. Draper MS. AJ 37a-47a; 40 J 33-39; Isaac J. Cox: "General Wilkinson and his later intrigues," *Am. Hist. Rev.*, 19:794-812 (1914); files of the *Western World* (Frankfort, Ky.), Harry Emerson Wildes: *Anthony Wayne*, p. 432.

47.2. *Simcoe Papers*, II, 222-223; *Mich.*, XXIV, 659-660; Canad. Arch., Q 69-1, p. 33.

50.1. *Simcoe Papers*, III, 19-21; Weld, *loc. cit.*; Draper MS. 16 U 29. MVHR, 1:429 (1914).

50.2. Oskison, *op. cit.*, p. 78.

51.3. Mich. XXV, 71-72.

52.1. The episode at Fort Miamis is described in *Simcoe Papers*, XX, 406-408, III, 98-99; Weld, *op. cit.*

53.3. Canad. Arch., C 688, fol. 37; William Wood: *Select Docs.*, III, 534.

54.1-2. Diary, Filson Club; NA: AGO. Post-Rev. War Rec., Env. 84.

54.3. Clark to O'Fallon, May 9, June 5, July 5, 1795, Filson Club.

56.3. Leland D. Baldwin: *Whiskey Rebels*, p. 49-57; William Findley: *Hist. of the Insurrection;* Asa Earl Martin and Hiram Herr Shenk: *Pa. Hist. told by contemporaries*, pp. 156-159.

57.2. ASP, XX (Misc. X), No. 56, pp. 83-85; Martin and Shenk, *op. cit.*, pp. 162-166; Brackenridge, *op. cit.*, p. 265.

58.4. Lewis's letters for this period are in MoHS. Photostat copies are in VaSLib and author's collection.

60.4. Clark to Biddle, Aug. 15, 1811 (LC); Coues, I, lxxii.

61.1. Clark's diary and reports are in the Voorhees Coll., MoHS.

68.2. Will of John Clark, July 24, 1799, Book I, p. 86, Louisville; transcript in Voorhees Coll., MoHS, which also has property return of July 5, 1802. See also tax receipts in Jonathan Clark Papers, Filson Club.

69.1. Draper MSS. 11 CC 27; 29 J 39.

69.2. Voorhees Coll., MoHS.

69.4. Taylor to Dye, n.d., Dye MSS.

70.1. Lewis Memorandum Book, MoHS; Account No. 3087, Account Book, Craig Papers, AA/Craig/III.c. For another Lewis reference, see credit to Peter Audrain, Dec. 16, 1796, VII.A.

70.2. Lewis to Johnson, May 2, 1797; Lewis to Marks, June 14, July 24, 1797, MoHS; Albemarle Deed Book 12, pp. 214-215, 326, 530-531; Deed Book 13, p. 253; Deed Book 15, pp. 330-331; Receipt Book, Lewis Papers, MoHS; on Fort Pickering, see EWT, IV, 293; *Tenn. Hist. Mag.*, V, 110, 124, 127 (1919-1920); VIII, 284-285 (1924-1925); J. M. Keating: *Hist. Memphis, passim;* Samuel C. Williams: *Beginnings of West Tennessee*, pp. 58-59, NA: War File 811-2, 1799, LC. 143-7.

70.3. Lewis Memorandum Book, Am. Philos. Soc., Lewis and Clark Papers, Vol. VI; Craig Papers, AA/Craig/VII.E; XII, Sept. 15, 1800; XIV, fols. 39-40; T. to F. Bates, Sept. 8, 21, 1800. On his argument with the officer, see Bond to Bates, Dec. 24, 1808, MS/Bates, F, Letters Sent Vol. I. Photostat, Detroit Public Library.

71.1. On Tarleton Bates, see T. to F. Bates, July 20, 1801; Forward to Bates, Feb. 4, 1806, MoHS; Craig Papers, Receipts Nos. 3137, 3248, 111, 278, 470, 3137, 3238 (1797-1798), Craig Papers, AA/Craig/III.c.; Mrs. Elvert M. Davis: "Letters of Tarleton Bates," *West. Pa. Hist. Mag.*, 12:32-53 (1929); T. L. Rodgers: "Last Duel in Pennsylvania," *Ibid.*, pp. 54-56; Onward Bates: *Bates, et al., passim;* Craig Papers

AA/Craig/XIV, fols. 39-40; GAO, Misc. Treas. Acct. No. 17990: 1806.

71.3. *Memoirs and letters of Dolly Madison* (Ed. 1886), pp. 30-31.

72.3. Margaret Bayard Smith: *Wintering in Washington*, I, 63; *First forty years*, pp. 13-14; Sarah N. Randolph: *Domestic life of Thomas Jefferson, passim.*

75.1. Jefferson to Burwell, Mar. 26, 1804, Ford: *Correspondence* (1916), pp. 105-106.

75.2. MS. Account Books in NYPL.

76.1. Lewis to Gilmer, June 18, 1801, MoHS.

78.3. Hough's letter is in the possession of Mrs. George Gordon, Stafford, Va. Photostat in author's collection.

80.2. James D. Richardson: *Compilation of messages and papers of the Presidents*, I, 352-354; Thwaites, V, 206-209.

83.2. Draper MS. 52 J 93; Thwaites, I, xx; VII, 193-194.

85.2. Jared Sparks: *Life of Ledyard*, p. 277.

85.5. Colton Storm: "Lieutenant Armstrong's expedition," *Mid-America*, 25 (OS) 14 (NS): 180-188 (1943); Thwaites, VII, 198-199. Original papers are in the Clements Library, University of Michigan.

86.3. EWT, III, 12-13; Michaux's Journal, *Proc. Am. Philos. Soc.*, XXIV, No. 129, entry of Sept. 10, 1793.

87.4. Robidoux to de Lemos, Mar. 7, 1798, Bancroft-Pinart MSS., University of California; F. J. Billon: *Annals* (1886), p. 283.

90.2. Jefferson to Monroe, May 26, 1801; Ford: *Writings*, VIII, 58.

91.2. Jefferson to Breckenridge, Aug. 12, 1803.

95.2. Lewis to Irvine, Apr. 5, 1803. The letter is summarized in a catalogue of the American Autograph Shop, Merion Station, Pa. The shop has since gone out of business and the letter has disappeared. Extracts from the catalogue are in MoHS and author's collection.

96.2. NA: Mil. Book 2, fol. 15; WSHP, 22:39 (1916).

97.3. Lewis to Jefferson, July 26, 1803 (LC); Thwaites, I, xx; VII, 264-265; T. Bates to F. Bates, Oct. 13, 1803, MoHS; West. Pa. Hist. Mag., 12:47 (1929); 13:150, 170 (1930); Craig Papers, Craig to Swan, Nov. 11, 1803, AA/Craig/II.F, fols. 263-264; Dec. 16, 1803, fol. 266; Pittsburg *Gazette*, Jan. 2, Feb. 13, 1801; Heitman, p. 348; NA: Mil. Book 2, fol. 13; Mil. Book 1, fols. 26, 371; H. 143 (3), 170 (3), 171 (31), 172 (3).

98.3. Draper MS. 2 J 101. Clark's letter now exists only in a rough draft in MoHS.

100.2. Jefferson to R. Lewis, Nov. 6, 1804, Huntington; Ford: *Correspondence* (1916), p. 109.

101.1. These documents, formerly in the Quartermaster Depot, Philadelphia, are now somewhere in the National Archives, unclassified. There are also some references to supply in the QM Ledger there.

See *Quartermaster Review*, 4:44 (1925) and Thwaites, VII, 231-246.

101.2. NA: Military Book 2, fol. 15. Lewis's Journal for the Ohio River trip is in WHSP, Vol. 22.

102.1. WHSP, 22:31 (1916); EWT, IV, 93.

103.1. Photostat in Filson Club.

103.2. Drouilliard's signature shows that he spelled his name with a second "i", which his collateral descendants omit.

105.1. NA: Military Book 2, fol. 15. On Gass, see Dye MSS.

106.2. Detachment Orders, Feb. 20, 1804. Clark Papers, MoHS; Thwaites, I, 9-10.

107.1. Detachment Orders, Mar. 3, 1804; Thwaites, I, 13.

107.2. Lewis to SW, Jan. 15, 1807, ASP (Mil. Aff. I), No. 68, pp. 207-209; Thwaites, VII, 358. The original, in NA, is now almost illegible.

108.2. *Mo. Hist. Colls.*, VI, 320 (1931); III, 44 (1908-1911); William Cothren: *Hist. Ancient Woodbury*, I, 456-459; F. L. Billon: *Annals* (1888), p. 1; Stoddard to SW, Mar. 15, 17, 1804; Stoddard to Claibourne, Mar. 6, 1804, *Glimpses of the Past*, II, 93, 94, 96 (1935).

108.5. Le Raye in Jervase Cutler: *Topographical Description, passim; SD Hist. Colls.*, 4:150-180 (1908); MVHR, 16:523-524 (1929-1930).

109.1. ASP X (Misc. I), No. 164, pp. 344-356; *Niles' Register* (1817), pp. 293-294.

111.3. NA: Military Book, p. 202; Billon, *op. cit.*, p. 53.

112.2-3. Clark to Biddle, Aug. 15, 1811 (LC); Coues, I, lxxii.

116.3. Flogging remained as a punishment in the U.S. Army until well on in the nineteenth century, though the number of strokes was eventually reduced to fifty. The British Army did not give it up until 1881. Sentences of 1500 strokes were not unknown and there is record of one sentence of 12,600 in seven applications. See B. H. Liddell Hart: *Europe in Arms*, pp. 163-164.

117.3. Annie Heloise Abel: *Tabeau's Narrative*, p. 29. This is based on two of Tabeau's MSS., one formerly in the Archepiscopal Archives, Montreal (now lost), and the other in the Library of Congress. A third MS. is in the Coe Collection, Yale Library. On Labeaume, see *Mo. Hist. Colls.*, 3:250-n; Billon: *Annals* (1888), pp. 13, 14, 199, 361; EWT V, 253.

118.1. Loisel's memorial to De Lassus, May 28, 1804, in Houck Papers, 1784-1805, WSHS and MoHS; J. A. Robertson: *Louisiana under Spain, France, and the U.S.*, p. 338; Wilkinson to SW, Oct. 19, 1805, enc. to Wilkinson to SW, Oct. 22, 1805, NA: WD/SWDF; Carter, XIII.

119.2. Draper MS. 50 J 34.

121.1. EWT, V, 75-76; Olin D. Wheeler: "One of Lewis and Clark's men," *Wonderland*, 1901, pp. 89-90; Bruff to Wilkinson, enc. to Wilkinson to SW, Dec. 13, 1804, NA: WD/SWDF; Carter, XIII.

122.4. The location of the council is disputed and there are rival markers at Council Bluffs, Iowa, and Fort Calhoun, about seven miles north of Omaha. See *Omaha Weekly Herald*, Apr. 26, 1867, in Omaha Public Library.

123.3. The original MS. of the Floyd letter was sent to the Floyd Memorial Association, Sioux City, Iowa, by Mrs. Susan Floyd Gunter, of Louisville, who had found it among old family papers. It has since been lost but is reprinted in Albert M. Holman and Constant R. Marks: *Pioneering in the Northwest*, p. 73.

124.1. *Reports of the Floyd Memorial Association*, 1897, 1901, Sioux City Public Library; Thwaites, I, 114; Holman and Marks, *op. cit.*, pp. 69-72.

126.1. Le Raye, *op. cit.*

129.1. *SD Hist. Colls.*, 9:534-537 (1918); Robinson to Dye, Mar. 15, 1902, Dye MSS. A medal formerly owned by Strike-the-Ree is in the Museum, Sioux City.

129.3. MS. autobiography of Capt. Samuel Hill, NYPL; *Trans. Royal Soc. Canada*, 3rd ser. 26:49 (1932).

129.4. *SD Hist. Colls.*, 9:543-548 (1918).

132.4. Abel, *op. cit.*, p. 105; *SD Hist. Colls.*, 9:556 (1918).

133.1. Abel, *op. cit.*, pp. 110-111, 115.

139.1. Ibid., p. 172.

142.2. Ibid., p. 154-n, 158, on tobacco, and p. 171 on liquor. Cf. EWT, XXVIII, 263.

145.1. Coues: *New Light*, I, 322, 329; III, 1128; Wheeler, *op. cit.*, I, 180-183, 197; *SD Hist. Colls.*, 4:286 (1908); EWT, V, 162.

145.3. On Jussome, see Abel, *op. cit.*; David Thompson's *Narrative* (Ed. 1916), pp. 209, 212, 226; Coues: *New Light*, I, 333, 401; Maximilian of Wied: *Travels* (Paris, 1841), II, 371-n; Thwaites, I, 233; EWT, V, 155, 156, 167; XV, 59. See also Record Book B (original MS.), fol. 271 (Vault, Recorder of Deeds' Office, City Hall, St. Louis). The name is variously spelled. The spelling here used is from a signature, though this may have been written for Jussome, who is said to have been illiterate. See *Mo. Hist. Colls.*, 4:234-235 (1912-1923).

147.3. Henry's Journal, Canad. Arch., fol. 457.

148.2. Ibid., fol. 493.

148.3. Coues: *New Light*. I, 329, 331; EWT, VI, 137.

149.1. Abel, *op. cit.*, pp. 129, 136; *Am. Hist. Rev.*, 19:322-324 and note 62. On Indian poisoners, see John Tanner: *Narrative* (1830), p. 192 and Thwaites's ed. of La Hontan, II, 459.

149.3. EWT, VI, 137.

150.3. Thwaites, I, 217-n. The general location is now marked by a Masonic monument.

152.3. Masson, I, 308; Biddle, I, 128-129; Abel, *op. cit.*, p. 129-n; Abel: Journal at Fort Clark, pp. 310-311.

153.1. Le Raye, *op. cit.*

155.1. The spelling and accent Sacagáwea is that of the Bureau of American Ethnology, the U. S. Geographical Board, and the DAB. The name has been much disputed. See *SD Hist. Colls.*, 12:82-84 (1924); the MS. files B/Sal/2, 3, and 4 in Historical Society of Montana; Charles Larpenteur: *Forty years a fur trader*, I, 141-n. If it is a Minnetaree word, it is derived from *tsa-kaka*, "bird," and *wea*, "woman." If it is Shoshone, it is derived from *sac*, "boat," *a*, "the," and *ja-we*, "launcher."

153-160. The Canadian material is from Masson, I, 302-336.

156. On Larocque and McKenzie, see W. Stewart-Walker: *Documents relating to the N. W. Company*, p. 460.

158.4. Abel, *op. cit.*, p. 88-n.

160.1. See also Merrill G. Burlingame: *Montana frontier*, pp. 12-13; Daniel William Harmon: *Journal* (1820), pp. 136-137; Coues: *New Light*, I, 187-188, 299-n; F. F. Victor: *All over Oregon* (1872), p. 27, and *Atlantis arisen* (1891), p. 24; *Portfolio*, 7:448-449 (1812). Larocque's Journal is also in Ruth Hazlitt: *Sources of N. W. history* (No. 20, 1934).

162.2. MS. by Mrs. Albert Chesterson (Maud J. Bratton), Waynetown, Ind., William Bratton's great-grandmother.

166.1. J. G. Jacob: *Life and Times of Patrick Gass*, p. 61, supplements the various journals' account of the Sioux raid.

166.3. John Tanner: *Narrative* (1830), pp. 113, 253-256. On the Mouse River Post, see *His. and Sci. Soc. Manitoba, Trans.*, No. 5, July, 1930.

168.1. *Doc. Hist. N. Y.*, I, 16.

169.2. Coues: *New Light*, I, 367; Masson, I, 294; EWT, V, 134.

170-172. Abel, *op. cit.*, pp. 179-182; Biddle, I, 232; Coues: *New Light*, I, 381; Taliaferro TS., VII, 13, MinnSHS.

173.1-2. *SD Hist. Colls.* 9:534-537 (1918); Robinson to Dye, Mar. 15, Oct. 13, 1902, Dye MSS.

176.1. Biddle, I, 157; Gerard to Dye, Nov. 1, 1889, Dye MSS.

177.1. David Thompson, *op. cit.*, pp. 234-235; Heinrich von Martels: *Briefe über d. westlichen Theile d. Vereinigten Staaten* (1834), p. 75 (NYPL). See also *Mo. Hist. Rev.*, 17:345 (1923).

178-179. Abel, *op. cit.*, pp. 196-197. Translation here is from the Montreal text, original of which is now lost, though portions are reproduced by Abel.

180.1. Coues: *New Light*, I, 326-327. See also George Catlin: *Folium reservatum* (NYPL).

181.3. Copies of Ordway's letters are in *Mo. Hist. Rev.* 2:279-283 (1908) and in Dye MSS.

185.1. Jefferson to R. Lewis, July 10, 1805, Huntington. Various individuals who later claimed to have been with the expedition but whose names do not appear in the records may have been in this group. See "F. X. Matthieu: Refugee, trapper & settler," Bancroft MS. A.49, University of California.

195.3. Julia Hancock was often called "Judy" and even "Judith." See Hancock to Clark, Feb. 14, July 30, 1811, MoHS; Coues, I, lxvi. One of her portraits is said to have been marked "Judith."

197.3. Washington Matthews: *Grammar and dictionary of the language of the Hidatsas*, p. ix.

199.1. Thwaites, II, 142; EWT, XXIII, 84.

201.1. *Narrative of Zenas Leonard* (Ed. 1934), p. 180.

202.2. William H. Wright: *The grizzly bear*, p. 14; Victor H. Cahalane: *Mammals of North America*, pp. 144-150. The latter states grizzlies have been recorded weighing 1650 pounds.

204.2. *Narrative of Zenas Leonard* (Ed. 1934), p. 180.

205.4. William H. Wright: *The grizzly bear*, pp. 237-238.

207.1. Elliott Coues (ed.): *Journal of Jacob Fowler*, pp. 41-45.

213.1. Hebard to Drumm, Jan. 21, 1928, B/Sal/4, Montana HS.

225.1. Philanthropy River is now usually called Ruby Creek, Philosophy River, Willow Creek. See U. S. Geol. Survey map, 1:250,000, Dillon (Mont.) Sheet; Thwaites, II, 316; *Wonderland*, 1900, p. 39; *Pacific R.R. explorations* (1855), House Doc. 129, Vol. I, pp. 340, 351.

236.5. T. J. Farnham: *Travels* (Ed. 1843), II, 46-47; Wheeler, *op. cit.*, II, 48-49.

243.1. Jeannette Mirsky: *Westward crossings*, p. 137.

260.2. *Wonderland*, 1900, pp. 43-45; for a squaw's account of the same episode, see TS. 978.6/N87 in Montana HS. See also Edwin T. Denig: *Indian tribes of the Upper Missouri*, p. 395 (46th Annual Report of the Bureau of American Ethnology, 1928-1929); Peter Ronan: *Hist. Sketch of the Flathead Indian nation*, pp. 41-42; L. B. Palladino: *Indian and White in the Northwest* (Ed. 1922), p. 3.

266.4. Lawyer told his tale to C. T. Stranahan, Esq., of Lewiston, Idaho, who told it to the author in 1946.

267.2. Information from C. T. Stranahan, Esq., who had it orally from the Nez Percé visit, see statement of Peo-peo-tah-likh, Feb. 25, 1935; of Many Wounds (Samuel Lott), May 25, Nov. 28, 1935, Evans MSS.; of Billy Chinook in Walker to Dye, Feb. 11, 1902, Dye MSS.; Kate C. McBeth: *Nez Percés since Lewis and Clark*, *passim.*; author's interview (MS.) with C. T. Stranahan.

265-266. C. T. Stranahan heard this story from the Nez Percés as early as 1879. It is also given in McBeth, *op. cit.*; Thwaites, II, 83-n; Wheeler, *op. cit.*, 113-114; statement of Peo-peo-tah-likh in Evans MSS.; statement to author of Wade Wilson, Kamiah, Idaho, where it is a local tradition of long standing. The 1946 vision story is from Mr. Stranahan.

268.2. Robert G. Bailey: *River of no return*, pp. 23-24, with a picture of the cap, which still exists. C. T. Stranahan also heard a squaw describe being strapped, as a child, to a horse and taken to see Lewis and Clark.

268.5. The word "To-to-kean" is *toquen* in modern Nez Percé. Its real meaning is "person," but to the Nez Percés of Lewis and Clark's day a "person" was usually an Indian, very rarely a white man, and never before York's arrival a black man.

270.2. Mr. Stranahan's statement to author, Nov. 30, 1946. Mr. Stranahan, conversing in the Chinook jargon, heard this story repeatedly from the Indian, who had it directly from his father.

277.3. Father Cataldo's MS. "Sketch of Spokane mission, 1865-1886," fol. 13, Jesuit Archives, Oregon Province, Mt. St. Michael's, Spokane, Wash.

281.1. Thomas Nelson Strong: *Cathlamet on the Columbia* (Ed. 1930), pp. 5-6.

282.1. Biddle (II, 264-265) gives a more extended account of this episode than the Original Journals (Thwaites, III, 224-229), since he had Shannon as an editorial assistant.

287.3. OreHS *Annual Report*, 1900, p. 22; Strong to Dye, June 17, 1904, Dye MSS.

288.3. OreHS *Annual report*, 1900, p. 20; Wheeler, *op. cit.*, II, 197.

289.2. Clark's Order Book, Jan. 1, 1806, MoHS.

290.1. *Morning Oregonian*, Nov. 18, 1899 and Wheeler, *op. cit.*, II, 197, based on statement of Coboway's grandson.

290.2. The salt works were on Avenue Q, between South Promenade and Beach Streets, Seaside, Ore. The site was identified by Silas B. Smith, grandson of Coboway, and by a squaw, whose mother saw the white men working there. See OreHS *Annual report*, 1900, pp. 16-17.

293.4. Lewis to an unknown individual, Sept. 29, 1806. The letter is preserved in David Thompson notebooks in the Vancouver (B.C.) Public Library.

296.2. Wheeler, *op. cit.*, II, 220.

297.1. Ross Cox: *Adventures on the Columbia* (1832), p. 151; Coues: *New Light*, II, 768.

298.2. *Ore. Hist. Qy.*, 27:268 (1926).

302.2. Captain Hill's MS. *Autobiography* (NYPL); *Ore. Hist. Qy.*, 2: 275 (1926); Coues, III, 903-904; Biddle, III, 16.

304.2. OreHS *Annual report*, 1900, p. 20.

305.2. George Gibbs, U. S. Geol. Survey, *Contrib. N. American Ethnol.*, I, 238; Thwaites, IV, 196-n; Ross Cox (1831), II, 134; Wheeler, *op. cit.*, II, 196-197; Frederick V. Homan: "Lewis and Clark Expedition at Fort Clatsop," *Ore. Hist. Qy.*, 27:267 (1926); *Morning Oregonian*, Nov. 18, 1899; OreHS *Annual report*, 1900, p. 22.

305.3. John K. Townsend: *Narrative* (1839), p. 256; H. H. Bancroft: *Hist. N. W. Coast*, II, 55n; Coues, III, 904-n; Wheeler, *op. cit.*, II, 188; OreHS *Annual report*, 1900, pp. 16 ff.; D. Curtis Freeman: "Location of historic Fort Clatsop," *Lewis and Clark Journal* (Portland Exposition publication), 1:15 F 1904; F. F. Victor: *All over Oregon* (1872), p. 27; F. F. Victor: *Atlantis arisen* (1891), p. 24.

306.4. Wilhelm's *Military and Naval Encyclopaedia* (1879).

311.2. *Portland Telegram*, under dateline Nov. 11, 1904. Clipping in OreHS.

316.4. Kate C. McBeth: *Nez Percés since Lewis and Clark*, p. 23.

318.2. Harold W. Gregg: "Sidelights on early Montana medical history," *Journalist-Lancet*, 1938, pp. 69-74; *SD Hist. Colls.* 12:53-66 (1924).

332.3. Wheeler, *op. cit.*, II, 292; EWT, XXVII, 269-n; XXIX, 340.

336.3. *Adventures of Zenas Leonard* (Ed. 1934), pp. 15-16.

346.2. Wheeler, the most careful student of the route, thinks Clark traveled: Bitterroot River—Ross's Hole—Camp Creek—Big Hole (Wisdom) River—Gibbon's Pass—Bald Mountain—Grasshopper (Willard's) Creek—Bannack—Shoshone Cove—Jefferson's River—Three Forks—Bozeman Pass—Yellowstone. See II, 317-333.

347.3. Abel, *op. cit.*, pp. 78-80.

348.3. EWT, XXI, 54-55.

349.2. The Tower is located near Pompey's Pillar, Mont., just off route 10, at the bridge over the Yellowstone. The Masons and the DAR have added plaques. See Larocque's *Journal* (Ed. Ruth Hazlitt, 1934), p. 22; Merrill G. Burlingame: *Montana frontier*, pp. 12-13; J. A. Hosmer: *Trip to the States in 1865* (1867), pp. 18-19; *Frontier*, 12:155 (1932); Joseph Mills Hanson: *Conquest of the Missouri*, p. 16; W. F. Raynolds: *Report on the exploration of the Yellowstone River* (1868); James W. Forsyth: *Report of an expedition up the Yellowstone*, p. 8; statement of Captain Grant Martin, clipping in Lewis and Clark file, Billings (Mont.) Public Library; *Personal memoirs of Major General D. S. Stanley*, pp. 240-251, 267.

349.3. Ghent to Hebard, Mar. 2, 1933, B/Sal/4 in Mont.HS; Hebard to Robinson, Feb. 3, 1928, ibid.; TS. by John G. Brown, 978/L58B in Mont.HS.

350.1. *Journal of Negro History*, 12:347-348 (1927).

353.3. Wheeler, *op. cit.*, II, 311-313; Clark Wissler: "Material culture of the Blackfoot Indians," *Anthropological papers*, (Am. Mus. Nat. Hist.), Vol. V, Part I, pp. 10-11 (1910); Biddle to Atkinson, Oct. 29, 1819, ASP (Ind. Aff. II, 201); Grinnell: *Trails of the pathfinders*, p. 200.

354.1. David Thompson: *Narrative* (Champlain Soc. ed.), p. 375. **On**

subsequent Blackfoot hostility, see W. J. Snelling: "Oregon territory" in A. B. Hulbert: *Call of the Columbia*, p. 78.

360.5. The trappers were Joseph Dixon and Forrest Hancock. See WSHP, 22: 390-n (1916); *Wis. Hist. Colls.*, V, 315-317.

370.2. EWT, VI, 185; XXII, 278; Wheeler, I, 85-90; *Reports* of the Floyd Memorial Association, 1897, 1901 (Sioux City Public Library); Albert M. Holman and Constant R. Marks: *Pioneering in the Northwest*, pp. 77-90.

372.3. On Capt. McClallan's real errand, see Wilkinson to SW, Sept. 8, 1805, NA: WD/SWDF; Carter, XIII.

374.5. *Glimpses of the Past*, 1:48 (1934); Joseph Kinsey Howard: *Montana Margins*, p. 51.

378.1. The documents are in Deed Book (Original) A, fols. 346-349, and B (Original), fols. 152-156. These are kept in the Vault of the Recorder of Deeds, City Hall, St. Louis.

378.2. Clark to Dearborn, Oct. 10, 1806. MoHS: Coues, I, lxxi.

378.3. Photostat of Jonathan Clark's diary is in the Filson Club. The original is in the possession of Mrs. John C. Doolan, Louisville.

379.2. *Cal. Va. S. P.*, IX, 504-506.

380.2. *National Intelligencer*, Jan. 16, 1807; *Monthly Anthology*, 4: 143-144 (1807). Copies of the poem in Dye MSS. and MoHS. See also Sidney Greenbie: *Furs to furrows*, p. 137.

380.3. The original is NA: L 100 (3) LMisc. (1807). It is dated Jan. 15, 1807. See also ASP. V (Mil. Aff. I), No. 68, pp. 207-209; Thwaites, VII, 357-359. Lewis's MS. is now nearly illegible and a MS. transcript in NA is very inaccurate.

381.2. *Annals of Cong.*, 9 Cong. 2 Sess. 1278; Clark's receipt to Lewis, Mar. 9, 1807, MoHS.

382.1. Lewis's resignation from the Army is NA; L.124 (3). See also Burbeck to Cushing, Mar. 8, 1807, NA: AGO (1806 —sic). Lewis began to draw pay as governor in March, 1807. See GAO: Misc. Treas. Acct. No. 19507 (1807); Billon: *Annals* (1888), pp. 384-385. On Clark, see Charles K. Gardner: *Dict. of . . . Army* (1860), p. 115; A. W. Greeley: *Explorers and travelers*, pp. 160-161; SW to P. Chouteau, Mar. 7, 1807.

382.2. Rodney H. True: "Some neglected botanical results of the Lewis and Clark Expedition." Am. Philos. Soc., Apr. 24, 1925; McMahon to Lewis, Apr. 5, 1807, MoHS.; Frederick Pursh: *Flora Americae Septentrionalis*, pp. 260, 368; Thwaites, VI, 151-153; Lewis Account Book, May 10, 1807, MoHS: Jefferson to Countess de Tesse, Ford, IX, 439.

383.1-2. Draper MS. 2 L 60; Clark to Lewis, March 11 (?), 1807, MoHS. This letter survives only in Clark's pencil draft on the back of Lewis's letter of March 11.

383.3. Photograph of the jewels is in MoHS. The originals are now in Denmark. See William Hancock Clark to Dye. Dye MSS. (Conquest envelopes).

384.4. R. Lewis to Mary Marks, Nov. 29 [1807], MoHS.

388.1. Lewis to Clark, Mar. 13, 15, 1807, MoHS; Bates to Jefferson, May 6, 1807 (LC).

389.1. Clark's "doodles" are on Clark to Dearborn, June 8, 1807, MoHS.

390.2. The statement, sometimes made, that Lewis reached St. Louis in 1807 is an error. See Marshall, I, 312-n, and 304; Lewis to SW, July 14, 1808, NA: L.112/WD/(4).

391.1. Lewis to Hunt, May 26, 1808, Bissell MS. 19, Mercantile Library, St. Louis.

391.5. Jonathan Clark's Diary, Filson Club; Sullivan to —? June 2, 1808, Filson Club MS. A.C.592c/1; Clark to SW, July 17, Oct. 23, 1807, NA: C.308/WD/(3) and C.347/WD/(3).

392.2. Bates to R. Bates, July 14, 1809; Marshall, II, 69.

394.1. Lewis to Boilvin, May 14, 1808. Bissell MS. 17, MoHS.

394.2. ASP II (Ind. Aff. I), No. 129, p. 766; *Mo. Hist. Rev.* 3:215-218, 281 (1909); 4:12 (1909); 23:5-6 (1938).

394.3. EWT, XVI, 168; *Mo. Hist. Rev.* 3:251 (1909).

395.1-2. Charles Elihu Slocum: *Ohio country*, pp. 176-179; Carter, XIII, XVI; Sibley to Sibley, Sept. 26, 1806, Sibley Papers, MoHS; Boilvin to SW, Sept. 8, 1807; Clark to SW, Sept. 12, 1807; Courtin to Bates, June 22, 1807, enc. in Bates to SW, Aug. 2, 1807, all in NA: WD/SWDF. There are many more. See also *Missouri Gazette*, files, original in MoHS, photostat in NYPL.

396.2. Billon: *Annals* (1888), p. 15.

397.1. Bates to R. Bates, Nov. 9, 1809; to Scott, Smith, and R. Bates (letter book, MoHS); Marshall, I, 300. The other Bates letters here quoted are in his letter books and the Bates Papers, MoHS. Most of them are more easily accessible in Marshall. See also Georganne Tracy: *Frederick Bates and his administration of Louisiana Territory* (Washington University M.A. thesis, 1925).

399.6. Bates to R. Bates, July 14, 1809 (letter book); Marshall, II, 68.

400.1-3. Bates to R. Bates, Nov. 9, 1809 (letter book); Marshall, II, 110.

400.4. On Carr, see Billon: *Annals* (1888), pp. 201-202.

401.1. Lewis Account Book, MoHS; Lewis to Lucy Marks, Dec. 1, 1808, MoHS; SW to Lewis, July 15, 1809 NA: Military Book 4; Lewis to SW, Aug. 18, 1809, NA:WD/SWDF/L.328 (4). Lewis's land purchases are easily traced through "Collet's Index" to St. Louis land records, City Hall, St. Louis. Most of them are in Book C (Original), in the vault of the Recorder of Deeds Office.

401.3. Lewis Account Book, MoHS.

402.1. Copy of bond, May 13, 1809, MoHS.

402.2. M'Clelan to Lewis, Apr. 5, 1807, MoHS.

402.3. Lewis to SW, Mar. 7, 1809, NA: L.273 (4); SW to Clark, Mar.

9, 1809, NA: OIA, SW, Book B; Cater XIII; Clark to SW, Oct. 24, 1807, C.346/WD/(3); Clark to SW, May 18, 1807, NA: C.280/WD/(3); Clark's bill of exchange, May 25, 1807, NA: C.Misc. (1807); A. P. Chouteau to Bates, Oct. 6, 1807, MoHS; Rowse, pp. 202-206; H. M. Chittenden: *Hist. Am. Fur Trade*, I, 120; *SD Hist. Colls.*, 9:594-596; Kimball to Clark, n.d., NA: C.384/WD/(3). Chouteau's identity is established by Jussome to Jefferson, Dec. 4, 1807, printed in *Mo. Hist. Colls.*, 4:234-235 (1912-1923).

403.1. Pryor to Clark, Oct. 16, 1807, NA: C.350/WD/(3); printed in *Annals of Iowa*, 3rd ser., 1:613-620 (1894); Bates to Clark, Dec. 1807; Marshall, I, 250; Chouteau to SW, Sept. 1, 1809, NA: WD; Lewis to SW, Mar. 7, 1809, NA: L.273 (4); Clark to SW, Dec. 3, 1807, NA: WD/SWDF; Clark to SW, May 18, 1807, NA: C.280/-WD/(3); Chouteau to SW, Dec. 14, 1809, Pierre Chouteau MSS., MoHS. *SD Hist. Colls.*, 9:584 (1918); Carter, XIII; Clark to SW, Oct. 24, 1807, photostat in MoHS.

405.3. On Shannon's wound, see Bates to Clark, Dec. 7, 1808, Marshall, I, 248; SW to Clark, Aug. 7, 1809, NA: OIA/SW Letters Sent, Book C; NA: Old War Invalid File, 24807; Lewis Account Book, MoHS.

406.2. Bates to Clark, Dec. 1807; Marshall, I, 250; Bates to Woodward, Oct. 20, 1807; TS. in MoHS; James (Ed. 1916), p. 18; Chittenden, *op. cit.*, I, 138 ff.; Lewis Account Books, MoHS; Lewis to SW, May 13, 1809, NA: L.Misc. (1809); Clark to SW, June 1, 1807, NA: C.282/WD/(3).

407.1. DAB, IV, 93; David Thompson's *Narrative* (Champlain Soc. ed.), p. 226; Wheeler, *op. cit.*, I, 121-122; *Missouri Gazette*, Mar. 8, Sept. 26, Nov. 16, 23, 1809; Abel, *op. cit.*, p. 178-n; EWT, VI, 137; James (Ed. 1916), p. 229; F. W. Hodge: *Hbk. of Am. Inds.* (1910), II, 518; *ND Hist. Colls.*, 2:470-471 (1908). J. A. Medaris, Fort Berthold Agency, to author, June 9, 1947.

409.2. Unfinished letter of Lewis, dated July 8, 1809, Dye MSS. (copy); Wallis to Bates, Sept. 1, 1808; Marshall, II, 23-24; Anderson to Dye, Feb. 15, 1902, Dye MSS.

409.3. SW to Lewis, July 15, 1809, NA: Military Book 4.

410.2. Lewis to SW, Aug. 18, 1809, NA: WD/SWDF/ L.324 (4); Carter, XIII; P. Chouteau fils to SW, Sept. 1, 1809, NA: WD/SWDF; same, Dec. 14, 1809, photostat in MoHS.

410.3. Billon: *Annals* (1888), p. 53.

410.4. Fol. 43, MS. "Journal of Proceedings," K 8762/1808, Mercantile Library, St. Louis; Lewis Memorandum Book, MoHS; File 1809. WSHS.

411.5. Thwaites, VII, 368.

412.2. *Missouri Gazette*, Oct. 4, 1809. His death is reported Nov. 2.

413.1. Howe to Bates, Sept. 28, 1809. MoHS; *Missouri Gazette*, Oct. 19, 1809.

413.2. *Missouri Gazette*, Oct. 4, Nov. 2, 1809.

413.3. Draper MS. 1 O 81 (4-5). On Lewis's route, see *Natchez Trace Parkway Survey*, 76th Cong., 3rd Sess., Document No. 148, p. 73.

414.2. The Louisiana and Mississippi Almanac, 1819, lists James Perry's stand near Houston, Miss., on the Natchez trace. The 1821 edition lists Isaac Perry's, 15 miles North of the Choctaw-Chickasaw line. Neither was on the direct route to Nashville, but Neeley's Indian business may have necessitated divergence from it. There is, however, no evidence that either stand existed in 1809.

417.2. J. H. Moore: "Death of Meriwether Lewis," *Am. Hist. Mag. and Tenn. Hist. Soc. Qy.*, 9:218-230 (1904).

418.3. *National Intelligencer*, Nov. 15, 1809 (LC). See also *New York Dispatch*, Feb. 1, 1845; *Charlottesville Dispatch*, Jan. 7, 1879, Dye MSS.

419.3. J. A. Cunningham in T/920, Tennessee State Library.

419.4. The post-rider, Robert O. Smith made no written report and Post Office Department records do not allude to the affair. See letters by William J. Webster and F. C. Frierson in "Tennessee Crockett Houston Lewis" (T/920) in Tennessee State Library.

420.1. Webster Papers, File 101-05, MLNM.

420.3. MS. copy of a letter from Hugh Lee Webster, son of William J. Webster, who has continued his father's studies, to Mrs. Robert H. White, Jan. 29, 1932. File 101-05, MLNM. Maury County officials and the author's personal search in the Court House confirm the disappearance of the papers.

420.4. The Frierson statement is in the Tennessee State Library.

421.2. File 101-09, MLNM.

421.3. Hickman County Deed Book (Old) C, p. 31. It has been transcribed in a new Deed Book, ABC, p. 141.

421.4. Statement of Sallie Walker, TS. in Tennessee State Library.

422.4. Anderson to Dye, Feb. 6, 1903, Sept. 1902, Dye MSS.

424.3. Lewis Account Book, entry of Sept. 27, 1809, MoHS.

425.1. Anderson to Dye, Dec. 4, 1901, Feb. 6, 1903, Dye MSS.

425.2. Albemarle Will Book 5, p. 66.

425.3. Extract from F. H. Smith Papers, File 101-05, MLNM. See also No. 15 in "Tennessee Crockett Houston Lewis" (T/920) in Tennessee State Library.

426.4. These letters are in MoHS.

427.3. The Bryan & Schlatter letter is in Chouteau-Maffitt Papers, MoHS.

427.4. Estate papers are in Bundle No. 77, Probate File Room, Civil Courts Building, St. Louis. Colter vs. Hempstead, adm., is No. 38 in the November Term, 1810, Court of Common Pleas.

428.2. Marks to R. Lewis, Jan. 22, 1812, draft in possession of Mrs. George Gordon, Stafford, Va. TSS. in UVaLib, WSHS, and author's collection.

See also "Estate of Meriwether Lewis" in the 1801-1810 envelope, Clark Papers, MoHS and Book A, 1806-1821, fols. 37, 38, 41, 47 in safe of Cashier's Office, Probate Court.

429.2. Clark to Jonathan Clark, Oct. 28, 1809, Bodley Papers, 5 Cook 252, Filson Club. This is a copy made for Temple Bodley from an unknown original.

430.1. Taylor to Dye, n.d., Dye MSS.

430.2. Meriwether to Marks, Jan. 5, 1810; Meriwether to Clark, Jan. 22, 1810; E. Clark to W. Clark, Feb. 3, 1810; Rogers to Clark, Jan. 3, 1810, MoHS; Clark to SW, Dec. 20, 1810, NA: C.5.

431.2. Monroe to Brent, Feb. 25, 1810. *Writings of James Monroe* (1901), V, 109. On Howard's appointment, see Billon: *Annals* (1888), pp. 8,100; Floyd Duckworth Welch: *Work of Indian agents in the Louisiana Purchase* (Washington University M.A. Thesis, 1926), pp. 87-88.

432.3. Mrs. Clark to Hancock, Feb. 7, 1814, MoHS; Clark to Edmund Clark, Dec. 25, 1814, Filson Club MS. A.C592c/1; Clark to SW, Sept. 12, 1813, NA: C. 232 (7).

432.4. Clark to Howard, May 5, 1814, NA: WD/SWDF; Clark to SW, June 5, 1814, NA: WD/SWDF.

433.1. William Wood: *Select Docs.*, I, 112-113; III, 253-256, 532-536.

434.3. Draper MS. 2 M 21; Clark MSS. Vol. VI, fol. 293, KasSHS. There is much material in NA: C. 110 on the work of the peace commission. See also Carter, XVI.

435.3. William J. Petersen: *Steamboating on the Upper Mississippi*, pp. 108-113; Clark MSS., "Book of accounts . . . 1828 to 1836," p. 74, KasSHS; McKenny to Clark, Apr. 5, May 26, July 23, 30, NA: OIA, Book 6, fols. 444-445, 499, 501.

435-436. *Oregon Spectator*, Dec. 12, 1850, p. 1, col. 2, OreHS; Jarret to Clark, July 18, 1810, NA: Misc. 1810; Taliaferro to Clark, June 10, 1833, MinnSHS.

436.3. Clark to Cass, Nov. 20, 1831, Clark MSS. Vol. IV, pp. 294-304; Street to Clark, Sept. 30, 1830, Ibid., Vol. VI, pp. 19-20, KasSHS.

437.1. Clark to Herring, Dec. 3, 1831, Clark MSS. IV, 306, KasSHS; Draper MS. 6 T 13; Joseph Peter Donnelly: *Liquor traffic among the aborigines of the new Northwest* (St. Louis University Diss., 1940).

437.1. Clark to SW, Sept. 22, 1830, Clark MSS., Vol. VI, fol. 5, KasSHS.

437.3. David Thompson: *Narrative* (Champlain Soc. ed.), p. 396.

438.2-3. Jussome to Clark, Aug. 29, 1812, MoHS; Orphans' Court, Book A, 1806-1821; Grace Raymond Hebard: *Sacajawea*, pp. 115, 221-22; James Haley White: "Early days in St. Louis," *Glimpses of the Past*, 6:11-12 (1929); Mo. Hist. Colls., 4:234-235 (1912-1923); Clark's Accounts, 1820, ASP (Ind. Aff. II), No. 5, p. 289.

439.2. There is much MS. material in the Jesuit Archives (Oregon Province) at Mt. St. Michael's, Spokane, Wash., especially the MSS.

of Fathers Cataldo, Joset, Muset, Mengarini and Palladino. See also George Catlin: North American Indians (1841), II, 109; Francis Haines: "Nez Percé delegation to St. Louis in 1831," *Pacific Hist. Rev.*, 6:71-78 (1937) and subsequent comment; L. B. Palladino: *Indian and White in the Northwest* (1922), pp. 3, 16-17; *Wonderland*, 1894, p. 75; EWT, XXVI, 14; The literature is voluminous, the best summary being Gilbert J. Garrigan: *Jesuits in the Middle United States*, Vol. II. The account of Kate C. McBeth: *Nez Percés since Lewis and Clark* is not very critical.

441.3. Bates to R. Bates, Dec. 17, 1807 (letter book); Marshall, I, 237-247.

442.1. Taylor to Dye, n.d., Dye MSS.

442.2. EWT, XV, 147. An interpolation omitted.

442.3. Washington Irving's *Journal* (Ed. J. F. McDermott, 1944), p. 103.

444.1. Taylor to Dye, n.d., Dye MSS.; Catlin, *op. cit.*, II, 30.

444.2. Irving's Journal, pp. 81-82.

444.5. G. W. Featherstonhaugh: *Excursions through the slave states* (1844), p. 69.

445.1. Thomas L. M'Kenney: *Memoirs*, I, 147-148.

445.2. Taylor to Dye, n.d., Dye MSS.; Audubon to Clark, Oct. 19, 1811, MoHS; Lee to Kayser, Mar. 9, 1838, Feb. 1, 1839, *Glimpses*, 3:5, 7, 27 (1936) and extract from Lee Papers, Richmond, in MoHS; John Tanner: *Narrative* (1830), p. 253.

446.2-3. Henry Shaw in New York *Evening Post*, Nov. 3, 1893; Taylor to Dye, n.d., Dye MSS.; Charles Augustus Murray: *Travels* (1854), I, 196; Jones to Dye, Aug. 5, 1901, Dye MSS.; Featherstonhaugh, *op. cit.*, p. 65. See also pp. v, 71.

448-449. Taylor to Dye, n.d., Dye MSS. Mrs. Dye in a letter to a "Mrs. Clark," July 28, 1902, states she has confirmation of this incident from four different sources.

450.2. Kennerly to Clark and Kennerly, Feb. 22, 1838, Kennerly Papers, MoHS.

450.3. Taylor to Dye, n.d., Dye MSS.; *Daily Argus*, Sept. 3, 4, 1838; *Missouri Republican*, Sept. 3, 1838; Draper MSS. 2 CC 24; 27 CC 28; 29 CC 64; 26 CC 24-25.

452.2. *Missouri Gazette*, Oct. 12, 1808. The lives of the other men are largely covered in Wheeler, *op. cit.*, in the Clark Papers, MoHS, and in the Dye MSS. There are military records for Gass and Windsor but the other records seem to have been among those burned by the British.

453.3. Gass's speech is preserved in the Dye MSS.

455.1. Luttig's original MS. is in MoHS, which also has a copy of Pilcher's letter. Bull's Eye's story is preserved in Montana HS The Nez Percé traditions of Sacagawea are in the Evans MSS. The story of the Wyoming Sacagawea has been told in Grace Raymond Hebard's *Sacajawea*.

Index

A CATALOG OF SELECTED
DOVER BOOKS
IN ALL FIELDS OF INTEREST

A CATALOG OF SELECTED DOVER
BOOKS IN ALL FIELDS OF INTEREST

CONCERNING THE SPIRITUAL IN ART, Wassily Kandinsky. Pioneering work by father of abstract art. Thoughts on color theory, nature of art. Analysis of earlier masters. 12 illustrations. 80pp. of text. 5⅜ x 8½. 23411-8

ANIMALS: 1,419 Copyright-Free Illustrations of Mammals, Birds, Fish, Insects, etc., Jim Harter (ed.). Clear wood engravings present, in extremely lifelike poses, over 1,000 species of animals. One of the most extensive pictorial sourcebooks of its kind. Captions. Index. 284pp. 9 x 12. 23766-4

CELTIC ART: The Methods of Construction, George Bain. Simple geometric techniques for making Celtic interlacements, spirals, Kells-type initials, animals, humans, etc. Over 500 illustrations. 160pp. 9 x 12. (Available in U.S. only.) 22923-8

AN ATLAS OF ANATOMY FOR ARTISTS, Fritz Schider. Most thorough reference work on art anatomy in the world. Hundreds of illustrations, including selections from works by Vesalius, Leonardo, Goya, Ingres, Michelangelo, others. 593 illustrations. 192pp. 7⅛ x 10¼. 20241-0

CELTIC HAND STROKE-BY-STROKE (Irish Half-Uncial from "The Book of Kells"): An Arthur Baker Calligraphy Manual, Arthur Baker. Complete guide to creating each letter of the alphabet in distinctive Celtic manner. Covers hand position, strokes, pens, inks, paper, more. Illustrated. 48pp. 8¼ x 11. 24336-2

EASY ORIGAMI, John Montroll. Charming collection of 32 projects (hat, cup, pelican, piano, swan, many more) specially designed for the novice origami hobbyist. Clearly illustrated easy-to-follow instructions insure that even beginning papercrafters will achieve successful results. 48pp. 8¼ x 11. 27298-2

THE COMPLETE BOOK OF BIRDHOUSE CONSTRUCTION FOR WOODWORKERS, Scott D. Campbell. Detailed instructions, illustrations, tables. Also data on bird habitat and instinct patterns. Bibliography. 3 tables. 63 illustrations in 15 figures. 48pp. 5¼ x 8½. 24407-5

BLOOMINGDALE'S ILLUSTRATED 1886 CATALOG: Fashions, Dry Goods and Housewares, Bloomingdale Brothers. Famed merchants' extremely rare catalog depicting about 1,700 products: clothing, housewares, firearms, dry goods, jewelry, more. Invaluable for dating, identifying vintage items. Also, copyright-free graphics for artists, designers. Co-published with Henry Ford Museum & Greenfield Village. 160pp. 8¼ x 11. 25780-0

HISTORIC COSTUME IN PICTURES, Braun & Schneider. Over 1,450 costumed figures in clearly detailed engravings–from dawn of civilization to end of 19th century. Captions. Many folk costumes. 256pp. 8⅜ x 11¾. 23150-X

STICKLEY CRAFTSMAN FURNITURE CATALOGS, Gustav Stickley and L. & J. G. Stickley. Beautiful, functional furniture in two authentic catalogs from 1910. 594 illustrations, including 277 photos, show settles, rockers, armchairs, reclining chairs, bookcases, desks, tables. 183pp. 6½ x 9¼. 23838-5

AMERICAN LOCOMOTIVES IN HISTORIC PHOTOGRAPHS: 1858 to 1949, Ron Ziel (ed.). A rare collection of 126 meticulously detailed official photographs, called "builder portraits," of American locomotives that majestically chronicle the rise of steam locomotive power in America. Introduction. Detailed captions. xi+ 129pp. 9 x 12. 27393-8

AMERICA'S LIGHTHOUSES: An Illustrated History, Francis Ross Holland, Jr. Delightfully written, profusely illustrated fact-filled survey of over 200 American light-houses since 1716. History, anecdotes, technological advances, more. 240pp. 8 x 10¾. 25576-X

TOWARDS A NEW ARCHITECTURE, Le Corbusier. Pioneering manifesto by founder of "International School." Technical and aesthetic theories, views of industry, economics, relation of form to function, "mass-production split" and much more. Profusely illustrated. 320pp. 6⅛ x 9¼. (Available in U.S. only.) 25023-7

HOW THE OTHER HALF LIVES, Jacob Riis. Famous journalistic record, exposing poverty and degradation of New York slums around 1900, by major social reformer. 100 striking and influential photographs. 233pp. 10 x 7⅞. 22012-5

FRUIT KEY AND TWIG KEY TO TREES AND SHRUBS, William M. Harlow. One of the handiest and most widely used identification aids. Fruit key covers 120 deciduous and evergreen species; twig key 160 deciduous species. Easily used. Over 300 photographs. 126pp. 5⅜ x 8½. 20511-8

COMMON BIRD SONGS, Dr. Donald J. Borror. Songs of 60 most common U.S. birds: robins, sparrows, cardinals, bluejays, finches, more—arranged in order of increasing complexity. Up to 9 variations of songs of each species.
Cassette and manual 99911-4

ORCHIDS AS HOUSE PLANTS, Rebecca Tyson Northen. Grow cattleyas and many other kinds of orchids—in a window, in a case, or under artificial light. 63 illustrations. 148pp. 5⅜ x 8½. 23261-1

MONSTER MAZES, Dave Phillips. Masterful mazes at four levels of difficulty. Avoid deadly perils and evil creatures to find magical treasures. Solutions for all 32 exciting illustrated puzzles. 48pp. 8¼ x 11. 26005-4

MOZART'S DON GIOVANNI (DOVER OPERA LIBRETTO SERIES), Wolfgang Amadeus Mozart. Introduced and translated by Ellen H. Bleiler. Standard Italian libretto, with complete English translation. Convenient and thoroughly portable—an ideal companion for reading along with a recording or the performance itself. Introduction. List of characters. Plot summary. 121pp. 5¼ x 8½. 24944-1

TECHNICAL MANUAL AND DICTIONARY OF CLASSICAL BALLET, Gail Grant. Defines, explains, comments on steps, movements, poses and concepts. 15-page pictorial section. Basic book for student, viewer. 127pp. 5⅜ x 8½. 21843-0

THE CLARINET AND CLARINET PLAYING, David Pino. Lively, comprehensive work features suggestions about technique, musicianship, and musical interpretation, as well as guidelines for teaching, making your own reeds, and preparing for public performance. Includes an intriguing look at clarinet history. "A godsend," *The Clarinet*, Journal of the International Clarinet Society. Appendixes. 7 illus. 320pp. 5⅜ x 8½. 40270-3

HOLLYWOOD GLAMOR PORTRAITS, John Kobal (ed.). 145 photos from 1926-49. Harlow, Gable, Bogart, Bacall; 94 stars in all. Full background on photographers, technical aspects. 160pp. 8⅜ x 11¼. 23352-9

THE ANNOTATED CASEY AT THE BAT: A Collection of Ballads about the Mighty Casey/Third, Revised Edition, Martin Gardner (ed.). Amusing sequels and parodies of one of America's best-loved poems: Casey's Revenge, Why Casey Whiffed, Casey's Sister at the Bat, others. 256pp. 5⅜ x 8½. 28598-7

THE RAVEN AND OTHER FAVORITE POEMS, Edgar Allan Poe. Over 40 of the author's most memorable poems: "The Bells," "Ulalume," "Israfel," "To Helen," "The Conqueror Worm," "Eldorado," "Annabel Lee," many more. Alphabetic lists of titles and first lines. 64pp. 5³⁄₁₆ x 8¼. 26685-0

PERSONAL MEMOIRS OF U. S. GRANT, Ulysses Simpson Grant. Intelligent, deeply moving firsthand account of Civil War campaigns, considered by many the finest military memoirs ever written. Includes letters, historic photographs, maps and more. 528pp. 6⅛ x 9¼. 28587-1

ANCIENT EGYPTIAN MATERIALS AND INDUSTRIES, A. Lucas and J. Harris. Fascinating, comprehensive, thoroughly documented text describes this ancient civilization's vast resources and the processes that incorporated them in daily life, including the use of animal products, building materials, cosmetics, perfumes and incense, fibers, glazed ware, glass and its manufacture, materials used in the mummification process, and much more. 544pp. 6⅛ x 9¼. (Available in U.S. only.) 40446-3

RUSSIAN STORIES/RUSSKIE RASSKAZY: A Dual-Language Book, edited by Gleb Struve. Twelve tales by such masters as Chekhov, Tolstoy, Dostoevsky, Pushkin, others. Excellent word-for-word English translations on facing pages, plus teaching and study aids, Russian/English vocabulary, biographical/critical introductions, more. 416pp. 5⅜ x 8½. 26244-8

PHILADELPHIA THEN AND NOW: 60 Sites Photographed in the Past and Present, Kenneth Finkel and Susan Oyama. Rare photographs of City Hall, Logan Square, Independence Hall, Betsy Ross House, other landmarks juxtaposed with contemporary views. Captures changing face of historic city. Introduction. Captions. 128pp. 8¼ x 11. 25790-8

AIA ARCHITECTURAL GUIDE TO NASSAU AND SUFFOLK COUNTIES, LONG ISLAND, The American Institute of Architects, Long Island Chapter, and the Society for the Preservation of Long Island Antiquities. Comprehensive, well-researched and generously illustrated volume brings to life over three centuries of Long Island's great architectural heritage. More than 240 photographs with authoritative, extensively detailed captions. 176pp. 8¼ x 11. 26946-9

NORTH AMERICAN INDIAN LIFE: Customs and Traditions of 23 Tribes, Elsie Clews Parsons (ed.). 27 fictionalized essays by noted anthropologists examine religion, customs, government, additional facets of life among the Winnebago, Crow, Zuni, Eskimo, other tribes. 480pp. 6⅛ x 9¼. 27377-6

FRANK LLOYD WRIGHT'S DANA HOUSE, Donald Hoffmann. Pictorial essay of residential masterpiece with over 160 interior and exterior photos, plans, elevations, sketches and studies. 128pp. 9¼ x 10¾. 29120-0

THE MALE AND FEMALE FIGURE IN MOTION: 60 Classic Photographic Sequences, Eadweard Muybridge. 60 true-action photographs of men and women walking, running, climbing, bending, turning, etc., reproduced from rare 19th-century masterpiece. vi + 121pp. 9 x 12. 24745-7

1001 QUESTIONS ANSWERED ABOUT THE SEASHORE, N. J. Berrill and Jacquelyn Berrill. Queries answered about dolphins, sea snails, sponges, starfish, fishes, shore birds, many others. Covers appearance, breeding, growth, feeding, much more. 305pp. 5¼ x 8¼. 23366-9

ATTRACTING BIRDS TO YOUR YARD, William J. Weber. Easy-to-follow guide offers advice on how to attract the greatest diversity of birds: birdhouses, feeders, water and waterers, much more. 96pp. 5³⁄₁₆ x 8¼. 28927-3

MEDICINAL AND OTHER USES OF NORTH AMERICAN PLANTS: A Historical Survey with Special Reference to the Eastern Indian Tribes, Charlotte Erichsen-Brown. Chronological historical citations document 500 years of usage of plants, trees, shrubs native to eastern Canada, northeastern U.S. Also complete identifying information. 343 illustrations. 544pp. 6½ x 9¼. 25951-X

STORYBOOK MAZES, Dave Phillips. 23 stories and mazes on two-page spreads: Wizard of Oz, Treasure Island, Robin Hood, etc. Solutions. 64pp. 8¼ x 11. 23628-5

AMERICAN NEGRO SONGS: 230 Folk Songs and Spirituals, Religious and Secular, John W. Work. This authoritative study traces the African influences of songs sung and played by black Americans at work, in church, and as entertainment. The author discusses the lyric significance of such songs as "Swing Low, Sweet Chariot," "John Henry," and others and offers the words and music for 230 songs. Bibliography. Index of Song Titles. 272pp. 6½ x 9¼. 40271-1

MOVIE-STAR PORTRAITS OF THE FORTIES, John Kobal (ed.). 163 glamor, studio photos of 106 stars of the 1940s: Rita Hayworth, Ava Gardner, Marlon Brando, Clark Gable, many more. 176pp. 8⅜ x 11¼. 23546-7

BENCHLEY LOST AND FOUND, Robert Benchley. Finest humor from early 30s, about pet peeves, child psychologists, post office and others. Mostly unavailable elsewhere. 73 illustrations by Peter Arno and others. 183pp. 5⅜ x 8½. 22410-4

YEKL and THE IMPORTED BRIDEGROOM AND OTHER STORIES OF YIDDISH NEW YORK, Abraham Cahan. Film Hester Street based on *Yekl* (1896). Novel, other stories among first about Jewish immigrants on N.Y.'s East Side. 240pp. 5⅜ x 8½. 22427-9

SELECTED POEMS, Walt Whitman. Generous sampling from *Leaves of Grass*. Twenty-four poems include "I Hear America Singing," "Song of the Open Road," "I Sing the Body Electric," "When Lilacs Last in the Dooryard Bloom'd," "O Captain! My Captain!"—all reprinted from an authoritative edition. Lists of titles and first lines. 128pp. 5³⁄₁₆ x 8¼. 26878-0

THE BEST TALES OF HOFFMANN, E. T. A. Hoffmann. 10 of Hoffmann's most important stories: "Nutcracker and the King of Mice," "The Golden Flowerpot," etc. 458pp. 5⅜ x 8½.   21793-0

FROM FETISH TO GOD IN ANCIENT EGYPT, E. A. Wallis Budge. Rich detailed survey of Egyptian conception of "God" and gods, magic, cult of animals, Osiris, more. Also, superb English translations of hymns and legends. 240 illustrations. 545pp. 5⅜ x 8½.   25803-3

FRENCH STORIES/CONTES FRANÇAIS: A Dual-Language Book, Wallace Fowlie. Ten stories by French masters, Voltaire to Camus: "Micromegas" by Voltaire; "The Atheist's Mass" by Balzac; "Minuet" by de Maupassant; "The Guest" by Camus, six more. Excellent English translations on facing pages. Also French-English vocabulary list, exercises, more. 352pp. 5⅜ x 8½.   26443-2

CHICAGO AT THE TURN OF THE CENTURY IN PHOTOGRAPHS: 122 Historic Views from the Collections of the Chicago Historical Society, Larry A. Viskochil. Rare large-format prints offer detailed views of City Hall, State Street, the Loop, Hull House, Union Station, many other landmarks, circa 1904-1913. Introduction. Captions. Maps. 144pp. 9⅜ x 12¼.   24656-6

OLD BROOKLYN IN EARLY PHOTOGRAPHS, 1865-1929, William Lee Younger. Luna Park, Gravesend race track, construction of Grand Army Plaza, moving of Hotel Brighton, etc. 157 previously unpublished photographs. 165pp. 8⅞ x 11¾.
                                                              23587-4

THE MYTHS OF THE NORTH AMERICAN INDIANS, Lewis Spence. Rich anthology of the myths and legends of the Algonquins, Iroquois, Pawnees and Sioux, prefaced by an extensive historical and ethnological commentary. 36 illustrations. 480pp. 5⅜ x 8½.   25967-6

AN ENCYCLOPEDIA OF BATTLES: Accounts of Over 1,560 Battles from 1479 B.C. to the Present, David Eggenberger. Essential details of every major battle in recorded history from the first battle of Megiddo in 1479 B.C. to Grenada in 1984. List of Battle Maps. New Appendix covering the years 1967-1984. Index. 99 illustrations. 544pp. 6½ x 9¼.   24913-1

SAILING ALONE AROUND THE WORLD, Captain Joshua Slocum. First man to sail around the world, alone, in small boat. One of great feats of seamanship told in delightful manner. 67 illustrations. 294pp. 5⅜ x 8½.   20326-3

ANARCHISM AND OTHER ESSAYS, Emma Goldman. Powerful, penetrating, prophetic essays on direct action, role of minorities, prison reform, puritan hypocrisy, violence, etc. 271pp. 5⅜ x 8½.   22484-8

MYTHS OF THE HINDUS AND BUDDHISTS, Ananda K. Coomaraswamy and Sister Nivedita. Great stories of the epics; deeds of Krishna, Shiva, taken from puranas, Vedas, folk tales; etc. 32 illustrations. 400pp. 5⅜ x 8½.   21759-0

THE TRAUMA OF BIRTH, Otto Rank. Rank's controversial thesis that anxiety neurosis is caused by profound psychological trauma which occurs at birth. 256pp. 5⅜ x 8½.   27974-X

A THEOLOGICO-POLITICAL TREATISE, Benedict Spinoza. Also contains unfinished Political Treatise. Great classic on religious liberty, theory of government on common consent. R. Elwes translation. Total of 421pp. 5⅜ x 8½.   20249-6

MY BONDAGE AND MY FREEDOM, Frederick Douglass. Born a slave, Douglass became outspoken force in antislavery movement. The best of Douglass' autobiographies. Graphic description of slave life. 464pp. 5⅜ x 8½. 22457-0

FOLLOWING THE EQUATOR: A Journey Around the World, Mark Twain. Fascinating humorous account of 1897 voyage to Hawaii, Australia, India, New Zealand, etc. Ironic, bemused reports on peoples, customs, climate, flora and fauna, politics, much more. 197 illustrations. 720pp. 5⅜ x 8½. 26113-1

THE PEOPLE CALLED SHAKERS, Edward D. Andrews. Definitive study of Shakers: origins, beliefs, practices, dances, social organization, furniture and crafts, etc. 33 illustrations. 351pp. 5⅜ x 8½. 21081-2

THE MYTHS OF GREECE AND ROME, H. A. Guerber. A classic of mythology, generously illustrated, long prized for its simple, graphic, accurate retelling of the principal myths of Greece and Rome, and for its commentary on their origins and significance. With 64 illustrations by Michelangelo, Raphael, Titian, Rubens, Canova, Bernini and others. 480pp. 5⅜ x 8½. 27584-1

PSYCHOLOGY OF MUSIC, Carl E. Seashore. Classic work discusses music as a medium from psychological viewpoint. Clear treatment of physical acoustics, auditory apparatus, sound perception, development of musical skills, nature of musical feeling, host of other topics. 88 figures. 408pp. 5⅜ x 8½. 21851-1

THE PHILOSOPHY OF HISTORY, Georg W. Hegel. Great classic of Western thought develops concept that history is not chance but rational process, the evolution of freedom. 457pp. 5⅜ x 8½. 20112-0

THE BOOK OF TEA, Kakuzo Okakura. Minor classic of the Orient: entertaining, charming explanation, interpretation of traditional Japanese culture in terms of tea ceremony. 94pp. 5⅜ x 8½. 20070-1

LIFE IN ANCIENT EGYPT, Adolf Erman. Fullest, most thorough, detailed older account with much not in more recent books, domestic life, religion, magic, medicine, commerce, much more. Many illustrations reproduce tomb paintings, carvings, hieroglyphs, etc. 597pp. 5⅜ x 8½. 22632-8

SUNDIALS, Their Theory and Construction, Albert Waugh. Far and away the best, most thorough coverage of ideas, mathematics concerned, types, construction, adjusting anywhere. Simple, nontechnical treatment allows even children to build several of these dials. Over 100 illustrations. 230pp. 5⅜ x 8½. 22947-5

THEORETICAL HYDRODYNAMICS, L. M. Milne-Thomson. Classic exposition of the mathematical theory of fluid motion, applicable to both hydrodynamics and aerodynamics. Over 600 exercises. 768pp. 6⅛ x 9¼. 68970-0

SONGS OF EXPERIENCE: Facsimile Reproduction with 26 Plates in Full Color, William Blake. 26 full-color plates from a rare 1826 edition. Includes "The Tyger," "London," "Holy Thursday," and other poems. Printed text of poems. 48pp. 5¼ x 7. 24636-1

OLD-TIME VIGNETTES IN FULL COLOR, Carol Belanger Grafton (ed.). Over 390 charming, often sentimental illustrations, selected from archives of Victorian graphics—pretty women posing, children playing, food, flowers, kittens and puppies, smiling cherubs, birds and butterflies, much more. All copyright-free. 48pp. 9¼ x 12¼. 27269-9

PERSPECTIVE FOR ARTISTS, Rex Vicat Cole. Depth, perspective of sky and sea, shadows, much more, not usually covered. 391 diagrams, 81 reproductions of drawings and paintings. 279pp. 5⅜ x 8½. 22487-2

DRAWING THE LIVING FIGURE, Joseph Sheppard. Innovative approach to artistic anatomy focuses on specifics of surface anatomy, rather than muscles and bones. Over 170 drawings of live models in front, back and side views, and in widely varying poses. Accompanying diagrams. 177 illustrations. Introduction. Index. 144pp. 8⅜ x11¼. 26723-7

GOTHIC AND OLD ENGLISH ALPHABETS: 100 Complete Fonts, Dan X. Solo. Add power, elegance to posters, signs, other graphics with 100 stunning copyright-free alphabets: Blackstone, Dolbey, Germania, 97 more—including many lower-case, numerals, punctuation marks. 104pp. 8⅛ x 11. 24695-7

HOW TO DO BEADWORK, Mary White. Fundamental book on craft from simple projects to five-bead chains and woven works. 106 illustrations. 142pp. 5⅜ x 8. 20697-1

THE BOOK OF WOOD CARVING, Charles Marshall Sayers. Finest book for beginners discusses fundamentals and offers 34 designs. "Absolutely first rate . . . well thought out and well executed."–E. J. Tangerman. 118pp. 7¾ x 10⅝. 23654-4

ILLUSTRATED CATALOG OF CIVIL WAR MILITARY GOODS: Union Army Weapons, Insignia, Uniform Accessories, and Other Equipment, Schuyler, Hartley, and Graham. Rare, profusely illustrated 1846 catalog includes Union Army uniform and dress regulations, arms and ammunition, coats, insignia, flags, swords, rifles, etc. 226 illustrations. 160pp. 9 x 12. 24939-5

WOMEN'S FASHIONS OF THE EARLY 1900s: An Unabridged Republication of "New York Fashions, 1909," National Cloak & Suit Co. Rare catalog of mail-order fashions documents women's and children's clothing styles shortly after the turn of the century. Captions offer full descriptions, prices. Invaluable resource for fashion, costume historians. Approximately 725 illustrations. 128pp. 8⅜ x 11¼. 27276-1

THE 1912 AND 1915 GUSTAV STICKLEY FURNITURE CATALOGS, Gustav Stickley. With over 200 detailed illustrations and descriptions, these two catalogs are essential reading and reference materials and identification guides for Stickley furniture. Captions cite materials, dimensions and prices. 112pp. 6½ x 9¼. 26676-1

EARLY AMERICAN LOCOMOTIVES, John H. White, Jr. Finest locomotive engravings from early 19th century: historical (1804–74), main-line (after 1870), special, foreign, etc. 147 plates. 142pp. 11⅜ x 8¼. 22772-3

THE TALL SHIPS OF TODAY IN PHOTOGRAPHS, Frank O. Braynard. Lavishly illustrated tribute to nearly 100 majestic contemporary sailing vessels: Amerigo Vespucci, Clearwater, Constitution, Eagle, Mayflower, Sea Cloud, Victory, many more. Authoritative captions provide statistics, background on each ship. 190 black-and-white photographs and illustrations. Introduction. 128pp. 8⅞ x 11¾. 27163-3

CATALOG OF DOVER BOOKS

LITTLE BOOK OF EARLY AMERICAN CRAFTS AND TRADES, Peter Stockham (ed.). 1807 children's book explains crafts and trades: baker, hatter, cooper, potter, and many others. 23 copperplate illustrations. 140pp. 4⅝ x 6.   23336-7

VICTORIAN FASHIONS AND COSTUMES FROM HARPER'S BAZAR, 1867–1898, Stella Blum (ed.). Day costumes, evening wear, sports clothes, shoes, hats, other accessories in over 1,000 detailed engravings. 320pp. 9⅜ x 12¼.   22990-4

GUSTAV STICKLEY, THE CRAFTSMAN, Mary Ann Smith. Superb study surveys broad scope of Stickley's achievement, especially in architecture. Design philosophy, rise and fall of the Craftsman empire, descriptions and floor plans for many Craftsman houses, more. 86 black-and-white halftones. 31 line illustrations. Introduction 208pp. 6½ x 9¼.   27210-9

THE LONG ISLAND RAIL ROAD IN EARLY PHOTOGRAPHS, Ron Ziel. Over 220 rare photos, informative text document origin (1844) and development of rail service on Long Island. Vintage views of early trains, locomotives, stations, passengers, crews, much more. Captions. 8⅞ x 11¾.   26301-0

VOYAGE OF THE LIBERDADE, Joshua Slocum. Great 19th-century mariner's thrilling, first-hand account of the wreck of his ship off South America, the 35-foot boat he built from the wreckage, and its remarkable voyage home. 128pp. 5⅜ x 8½.   40022-0

TEN BOOKS ON ARCHITECTURE, Vitruvius. The most important book ever written on architecture. Early Roman aesthetics, technology, classical orders, site selection, all other aspects. Morgan translation. 331pp. 5⅜ x 8½.   20645-9

THE HUMAN FIGURE IN MOTION, Eadweard Muybridge. More than 4,500 stopped-action photos, in action series, showing undraped men, women, children jumping, lying down, throwing, sitting, wrestling, carrying, etc. 390pp. 7⅞ x 10⅝.   20204-6 Clothbd.

TREES OF THE EASTERN AND CENTRAL UNITED STATES AND CANADA, William M. Harlow. Best one-volume guide to 140 trees. Full descriptions, woodlore, range, etc. Over 600 illustrations. Handy size. 288pp. 4½ x 6⅜.   20395-6

SONGS OF WESTERN BIRDS, Dr. Donald J. Borror. Complete song and call repertoire of 60 western species, including flycatchers, juncoes, cactus wrens, many more—includes fully illustrated booklet.   Cassette and manual 99913-0

GROWING AND USING HERBS AND SPICES, Milo Miloradovich. Versatile handbook provides all the information needed for cultivation and use of all the herbs and spices available in North America. 4 illustrations. Index. Glossary. 236pp. 5⅜ x 8½.   25058-X

BIG BOOK OF MAZES AND LABYRINTHS, Walter Shepherd. 50 mazes and labyrinths in all—classical, solid, ripple, and more—in one great volume. Perfect inexpensive puzzler for clever youngsters. Full solutions. 112pp. 8⅛ x 11.   22951-3

PIANO TUNING, J. Cree Fischer. Clearest, best book for beginner, amateur. Simple repairs, raising dropped notes, tuning by easy method of flattened fifths. No previous skills needed. 4 illustrations. 201pp. 5⅜ x 8½.   23267-0

HINTS TO SINGERS, Lillian Nordica. Selecting the right teacher, developing confidence, overcoming stage fright, and many other important skills receive thoughtful discussion in this indispensible guide, written by a world-famous diva of four decades' experience. 96pp. 5⅜ x 8½.   40094-8

THE COMPLETE NONSENSE OF EDWARD LEAR, Edward Lear. All nonsense limericks, zany alphabets, Owl and Pussycat, songs, nonsense botany, etc., illustrated by Lear. Total of 320pp. 5⅜ x 8½. (Available in U.S. only.)   20167-8

VICTORIAN PARLOUR POETRY: An Annotated Anthology, Michael R. Turner. 117 gems by Longfellow, Tennyson, Browning, many lesser-known poets. "The Village Blacksmith," "Curfew Must Not Ring Tonight," "Only a Baby Small," dozens more, often difficult to find elsewhere. Index of poets, titles, first lines. xxiii + 325pp. 5⅜ x 8¼.   27044-0

DUBLINERS, James Joyce. Fifteen stories offer vivid, tightly focused observations of the lives of Dublin's poorer classes. At least one, "The Dead," is considered a masterpiece. Reprinted complete and unabridged from standard edition. 160pp. 5³⁄₁₆ x 8¼.   26870-5

GREAT WEIRD TALES: 14 Stories by Lovecraft, Blackwood, Machen and Others, S. T. Joshi (ed.). 14 spellbinding tales, including "The Sin Eater," by Fiona McLeod, "The Eye Above the Mantel," by Frank Belknap Long, as well as renowned works by R. H. Barlow, Lord Dunsany, Arthur Machen, W. C. Morrow and eight other masters of the genre. 256pp. 5⅜ x 8½. (Available in U.S. only.)   40436-6

THE BOOK OF THE SACRED MAGIC OF ABRAMELIN THE MAGE, translated by S. MacGregor Mathers. Medieval manuscript of ceremonial magic. Basic document in Aleister Crowley, Golden Dawn groups. 268pp. 5⅜ x 8½.   23211-5

NEW RUSSIAN-ENGLISH AND ENGLISH-RUSSIAN DICTIONARY, M. A. O'Brien. This is a remarkably handy Russian dictionary, containing a surprising amount of information, including over 70,000 entries. 366pp. 4½ x 6⅛.   20208-9

HISTORIC HOMES OF THE AMERICAN PRESIDENTS, Second, Revised Edition, Irvin Haas. A traveler's guide to American Presidential homes, most open to the public, depicting and describing homes occupied by every American President from George Washington to George Bush. With visiting hours, admission charges, travel routes. 175 photographs. Index. 160pp. 8¼ x 11.   26751-2

NEW YORK IN THE FORTIES, Andreas Feininger. 162 brilliant photographs by the well-known photographer, formerly with *Life* magazine. Commuters, shoppers, Times Square at night, much else from city at its peak. Captions by John von Hartz. 181pp. 9¼ x 10¾.   23585-8

INDIAN SIGN LANGUAGE, William Tomkins. Over 525 signs developed by Sioux and other tribes. Written instructions and diagrams. Also 290 pictographs. 111pp. 6⅛ x 9¼.   22029-X

ANATOMY: A Complete Guide for Artists, Joseph Sheppard. A master of figure drawing shows artists how to render human anatomy convincingly. Over 460 illustrations. 224pp. 8⅜ x 11¼. 27279-6

MEDIEVAL CALLIGRAPHY: Its History and Technique, Marc Drogin. Spirited history, comprehensive instruction manual covers 13 styles (ca. 4th century through 15th). Excellent photographs; directions for duplicating medieval techniques with modern tools. 224pp. 8⅜ x 11¼. 26142-5

DRIED FLOWERS: How to Prepare Them, Sarah Whitlock and Martha Rankin. Complete instructions on how to use silica gel, meal and borax, perlite aggregate, sand and borax, glycerine and water to create attractive permanent flower arrangements. 12 illustrations. 32pp. 5⅜ x 8½. 21802-3

EASY-TO-MAKE BIRD FEEDERS FOR WOODWORKERS, Scott D. Campbell. Detailed, simple-to-use guide for designing, constructing, caring for and using feeders. Text, illustrations for 12 classic and contemporary designs. 96pp. 5⅜ x 8½. 25847-5

SCOTTISH WONDER TALES FROM MYTH AND LEGEND, Donald A. Mackenzie. 16 lively tales tell of giants rumbling down mountainsides, of a magic wand that turns stone pillars into warriors, of gods and goddesses, evil hags, powerful forces and more. 240pp. 5⅜ x 8½. 29677-6

THE HISTORY OF UNDERCLOTHES, C. Willett Cunnington and Phyllis Cunnington. Fascinating, well-documented survey covering six centuries of English undergarments, enhanced with over 100 illustrations: 12th-century laced-up bodice, footed long drawers (1795), 19th-century bustles, 19th-century corsets for men, Victorian "bust improvers," much more. 272pp. 5⅜ x 8¼. 27124-2

ARTS AND CRAFTS FURNITURE: The Complete Brooks Catalog of 1912, Brooks Manufacturing Co. Photos and detailed descriptions of more than 150 now very collectible furniture designs from the Arts and Crafts movement depict davenports, settees, buffets, desks, tables, chairs, bedsteads, dressers and more, all built of solid, quarter-sawed oak. Invaluable for students and enthusiasts of antiques, Americana and the decorative arts. 80pp. 6½ x 9¼. 27471-3

WILBUR AND ORVILLE: A Biography of the Wright Brothers, Fred Howard. Definitive, crisply written study tells the full story of the brothers' lives and work. A vividly written biography, unparalleled in scope and color, that also captures the spirit of an extraordinary era. 560pp. 6⅛ x 9¼. 40297-5

THE ARTS OF THE SAILOR: Knotting, Splicing and Ropework, Hervey Garrett Smith. Indispensable shipboard reference covers tools, basic knots and useful hitches; handsewing and canvas work, more. Over 100 illustrations. Delightful reading for sea lovers. 256pp. 5⅜ x 8½. 26440-8

FRANK LLOYD WRIGHT'S FALLINGWATER: The House and Its History, Second, Revised Edition, Donald Hoffmann. A total revision—both in text and illustrations—of the standard document on Fallingwater, the boldest, most personal architectural statement of Wright's mature years, updated with valuable new material from the recently opened Frank Lloyd Wright Archives. "Fascinating"—*The New York Times.* 116 illustrations. 128pp. 9¼ x 10¾. 27430-6

PHOTOGRAPHIC SKETCHBOOK OF THE CIVIL WAR, Alexander Gardner. 100 photos taken on field during the Civil War. Famous shots of Manassas Harper's Ferry, Lincoln, Richmond, slave pens, etc. 244pp. 10⅝ x 8¼. 22731-6

FIVE ACRES AND INDEPENDENCE, Maurice G. Kains. Great back-to-the-land classic explains basics of self-sufficient farming. The one book to get. 95 illustrations. 397pp. 5⅜ x 8½. 20974-1

SONGS OF EASTERN BIRDS, Dr. Donald J. Borror. Songs and calls of 60 species most common to eastern U.S.: warblers, woodpeckers, flycatchers, thrushes, larks, many more in high-quality recording. Cassette and manual 99912-2

A MODERN HERBAL, Margaret Grieve. Much the fullest, most exact, most useful compilation of herbal material. Gigantic alphabetical encyclopedia, from aconite to zedoary, gives botanical information, medical properties, folklore, economic uses, much else. Indispensable to serious reader. 161 illustrations. 888pp. 6½ x 9¼. 2-vol. set. (Available in U.S. only.) Vol. I: 22798-7
Vol. II: 22799-5

HIDDEN TREASURE MAZE BOOK, Dave Phillips. Solve 34 challenging mazes accompanied by heroic tales of adventure. Evil dragons, people-eating plants, blood-thirsty giants, many more dangerous adversaries lurk at every twist and turn. 34 mazes, stories, solutions. 48pp. 8¼ x 11. 24566-7

LETTERS OF W. A. MOZART, Wolfgang A. Mozart. Remarkable letters show bawdy wit, humor, imagination, musical insights, contemporary musical world; includes some letters from Leopold Mozart. 276pp. 5⅜ x 8½. 22859-2

BASIC PRINCIPLES OF CLASSICAL BALLET, Agrippina Vaganova. Great Russian theoretician, teacher explains methods for teaching classical ballet. 118 illustrations. 175pp. 5⅜ x 8½. 22036-2

THE JUMPING FROG, Mark Twain. Revenge edition. The original story of The Celebrated Jumping Frog of Calaveras County, a hapless French translation, and Twain's hilarious "retranslation" from the French. 12 illustrations. 66pp. 5⅜ x 8½. 22686-7

BEST REMEMBERED POEMS, Martin Gardner (ed.). The 126 poems in this superb collection of 19th- and 20th-century British and American verse range from Shelley's "To a Skylark" to the impassioned "Renascence" of Edna St. Vincent Millay and to Edward Lear's whimsical "The Owl and the Pussycat." 224pp. 5⅜ x 8½. 27165-X

COMPLETE SONNETS, William Shakespeare. Over 150 exquisite poems deal with love, friendship, the tyranny of time, beauty's evanescence, death and other themes in language of remarkable power, precision and beauty. Glossary of archaic terms. 80pp. 5$\frac{3}{16}$ x 8¼. 26686-9

THE BATTLES THAT CHANGED HISTORY, Fletcher Pratt. Eminent historian profiles 16 crucial conflicts, ancient to modern, that changed the course of civilization. 352pp. 5⅜ x 8½. 41129-X

THE WIT AND HUMOR OF OSCAR WILDE, Alvin Redman (ed.). More than 1,000 ripostes, paradoxes, wisecracks: Work is the curse of the drinking classes; I can resist everything except temptation; etc. 258pp. 5⅜ x 8½. 20602-5

SHAKESPEARE LEXICON AND QUOTATION DICTIONARY, Alexander Schmidt. Full definitions, locations, shades of meaning in every word in plays and poems. More than 50,000 exact quotations. 1,485pp. 6½ x 9¼. 2-vol. set.

Vol. 1: 22726-X
Vol. 2: 22727-8

SELECTED POEMS, Emily Dickinson. Over 100 best-known, best-loved poems by one of America's foremost poets, reprinted from authoritative early editions. No comparable edition at this price. Index of first lines. 64pp. 5³⁄₁₆ x 8¼. 26466-1

THE INSIDIOUS DR. FU-MANCHU, Sax Rohmer. The first of the popular mystery series introduces a pair of English detectives to their archnemesis, the diabolical Dr. Fu-Manchu. Flavorful atmosphere, fast-paced action, and colorful characters enliven this classic of the genre. 208pp. 5³⁄₁₆ x 8¼. 29898-1

THE MALLEUS MALEFICARUM OF KRAMER AND SPRENGER, translated by Montague Summers. Full text of most important witchhunter's "bible," used by both Catholics and Protestants. 278pp. 6⅝ x 10. 22802-9

SPANISH STORIES/CUENTOS ESPAÑOLES: A Dual-Language Book, Angel Flores (ed.). Unique format offers 13 great stories in Spanish by Cervantes, Borges, others. Faithful English translations on facing pages. 352pp. 5⅜ x 8½. 25399-6

GARDEN CITY, LONG ISLAND, IN EARLY PHOTOGRAPHS, 1869–1919, Mildred H. Smith. Handsome treasury of 118 vintage pictures, accompanied by carefully researched captions, document the Garden City Hotel fire (1899), the Vanderbilt Cup Race (1908), the first airmail flight departing from the Nassau Boulevard Aerodrome (1911), and much more. 96pp. 8⅞ x 11¾. 40669-5

OLD QUEENS, N.Y., IN EARLY PHOTOGRAPHS, Vincent F. Seyfried and William Asadorian. Over 160 rare photographs of Maspeth, Jamaica, Jackson Heights, and other areas. Vintage views of DeWitt Clinton mansion, 1939 World's Fair and more. Captions. 192pp. 8⅞ x 11. 26358-4

CAPTURED BY THE INDIANS: 15 Firsthand Accounts, 1750-1870, Frederick Drimmer. Astounding true historical accounts of grisly torture, bloody conflicts, relentless pursuits, miraculous escapes and more, by people who lived to tell the tale. 384pp. 5⅜ x 8½. 24901-8

THE WORLD'S GREAT SPEECHES (Fourth Enlarged Edition), Lewis Copeland, Lawrence W. Lamm, and Stephen J. McKenna. Nearly 300 speeches provide public speakers with a wealth of updated quotes and inspiration–from Pericles' funeral oration and William Jennings Bryan's "Cross of Gold Speech" to Malcolm X's powerful words on the Black Revolution and Earl of Spenser's tribute to his sister, Diana, Princess of Wales. 944pp. 5⅜ x 8⅜. 40903-1

THE BOOK OF THE SWORD, Sir Richard F. Burton. Great Victorian scholar/adventurer's eloquent, erudite history of the "queen of weapons"–from prehistory to early Roman Empire. Evolution and development of early swords, variations (sabre, broadsword, cutlass, scimitar, etc.), much more. 336pp. 6⅛ x 9¼.

25434-8

AUTOBIOGRAPHY: The Story of My Experiments with Truth, Mohandas K. Gandhi. Boyhood, legal studies, purification, the growth of the Satyagraha (nonviolent protest) movement. Critical, inspiring work of the man responsible for the freedom of India. 480pp. 5⅜ x 8½. (Available in U.S. only.) 24593-4

CELTIC MYTHS AND LEGENDS, T. W. Rolleston. Masterful retelling of Irish and Welsh stories and tales. Cuchulain, King Arthur, Deirdre, the Grail, many more. First paperback edition. 58 full-page illustrations. 512pp. 5⅜ x 8½. 26507-2

THE PRINCIPLES OF PSYCHOLOGY, William James. Famous long course complete, unabridged. Stream of thought, time perception, memory, experimental methods; great work decades ahead of its time. 94 figures. 1,391pp. 5⅜ x 8½. 2-vol. set. Vol. I: 20381-6 Vol. II: 20382-4

THE WORLD AS WILL AND REPRESENTATION, Arthur Schopenhauer. Definitive English translation of Schopenhauer's life work, correcting more than 1,000 errors, omissions in earlier translations. Translated by E. F. J. Payne. Total of 1,269pp. 5⅜ x 8½. 2-vol. set. Vol. 1: 21761-2 Vol. 2: 21762-0

MAGIC AND MYSTERY IN TIBET, Madame Alexandra David-Neel. Experiences among lamas, magicians, sages, sorcerers, Bonpa wizards. A true psychic discovery. 32 illustrations. 321pp. 5⅜ x 8½. (Available in U.S. only.) 22682-4

THE EGYPTIAN BOOK OF THE DEAD, E. A. Wallis Budge. Complete reproduction of Ani's papyrus, finest ever found. Full hieroglyphic text, interlinear transliteration, word-for-word translation, smooth translation. 533pp. 6½ x 9¼. 21866-X

MATHEMATICS FOR THE NONMATHEMATICIAN, Morris Kline. Detailed, college-level treatment of mathematics in cultural and historical context, with numerous exercises. Recommended Reading Lists. Tables. Numerous figures. 641pp. 5⅜ x 8½. 24823-2

PROBABILISTIC METHODS IN THE THEORY OF STRUCTURES, Isaac Elishakoff. Well-written introduction covers the elements of the theory of probability from two or more random variables, the reliability of such multivariable structures, the theory of random function, Monte Carlo methods of treating problems incapable of exact solution, and more. Examples. 502pp. 5⅜ x 8½. 40691-1

THE RIME OF THE ANCIENT MARINER, Gustave Doré, S. T. Coleridge. Doré's finest work; 34 plates capture moods, subtleties of poem. Flawless full-size reproductions printed on facing pages with authoritative text of poem. "Beautiful. Simply beautiful."–*Publisher's Weekly.* 77pp. 9¼ x 12. 22305-1

NORTH AMERICAN INDIAN DESIGNS FOR ARTISTS AND CRAFTSPEOPLE, Eva Wilson. Over 360 authentic copyright-free designs adapted from Navajo blankets, Hopi pottery, Sioux buffalo hides, more. Geometrics, symbolic figures, plant and animal motifs, etc. 128pp. 8⅜ x 11. (Not for sale in the United Kingdom.) 25341-4

SCULPTURE: Principles and Practice, Louis Slobodkin. Step-by-step approach to clay, plaster, metals, stone; classical and modern. 253 drawings, photos. 255pp. 8⅛ x 11. 22960-2

THE INFLUENCE OF SEA POWER UPON HISTORY, 1660–1783, A. T. Mahan. Influential classic of naval history and tactics still used as text in war colleges. First paperback edition. 4 maps. 24 battle plans. 640pp. 5⅜ x 8½. 25509-3

THE STORY OF THE TITANIC AS TOLD BY ITS SURVIVORS, Jack Winocour (ed.). What it was really like. Panic, despair, shocking inefficiency, and a little heroism. More thrilling than any fictional account. 26 illustrations. 320pp. 5⅜ x 8½.

20610-6

FAIRY AND FOLK TALES OF THE IRISH PEASANTRY, William Butler Yeats (ed.). Treasury of 64 tales from the twilight world of Celtic myth and legend: "The Soul Cages," "The Kildare Pooka," "King O'Toole and his Goose," many more. Introduction and Notes by W. B. Yeats. 352pp. 5⅜ x 8½.

26941-8

BUDDHIST MAHAYANA TEXTS, E. B. Cowell and others (eds.). Superb, accurate translations of basic documents in Mahayana Buddhism, highly important in history of religions. The Buddha-karita of Asvaghosha, Larger Sukhavativyuha, more. 448pp. 5⅜ x 8½.

25552-2

ONE TWO THREE . . . INFINITY: Facts and Speculations of Science, George Gamow. Great physicist's fascinating, readable overview of contemporary science: number theory, relativity, fourth dimension, entropy, genes, atomic structure, much more. 128 illustrations. Index. 352pp. 5⅜ x 8½.

25664-2

EXPERIMENTATION AND MEASUREMENT, W. J. Youden. Introductory manual explains laws of measurement in simple terms and offers tips for achieving accuracy and minimizing errors. Mathematics of measurement, use of instruments, experimenting with machines. 1994 edition. Foreword. Preface. Introduction. Epilogue. Selected Readings. Glossary. Index. Tables and figures. 128pp. 5⅜ x 8½.

40451-X

DALÍ ON MODERN ART: The Cuckolds of Antiquated Modern Art, Salvador Dalí. Influential painter skewers modern art and its practitioners. Outrageous evaluations of Picasso, Cézanne, Turner, more. 15 renderings of paintings discussed. 44 calligraphic decorations by Dalí. 96pp. 5⅜ x 8½. (Available in U.S. only.)

29220-7

ANTIQUE PLAYING CARDS: A Pictorial History, Henry René D'Allemagne. Over 900 elaborate, decorative images from rare playing cards (14th–20th centuries): Bacchus, death, dancing dogs, hunting scenes, royal coats of arms, players cheating, much more. 96pp. 9¼ x 12¼.

29265-7

MAKING FURNITURE MASTERPIECES: 30 Projects with Measured Drawings, Franklin H. Gottshall. Step-by-step instructions, illustrations for constructing handsome, useful pieces, among them a Sheraton desk, Chippendale chair, Spanish desk, Queen Anne table and a William and Mary dressing mirror. 224pp. 8⅛ x 11¼.

29338-6

THE FOSSIL BOOK: A Record of Prehistoric Life, Patricia V. Rich et al. Profusely illustrated definitive guide covers everything from single-celled organisms and dinosaurs to birds and mammals and the interplay between climate and man. Over 1,500 illustrations. 760pp. 7½ x 10⅛.

29371-8